DAILY
Guideposts®
2003

O give thanks unto the LORD; for He is good; for His mercy endureth for ever.
1 CHRONICLES 16:34

IDEALS PUBLICATIONS
NASHVILLE, TENNESSEE

ISBN 0-8249-4608-1

Published by Ideals Publications, a division of Guideposts.

ACKNOWLEDGMENTS

All Scripture quotations, unless otherwise noted, are taken from *The King James Version of the Bible*.

Scripture quotations marked (NAS) are taken from the *New American Standard Bible*, © The Lockman Foundation, 1960, 1962, 1963, 1968, 1971, 1972, 1973, 1975, 1977. Used by permission.

Scripture quotations marked (NIV) are taken from *The Holy Bible, New International Version*. Copyright © 1973, 1978, 1984 International Bible Society. Used by permission of Zondervan Bible Publishers.

Scripture quotations marked (NKJV) are taken from *The Holy Bible, New King James Version*. Copyright © 1997, 1990, 1985, 1983 by Thomas Nelson, Inc.

Scripture quotations marked (RSV) are taken from the *Revised Standard Version of the Bible*. Copyright © 1946, 1952, 1971 by Division of Christian Education of the National Council of Churches of Christ in the U.S.A. Used by permission.

Scripture quotations marked (TLB) are taken from *The Living Bible*. Copyright © 1971 by Tyndale House Publishers, Wheaton, IL 60187. All rights reserved.

"Charley's Gifts" was written by Rick Hamlin.

"A Closer Walk" was written by Daniel Schantz.

"An Eye for Blessings" was written by Elizabeth Sherrill.

"Following Jesus" was written by Roberta Messner.

"A Heritage of Freedom" was written by Eric Fellman.

"Into the Wilderness" was written by Mary Brown.

"A Light from the Manger" was written by Shari Smyth.

"Out of the Shadows" was written by Libbie Adams.

"Sun, Moon and Stars" was written by Carol Knapp.

"The Walls of Cumbria" was written by John Sherrill.

"Reader's Room" by Fran Barker, Sally Edwards Christensen, Amy A. Dunlap, Helene C. Kuoni, Pat Loek, Lillian Henderson Miller, Rebecca Ann Murray, Debbie Stanley, Martha A. Suter, Marilyn Wagnon, Lisa Walkendorf and Hope Williams are reprinted with permission by the authors.

Gina Bridgeman's photo is copyright © 2002 by Michael Norton.

Julie Garmon's photo is copyright © 2002 Jeff Von Hoene.

Oscar Greene's photo is copyright © 2001 by Olan Mills, Inc.

Edward Grinnan's photo is by Julie Skarratt.

Rick Hamlin's photo is by Lilly Dong.

Van Varner's photo is by Steven Boljonis.

www.guidepostsbooks.com
Cover designed by Eve DeGrie
Cover photograph, Arctic National Wildlife Refuge, Alaska, © Carr Clifton
Text designed by Holly Johnson
Artwork by Jennie Yip
Indexed by Patricia Woodruff
Typeset by Planet Patti, Inc.
Printed in the United States of America

TABLE OF CONTENTS

TABLE OF CONTENTS

INTRODUCTION

We've been through a lot since September 11, 2001. We've experienced deadly attacks and economic hardship, sent our young men and women to fight in faraway places, and learned to live with uncertainty. But in the midst of change and upheaval, we need to keep in mind a few simple truths: God is with us. Every day, whatever that day may bring, is a day spent in His presence. Every day, in the activities that make up the texture of our lives, through the people we live and work with, He blesses us and upholds us, shares the bounty of His love and transforms us by His grace.

To help keep these truths in our hearts, our theme for *Daily Guideposts, 2003* is "Everyday Blessings." We've asked our fifty-four writers to let us know how God is with them each day, not in extraordinary and unusual events, but in the blessings of the day's routine. They've found God's blessings in sickrooms and in schoolrooms, waiting for a baby to be born or keeping vigil with a dying friend, starting a new job or adjusting to retirement. By seeing through their eyes and hearing through their ears, we'll be better able to recognize the everyday blessings in our own lives.

At the beginning of each month, Elizabeth Sherrill helps you rediscover the often overlooked wonders that surround you every day. In the middle of the month, Roberta Messner shows you how the familiar question "What would Jesus do?" is answered in the lives of people who seek to travel "in His steps." And throughout the year, Eric Fellman will take you with him to visit the monuments of our nation's capital as he reflects on our nation's heroes and the legacy they've left us.

Join Rick Hamlin in February as he visits an old friend stricken with Lou Gehrig's disease and discovers the blessings of a family's devotion and a dying man's courage. For Holy Week and Easter, Daniel Schantz shows you how Jesus' final words of comfort can soothe your daily cares and how His Resurrection can inspire you to dust off your dreams. In July, John Sherrill takes you to England's Lake District and shows you the spiritual lessons that the walls enclosing every field and lining every footpath can teach. In August, join Mary Brown on a three-day voyage of discovery into the meaning of love, the reality of aging and the comfort of faith. In October, Libbie Adams shows you how faith in God and the help of an extraordinary Christian therapist led her out of the shadows of anxiety and depression. In November, Carol Knapp shares some of the ways she's understood God's glory through the great lights He's placed in the sky. And this Advent and Christmas, let Shari Smyth kindle the lights of Christmas in your heart as she tells how Christ has transformed her own.

As always, we welcome back old friends whose lives have become so much a part of our own—Marilyn Morgan King and Fred Bauer, Oscar Greene and Drue Duke, Marion Bond West and Scott Walker, Van Varner and Fay Angus. And we've asked some new folks to join our family: Ted Nace of Poughquag, New York, Guideposts Director of Outreach, invites you to join him on an amusement-park ride you'll never forget; Julie Garmon, a mother of three from Snellville, Georgia, and the daughter of Marion Bond West, finds out that even a squeaking clothes dryer can be an everyday blessing; Joshua Sundquist, a student from Harrisonburg, Virginia, shares the story of his battle with cancer; Harold Hostetler, a roving editor for *Guideposts* magazine from San Diego, California, learns the limits of self-reliance from a leaky faucet; Evelyn Bence of Arlington, Virginia, finds a victory over disappointment in the encouragement of a persistent friend; and Ptolemy Tompkins of New York City, a staff editor at *Guideposts* and *Angels on Earth* magazines, gives you a whole new perspective on the clutter in your life.

Even as we welcome back old friends and meet new ones, we must say good-bye to two very precious members of our *Daily Guideposts* family, Marjorie Holmes and Arthur Gordon. Marjorie died on March 13, 2002, at the age of ninety-one; Arthur died on January 4, 2002, at the age of eighty-nine. Both Marjorie and Arthur joined our *Daily Guideposts* family in 1979; they were both marvelous writers, generous colleagues and caring friends, and we will miss them both very much. Please keep Marjorie and Arthur's families in your prayers.

For more than a quarter of a century, we readers and writers of *Daily Guideposts* have helped each other become more aware of God's presence and work in our lives through the stories of our writers and the often extraordinary letters of our readers. Every day, we've remembered each other in prayer. And, God willing, we'll be together on every day of this year of our Lord 2003 to share the good news of God's everyday blessings in our hearts, in our homes, in our nation and in the world.   —*THE EDITORS*

JANUARY

Blessed are the poor in spirit: for
theirs is the kingdom of heaven.
—Matthew 5:3

S	M	T	W	T	F	S
			1	2	3	4
5	6	7	8	9	10	11
12	13	14	15	16	17	18
19	20	21	22	23	24	25
26	27	28	29	30	31	

AN EYE FOR BLESSINGS

Everyday blessings: Does their very dailiness take away our wonder at them? Elizabeth Sherrill says this was certainly true for her—and invites you to join her on a yearlong adventure in rediscovering the wealth that's all around us. —THE EDITORS

1 / WED   SEEING ANEW

"Lord, let our eyes be opened." —MATTHEW 20:33 (RSV)

During a week's hospital stay, I had enjoyed a colorful Gauguin Tahiti scene on the wall of my room. So I was dismayed when a beaming hospital volunteer stepped in one morning and took it down.

The lady must have caught my expression. "I'll be right back!" she promised.

A few minutes later she wheeled in a cart filled with framed prints: landscapes, flowers, ballet dancers, galloping horses. "When you look at something every day," she explained, "you stop seeing it. That's why we change the pictures around."

I chose Renoir's *Boating Party*. But her words had started me thinking. Had I really stopped seeing the things I saw every day?

Back home, I walked through the house with newly opened eyes. It was true: the wallpaper in the kitchen, the china figurine on the bedroom bureau, my sister's watercolor over the piano. How long since I'd really looked at any of them? Because they were always there, they had become invisible.

It wasn't only decorative things. The refrigerator, the telephone —the more often I used an object, the less I seemed to notice it. If I had never owned two pairs of shoes or a sink with running water, as half the world does not, how I would thank God if I ever obtained them! Shouldn't an abundance of material blessings make me more grateful, not less? Why not change—not the pictures on the wall—but the way I looked at them?

That morning I made a New Year's resolution: to thank God each day for something in common use and view. What began as a simple exercise in awareness has become a daily adventure as I discover God's blessings in the commonplaces of my life.

Open my eyes all this year, Father, to Your gifts in the every day.
—ELIZABETH SHERRILL

EDITOR'S NOTE: Throughout the year ahead, please take time to write down some of the ways God is blessing you day by day. You'll find a place for your reflections in the "My Daily Blessings" pages at the end of every month.

2/THU *How precious also are thy thoughts unto me, O God! How great is the sum of them! If I should count them, they are more in number than the sand....* —PSALM 139:17–18

Have you ever selected a particular Bible verse, one that you consider your very own, one that you determine to count on "through thick and thin"?

Every January I choose my "verse for the year." Then, whatever happens, good or bad, I count on my particular verse, which I consider to be my promise from God, a steadying, calming influence, my bedrock-solid foundation. My verse for this year is "What time I am afraid, I will trust in thee" (Psalm 56:3). You may wish to use it also. If not, how about one of the following?

- "Wait on the Lord: be of good courage, and he shall strengthen thine heart: wait, I say, on the Lord" (Psalm 27:14).
- "The Lord is good unto them that wait for him" (Lamentations 3:25).
- "What doth the Lord require of thee, but to do justly, and to love mercy, and to walk humbly with thy God" (Micah 6:8).
- "This is my commandment, That ye love one another" (John 15:12).
- "Be not overcome of evil, but overcome evil with good" (Romans 12:21).
- "We then that are strong ought to bear the infirmities of the weak, and not to please ourselves" (Romans 15:1).
- "Let us not be weary in well doing: for in due season we shall reap, if we faint not" (Galatians 6:9).

I've never counted the verses in the Bible, but according to those who have, there are 23,214 in the Old Testament and 7,959 in the New Testament, for a total of 31,173 in the King James Version! So while you browse through the Scriptures to choose your personal verse for the year, you may have trouble selecting just one from the many precious promises you'll come across. I know I did!

Lord, with the Psalmist I marvel that You, the Great Creator, care even about me. —ISABEL WOLSELEY

3/FRI   *Use hospitality one to another....*
—I PETER 4:9

When I was a child, people often stopped by our house completely unannounced. The doorbell would ring, and I'd fly to the door yelling, "We've got company!" It might be an aunt, an uncle and a cousin or two; it might be our favorite older couple, Mr. and Mrs. Solomon; it might be someone who worked for my father or played golf with my mother. It could be just about anyone!

Back then, my mother made a cake every week and our pantry always held some extra snacks, but most often I remember my father dashing for the car and speeding down to the Toddle House. Within minutes he was back with one of the delights of my childhood, a Toddle House pie. Our company never left hungry!

In our first years of marriage, David and I went as missionaries to a tiny coal mining town in eastern Kentucky. I had never seen people who lived with so little. And yet, they always had so much to share. I love recalling our visits to the tiny home of two of our favorite parishioners, Taft and Beulah Sargent. We always left with our arms full of homemade jelly or honey fresh from the hive or just-churned butter.

"Oh, we can't take all this from you," we'd argue.

"Hush now," Beulah would say. "We're just so happy we have it to give." The Sargents' home was one of the most humble I have ever entered, yet in my memory it is one of the finest, most hospitable places I have ever been.

It's true that people just don't "drop in" much anymore, but there are many who would count it a privilege to be invited to your home. So put out the welcome mat, dash out for a local version of a Toddle House pie, and share some simple hospitality with whomever God sends your way.

Father, help me reach out beyond my friends to share my table and my life with others. —PAM KIDD

4/SAT   *I will remember the works of the Lord: surely I will remember thy wonders of old.* —PSALM 77:11

Word reached me today that my old friend Arthur Gordon had died at age eighty-nine in his beloved Savannah, Georgia. I had talked with Arthur just a short time before and we had made plans for dinner, but, alas, that will not come to pass.

When the news reached me, I went to my bookshelves and took down one of Arthur's creations, the classic *A Touch of Wonder.* In it, he shares some of the philosophy and faith that made his art of living stories so memorable. A Yale graduate and a Rhodes Scholar, Arthur credited, among others, his Aunt Juliette Gordon Lowe, the founder of the Girl Scouts of America, with planting in him the seeds of curiosity and adventure that so marked his life. His passions were many, his interests varied and his friendships vast.

I first met Arthur when I came to Guideposts from Ohio in 1962. He was already an accomplished writer, and I was more than a little flattered when he took an interest in some of the things I wrote. Eventually, Arthur became editorial director of Guideposts, and I served as his executive editor. It was a great learning experience for me, working for a few years with a master storyteller who had few peers.

Perhaps the thing that had the most lasting impact on me was a piece he once wrote about not being afraid to take chances, stepping out in faith and risking all. The article was entitled "Be Bold and Mighty Forces Will Come to Your Aid." It resonated strongly with me and has become a family motto. My kids have heard me repeat it so often that they raise a knowing eyebrow whenever I launch into it. But I can't think of a better epitaph for Arthur's fruitful life: *Be bold, and mighty forces will come to your aid.*

Thank You, Lord, for writers who with their words inspire, Who teach us, beseech us, to reach out and aspire.
—FRED BAUER

5/*SUN*   *"Remember the Sabbath day by keeping*
it holy."   —EXODUS 20:8 (NIV)

A blast of cold, damp air pushed me through the doors of the grocery store. *Great,* I thought, pulling my jacket tighter around me.
It's as cold in here as it is outside. I quickly walked down the aisle to
pick up my favorite brand of orange juice. The compartment was
empty. TEMPORARILY OUT, the sign read.

"Oh, no!" I moaned, fumbling for a tissue. "And I'm catching a
cold." I snatched up another brand of juice and threw it into my
basket. I began to sneeze.

At that moment a gray-haired lady wrapped in a brown woolen
shawl shuffled past me, softly singing my favorite childhood hymn:

> *Come to the church in the wildwood,*
> *Oh, come to the church in the vale;*
> *No spot is so dear to my childhood*
> *As the little brown church in the vale.*

Memories overwhelmed me. I recalled the little white clapboard
church where I sang in the youth choir on Sunday mornings and
ate potluck dinners in the fellowship hall on cold Sunday nights. I
had my answer: I needed to go to church. I had missed services
the past few weeks because I had been trying to juggle graduate
school and a demanding job. I closed my eyes and prayed, *Lord, I
get the message. I'll be in church on Sunday. Nothing is more important
than You.*

That Sunday I did not go to my regular church. Instead, I drove
thirty miles to the church of my childhood, where I had sung my
first hymn, memorized my first Scripture and stood in front of the
congregation and given my life to Jesus.

At the altar call that morning, when the congregation sang the
words, "O Lamb of God, I come," I prayed:

**Lord, thank You for always being ready to welcome me back to
the fold. Enfold me in Your redeeming love.**

                                        —MELODY BONNETTE

6 / MON   *To every thing there is a season . . . a time to keep, and a time to cast away.* —ECCLESIASTES 3:1, 6

The day that I always wish would never come has arrived. I am "downloading" the Christmas tree. I love putting the decorations on, and I loathe taking them off. But the sanitation service will only collect trees through this week. That means I have a deadline.

An empty box sits on the floor, waiting to hold the ornaments until next season. First, there's my angel collection. One perches on a red ceramic heart that bears my name. My friend Mary sent it the year I moved away. The handblown indigo glass angel with translucent wings came from our daughter Kelly on the last Christmas before she married. My Montana friend Cathy sent the felt cowgirl angel. The frowning, yellow-painted wooden one was purchased by another friend Mary, who saw me admiring it in an airport gift shop. Mary died just two months ago.

Then there is a cheerful alpine fellow whom Mom brought back from a trip to Germany. The white-threaded alpaca wearing a woven blanket is from Janet, who owns an alpaca farm. A smiling, rosy-cheeked boy wrapped in a knitted muffler and cap stood on our son Phil's twelfth birthday cake. It has a trace of frosting still stuck to its foot. Our daughter Brenda gave me the pink porcelain fairy rising from a flower after competing at Disney World with her high-school cheerleading team.

Each ornament tells a story; many bring to mind someone dear to us who is no longer nearby. Maybe that's why I'm sad when it's time to take down the tree: I feel like I'm packing away my family and friends. I'm a lingerer, but even a lingerer must move ahead. If I don't, I'll have no new ornaments to add to my tree, no new stories, no new friends.

Okay, Lord, now that I'm done talking about taking down the Christmas tree, help me to quit dawdling and go do it! New possibilities await!   —CAROL KNAPP

7 / TUE   *I can do everything through him who gives me strength.* —PHILIPPIANS 4:13 (NIV)

I sat in a Chicago airport waiting for my flight. The gate was packed and noisy; a confusing jumble of voices spun around me and over the loudspeaker. In the seat next to me, a young mother held a child with curly, dark hair, who was wriggling to get down.

"You have your hands full," I said to the mother. She laughed and set the child down a short distance from her.

"Anna's just learning to walk. She's itching to practice." The mother held out her arms. "Come on, Anna. Come to Mommy."

But Anna's tiny sneakered feet froze on the strange floor. She looked around, her dark eyes growing large at all the noise. "Come on," the mother coaxed again, holding out her arms.

Back on track, Anna toddled a few steps. "Oh, no, she's going to fall," a well-meaning lady called. Anna looked toward the voice and fell. She cried, a long, sobbing wail. Mother picked her up, kissed her and put her back on track.

"You can do it, Anna," the mother insisted gently. "Come on. Just take a step." And this time she did. Squinting straight ahead, she walked the whole two yards right into her mother's arms.

I was embarking on a new project that both terrified and excited me. I was sure I could do it. Yet doubts pounded me till I stood frozen, listening to all the discouraging voices inside me. *Where is Your voice?* I kept asking God. *Why don't You show me how to do this? I don't even know where to start.*

But right here in this noisy airport, God did show me. Not how to do it, but how to know His voice. The child in me stood still, listening through the confusing jumble of doubt. Sure enough, His voice came soft and insistent: *You can do it. Just take the first step.*

Father, with each toddling step, help me to keep focused on Your soft, encouraging voice. —SHARI SMYTH

8/ WED   *And I have filled him with the spirit of God, in wisdom, and in understanding, and in knowledge, and in all manner of workmanship.* —EXODUS 31:3

At last I've found a restaurant to take the place of the defunct hotel coffee shop, which was reasonably priced (well, cheap) and where I ate dinner once or twice a week. It's only another block away, on Amsterdam Avenue. The reason I didn't try it before was that it was so small and so packed, with lines of young people waiting outside. By going early, about five o'clock, I don't have to worry about getting in, and the diners are mostly older people, or very young children with their parents. I'm getting to know a lot of the regulars, and one woman paid me a compliment, I think, when she said, "I know you. You were in the theater." Too bad. She had to settle for an ex-editor.

The restaurant is very different from the coffee shop. For one thing, it's Chinese. Pretty, ponytailed Chinese waitresses bring me a large glass of Pepsi as I settle into a table by the window. I dip a crispy noodle into the orange duck sauce and order the same as usual: egg-drop soup and General Tso's chicken (I don't know who he was, or is, but his dish of crispy chunks of chicken, sautéed with fresh vegetables in a spicy brown sauce, is great). There's always too much for me to eat, which means that a doggie bag is necessary, which means that my dog Shep will be waiting at home, frantic with anticipation.

There's one thing I truly miss: the conversations about religion with Rumi and Roni, the Pakistani brothers at the coffee shop. Here, the waitresses are too busy (they are preparing the snow peas when not waiting on tables), but I would like to talk to someone about the fortune cookie that comes as complimentary dessert (with orange slices and pineapple). It is pleasant to receive word that "Money is coming your way" or that "Your happiness is intertwined with your outlook on life," but I wonder about a statement I received that read: "Trust your intuition. The universe is guiding your life." Whom can I tell that there is Someone guiding my life, exerting His power in subtle ways. Whom can I tell about God?

Lord, why not just once have a fortune cookie that says it Your way? —VAN VARNER

9/*THU* *We give thanks to God always for you all, making mention of you in our prayers.* —I THESSALONIANS 1:2

Mable Sharpston, who helps my neighbor Ina, was driving the three of us to the grocery store. As we turned into the parking lot, Mable asked me, "Mrs. Duke, will you pray for my son and me?"

From the backseat, I answered, "Of course, I will. Is there something in particular I should pray about?"

"I want to hear from him," she said. "He's moved, and I don't know where he is. I just need for him to call me." She parked the car and turned to face me. "I want to hear from him," she repeated, "and know that he's all right."

"Have you put him in God's hands?" I asked her. On her face, I saw the anguish of a frightened mother. "I will pray constantly," I promised her, "but you must pray, too. And you should stop fretting. You could make yourself sick."

As we shopped, I prayed silently. And at home, the rest of that day and the next, I talked to God—over the dishpan, the vacuum cleaner, with everything I did.

Bright and early the following morning, the telephone rang, and I heard Mable's voice ringing with joy. "He called me!" she said. "He didn't realize it had been so long or that I would be so worried. Thank you very much for praying for me!"

"I feel honored that you asked me," I told her. "Now let's both remember to thank our Lord."

Thank You, Father, for this and the many prayers You hear and answer. Let me always be ready to come to You when there is a problem. Amen. —DRUE DUKE

10/ FRI *In everything . . . he sought his God and worked wholeheartedly. And so he prospered.*
—II CHRONICLES 31:21 (NIV)

"Oh, that holiday food—and now another year, another diet. I don't have the equipment, the space or the time to exercise. When will I get it together? How will I get it together? It just feels hopeless." Thanks to the miracle of modern technology, I'm whining by e-mail to a friend who has had some success in the battle against encroaching pounds.

In a few minutes, my friend Angela responds, "Sharon, don't try to do too much. Just do something small, consistently. That's the key—small, daily acts of obedience."

She's right. I know she is.

When I began writing, I worked full-time and was the full-time caretaker for my son Chase. Perhaps my writing might somehow bless others, but for years I told myself it was too hard. There came a time, though, when I stopped relying on myself and prayed. I couldn't visualize the end, and I had no plan. But through prayer, I discovered that I could commit to do something each day—

a small daily act of obedience. I could stop focusing on what I couldn't do and, instead, capitalize on what I could do.

Each morning, I rose at five o'clock and devoted a half-hour to writing before I stopped to get ready to go to my real job. My living room became my office. I prayed each morning before I began, then wrote longhand on steno notepads. I did what I could every day—small daily acts of obedience.

Soon, I had filled several notepads. As I worked, my children encouraged and supported me. Friends lent me a word processor; a kind stranger gave me a computer. Those pages ultimately became my first novel, *Passing by Samaria*. Since then, I have written a second novel, and I am working to finish a third.

What's true for writing is also true for losing weight: I don't have to rely on any special willpower. Those small acts of obedience will do the trick. Starting today.

God, help me to apply the lesson of daily obedience to all areas of my life. —SHARON FOSTER

11 / SAT   *O Lord my God, I cried unto thee, and thou hast healed me.* —PSALM 30:2

Like most animals, my dog Tara does not enjoy going to the veterinarian. So there we were in the waiting room, Tara shaking while I tried to reassure her. "It's going to be okay," I told her, holding her close to me. "It's just a simple blood test."

Easy for me to say. I knew what a blood test involved. But Tara had no idea what was going to happen.

I was worried, too. An earlier X ray of Tara's heart showed some suspicious dark areas that might have indicated heartworm disease, a serious condition that is often fatal. I always had her inoculated against heartworm disease, but I didn't know what had gone on in her life before I adopted her. The disease was capable of hiding out in the body for years.

"This won't take long," said Penny, the vet tech, as she reached for Tara's leash and took her to one of the examining rooms. A few minutes later, the door opened and Penny beckoned to me. "I think Tara will be calmer if you're with her," she said. "I have to draw some blood, and she won't hold her leg still."

Tara was standing on the floor, trembling. I crouched down

alongside of her and put my arm around her. "It's okay, honey. I'm right here," I said.

I could feel her calming down, and I told her to sit. When Penny lifted her left front leg up and deftly inserted the needle into a vein, Tara didn't pull back. I kept talking to her and the trembling stopped. When it was all over, I gave her a big hug.

Tara's blood test revealed traces of an early presence of heart-worm disease. The shadowy areas in the X ray were like scar tissue; they meant that she had survived the attack. The good news was that there was no threat to her any longer.

Lord, I thank You that whenever I have to go through something strange and scary, I have a loving Father by my side. Amen.

—PHYLLIS HOBE

12/SUN   A man approached Jesus and knelt before him. "Lord, have mercy on my son," he said. . . .

—MATTHEW 17:14–15 (NIV)

Bless them, I silently prayed as I walked into church and saw two strangers among us, up near the front. The Hillearys had adopted brothers, aged five and four. Just arrived in Virginia from Cambodia, they understood hardly a word of English. During the songs, the curious boys surveyed the congregation, each perched on his specially reserved seat: the hipbone of a new parent. Throughout the Scripture readings and the sermon, the brothers didn't say a word or make a fuss.

When the sermon was over, I opened my *Book of Common Prayer* to the "Prayers of the People," which start with the invitation, "With all our heart and with all our mind, let us pray to the Lord, saying, 'Lord, have mercy.'"

From a front pew, a woman read a petition: "For the peace from above . . . let us pray to the Lord." She paused.

"Lord, have mercy," we responded.

She took a breath and then read another line: "For the peace of the world . . . let us pray to the Lord."

"Lord, have mercy."

The rhythm was quickly obvious, even if you'd missed the instructions. So I was surprised to hear the pattern broken after the sixth response. It was the older Hilleary brother. In the brief silence between the response and the next prayer, he went solo: "Lord, have mercy."

Then again and again, for the next six petitions. After the congregation asked for a common mercy, the child echoed his own private request. The boy, embarking on a new life—in a new land, with a new family—didn't know the meaning of his prayer. But that only made his final echo more striking—for him and for every child of God of every age.

> *"Defend us, deliver us and in thy compassion*
> *protect us, O Lord, by thy grace."*
> *"Lord, have mercy."*
> *"Lord, have mercy."* —EVELYN BENCE

*13/*MON *"Remember, therefore, what you have received. . . ."* —REVELATION 3:3 (NIV)

It's 7:00 A.M., and I'm trying to be quiet as I rummage around for my razor in the bathroom I share with my wife and my stepdaughter Mara.

Everyone in New York City has space complaints, and after years of marriage I'm used to the fact that the three of us might as well be living on a submarine. But the bathroom is the one place where I still lose patience. Papaya-scented clarifying solution, mango-essence rejuvenating cream. Each day I seem to be confronted with another new substance that Mara has decided is essential for her appearance. "For heaven's sake," I said to her recently, "you're fifteen! Why don't you at least wait till you're old and have some wrinkles to cover up before buying all this junk?"

Crash! In my haste I knock a big container of moisturizing lotion off the sink. It lands amid a phalanx of half-used shampoos and conditioners wedged up against the tub. Reaching down to retrieve it, my fingers touch something unfamiliar. I straighten back up and bring the object into the light: a Fisher-Price milkman with movable arms and legs and a hardy smile painted across his face. I haven't seen this figure in years, though I used to run into it just about every day. Instantly, I'm brought back to the first months of my marriage, when my new stepdaughter was seven and this bathroom was just as cluttered as it is now, but with altogether different items: plastic dinosaurs; animal-shaped sponges; and innumerable action figures like this one that Mara had long dialogues with as she sat in the tub. I look at that little figure and wonder at all the time that has gone by, and I pray:

Thank You, Lord, for the clutter in my life—every last piece of it.

—PTOLEMY TOMPKINS

FOLLOWING JESUS

In the novel In His Steps, *written by Charles Sheldon in 1896, the pastor of an affluent church challenges his congregation to do nothing for an entire year without first asking the question "What would Jesus do?" In the course of her life,* Daily Guideposts *writer Roberta Messner has encountered many people who truly follow "in His steps," emulating their Savior in simple yet profound ways. This year, join Roberta each month and discover the everyday people who have transformed her life—and can help you discover the challenge and the blessing of being a sign of His presence in the world.* —THE EDITORS

14/ *TUE* NEW BEGINNINGS

Clothe yourselves with the Lord Jesus Christ. . . .

—ROMANS 13:14 (NIV)

Last fall, I went to St. Mary's Hospital to have a CAT scan of my sinuses. When I checked in, the clerk began the tedious process of verifying my insurance information. "Don't you have that on file?" I asked, an edge of annoyance in my voice.

"I'm sorry," she said. "It does seem like we ask the same questions a dozen times."

In my many trips to St. Mary's, I'd often encountered this same clerk, with her glistening black hair, rings on every perfectly manicured finger and a perennial smile. She was the kind of person you knew had it all together. That morning, as my eyes fell to her new little white-beaded bracelet, inscribed with the letters *WWJD* ("What Would Jesus Do?"), I understood why.

"I love your bracelet," I said, embarrassed to admit I was a Christian after my bout of impatience. "I sure wish I could live up to those words. But I'm having a really down day." My doctor suspected that tumors were growing in my sinuses, and I'd fought a splitting headache for days. And with my feet cracked and bleeding from still more tumors, I felt as if I'd been walking on shards of glass.

"Oh, I fail Him, too," the clerk assured me. "Every day. But He understands. What matters is that our heart is bent toward Him. Then we're in the right position to start over."

The CAT scan technician gave my chin an upward tilt. "There, now, perfect position, Roberta. Lie still so the pictures won't be blurry." And there in the stillness, with my heart bent toward God, it was just as the clerk had promised. I was in the perfect position for a brand-new beginning.

Loving Father, thank You for the people You place in my life to point me toward You. Help me to notice each one You place in my path.
—ROBERTA MESSNER

15/WED   *Here there is no . . . slave or free, but Christ is all, and is in all.*   —COLOSSIANS 3:11 (NIV)

My nine-year-old John ordered a paperback from the school book club entitled *I Have a Dream—Dr. Martin Luther King, Jr.* I was quite surprised when the book arrived to find that it was not a book *about* Dr. King, but an illustrated edition of the actual text of his most famous speech. I had been John's age myself when this historic speech was delivered.

As John and I looked through the book together, we came to a picture of a white mob pouring ketchup on the heads of African Americans seated at a lunch counter. John had many questions, and I had to admit the sad truth about our society's history of race relations. *What faith Dr. King must have had to believe that such monumental changes were possible,* I thought.

Then I read aloud a simple yet moving paragraph from the speech: "I have a dream that one day on the red hills of Georgia, the sons of former slaves and the sons of former slave owners will be able to sit down together at the table of brotherhood."

A shiver went down my spine as the words hit me like a prophecy fulfilled in my own life. We lived in the red clay hills of Georgia, and as difficult as it was to admit it, some of my ancestors had owned slaves. Yet Dr. King's dream had become a reality every time my family had sat down around our turn-of-the-century mahogany dining room table to share a meal with African American friends, co-workers and neighbors.

Finally I understood something of Dr. King's faith. Yes, he worked hard for new laws to bring about justice and change, but he also knew that the laws of the heart are the ones that revolutionize the world. Even monumental changes start small—one dining room table at a time.

Father, remake our life together in the image of Your love for us, one heart at a time—beginning with mine. —KAREN BARBER

16/THU *If I speak with the tongues of men and of angels, but do not have love, I have become a noisy gong or a clanging cymbal.* —I CORINTHIANS 13:1 (NAS)

My friend Ed Streetman was eighty-three years old when he died last week. He lived a good life and accomplished much. A generous man, he gave back to life far more than he received.

The day after his death, I visited with his family. I have been Ed's pastor for eight years, and they asked me to conduct his funeral. With his wife and two middle-aged children gathered around the dining room table, we began to plan his funeral service. Looking at his daughter Helen, I asked, "Look back through your years with your father. What are some of the most important lessons that he taught you?"

Without hesitation, Helen quickly answered, "He taught me to ride a bicycle, and I've never forgotten how."

For a minute I sat there stunned. Surely there must have been a parental lesson more memorable, a teaching more profound. Then I realized that Helen was serious. The memory of her father teaching her to ride a bicycle, gently picking her up when she fell, was a symbol of a lifelong loving relationship.

Later, as I drove home, I thought about my own three children. *When all is said and done, what will they say are the most important lessons I have taught them?* Probably not the ones I thought most important: the principles of financial management, how to study, good manners or how to succeed. I hope they will remember that I loved them, taught them to do things they really enjoyed, and picked them up when they fell and hurt themselves.

The small things in life most reveal our heart. The big things are more easily taught.

Lord, help me take the time to do the little things for my loved ones. Amen. —SCOTT WALKER

READER'S ROOM

How has God been reaching out to me this year? With His all-powerful hand!

In January, I fell on the ice and broke my wrist—my first experience with broken bones. After nine weeks, I am out of the cast and have completed two weeks of physical therapy.

I am so thankful every time I master a new task. At first, I rejoiced before the Lord every time I buttoned a button, turned a knob or signed my name. Now I thank Him that I can type with both hands and play the piano again. I also thank Him for the ability to wash the dishes, vacuum the floors, make the beds and cook dinner. I thank Him that I can turn a key in a lock and open a door.

I also thank Him for what I see others doing. When I attended a symphony orchestra concert this weekend, I studied the musicians and marveled at everything the human hand can do. And I marvel at the hand of God knitting my bones back together when they were hidden in the cocoon of a cast. —HELENE C. KUONI, BASKING RIDGE, NEW JERSEY

17 / *FRI*   *Whoever is kind to the needy honors God.*
—PROVERBS 14:31 (NIV)

When our family lived in South Africa, we were approached almost daily on the street or at our door by beggars pleading for a job, food, clothing or money. We were living in a small apartment with only the contents of our suitcases and little money, and I sorely felt our inability to help them.

One day I shared my frustration with the priest at the church we were attending. "Remember," Father Panteleimon said, "the greatest of all virtues is charity. Be grateful for any opportunity to show kindness to someone. See each request as a privilege, a chance to give to Christ coming to you in the 'least of His brethren.' Try to give what you can, even a few coins or a little food, a kind word and a prayer."

One evening shortly after our talk, I walked to the store "just to get milk"—and headed home with two bags. A woman in a maid's uniform, on her way home from work, approached me. "Oh, madame," she pleaded, "could you give me money for my children? I don't get paid until next week and we have no more food."

About to say, "Sorry, I have no money left," I remembered Father Panteleimon's words.

"Here, take these." I handed her the bags, after pulling out a carton of milk. "This is all I really need tonight."

She protested, but I put the sacks in her hands. "It's not much," I insisted, "just bread, cheese, meat and custard."

"Oh, madame, thank you, thank you!" Her face beamed. "My children will be so happy." I floated to our apartment, profoundly grateful that God had put her in my path.

Now I'm back home in the suburbs, and no beggars approach me for food. But God gives me other opportunities to make small sacrifices. A friend calls late at night needing to talk. Reluctantly leaving the recliner and my favorite TV show, I listen, offer some encouragement and then head to bed renewed.

Lord, help me recognize each opportunity today to show You kindness.
—MARY BROWN

18/SAT

And thou shalt rejoice, thou, and thine household. —DEUTERONOMY 14:26

I've had some health problems this year that have caused me to look at life in new ways. I'm more and more aware of my aging body and of the fact that my life on earth will indeed come to an end someday. (There's always been some denying part of me that hasn't quite believed this would actually happen to *me*.)

This very day, at this very moment, my body is operating up to speed. I can walk up the mountain road behind our house, past the winter-vacant cabins on Falls Avenue, where I stop to gaze at the doe and her three fawns who have stopped to gaze at me in the stillness. I can come home to savor stuffed peppers from the Crock Pot. I can look out our picture window and enjoy the gently falling snow as it lays down a white carpet over the now-brown grass. I can listen to music in the dark with my husband Robert and enjoy resting my head on his shoulder. I can relish the scent of pine from the fire in our wood-burning stove that reminds us that we're warm and safe from the winter cold outside.

More frequently now than ever before, I find myself thinking, *Amazing! I'm here! Now! This moment!* And at those wake-up instants, I give thanks just for the miraculous fact of being alive.

As I walk through this day, Loving Christ, please keep me awake to those everyday blessings I so often take for granted.

—MARILYN MORGAN KING

19/SUN

His work is perfect. . . .—DEUTERONOMY 32:4

I pride myself on having a very clear awareness of my failings. I keep a mental list under the heading "Fix These." I also know what I'm good at, and this much smaller list falls under the heading "Acceptable Behavior." I've filed "Good Organizer" in the "Acceptable Behavior" column, and I use my almost-daily walking time to hone this skill.

This past Sunday my husband Charlie accompanied me on my walk. At six feet, four inches tall, he's got quite a leg-span advantage over me, but he had to pay attention to match my determined stride. Where he might have meandered, I sped along, dragging him with me. As we passed ice-covered inlets, snow-brushed marshes, deserted winter beaches and warmly lit houses, I plunged ahead with my agenda, talking nonstop about our budget. How much will our vacation cost? Will we have enough saved by then? Do we have enough frequent-flyer miles for a free ticket? What about two free tickets? Has he made the reservations yet?

Suddenly, Charlie interrupted me, "Marc, look at the Canada geese on the ice!"

Without even glancing to where he was gesturing, I snapped, "Are you even listening to me?"

Charlie gently took me by the shoulders and turned me toward the cove. I gasped in surprise: There were more than a hundred Canada geese waddling around on top of the ice as if waiting for the sun to melt it and restore order in their lives.

I put my arms around Charlie. When we got home, I would have to make a few changes to my "Acceptable Behavior" list.

Lord, You've given us so much! Open my senses to Your many gifts.　　　　　—MARCI ALBORGHETTI

20/MON You shall eat the fruit of the labor of your hands; you shall be happy, and it shall be well with you. . . . May you see your children's children! . . .　　—PSALM 128:2, 6 (RSV)

For a long time I fretted that by the time my children decided to have babies, my arthritis would be so bad I wouldn't be able to knit. Last winter I decided to knit anyway; whatever I came up with could easily wait. I was almost finished with an elaborate pink dress when I chanced to go over to my daughter's house. She handed me a gift. "What's this?" I asked.

Heather just smiled. I looked over to her husband. "A Happy Monday present," Dallas singsonged mysteriously.

"Am I supposed to open it now?"

They curled up on the sofa; I took the rocking chair. Pulling back the wrapping of a small photo album, I read, *Grandmother's Brag Book.* I sat a moment uncomprehending, then I sprang off the rocker onto the sofa and hugged my daughter over and over. *A baby!*

Four months later I was nursing a sore throat, buried beneath a blanket on the sofa, when my son and his wife came over with some Popsicles for me. Phil came around and perched on the sofa arm behind my head, but instead of handing off a Popsicle, he gave me a book. "See what Katie's dad just gave me?" he said, pleased as punch. Up I popped like jack-in-the-box! I was staring at Bill Cosby's *Fatherhood.*

"*You're* pregnant, too, Philly?"

"Well, Katie is."

Katie gave me a smile that made me grin big time. *Two babies!* "Good thing I got started knitting!"

Heather is due the end of January, Katie the end of May, on my fiftieth birthday. I called my youngest child, still at Wheaton College in Chicago, to tell him the good news. Blake always manages to say what's in my heart. "*Yes!*" he shouted into the phone. That's exactly how I feel. *Yes!*

Dear Lord, I am at last eating the fruit of my labor—for I am happy, it is well with me, and soon I will see my children's children. Yes!   —BRENDA WILBEE

21/TUE   *"You shall love the Lord your God with all your heart, and with all your soul, and with all your mind. . . . You shall love your neighbor as yourself."*

—MATTHEW 22:37, 39 (RSV)

I'd forgotten my promise to visit a sick friend at the hospital, and now he was dead.

"I couldn't even remember to visit my dying friend!" I told another friend. "Maybe I should give my pew at church to someone who really loves his neighbor as himself."

My friend just smiled and shook his head. "Keith, no one can live perfectly enough to earn God's love. That's why Jesus had to die for us."

"I know that," I said, "but if I love God with all my heart and soul and mind, then why can't I love my neighbor as myself?"

My friend looked at me a few seconds. "Keith," he said, "I don't know about you, but if I really loved God with all my heart and soul and mind, I'd have more time to pray and read the Bible, and I'd be a lot more focused on loving other people."

"Well, then," I said quietly, "how do I change?"

"When I realize I've forgotten to keep a promise," my friend said thoughtfully, "I look at exactly what I was doing when I forgot, because it was obviously more important to me than loving people for God. Then I can ask God to help me surrender that absorbing thing I was doing to Him."

I thought about the day I forgot to see my friend. I was working to get a project finished, and I didn't take time to pray or read the Bible or listen to the people around me who needed love and attention. At the center of my life, I'd replaced God with an idol—my work. I was heartbroken; it was time to ask God to help me change my priorities and surrender them to Him.

Lord, help me put You in the center of my life—and when I forget, please do whatever it takes to remind me. Amen.

—KEITH MILLER

22 / WED Remember me, O my God, concerning this, and wipe not out my good deeds that I have done. . . .

—NEHEMIAH 13:14

Some of my grandchildren were almost grown before it dawned on me that I'd made huge mistakes as a mother. As I watched my children raise their own children and had some honest, often painful discussions with them, I realized I probably could have qualified for Unmother of the Year. My children were very specific:

"You were always helping others."

"You were always working."

"You locked us out of the house during the summer and told us to drink out of the hose."

"You screamed a lot."

"You didn't smile much."

"You almost never seemed happy."

"You weren't much fun."

"We never got to have sleep-over company."

"You said no most of the time."

Recently, I saw an unforgettable picture in the newspaper: A mother, her face all aglow, followed her young daughter into a garden to gather tomatoes. One look at the child's expression said it all: "I've got the best mother in the world!" I made copies of the picture and mailed them to my children, writing, "I wish you had memories like this."

The first response came in today's mail in a hastily scrawled letter I'll always keep: "In bed two nights ago, I remembered the day you taught me 'Annabelle Lee.' I remember knowing even then that I loved the strings of words that moved my heart. You taught me to love words, to put them together like sewing an outfit. Maybe the best memory ever was when we could go downtown to the Athens library on a Sunday afternoon. Nothing could be better than that! Libraries, books, words—you taught me to appreciate the written word. And lately, you've taught me to have fun! Thanks, friend o' mine!"

Lord, even though we're all adults, I pray it's not too late for You to show me how to make more memories with my children.

—MARION BOND WEST

23/THU Do not put out the Spirit's fire. . . . Hold on to the good. Avoid every kind of evil.

—I THESSALONIANS 5:19, 21-22 (NIV)

My friend and I arrived early for the performance by the Abbotsford Symphony. "Shall we sit here?" she asked, stopping at a row of seats near the front.

I looked up and wanted to shout, "Not here, please." For in the very next row sat Susan, my former head nurse, who had been responsible for my losing a job.

"You've decided to forgive her," a small Voice whispered. *"So why not sit here?"*

She'll turn around and I'll have to speak with her, I argued back. Not wanting to upset my friend, I reluctantly sat down.

But I didn't get the full benefit of the wonderful performance by the orchestra. Other voices clamored for my attention: *"What she did was downright mean. She deserves to be shunned."* And yet I knew that forgiveness is like a very narrow gate leading to a garden where God dwells. If you want to enter it, you can't hang on to extra baggage like resentment and bitterness. You must give up your right to be hurt.

I want to forgive, Jesus, but it's so hard. Please, help me.

During intermission I watched Susan rise and reach for what I thought was a clipboard. *How typical,* I thought. Always looking for new ideas to improve the efficiency of her ward, superorganized Susan often carried a clipboard as she made careful notes and charts of everything.

I tapped her on the shoulder. "Susan, did you take your clipboard to the *symphony*?" I asked in mock horror.

"Not on your life," she shot back with a laugh.

For a few moments, we chatted amiably the way forgiven people do, then Susan joined her friends.

This is the only way to live, I thought as I settled in to enjoy the second half of the concert. *Life is too short for keeping grudges and spoiling symphonies.*

Lord Jesus, help me to forgive others as You have forgiven me.

—HELEN GRACE LESCHEID

℮〜

24/*FRI* *I am listening carefully to all the Lord is saying.*... —PSALM 85:8 (TLB)

I love a good movie. I've lost count of the many times I've seen television reruns of *The Sound of Music*, *My Fair Lady*, *Chariots of Fire* and Sir Anthony Hopkins playing C. S. Lewis in *Shadowlands*, to name a few. Currently, I've taken to watching a TV program that features actors, actresses and directors in hour-long interviews that give inspirational insights into their childhoods and their struggles to get to where they are.

The high point of the program comes toward the end, when as part of the regular format, the featured personality is asked, "When you get to heaven, what do you want God to say to you?"

The answers vary from, "Whew, I'm glad you made it!" to "Welcome, come on in" or, as in one original response, "We're not ready for you yet. Go back down to earth!"

The answer that left the greatest impression on me came from the director who said that throughout his childhood, in his home, the Scriptures were read aloud every day. He wasn't given a choice. Day in and day out, he had to sit and respectfully listen to the Word of God, so much so that when he gets to heaven he would like God to say to him, "Thanks for listening!"

I've thought a lot about that director's answer. Because the Word of God is the voice of God to me, I've now taken to reading my daily devotional passages of Scripture aloud so that I might better listen, not only with my inward ear, but also with my outer ear. When I get to heaven, I hope God also says to me, "Thanks for listening!"

What an awesome and magnificent voice You have, O Lord! Help me listen daily to the beauty of the Psalms, the wisdom of Proverbs, the promises spoken through the prophets and, most of all, the voice of Christ. —FAY ANGUS

25/SAT *Therefore shall a man leave his father and his mother, and shall cleave unto his wife: and they shall be one flesh.* —GENESIS 2:24

My wife Sandee likes to say that Saturday is "Daddy's day to bond with the kids," which is code for "You're on your own, pal."

Mostly I enjoy it, although I would appreciate a nap. Inevitably I plan the day poorly, and we end up at McDonald's for dinner. Besides, Grace, the five-year-old, loves the Playland.

There are often other fathers at McDonald's Playland. Some of them I know; they're in the same boat with me—single for a day. Others, though, are single on a more permanent basis. And I begin to realize that this is "their weekend to have the kids." I hear the fathers' flat voices echo against the hard plastic:

"Sarah, leave your brother alone."

"Either eat or play."

"Adam, put your socks back on, or we're going."

I'm having fries with my oldest daughter Faith, while she does her homework. And I start thinking, *We're here by choice—because I'm too lazy to cook. We're not here by court order: Wednesday afternoons and every other weekend, plus rotating holidays as agreed.*

Faith is learning a new word: *leaving.* Reading her third-grade script upside down, I add a thin letter to her new word. She stares at the result.

"What's *cleaving*?" she asks.

"To join," I tell her, "or to split."

Now she looks at me, and for that moment I feel like the last married father in McDonald's, the last married father in America, and I'm afraid of what she might ask. Instead she asks me if she can go play.

So I sit there in my bright little chair, next to a statue of Ronald

McDonald, wondering about the thin line that separates *leaving* from *cleaving*, as my daughter—*our* daughter—negotiates with Adam and his one sock, deciding who can and cannot play in the little room with the plastic balls.

Thanks, Lord, for a day out with our girls. And give all of us the strength to face the many challenges of parenthood—and marriage.   —MARK COLLINS

26/SUN   *Thy testimonies are very sure: holiness becometh thine house, O Lord, for ever.*   —PSALM 93:5

The tears rolled quietly but steadily down her face and dripped onto her blouse, making a dark mark. We were standing around the Communion table at an early morning service, and I didn't know if her tears came from sorrow or from the wonder of worship. I had never seen her before. Big city churches welcome many strangers.

I am both reserved and shy—foolish at this stage in my life, but a fact. So it surprised, almost shocked me to see my hand stretch out and take hers. The serene voices of the choir continued to sing:

> *Here I am, Lord.*
> *Is it I, Lord.*
> *I have heard You calling in the night.*

And the weeping stranger and I held hands. The hymn ended. The congregation greeted one another. She squeezed my hand, said "Thank you" almost in a whisper and walked out of my life.

Afterward, I thought about those few moments. I wondered what gave me the confidence to reach out and take her hand. I just never do things like that; I never ask questions at lectures or offer my opinion unsolicited.

The explanation is so simple that it took awhile for me to realize it: I was in God's house, and when you're in someone's house, you follow His rules.

Lord, let me listen always for Your voice and do what You ask of me.   —BRIGITTE WEEKS

27 / MON   As cold water to a weary soul, So is good news
from a far country.   —PROVERBS 25:25 (NKJV)

"The mail is here!" my wife shouts, and we race each other to the box, laughing. From a good friend of ours I've learned just what it takes to get a letter to us.

Carolyn Ferguson is a bright brunette with a talk-show personality, and she works as a rural mail carrier in Mississippi. Wearing a "Rejoice" T-shirt, Carolyn pilots her little white truck with her left hand and stuffs boxes with her right. Taped gospel music sets the pace for her demanding job of filling almost seven hundred boxes. Many dangers lurk on those pretty country roads: flash floods, auto accidents, road construction and flat tires. Her *ooga* horn helps her avoid stray cows and crossing deer.

The big dread of every mail carrier is the dog: pit bulls, Rottweilers and other incredibly friendly canines. Some mail carriers might just drive on or even use a chemical repellent, but Carolyn keeps a box of dog biscuits on her seat. She throws a biscuit to the dog and calls it by name. "Easy, Trapper!" "Down, Bubba!" Names she learns from listening to the owners. The dogs become docile.

What gives Carolyn patience with her exhausting task is her overwhelming sense of mission—the mail must go through. She sees herself as a distributor of happiness, and she envisions all the smiling faces waiting for their packages and letters.

It's a principle I need to keep in mind when I face the "big dogs" of my work. When students attack me about low grade reports, I need to see them not as enemies but as future leaders, if I can guide them to maturity. Some tasks are just too important to let barking people interfere. Whether you are a teacher, a parent or a stockbroker, the mail must go through.

Lord, keep my mind focused on my mission of service to others.
                                        —DANIEL SCHANTZ

28 / TUE   *"I will send down showers in season; there
will be showers of blessing."*   —EZEKIEL 34:26 (NIV)

"Bless you!" a stranger said to me as I sneezed loudly in the supermarket once again. It must have been the tenth time I'd heard it that day as I suffered with yet another winter cold. *I don't feel all that blessed,* I thought, sniffling and reaching for another tissue. I appreciated her kindness, but suddenly the phrase seemed silly. Who's really thinking about God's blessings when somebody sneezes? I've read that the origins of this tradition go far back in history, to a superstitious belief that an evil spirit could enter the body to steal the soul or to the fear that a sneeze signaled oncoming illness, requiring God's protection for the sneezer. Whatever its origin, the average "Bless you" is little more than a courtesy today.

Still, all those "bless yous" made me think about the many times each day when I do feel blessed in small ways. I was blessed when a truck driver let me in ahead of him to make my left turn, instead of speeding up to beat me to the intersection. And I was blessed when a woman held the door open and waited for me as I struggled with my arms full of boxes for a school project. These weren't big events, but little kindnesses that eased my way and brought much-needed help.

Yet I've discovered something about these small, everyday blessings. They seem to mean the most to me when I'm on the giving end. The other day I was waiting in the checkout line with my full cart, and I let a man with a huge box of diapers go ahead of me. "Thank you. You're a blessing to me today," he said. But instead I felt blessed, privileged to be able to pass on even the tiniest bit of God's love that might make someone's day go a little smoother. It's one of God's wonderful ironies: The more blessings I give others, the more blessed I am myself.

Heavenly Father, show me the ways I might shower others with blessings as You have showered me. —GINA BRIDGEMAN

29/WED

Lord. . . ."   *"Blessed is the man who trusts in the Lord. . . ."* —JEREMIAH 17:7 (NAS)

I was working in my office when the phone rang. It was my son Reggie. "Dad," he said, "I need your advice." Now, Reggie hasn't asked me for advice in quite some time. In fact, there had been a few times over the past few years when he thought I was giving him more advice than he cared to have. So I was both surprised and glad to hear his request. *Now that he's twenty-five years old,* I thought, *maybe he's growing up.*

Reggie wanted to talk to me about buying a car. We'd given him an older car when he graduated from college, but it had finally broken down. He needed a new one, which would be the first car he purchased on his own. We talked about the style and make of car he was interested in, the price range he was looking at, how large a monthly car payment he could afford, and how the car payment would affect his budget.

For the next few days, my phone rang off the hook. I didn't really give Reggie much advice; mostly I listened to him and asked questions. And when he finally bought a car, I knew that he'd considered his decision carefully, and he knew that even though the car he bought was not the one I would have purchased, he had my support.

Best of all, I'd been able to trust Reggie to make a good decision. It isn't easy for a father to let go, but I learned that I could be available to my son without trying to control him. Even if it meant biting my tongue once or twice, I could listen, ask a few questions, and let God go to work in Reggie's life.

Lord, help me trust You in all things, even in the decisions of my children. —DOLPHUS WEARY

$30/$ THU   *"He will yet fill your mouth with laughter. . . ."*
—JOB 8:21 (NAS)

"Going out to plug in the car," my husband Leo called from the back doorway.

A good thing, too, for when I peeked through the heavily frosted window on that winter morning, the thermometer read thirty-two below. Pulling my cozy housecoat more snugly around me, I shuffled down the hall to turn up the thermostat. Murphy, our old ginger-colored cat, had just crawled out from under the covers of a warm bed and was sleepily sauntering toward the kitchen.

Suddenly, the back door creaked open and Leo jumped back inside, clouds of frosty air billowing around him, his big floppy overshoes squeaking on the snow. The plaid scarf tied around his head was knotted under his chin, and he had a decrepit old jacket pulled on over his pajamas.

In all of his nine lives, Murphy the cat had never encountered anyone wearing such odd-looking clothes so early in the morning.

Hissing and arching his back, his tail extended like a bottle brush, he attempted a speedy getaway, his claws screeching on the slippery floor. Bolting down the hallway, he skidded around the corner and disappeared from view.

"What was that?" exclaimed Leo, peering at me through hoarfrosted glasses.

"The cat. He took exception to your dress code!"

We both burst into belly laughs. "I bet he hasn't moved that fast in a year!" Leo said.

"And he may not surface for that long either!" I replied. We laughed all over again.

Poor Murphy! Not until mid-morning did his hunger finally overcome his hesitancy. Very warily, he crept out to his dish, but he's still a little skittish when the back door opens on a winter morning.

Father God, thank You for the humorous little episodes that warm me up inside, even on the coldest days of the year.

—ALMA BARKMAN

31 / FRI   *A cheerful heart is a good medicine, but a downcast spirit dries up the bones.*   —PROVERBS 17:22 (RSV)

"Linda, can you cover the music department tonight? We're short-staffed."

I gulped and said yes to my frazzled bookstore manager. But I knew—as he did—that I'd be in trouble. While I love books, my knowledge of music is limited to the fact that there were four Beatles. And isn't there a crooner named Frank Sinatra? The customers who poured in that Friday night—mostly teenagers in giggling groups—were sure to expose me as the tin-eared musical ignoramus I am. *Not if I can help it,* I decided.

So all night I managed to field questions with an officious sounding "Let me look that up on the system." Names of singers— or were they groups—I certainly didn't know flew by my head like strange tunes: Blink 182? Metallica? Barenaked Ladies? I managed to hide my shock at that one, though my eyes opened wide. *God, just help me not to show my ignorance,* I breathed in a silent prayer. *Oh, and could You never put me in the music department again?*

Apparently I hid my ignorance well, for I managed to direct all the kids to the right areas, ring up their sales and bag their purchases.

"Enjoy your records!" I said, smugly handing them the white plastic bags across the counter. I heard them giggling, and my face flamed.

"Records!" I heard one say, laughing as they exited. "Did she say 'records'? That is *so* totally seventies!"

I felt confusion for a moment, then I laughed. Of course! We haven't sold records for years. They're all CDs now. I *am* so seventies, I suppose. So sixties, even.

As I stood there smiling, my manager came by. "You seemed nervous, but it looks as if you're doing okay," he said.

I nodded. "I think I handled it fairly well for someone who is so totally seventies," I commented. Then I added, "You can put me in music again anytime. It's 2003, and I guess it's time for me to move up to the eighties, at least in my musical knowledge."

God, thank You for letting me know it's okay not to know all the answers—sometimes not even to understand the questions! Make me open to learning more every day. —LINDA NEUKRUG

My Daily Blessings

1 _____

2 _____

3 _____

4 _____

5 _____

6 _____

7 _____

8 _____

9 _____

10 _____

11 _____

12 _____

13 _____

14 _____

15 _____

16 _____

17 _____

18 _____

19 _____

20 _____

21 _____

22 _____

23 _____

24 _____

25 _____

26 _____

27 _____

28 _____

29 _____

30 _____

31 _____

FEBRUARY

Blessed are they that mourn: for
they shall be comforted.
—Matthew 5:4

S	M	T	W	T	F	S
						1
2	3	4	5	6	7	8
9	10	11	12	13	14	15
16	17	18	19	20	21	22
23	24	25	26	27	28	

AN EYE FOR BLESSINGS

*1/*SAT   THE LANGUAGE OF LOVE
For God so loved the world that he gave his only Son. . . .
—JOHN 3:16 (RSV)

The first valentine card came in the mail today. Because my birthday is on Valentine's Day, I've probably received more than my share of these over the years! When I was growing up, I saved them in a heart-shaped candy box covered in red satin, marveling that there could be so many different rhymes for the same message.

How many means of expressing love? I look around and see the footstool with my mother-in-law's needlepoint cushion, the hammered-brass kettle from her home in Holland that Corrie ten Boom brought us on her last visit, the quilt on the wall that family members worked in secret for a year to give us on our fiftieth anniversary.

How many ways to say "I love you"? On the bed upstairs is the green bathrobe made by my friend Mary Lynn Windsor. On the dresser, the photo our friend Sandy LeSourd took of my husband and me in Florida; before sending it, Sandy glued two dozen seashells to the frame.

Since January 1, I've been trying to be more aware of the things around me every day. But the blessings, I thought as I carried the valentine from room to room, are so much more than the physical things themselves! Object after object evoked a face, a voice, a loving hand. Next to the seashell frame on the dresser is a wooden plaque with the single word *Jesus*. Of all the ways there are to say love, God chose the one that says it best.

In this month of valentines, Lord, help me find new ways to speak Your language of love.   —ELIZABETH SHERRILL

2/SUN   *Now the God of hope fill you with all joy and peace in believing, that ye may abound in hope, through the power of the Holy Ghost.* —ROMANS 15:13

Just before my husband Norman Vincent Peale retired as minister of New York City's Marble Collegiate Church, I attended a brunch for members of the congregation. I found myself sitting next to a woman from out of town who told me that her husband could have used Norman's sermon on joy that day.

"What's troubling him?" I asked.

"Everything bothers him!" she answered. "The state of the world, the state of his health, his job. Life in our house is one long gloom."

When I asked the woman why she couldn't change that, she looked at me with astonishment. "Why, what can I do?" she asked.

"Everything," I responded as I sipped my tea.

"Oh, come now, Mrs. Peale," she said. "It's easy for you to talk. You're married to one of the world's greatest optimists."

She was right about one thing: Norman was one of the world's great optimists. But she was dead wrong in thinking I didn't understand her situation. Norman, too, had his moments of discouragement.

"I try to help Norman through his darker days by encouraging him to talk out his feelings," I told her. "As I listen, I try to absorb some of his gloominess, as if I were made of emotional blotting paper.

"You need to discover your own ways to help your husband. The human mind can't hold two sets of ideas at the same time, so if you can help him to focus his mind on something good and positive, he won't be able to dwell on the bad and negative things."

As we stood to leave the fellowship hall, I encouraged her to try for forty days to help her husband have fun and be positive. "Ask God to guide you and make the best out of every day of your marriage," I told her. "I know He'll hear your prayer."

Lord, help me to greet each day joyfully and to share my joy with others. —RUTH STAFFORD PEALE

3/MON   *Let this mind be in you, which was also in Christ Jesus: Who, being in the form of God . . . took upon him the form of a servant, and was made in the likeness of men.*
—PHILIPPIANS 2:5–7

Yesterday was Sunday, an unseasonably bright, warm February day. On the way home from church, I asked five-year-old John if he'd like to go to the park with me. I've been struggling hard to understand what's been going on with John lately. With a new baby in the family, the occasional misbehavior he showed at three and four has given way to tantrums. The usual disciplinary strategies only seem to fuel them, and I find myself fighting my own anger and frustration.

"Can we play American Revolution?" John asked excitedly.

"Sure," I answered. John loves birds and music, but most of all he loves history, especially if it involves battles. So after lunch, we headed for Fort Tryon Park. Our New York City neighborhood was the site of the battle for Fort Washington, an American defeat that sent George Washington's army retreating across New Jersey, and the park is built on the site of a British redoubt.

"You can be the British," John announced. "I'll be the Americans."

For three hours, John and I were playmates. We ran back and forth maneuvering our troops, charging and repulsing attacks. Then John decided we would both be Americans, and he spun out complicated scenarios in which joggers were regiments of Hessians, dog walkers were Loyalist spies, and football players were the British Army.

Our afternoon in the park hasn't solved John's behavior problems. But it has given him a chance to see his daddy, not as the man who puts him in time-out, but as a fellow citizen of his own imaginative world. And it's reminded me that behind the storm clouds, John is still the sweet and enthusiastic boy he was before his troubles started.

Lord, thank You for the love that sent You to live and die as a citizen of our broken world.   —ANDREW ATTAWAY

4/ TUE   *Very early in the morning, while it was still dark, Jesus got up, left the house and went off to a solitary place, where he prayed.*   —MARK 1:35 (NIV)

Years ago I heard it called a "California rolling stop." When approaching a stop sign or making a right turn at a red light, a driver would slow down just enough to see if the coast was clear, then speed up without making the mandatory stop. Today while I was on my morning walk, I felt anger begin to simmer as I witnessed a driver hardly hesitate before darting past a stop sign. Here in California, it seemed to me, running red lights and stop signs has become an epidemic.

But as I continued pushing myself in a brisk walking pace, a different perspective started to take shape: Motorists are not the only ones who fail to stop when they should. In my own life, I've often plunged ahead when I ought to have stopped to see if it was okay to proceed. For instance, there was the evening I was lost for two hours driving around Washington, D.C. I'd rushed away from the Baltimore airport rental car counter with the wrong map—it was for Baltimore.

More than anything, though, I found myself thinking of the times I'd done the wrong thing because I failed to stop and pray. Once, I taped a nasty note to a neighbor family's door after they'd gone away, leaving their dog barking outside. If I'd stopped to pray, I would have waited and reasoned with them later in person. I finally did, successfully, after my first complaint backfired with angry words.

I finished my walk that morning not angry, but thankful—and with plenty to pray about.

Father, help me not only to stop and think, but also to pray before I act.   —HAROLD HOSTETLER

5/ WED   *"I have come to bring fire to the earth, and, oh, that my task were completed! There is a terrible baptism ahead of me, and how I am pent up until it is accomplished!"*   —LUKE 12:49–50 (TLB)

I'm not an autograph collector, but in our home we do have one framed autograph. I got it for my youngest son Andrew in 1991 when I was working for a radio station in Milwaukee, Wisconsin.

One day, baseball great Hank Aaron came to the station to promote his book *I Had a Hammer: The Hank Aaron Story*. During a commercial break, I asked Hank for his autograph. He smiled and wrote his name in big letters across a sheet from my radio station notepad.

Of course, Andrew was thrilled. After all, Hank Aaron still holds Major League Baseball's record for the most home runs hit by any player. Though I'm not a diehard baseball fan, I was even more thrilled than Andrew to have this man's autograph. Why? Because of the struggles Hank Aaron had during his career. He began playing at a time when few African American athletes even made it into the big leagues. And because of racism, he had to struggle against the odds time and again, often facing taunts and jeers from the world outside the baseball field.

Do you ever feel you're battling a war against all odds? Do pressures in your home or job make you feel you're not accomplishing anything worthwhile? Next time you feel that way, think about Hank Aaron. For more than twenty years he just "hammered" away, facing the struggles head-on, until he beat Babe Ruth's record by forty-one home runs!

By the way, today, is "Hammerin' Hank's" birthday.

Heavenly Father, when I feel as if I'm not accomplishing anything, give me the grace and determination to keep hammerin' away and remind me that someday, with Your help, I will have accomplished something great. —PATRICIA LORENZ

6/THU   *O give thanks unto the Lord; for he is good: for his mercy endureth for ever.* —PSALM 106:1

"Please, Lord, help me see the circumstances of this day as gifts from You," I prayed as I sat in a dreary motel room on a drab winter morning, far from home. For the last two days, I'd been at a conference and now it was my husband's birthday, and I just wanted to get home. But because of airline problems, I couldn't get a flight until afternoon, and now it was snowing . . . hard.

So I packed my bags, caught a shuttle and got to the airport early. Upon checking in, I found that all the flights were oversold, and even though I had a ticket, I didn't have a seat. "You're on the waiting list," the ticket agent told me. "I think you'll be fine."

I didn't want to be "fine." I wanted to be on the plane. I wanted to throw a tantrum. I wanted to talk about "being fair." But instead I merely sat down in the waiting area where I watched dozens of people board the flight. At least a dozen more waited, just like me, hoping for seats. Lots of names were called, and people went forward to get their boarding passes, including people who had checked in after I did.

Please, Lord, let me see these circumstances as gifts from You, I repeated, thinking maybe God hadn't heard me the first time.

At last my name was called, and I went up to the gate. "We're out of room in coach," the boarding agent said, "but we've found a seat for you."

An hour later, I was sitting on the plane with a white linen cloth covering my tray table, enjoying an elegant three-course meal, while stretching out to enjoy the extra space (and grace!) of my first-class seat. It seems they had run out of seats in coach and being last had made me first—for first-class.

Lord, even when my circumstances don't include first-class, may I see them as Your gifts, intended for good.

—CAROL KUYKENDALL

7 / FRI   *I have been reminded of your sincere faith, which first lived in your grandmother . . . and, I am persuaded, now lives in you also.*   —II TIMOTHY 1:5 (NIV)

My grandmother had fallen—again. The first time she had broken her hip. Now, at ninety-seven, she had fractured her shoulder. After two days, the hospital was discharging her, and since her arm was immobilized in a sling, she couldn't use her walker. She needed twenty-four-hour care. Mamie, her regular daytime nurse, arranged for a nighttime nurse to start on Monday, but today was Friday. For the upcoming weekend, I would stay with Gamma at night, while Mamie would be with her during the day.

Ten minutes into my first shift, I was washing dishes when I heard a knock. I peeked into Gamma's room. She was reaching out to the table and swinging her knees off the bed.

"Gamma, what are you doing?"

"I need to go to the bathroom. I thought that as long as I could just touch something, I would be okay."

"Let me help you," I said.

After she was settled back into bed, I explained, "Gamma, the doctor told you to walk only with someone helping you."

"I know. I just don't want to be an inconvenience."

"You're not an inconvenience. You're my grandmother." She slept through the night while I hardly slept at all.

My brother David and I had often spent weekends with Gamma when we were children. At night, she would calm us down from nightmares, pour us a glass of water or just sit watching us fall asleep.

For three nights, I cared for my grandmother. Monday came, and with it came the nighttime nurse. Before I left, Gamma gave me a narrow vertical frame that had lost its place on her wall to a night-light. The frame held six small black-and-white photographs of my brother and me playing in her backyard.

Lord, thank You for the caring that makes us a family, and for the opportunity to give some of it back. —BILLY NEWMAN

8/SAT   *"Their children will see it and be joyful; their hearts will rejoice in the Lord."* —ZECHARIAH 10:7 (NIV)

"That's you on lead guitar?" I asked my son when he played a selection from his band's new CD.

"I told you I've been practicing," Ted answered. I watched my son finger imaginary guitar strings as we listened to the music. His fingers were strong, sure and blindingly quick.

The first time I noticed that quickness was when he was eight years old. We had just adopted him a year before, and Ted seemed comfortable when he was around me. I had almost forgotten that he was nearby while I was cutting some door casing on my table saw. I shut off the switch, and the saw blade continued to spin.

Ted noticed that the leftover wood was still vibrating on the saw table. He reached out to retrieve it before I could even think of crying out. Never have I moved so fast and felt so slow. Ted dropped the wood in wide-eyed alarm when he saw me lunge for him. I grabbed his skinny wrists hard and yanked his hands to eye-height. Fear turned to relief and relief to anger. "Never, ever touch my table saw when the blade is still turning. Just don't get near my tools at all! Ever! Do you understand?"

Ted glared at me. We stared at each other, two strangers, one helpless, the other not knowing how to be helpful.

"Dad," he said, angrily, "when you were a little boy, did you ever hate your dad?"

"Yes, I did," I said. "Especially when he was mad at me."

"What did your dad do when you hated him?"

"He loved me," I said.

Ted didn't understand my answer or the joy that I felt as I held his perfect hands in mine. I like to think that it was a small measure of the joy our Father feels when we first begin to realize He loves us, even when we don't understand what He is doing.

Dear God, help me to understand Your will for me, and thank You for loving me when I don't love You. —TIM WILLIAMS

9/ SUN   *Each man should give what he has decided in his heart to give, not reluctantly or under compulsion. . . .*
—II CORINTHIANS 9:7 (NIV)

February is birthday month in our family. The birthdays begin with my sister Jane on the third, then Mother on the tenth, Aunt Ruth on the eleventh, our grandson Shawn on the twelfth and my wife Ruby on the twentieth. And Valentine's Day, of course, is the fourteenth. Mother and Aunt Ruth are with the angels, but the others have to be remembered.

As each birthday comes up, I shudder. What should I give? All of the people on my list have more than they can say thanks over. Besides, I'm not a good shopper. So every February my worries escalate.

Then one Sunday our pastor suggested we read Romans 12:6–12. "Ask yourselves the following questions," he said. "What are my gifts? Am I using them effectively? Am I sharing genuine love with others? Do I concentrate on what is good? Am I giving presents instead of sharing gifts?" I knew I had work to do.

As I asked myself those questions, I discovered that my attitude was the problem. I treated shopping for birthday gifts as a chore rather than a privilege. I failed to see that the way I gave was more important than the giving. I knew each person well, yet I never listened for clues to appropriate gifts during conversations, and I ignored their wish lists. I was concentrating on myself and not on my loved ones.

As I worked to change, I discovered that pleasing others brought me enjoyment, too. Giving with a smile, good manners and consideration brought delight to me as well as to my family and friends. I'm even beginning to look forward to February!

Giving Lord, help me always to ask, "What can I give today?"
—OSCAR GREENE

$$\mathscr{C}\!\!\sim$$

10/MON   *"My God, in whom I trust!" For it is He who delivers you from the snare. . . .*   —PSALM 91:2–3 (NAS)

I'd had it with Willie, our fat gray-and-white tomcat. If we let him sleep inside during the night, he'd wake me up around one o'clock with a constant *mmeeeeeeoow* until I let him out. Then, promptly at four o'clock, he'd stand at the front door and demand to come back inside. When I let him in, he'd meow relentlessly at the side of our bed until I stomped upstairs and topped off his bowl with a few more pieces of dry food. During the day, Willie paced in my kitchen window boxes, trampling through my flowers, his wide eyes seeming to say, "Meet my needs. Meet my needs."

I complained to Jamie, our twenty-year-old daughter, who had just finished house-sitting for us for a weekend. "I don't know what you're talking about, Mom. While I was in charge, Willie behaved like a perfectly normal cat. He slept at the foot of my bed all night. I fed him once each morning. He purred a lot, but I don't think he meowed much at all."

Is it just me, God? I prayed. *What am I doing wrong with Willie? Even our cat has begun to control me!* God's gentle spirit seemed to impress an unwelcome truth on me: Too often, I handled friends and family just the way I handled Willie. I'd zoom in to fix people's problems, until my constant "helping" made them think I was at their beck and call and left me feeling exhausted and irritable.

Then I came up with a simple plan: From now on, I'd shut our bedroom door at night and turn on the humidifier so I couldn't hear Willie. He could meow as much as he wanted; I wasn't going to jump up to get him more food. In a few days, Willie learned the new rules. So did I.

Lord, before I start trying to fix everything and everyone, remind me to pray and share my problem with You.

—JULIE GARMON

11 / TUE *You, O Lord, keep my lamp burning; my God turns my darkness into light.* —PSALM 18:28 (NIV)

For six months last year, I went through a time of terrible stress. Humbled by an inability to cope with circumstances and responsibilities suddenly thrust upon me, my self-confidence was shattered. My coping skills went to zero as I struggled to survive from day to day. Although I faced a situation that many people seem to adjust to easily, I simply could not. In the midst of this, my cousin Lee Schaffer sent me an e-mail. Lee was well into her fourth year after a bout with cancer, and she shared with me one of the ways she'd been able to find stability in emotional turmoil.

"I know your life seems like a roller coaster and a nightmare right now. It might help to make a list of 'little lights,' hoping to list just one thing you're grateful for at the end of each day. Some days it's hard, but I can always find something. And it's amazing what tiny things are on that list! A wee new daffodil or a door being held for me at the store."

Little lights, I thought. *Yes, a wonderful idea! Small blessings, small rays of delight in this difficult time. But how can I do it with my too-full schedule?*

The next day *Daily Guideposts* gave me the answer. The you-do-it section at the end of each month—what a convenient place to stick an extra bookmark and every day write in a "little light."

I began at once, and over the months I've jotted in things such as "rain in the porch gutters," "finding the wrist-rest for Sheila," "small blue flowers by the front path," "Bill (and the other driver) spared in a car crash in front of him," "tea in Glenda's sunroom" and "soft night winds with lightning over the western mountains."

The bad time is past, but my monthly end-pages in *Daily Guideposts* are still being filled with the small and big praises of the day, a record of the blessings, the "little lights" of God.

Father, thank You for helping me become conscious of the small blessings You pour into my life each day. —ROBERTA ROGERS

A HERITAGE OF FREEDOM

In the days following September 11, 2001, Americans across the country gathered spontaneously to hold hands, pray and sing the old hymns of faith and country. In Washington, D.C., Daily Guideposts contributor Eric Fellman joined such a gathering on the steps of the Lincoln Memorial. As nighttime came, and thousands of candles were lit against the dark, Eric's eyes were drawn to the National Mall, stretching down to the Capitol dome and framed by monuments. A few days later, he walked among them and found anew the inspiring heroes who defined our faith and values as a nation. This year, join Eric on some of our national holidays and rediscover the faith of our Founding Fathers.

—THE EDITORS

12/WED   THE LINCOLN MEMORIAL
And the work of righteousness shall be peace....—ISAIAH 32:17

I was born in Illinois, the "Land of Lincoln," and I've been studying our sixteenth president all my life. For me, he was the wisest and most spiritual of our presidents. He was also one of only a few who have been in office when acts of war brought death and destruction to American soil.

Carved in the marble walls of the Lincoln Memorial are these eloquent words from Abraham Lincoln's second inaugural address:

> With malice toward none; with charity for all; and with firmness in the right, as God gives us to see the right, let us strive on to finish the work we are in; to bind up the nation's wounds; to care for him who shall have borne the battle, and for his widow, and his orphan—to do all which may achieve and cherish a just and lasting peace among ourselves, and with all nations.

Our family explored what it means to seek peace when we invited a young Muslim student to dinner in our home a few months after September 11, 2001. As the meal progressed, one of our sons asked our guest how she came to be in America.

"My father came here on a work visa," she replied. "When the trouble came, he told us to pack to return home, because he was afraid of how Americans might treat us. Then, a few nights before we were to leave, he was watching the news on television. There was a group of people outside the White House, protesting American military action. A large, hostile crowd watched the protesters, and between the two groups were dozens and dozens of police. My father watched for a long time and then turned to the family and said, 'Go unpack your bags. We are staying. Nowhere else in the world would the police protect the protesters. This is the freest land on earth, and we will make it our home.'"

Lord, as I remember Abraham Lincoln, let me remember the blessings of freedom we share with all who come to our shores.

—ERIC FELLMAN

13 / THU   *As newborn babes, desire the sincere milk of the word, that ye may grow thereby.*   —I PETER 2:2

Animal crackers. You'll probably think it's silly, but I'm serious about it. I hadn't seen them since I was a kid (only about seventy-five years ago), but there they were on the shelves of the supermarket. They brought back a story a friend once told me about his mother, who had six children, all of whom were grown and away from home. When she happened on a box of Barnum's Animals, she picked it up and burst into tears.

Hmmm. I looked at the box, still the same red and yellow one simulating a circus wagon, with a string attached for carrying it. Barnum's Animals they were still called, and at the top was the announcement: 100TH BIRTHDAY—1902–2002.

"For your grandkids?" asked a jocular woman at the checkout counter.

"Well, I . . ." I stumbled and finally lied, embarrassed.

With the box before me on the desk at home, I took out a lion and then an elephant, a gorilla and a polar bear. I didn't eat them; instead I found myself swept away to a childhood territory I hadn't visited for years. Poems and prayers came rushing back, and I recited them out loud:

> *In winter I get up at night,*
> *And dress by yellow candlelight . . .*
>
> *Rain, rain, go away;*
> *Come again another day . . .*
>
> *Now I lay me down to sleep.*
> *I pray Thee, Lord, my soul to keep.*

For hours I was a child again, and loving it. My embarrassment vanished. Why not? Didn't Jesus say, "I tell you as seriously as I know how that anyone who refuses to come to God as a little child will never be allowed into his Kingdom" (Mark 10:15, TLB).

Father, let me keep my childlike faith in You. —VAN VARNER

14/FRI *"Haven't you heard . . . the two will become one flesh? So they are no longer two, but one. . . ."*
—MATTHEW 19:4–6 (NIV)

Long-stemmed red roses, thick boxes of chocolates, huge stuffed bears holding plush hearts—it was easy to see that Valentine's Day was just around the corner! But as I stood in the card aisle of the grocery store that morning, I wasn't there to buy sentimental verse or romantic humor. I was there to choose a get-well card for our friend Jan who had suffered a bad fall, breaking both her arm and pelvic bone.

Jan and her husband Dwight work together, building beautiful homes in our community. They had been finishing up one that they were going to move into when, late one evening, Jan misjudged the position of the second-story stairway and fell eleven feet onto the hardwood floor below. Dwight called for help and stayed beside her until the ambulance arrived.

When my husband Gary and I went to visit her, we found Jan sitting in a wheelchair in the kitchen of the duplex where they were living. "Oh, Jan, we're so sorry you're hurt!"

Jan laughed. "Oh, it could have been lots worse!"

A hospital bed took up most of the living room. Dwight hovered nearby, eager to get her a glass of water or reposition her cushions. He spoke in hushed tones about how scared he had been when she fell. Then, as we were leaving, I noticed a small mattress leaning up against the wall by the front door. Dwight smiled. "That's my bed. I put it on the floor beside her in case she needs anything in the night."

Flowers and cards and even plush bears are fine. But I knew that what I'd just witnessed went way beyond those. This was true romance. I slipped my hand into Gary's. "Happy Valentine's Day," I whispered.

You are the source of all real love, God. Thank You!

—MARY LOU CARNEY

READER'S ROOM

My husband Barry and I renewed our wedding vows on February 17, 2001. When we got married ten years ago, many people gave us advice on what to expect. It was mostly warnings, such as "Couples are in their comfort zone for the first five years, and then they run into trouble." We tried to look past these negative words, and we promised each other that if our marriage lasted ten years, we would renew our vows.

Well, thanks to God our Lord and Savior, we made it! What a joy it was to see our friends, family members, and especially our children Barry and Tiffany smiling at us as we renewed our vows in the presence of the Lord.

I thank God for the challenges we've met, and I look forward to approaching each future milestone in a positive way.

—HOPE WILLIAMS, PHILADELPHIA, PENNSYLVANIA

FOLLOWING JESUS

15/*SAT*   SECRET GIVING

"And your Father, who sees what is done in secret, will reward you." —MATTHEW 6:18 (NIV)

During the last year of my mother's life, she only left the house to go to the doctor or to get her hair done. My dad had always loved Mother's hair, and he couldn't wait for her to return from the hairdresser so he could award her hairdo his seal of approval. I'd no sooner help her into the house than he'd kiss her on the cheek, stroke her shiny gray hair, get a faraway look in his eyes and say, "That hairdresser fixes my Bunnie Pie up as pretty as the first time I laid eyes on her."

But I didn't learn the full story of Mother's shimmering hair until right after she died. As a special gift, her hairdresser Linda Sue had gone to the funeral home to fix Mother's hair, and now, just before the funeral, she was doing mine. We were reminiscing about Mother when Linda Sue pointed to a white squeeze bottle and asked, "Okay if I use this on you? It always made your mother's hair so pretty and shiny."

"I thought that was Mother Nature," I answered, smiling for the first time in days. "And wait a minute, she never paid you for any extra treatments. Even when your price went up, you wouldn't take a penny more."

"I snuck some of that rinse on your mother's hair when it first came out, just to see what it would do," she said. "Then I got such a kick when she told me about your dad that I couldn't stop. She'd look into the mirror and say, 'My hair does have a sheen to it, doesn't it?' It became my little secret, and I never enjoyed anything more."

Only your hairdresser—and God—knows for sure. Oh, the power of a secret gift to soothe the saddest of days!

Thank You, Lord, for those who conspire with You in secret to give from the heart. —ROBERTA MESSNER

16/SUN *Surely the Lord is in this place; and I knew it not.* —GENESIS 28:16

Though my youngest child always genuinely enjoyed attending and participating in worship services, my older children reached a point where they would dream up every excuse imaginable to avoid accompanying me to church. As a single parent, it took me a little while to catch on.

I quickly learned to tell who was sound asleep and who was pretending. Diagnosing diseases proved harder. Sometimes my children suffered from mysterious ailments that miraculously disappeared by the time I arrived back home to find them cheerfully curled up with the Sunday comics. Other times, thoroughly planned disorganization took its toll:

"I can't find my shoes."

"There's no time to shower."

"No time to curl my hair."

"My alarm didn't go off."

Even if the children were ready, they moaned as I edged them into the car:

"It's boring."

"It's too long."

"I don't know what the pastor's talking about."

But one particular morning was the worst. My teenage sons reluctantly shuffled into church and pleaded to sit by themselves in the back. A little hurt, I agreed, rationalizing, *At least they're in church.* I sat with the girls in my customary seat up front. When I didn't see the boys in the Communion procession, I became suspicious. Much later I learned that they had slipped out of church shortly after the entrance hymn, hiked a mile to a fast-food joint for cocoa and hot-footed it back to church in time to stroll out with the congregation after the recessional.

It was nearly the same story five years later, when my older daughter Tess, by then a mother herself, paid her younger brother's airfare so he could join her at Christmas. She wanted family time on Christmas Eve; he wanted time with old friends. Tess stood her ground: "First, you *have* to go with me to the vigil service. Afterward, we'll have a turkey dinner with all the fixings. *Then* you can go see your friends."

"You sound just like Mom!" he thundered.

Tess admits she was delighted by the accusation.

Father of all, give me the stamina to teach my children the way they should go—even when they don't like it very much.

—GAIL THORELL SCHILLING

$17/_{\text{MON}}$ *Continue in prayer, and watch in the same with thanksgiving.* —COLOSSIANS 4:2

Last February I went to the National Prayer Breakfast in Washington, D.C. It was the fiftieth such annual gathering of our nation's spiritual and political leaders, and the first since the terrible events of September 11, 2001.

As is customary, the president was scheduled to attend and lead us in prayer. Security, tight in the best of times, was unprecedented. We lined up at 6:00 A.M. to pass through metal detectors and ID checkpoints before we were permitted to enter the grand ballroom of the Washington Hilton, one of the few venues large enough to accommodate the thousands of people from around the world who were invited. I took my seat at our table and couldn't help noticing the no-nonsense men and women with their telltale earpieces ringing the upper level of the ballroom. Somewhere up there, I'd heard, there was even a sharpshooter standing by in case of the unthinkable.

In addition to President Bush and the First Lady, the dais was crowded with luminaries, including Chief of Naval Operations Admiral Vern Clark, who rose to speak before the president. "Most people know that I'm a praying man," the admiral said. "I'll get an urgent call sometimes asking me to join in prayer with someone in crisis." Then he noted that he couldn't remember ever getting a call in the middle of the night asking him to join in a prayer of unbounded gratitude. There was a ripple of knowing laughter among the attendees.

The world has changed after the horrors of September 11. Few of us will ever be quite the same. Yet sitting on the train back to New York after the prayer breakfast, watching the scenes of everyday life sweep past the window—schoolyards, factories, neighborhoods, shopping malls, busy highways—the admiral's comment kept clicking away in my mind, and I found myself wishing I knew his phone number.

God, let me remember not just to come to You when the moment is dark, but to bow my head always in gratitude for Your goodness and Your blessings, which are boundless in both good times and bad.
                                                    —EDWARD GRINNAN

18/TUE

I will strengthen thee; yea, I will help thee. . . .
                                                    —ISAIAH 41:10

When my dad came to live with me some years ago, along with some other possessions he brought an old toolbox. Dad was a man who wasn't the least bit handy. He knew it, too, yet he always tried to repair whatever was broken, just because he wanted to be helpful. He never succeeded.

After Dad passed away, I would come across his toolbox in the closet every now and then and wonder what I ought to do with it. But I left it where it was.

Recently, while the inside of my house was being painted, I asked the painter to install some new curtain rods in the living room. When he opened the package, he found that a screw was missing.

"Would you happen to have anything like this?" he asked, holding up a screw. And, of course, I didn't. But I knew where I might find one!

I went to the closet and pulled out Dad's toolbox. As I lifted up the top, Mr. Gehman, the painter, came to look at what was inside. We both were astonished. There were all kinds of screws and nails and tacks neatly stored in little containers, each one carefully labeled.

After finding what he needed, Mr. Gehman looked at the tools.

"Look at this!" he said, pointing to a folding wooden rule. "What a fine rule—much better than you can get today," he said.

Suddenly I knew what to do. "Mr. Gehman, can you use a tool like this?" I asked.

"Sure could," he said.

I held it out to him. "Please, I'd like you to have it."

As I closed the toolbox and put it back in the closet, I had the comfortable feeling that Dad was pleased. He had finally helped to fix something that was broken.

Dear Lord Jesus, make me aware of those who need my help. Even when I can't do what needs to be done, I can always be by their side. —PHYLLIS HOBE

---

19 / WED   *There be three things which are too wonderful for me, yea, four which I know not: The way of an eagle in the air; the way of a serpent upon a rock; the way of a ship in the midst of the sea; and the way of a man with a maid.*

—PROVERBS 30:18–19

Now that I have achieved a certain age, I've learned to listen a little, and see small miraculous things and not be such an unadulterated rock-head.

And I've become a student of ways—the way that men's suit pants bunch up at the knees when they stand after kneeling in church; the way that strands of hair work loose from my wife's ponytail when she is working; the way some children sleep with one hand open and legs splayed like scissors; the way a knee is knobby; the way a face curves around a grin in middle age; the way a mouth opens slightly when a man or woman falls asleep in a chair by the fire, and the way they startle gently awake, their eyes wide with amazement.

These are the ways we are, the miracles we swim in, the fingerprints of the Maker.

Dear Lord, teach me to see, help me to smell, allow me to listen to the million miracles around me—the extraordinariness of the ordinary. For there You are, and there is peace and joy unending, if only I could sense it more than fitfully. —BRIAN DOYLE

20/THU   *Commit thy works unto the Lord, and thy thoughts shall be established.*   —PROVERBS 16:3

I've always loved music. As a child, I struggled with piano lessons, but my hands were too small to stretch an octave on the keys, and I never could seem to loosen their stiffness enough to make the music seem other than labored. I gave it up when I got old enough to protest against the lessons.

One year I shared a monastery guest house with a young man named Douglas, who wanted to be a jazz trumpeter. He moved in with hundreds of CDs and a shiny trumpet. I was eager to hear him play. Douglas practiced for four hours every day, two in the morning and two in the evening. But for the entire month I was there, he played only scales, every morning, every night. All those hours of practice went into nothing more than scales.

Just before I was due to leave, I asked him why he never played anything else. He answered, "I want to be a very good trumpet player, and I don't have a natural gift for it. So I have to work at the basics very hard for a very long time."

I went away humbled by his dedication to making music, aware that, just as I hadn't had the talent to play easily, I also hadn't had the gift of working hard enough to make up for my flaws. Douglas may not get the career he wants, but it won't be for any lack of trying. His God-given determination will carry him through obstacles that turn away a lesser heart.

Show me the gift You've given me, Lord, and give me the perseverance to pursue it.   —RHODA BLECKER

21/FRI   *And we know that all things work together for good to those who love God, to those who are the called according to His purpose.*   —ROMANS 8:28 (NKJV)

During the week before my amputation, I would lie awake at night, softly crying to myself, "I don't want to lose my leg. I don't want to lose my leg."

I would look down at my pillow and see that I had lost the last remaining bristles of my hair. I would look under the covers at my frail, sixty-five-pound body. Then I would wonder what other nine-year-olds were doing.

It had been three months since doctors gave me a fifty/fifty chance to live and I began chemotherapy. When tests showed that the tumor remained, amputation at the hip became the only option.

The day finally arrived. My parents and I got in the car and began the journey across the mountain to the hospital. As we drove, sadness hung in our minivan like a thick cloud. I was holding on to my leg with both arms. Then my parents read Romans 8:28. As I thought about the verse, I sat up: God was in control. Maybe I didn't understand why I'd never play soccer again, but He did.

After the amputation, I didn't look back. By the third day, I was running laps around the seventh floor of the hospital, worried nurses chasing close behind. Although doctors expected me to stay in the hospital for three weeks of recovery, I healed so quickly that they released me after five days.

Normally, when people lose limbs, they go through a grieving process. The doctors couldn't understand why I didn't show any such symptoms. They sent in a psychologist, but even she couldn't figure out where all of these feelings of grief were.

Of course, I knew where they were. I had given them to the only One Who was really in control.

Lord, help me to trust and follow Your plan for my life whenever life doesn't conform to my plan. —JOSHUA SUNDQUIST

22/SAT Just as we have borne the image of the man of dust, we shall also bear the image of the man of heaven.
—I CORINTHIANS 15:49 (RSV)

At age five, my son John is obsessed with the Revolutionary War. So it was no surprise that while we were in the Metropolitan Museum of Art today, he asked if we could go see *Washington Crossing the Delaware.* We took a detour through Medieval Art, passed Paul Revere's silver and entered the picture galleries of the American Wing. The kids breathed a deep sigh of admiration as we walked in: The painting is quite large and very dramatic.

"Hey, that's George Washington, too!" John said, glancing at the opposite wall. "Who is he talking to?" We turned to study a painting of Washington and Lafayette on the porch of Mt. Vernon. Curious about what else was in the collection, we wandered farther in until we came to a room chock-full of paintings of Washington. The kids sat down to take a better look.

"Which one do you like best?" I asked, as I glanced from one picture to another. In a full-length portrait, Washington looked debonair; in a smaller painting, he was commanding; in a third, he appeared serious and reserved. Each artist seemed to have captured a different person in paint.

Which is the real guy? I wondered. Over the years, I'd put my textbook image of him into a tidy little box labeled "Hero," and it was pleasantly startling to find he was much more human and complex than I'd imagined.

Sometimes, if I'm not careful, I can find myself doing the same thing with Jesus. Unfortunately, I'm quite capable of putting Him into a neat little box labeled "Lord," where I'm guided by my ideas about Him rather than by Jesus Himself. Yet Jesus wants more. He wants me to know Him in all His divine and human complexity. And He wants that knowledge to make me a living servant of the living God.

Lord Jesus, change my heart so fully that all who know me know You.   —JULIA ATTAWAY

*23/*SUN   *Give unto the Lord the glory due unto his name; worship the Lord in the beauty of holiness.* —PSALM 29:2

"Remember," our pastor said as he concluded the sermon, "worship is every bit as important to your spiritual well-being as breathing is to your physical health."

While he gave the closing prayer, I checked to see that the music for the postlude was in place and mentally reviewed the introduction to the last hymn. As I played the organ, a familiar feeling of guilt accompanied every note. I had a secret: Although I attended church every Sunday, I didn't worship. I was too busy concentrating on the details of the service.

I hope no one remembers I played the same prelude last month. Will the offertory be long enough? Should I slow down on the last verse of the

hymn? I enjoyed the Christian fellowship with my friends and neighbors, was inspired and challenged by the sermons, and missing church left a hole in my week. But I didn't worship.

Finally, I confessed to an older friend who was a professional musician as well as a church organist. Her response was definitely not what I expected. "Why do you think it's called the worship *service?*" she asked. "Because for many of us—the pastor, the acolytes, the musicians—it's definitely a time to serve. We worship through our work, too, you know. Still, it's important to find times when you're free of responsibility and can give your whole heart to worship."

Her advice helped me relax and let go of the guilt. I began to seek a few nontraditional opportunities for worship: an evangelism event; musical presentations; even an occasional TV service. And a strange thing happened: Although most Sunday mornings still find me on the organ bench, and sometimes every head is bowed and every eye closed except mine, there are plenty of times now when heart-worship happens.

Dear Lord, thank You for pastors, musicians, ushers, nursery workers and all who worship through service on Sunday.

—PENNEY SCHWAB

CHARLEY'S GIFTS

A friend's struggle with a terminal illness proved to be a trying time for Rick Hamlin. What he found were moments of grace in a life lived to its fullest, and this week he'll share them with you.

—THE EDITORS

24/MON DAY ONE: THE GIFT OF LIFE

To him that is joined to all the living there is hope. . . .

—ECCLESIASTES 9:4

At first Charley thought it was carpal tunnel syndrome—the ache in one hand and the way his fingers stopped operating efficiently. He expected a quick diagnosis and a few exercises; in no time he'd be back to writing long memos on his computer for the students he taught. But the doctors' tests dragged on for months. And the numb feeling moved up his arm to other parts of his body. Things stopped cooperating—his feet, his legs, his voice. When I spoke to him on the phone, his words came out slowly, as though he were a very old man, not the forty-five-year-old professor he was. By then the diagnosis was in: ALS, Lou Gehrig's disease. No cure, no hope, just a slow, irreversible deterioration.

He lived in Boston, and after receiving the news I dreaded visiting him. It seemed incredibly sad. What would his wife do? What about his four kids? Two sets of twins, two-year-olds and five-year-olds. Didn't they deserve to grow up knowing the vital, active, fun-loving man I had known? How unfair. *What's the purpose, God?*

But that first visit with Charley surprised me. He couldn't get up, he drawled words that had once come to him with lightning speed, but the wit was still there. We told stories, joked, remembered college days. And with those four children crawling all over him, darting up and down the stairs and in and out of the living room, there wasn't time to get depressed.

Later I spoke to his wife Lynn. She recalled someone visiting and telling her tearfully, "It's so sad to think of Charley dying." She looked at me sternly without a tear in her eye, "I don't see it that way, Rick. He's living. I don't know how much longer he'll be around, but every day it's life, and that's how we're getting through this."

I listened to the laughter of the children as Charley attempted to read to them. Life never seemed so precious. There was no answer to the why. Only that within the struggle, there was plenty of life left.

Lord, may I never lose my sense of how precious life is.

—RICK HAMLIN

25/*TUE* DAY TWO: THE GIFT OF SONG

We will sing my songs to the stringed instruments all the days of our life in the house of the Lord. —ISAIAH 38:20

In college, Charley and I sang together in a small, all-male *a cappella* group. He held the baritone line with musical sureness; I was second tenor. "Melody Hamlin," he used to call me. When he and I were traveling in London with a bass, he taught us a three-part cowboy song: "Out in Arizona where the bad men are, nothing there to guide you but the evening star. . . ." We sang with relish, our voices echoing beneath the arches of Regent's Crescent, three singing cowboys from America. We felt right at home.

I needed a song to sing while visiting Charley. I was helping out by giving the two-year-old twins their bath, and little Nicky was having none of it. He howled. Lynn had warned me, "He gets scared of water for some reason." Fear. It seemed a perfectly reasonable reaction to life with a father who had once run races and now could barely stand. Fear of the unknown. What would Daddy be like tomorrow? How much worse would he be then? "Let's sing," I said to Nicky. Out it came, the best song I could think of: "Out in Arizona where the bad men are, nothing there to guide you but the evening star. . . ."

Nicky looked at me, the tears slowing. I kept singing. Now he was smiling, splashing the water along with the beat: "He would moan, riding over the prairie alone, singing 'neath the Arizona sky. . . ."

"Sing along with me," I told him. "It's a song your dad taught me." *When you sing, the future always looks better*, I thought. *You can find that star to guide you 'neath the evening sky.*

"I heard you," Charley drawled. "I can't sing anymore."

Of course not. He didn't have the muscle control. "It's a good song," I said. "I'll teach it to him. You taught it to me. You helped me find my way in the darkness." And helped me remember that music puts me back in touch with God.

"Sing it for me," Charley said.

I lift up my voice, Lord, and feel Your goodness.

—RICK HAMLIN

26/WED   DAY THREE: THE GIFT OF SERVICE

We then that are strong ought to bear the infirmities of the
weak.... —ROMANS 15:1

When the news of Charley's illness spread, everyone had the same response: "What can I do to help?" It was a situation that made us all feel powerless. We couldn't reverse the course of the disease; we couldn't stop Charley from dying any more than we could stop his children from growing. We could only think of little ways to help. A neighbor offered her extra bedroom so Lynn could nap whenever caregivers allowed. A friend dropped by regularly to help clean up. Parents from the kids' schools brought by meals. Charley's students did grocery shopping. Family members did carpooling. People sent cards, letters, money. Lynn learned how to ask for what she needed and to accept favors with grace.

I went to Boston for another weekend. Doing things for the kids was an obvious way to help. I read them books, made peanut-butter-and-jelly sandwiches, took them to the playground. I played games with them and taught them songs. But what could I do for Charley? By now he was largely immobile, confined to a wheel-chair or bed. He could sip juice through a straw, but he couldn't raise a fork or a spoon, and chewing was an arduous process. Lynn spooned out scrambled eggs and rice for him as if she were feeding a child. Truth to tell, I was embarrassed to watch.

Then she had to get up from the table to help the kids. "Shall I?" I asked Charley timidly. He nodded. I spooned out a dollop of eggs and aimed for his mouth. It dribbled down his chin. I tried again. He strained to reach it, like a nestling stretching its neck. The third time, I landed the spoonful right in his mouth. He chewed contentedly. "You know, Charley, when we were back in college I never expected I'd be feeding you."

"You'll get better with practice," he said very slowly. I wiped his mouth with a napkin.

Lord, use my hands to serve You, however awkwardly I try.
—RICK HAMLIN

27 / *THU*   DAY FOUR: THE GIFT OF GIVING

They helped every one his neighbor; and every one said to his brother, Be of good courage.   —ISAIAH 41:6

On my last visit, Charley was confined to a hospital bed set up in his living room. He had round-the-clock nursing care and was fed through a feeding tube. He could no longer speak or move more than his index finger. The easiest way to communicate with him was by selecting letters from an alphabet board. I read off the alphabet and he stopped me at the right letter by nodding yes or no. "All I'm doing is breathing," he told me. It took about twenty minutes for me to get that sentence down, one letter at a time. And yet, Charley has remained hopeful where there has been little hope. He's been faithful where others would have given up.

On this visit, I gathered around his bedside with other fellows from our college singing group. We made a quartet and sang a couple of old songs, our efforts rewarded with smiles. Someone had to cover the baritone line, Charley's part.

Lynn has saved all the letters she has received. Insurance has long since stopped covering the monumental bills for home care. Donations have come from friends and family, none of them tax-deductible. "Share the care," she calls it. She has files of correspondence from people offering prayers. The daily support network, instead of exhausting itself, has increased. The food deliveries, the volunteers who clean, take care of the kids, shop, garden. And people like my college buddies and me who have come to sing for Charley.

Here we are: a doctor, a teacher, an editor, an officer of the Federal Reserve . . . and a baritone with no voice or movement. All of us have asked, *What purpose, God?* Here we have our answer. Charley has managed to have as big an influence from where he is as any of us have from our offices or classrooms. He's brought out the best in hundreds of people, their faith, their generosity. *What purpose, God?* I don't know, but I do know that life is about sharing the care.

I am richest, God, when I give.   —RICK HAMLIN

28/*FRI* DAY FIVE: THE GIFT OF HOPE

Be thou faithful unto death, and I will give thee a crown of life.
—REVELATION 2:10

We got the e-mail a few weeks before Christmas: "Charley died peacefully in his sleep, surrounded by his family." We could picture the scene so well: the big hospital bed surrounded by the machines that had made Charley's last two years possible and the people who had made that life livable. Still, it seemed unbelievable that it was over. I had grown used to the thought that I could drop by the house anytime, day or night, and find Charley just inside the front door, greeting me with a smile.

We went to the service prepared for tears, buckets of them. Of course, we cried. But there were also smiles and hugs and greetings between friends who'd made Charley part of their prayers for years. It was more like a wedding than a funeral, more Easter than Good Friday. We sang the hymns that Charley had picked and listened to the verses he wanted read. We formed our own pickup choir, rehearsing before the service. "May the Lord bless you and keep you. May the Lord make His face to shine upon you." *Yes,* I thought, *God's face is shining upon everyone who has lent a hand to Charley and his family.* The church was packed with them.

The family had a reception in the parish hall afterward. We ate, laughed and talked, the children scampering between our feet. People brought cameras to record the event. My favorite photo was of Lynn, Charley's wife, surrounded by all the daily caregivers, an indomitable bunch. Death had not triumphed here. It was "but the gate of life immortal," as one of the hymns said. At the last minute, a group of us gathered in a corner and sang one more tune for Charley: "Out in Arizona where the bad men are, nothing there to guide you but the evening star. . . ." I drove home beneath a winter sky filled with stars.

Guide me in this life, Lord, and in the life to come.

—RICK HAMLIN

My Daily Blessings

1 _____

2 _____

3 _____

4 _____

5 _____

6 _____

7 _____

8 _____

9 _____

10 _____

11 _____

12 _____

13 _____

14 _____

15 _____

16 _____

17 _____

18 _____

19 _____

20 _____

21 _____

22 _____

23 _____

24 _____

25 _____

26 _____

27 _____

28 _____

MARCH

Blessed are the meek: for
they shall inherit the earth.
—Matthew 5:5

S	M	T	W	T	F	S
						1
2	3	4	5	6	7	8
9	10	11	12	13	14	15
16	17	18	19	20	21	22
23	24	25	26	27	28	29
30	31					

AN EYE FOR BLESSINGS

1/SAT THE WONDER IN THE WIRES
Who can withstand his icy blast? —PSALM 147:17 (NIV)

It would have been such a nice photo—my husband John making his way across the yard after a record snowstorm—if only I hadn't gotten those ugly phone and electric lines in the picture! A cat's cradle of wires stretched right across the pristine snowscape, from the street to the side of the house. And then, holding the snapshot, I remembered another wintry scene. . . .

That year, it had been an ice storm—house, trees, telephone poles sheathed in an inch-thick coat. John was attending a conference in balmy Orlando, Florida, when the wind began that night. It screamed around the house, and with it came the rifle-shots of cracking wood.

I woke in the morning to a frigid house and a bizarre landscape. Weighted with ice, tall trees had snapped in two, jagged spars erect and treetops strewn over the ground. A dozen lay across the driveway like a giant heap of jackstraws.

After the uproar of the night, the house was eerily quiet. There was no rumble from the oil burner, no hum from the refrigerator, no radio or TV to tell me how widespread the storm had been or when road crews might reach our suburb. And there was no phone to let John know I was okay.

Sort of okay: There was no coffee—it's an electric pot; no hot oatmeal—electric stove; no power for the toaster; not even a way to count the passing hours on our four electric clocks. For nearly two days, before the road was cleared and a volunteer firefighter crawled over and under the obstacle course in the yard to get me to his truck and a motel, I kept a fire going in the living room and ate canned tuna.

I looked at the photo again. And thanked God for the blessings carried by those ugly wires.

Don't let me take the conveniences of modern life for granted, Father—or forget that human inventiveness is a gift from You.
—ELIZABETH SHERRILL

$2/_{SUN}$ *"You will call your walls Salvation and your gates Praise."*   —ISAIAH 60:18 (NIV)

I had recently moved from our country home of twenty-seven years to a condominium. It had been a gut-wrenching decision. Not only was I leaving a place where every nook and cranny had a precious memory of our happy family of seven, and where almost every bush and tree was one I had planted and nurtured to its blazing glory; the move from our family home also signaled the painful end of a marriage. I desperately needed a new beginning.

My care group from church wanted to give me a housewarming. "Could you make that a house blessing?" I asked. "Instead of gifts, each person can write out a personal blessing."

On that special night sixteen people crowded into my small condominium, their arms laden with food, their faces beaming goodwill. Here are some of the blessings they read to me:

"Even the sparrow has found a home, and the swallow a nest for herself . . . a place near your altar, O Lord Almighty" (Psalm 84:3, NIV).

"The crown of the home is godliness
The beauty of the home is order;
The glory of the home is hospitality
The blessing of the home is contentment
A good laugh is sunshine in a house
We wish you all of these in your new home."

"Trust in the Lord and do good. Live in this house and enjoy its safety."

Now, whenever the problems of my new life threaten to overwhelm me, I take out the carefully written blessings of my friends. As I reread them, I'm keenly aware that the God of blessing, Who delights to bless His children, is with me in this new venture.

Father, thank You for Your promise to watch over my comings and goings, both now and forevermore.

—HELEN GRACE LESCHEID

3/MON   *Choose the good.*   —ISAIAH 7:15

"I wish I had beautiful fingernails like you," I remember saying to Irene Solomon as I snuggled near her on the living room couch. Mrs. Solomon was a family friend who had come to stay with my brother Davey and me, so that my mother could go on a trip with my father. As far as I was concerned, everything about Mrs. Solomon, from her lovely red nails on, was perfectly wonderful.

Holding my seven-year-old hand in hers, she said, "Well, we can do something about that."

Soon Mrs. Solomon was patiently painting my scraggly fingernails that same bright red. "You know, Pamela," she said, "your fingernails are either being bitten off or they are growing long like mine. You can choose which way you want them to be."

I don't think I ever bit my fingernails again. And that's not all I learned from Mrs. Solomon. In the mornings, she put bright red cherries in the middle of our grapefruit; she let me wear my Sunday shoes to school; and at night she made us cola floats in my mother's crystal goblets. Later, on my eighth birthday, when everyone else was giving me useful things, she gave me an evening bag made of woven silver.

Though Mrs. Solomon worked well past retirement age in downtown Chattanooga, Tennessee, rode back and forth to work on a city bus, and lived in a tiny house in a modest neighborhood, she never stopped eating her cereal out of china bowls, painting her fingernails red, or (even in her late nineties) giving outlandish birthday presents to her friends.

The truth is, a cherry makes a grapefruit sweeter, china and crystal are made to be used, presents don't need to be practical, and you and I are either making life nicer or we're not. The choice is ours. Mrs. Solomon taught me that.

Father, in every moment of every day, a choice waits. Help us to choose the good. —PAM KIDD

A HERITAGE OF FREEDOM

4/*TUE*   THE FRANKLIN DELANO ROOSEVELT MEMORIAL

O righteous God, who searches minds and hearts, bring to an end the violence of the wicked. . . . —PSALM 7:9 (NIV)

Today is the seventieth anniversary of the first inauguration of Franklin Delano Roosevelt, whose memorial sits at the west end of the oval Tidal Pool. Near the center is a statue of the president who led us through the Great Depression and World War II, sitting in his high-backed wheelchair, arm raised as he makes a point to the nation.

I had never thought of FDR as a particularly religious man, but as I walked through the memorial's four outdoor galleries and read the quotations carved into the granite walls, I was struck by the frequent references to faith. Just two months prior to D-Day, he wrote, "The only limit to our realization of tomorrow will be our doubts of today. Let us move forward with strong and active faith." During the frantic days after Pearl Harbor he said, "We have faith that future generations will know that here, in the middle of the twentieth century, there came a time when men of goodwill found a way to unite, and produce, and fight to destroy the forces of ignorance, and intolerance, and slavery, and war."

As I read those words, it came to me that FDR was challenging future generations to believe that people of goodwill will always find a reason to unite against the forces of evil. I've been reflecting on what I can do in that battle:

- Never forget to be vigilant against evil.
- Tell my children and grandchildren the stories of heroes who have gone before.
- Speak up against the hatred and injustice that happen every day in neighborhoods, in schools, on the subway or around the office watercooler.

That's the start of my list. What's on yours?

Lord, thank You for the faith that has preserved our freedoms, and strengthen it so that I might hand it on to those coming after me. —ERIC FELLMAN

$5/$ WED   *I am in pain and distress; may your salvation, O God, protect me.* —PSALM 69:29 (NIV)

I'd been feeling sorry for myself. It was two months after I'd moved from Hartford, Connecticut, where I had lived for twenty years and made close friends, to a smaller town on the shore. I moved around Christmas, so I could understand when people failed to keep in touch. After all, it was the season: People couldn't keep up with their own schedules, never mind mine.

But now it was Ash Wednesday, the start of Lent, the darkest season of the year. I'd relied on my friends to get me through those short midwinter days. This year, no one was calling. And I was miserable.

I brooded, I cried, I shouted at the phone, I whined to my mother. But I didn't call the friends whose voices I so longed to hear. That just wasn't an option. After all, I'd supported them during their trials and tragedies. They had to know this move would be difficult. Where were they when I needed to talk, when I needed a little support?

I arrived home from church, marked with ashes, to a message from one of the offending friends on my answering machine. Mary had just returned from the hospital, where she'd waited alone while her husband was in surgery. Listening to her forlorn, aching voice, I knew that two months ago I would have waited with her at the hospital. I also knew that she still needed me.

Then I remembered something my mother had suggested—and I had immediately rejected—when I complained about my unfaithful friends. She said they were giving me room to make a new life before trying to fit themselves into it.

I picked up the phone.

Jesus, when I feel abandoned because no one seems to be reaching out, help me remember how You reached out and forgave those who truly abandoned You. —MARCI ALBORGHETTI

*6/*THU   *Not one of the good promises which the Lord had made to the house of Israel failed. . . .*

—JOSHUA 21:45 (NAS)

I didn't want to sell the old beige car. I had bought it shortly after I became a widow—the first one I ever bought by myself. Now my husband Gene thought I should have a newer, safer car. But the old car and I were good friends. Why, I had even driven it when I went to meet Gene for the first time. When I decided to see if I would like working in downtown Atlanta, I bravely and prayerfully drove it for six months through the snarling early-morning traffic. When my son Jeremy was in a terrible accident, my trusty car got me to him in record time. When my daughter Julie's newborn son died at birth, I found sanctuary in that faithful old car as Gene and I drove to the hospital and then to the cemetery the next day. When Julie delivered beautiful, healthy Thomas a few years later, I made the joyful drive to see them in my car. It was crammed full of memories, and its bumpers were covered with stickers that witnessed to the faith that had got me through.

In a moment of weakness, I took Gene's advice and bought a new car. But I absolutely refused to leave my old car on the lot, abandoned and unwanted. I drove it home slowly and thoughtfully, while Gene drove the snazzy new car with the sunroof. As I drove,

I asked God to send people to buy my car who would love it, be excited over it—and leave my bumper stickers on it. I could hardly believe it when He seemed to say, *Okay.* I parked my car in the yard and we put a FOR SALE sign on it, and I went inside to vacuum and try to work through my feelings.

I turned the vacuum off when Gene came running into the house with a fist full of money and explained, "This is a down payment. A couple stopped just as I parked your car. They've been praying—asking God to show them a car. They don't have a lot of money, but they have a lot of faith. They're in love with your car and, get this, they love your bumper stickers!"

Father God, help me to learn that when You say You'll do something, it's as good as done, no matter how trivial my request. Amen.   —MARION BOND WEST

7 / FRI   *Keep steady my steps according to thy* *promise.* . . .   —PSALM 119:133 (RSV)

When our youngest son Kyle was ready to learn to ride a bicycle, I thought I'd be off the hook. I had taught his brothers Ryan and Joel to ride, and now they would teach Kyle. But one evening my wife Cathy said sweetly, "Ted, I think it's a good time for you to teach Kyle to ride a bike."

I went down to the garage to get the red Columbia we had bought for Joel and let some of the air out of the tires so it would be easier for Kyle to stay upright. We walked the bike up to the field at the top of the hill and talked about our plan of attack: the ESB method.

"Kyle," I said, "ESB stands for Easy, Steady, Balance. If you can be easy in the seat, remain steady and calm, and balance the bike, you'll ride."

Kyle rode back and forth easily on the flattened tires, calling out "Easy! Steady! Balance!" as he rode. When our lesson was over, we walked the bike back down the hill. I took the path to the house and told Kyle to take the bike to the garage, where I'd help him put it away.

The phone was ringing when I got to the house, and it was awhile before I was able to go back outside. As I walked to the driveway, I could hear Kyle talking to himself. "Easy!" he said. "Steady! Balance! Easy! Steady! Balance!" I peeked around the corner of the house, and there he was, riding in circles on our driveway. "Easy!" he said. "Steady!" And then he fell.

Will he give up? I asked myself. *Will he cry?*

He did neither. Instead, Kyle picked up the bike by the handlebars and got back on. "Easy! Steady! Balance!" he said as he pushed with his legs to get started and glided down the drive.

Lord, when an old problem or a new challenge gets me down, remind me to take it easy, remain steady and maintain my balance. —TED NACE

8 / SAT   *"Let me inherit a double portion of your spirit," Elisha replied.* —II KINGS 2:9 (NIV)

We were at a school picnic when my dad began watching an Arizona Diamondbacks baseball game on his tiny three-inch television. My nephew Christopher peered over his shoulder and with the double-edged sword of innocence and boldness typical of an eight-year-old said, "Papa, can I have that when you die?" My dad had to laugh at his honesty.

I thought of that story recently when I ran across Elisha's reply to Elijah in the Old Testament. Before God takes Elijah up to heaven in a fiery chariot, Elijah asks Elisha what he might do for him. Elisha longs not for material wealth but for an inheritance of the great prophet's spirit. My first thought was, *Now that's what I'd like to inherit from my dad, a large measure of the indomitable spirit that keeps him working tirelessly for the causes he believes in.*

But then came the question: What kind of spirit might my children inherit from me? I remembered the promises my husband Paul and I made when our children were baptized, and I wondered how faithful I've been to those promises and what spirit I convey. I have taught them the Lord's Prayer—do I show a spirit of forgiveness? I bring them to church—do I show a spirit of community? I've placed the Scriptures in their hands—do I show the spirit of compassion Jesus taught?

Every day I have the opportunity to pass on so much more to my children—and to everyone I encounter—than a few material gifts. And going through the motions of worship and church life isn't enough. I need to show the gift of God's Spirit as it lives and works in me. That's a priceless inheritance.

Great God, give me as large a portion of Your Spirit as You think I can handle, and help me share it with everyone I meet.
—GINA BRIDGEMAN

9/SUN   *King David said . . . "I will not take for the Lord . . . which cost me nothing."* —I CHRONICLES 21:24 (RSV)

Recently I brought several casseroles over to church to be stored in the refrigerator for that evening's fellowship dinner. When I opened the appliance's door, I recognized "The Church Refrigerator." No matter what the denomination, it's always the same.

Every church refrigerator contains a bottle of Welch's grape juice, five bottles of partially used salad dressing (three without labels), two nearly empty jugs of Kool-Aid, a jar half full of pickle juice with a couple of slices swimming in it, a dried piece of cake and several plastic containers of something no longer identifiable. In the freezer section, there are three ice trays (two empty) and a carton of Neapolitan ice cream, sagging because the appliance had already seen its best days before it was donated, probably as a tax deduction.

When I turned to a nearby closet to store the cardboard box I'd carried the casseroles in, I recognized "The Church Missionary Barrel." I didn't paw through it, but I assumed that it contained items that their previous owners claimed "still have some good in them."

It was then that I recalled the Old Testament verse in which King David refused to offer something that cost him nothing to give to a holy, loving God.

Father, help me always to remember that what I give in Your name is being given to You, not merely to "someone less fortunate."
—ISABEL WOLSELEY

10/MON   *He that dwelleth in the secret place of the most High shall abide under the shadow of the Almighty.*
—PSALM 91:1

My youngest son John has completed his graduate work and has taken a position with a company in the Washington, D.C., area. The job is exactly right for him, and we were all delighted when he was offered the position. Then came September 11, 2001. To be honest, I worry about John. He's living in what is probably the least safe place in the country at this time, and there's nothing I can do to protect him.

I guess there comes a time when a mother has to let go and trust. But trust whom? The D.C. security forces? Can I really even trust God to keep my son safe? After all, I'm sure that many of those whose loved ones were killed on September 11 were praying people. Why should I believe that God would protect my son and not others?

The answer, as I see it, is there is no absolute certainty in this life. There is no physical place that is completely safe, and there never was. What I do know for sure is true safety is found only in God, and that His safety is of the soul and spirit, not necessarily of the body. Of course, I'll continue to pray for my son's physical safety, but I'm also trusting, in this unsafe world, that my children's souls will always be safe in the One Who created them. In the long view, that's all that really matters.

Holy Comforter, I entrust the souls of all those I love to Your unfailing care, now and always.   —MARILYN MORGAN KING

11/TUE   *I remember thee upon my bed, and meditate on thee in the night watches.*   —PSALM 63:6

When I was a child, said-aloud bedtime prayers were part of every day. Well, almost every day. Sometimes, when we got home from church especially late, or when we'd been in the hay fields all day, or when company stayed way past bedtime, Mother would tuck us in and say, "Pray yourself to sleep." And I always did. There, in the security of my room, bundled in handmade quilts, I would pray until I drifted off to dreams.

Several years ago, Mother had a stroke. By the time I could get to her, her powers of speech were gone. When I walked into her hospital room, she folded her hands and pointed her thumbs back toward herself. "Yes, Mother!" I assured her. "Many people are praying for you!"

I sat with her for six days, watching her slip further and further away. *What was she thinking? Could she hear me? Was she in pain?* I wrapped my prayers around her as I sat curled in a hospital chair near the foot of her bed. And when, on a cold March morning, Mother slipped easily into death, I was sure that—for the last time—she had prayed herself to sleep.

Whether we wake or sleep, You, O Lord, are God!

—MARY LOU CARNEY

12/WED   *"Though it linger, wait for it; it will certainly come and will not delay."*   —HABAKKUK 2:3 (NIV)

When I was in junior high, I was a reporter for the school newspaper. I sat behind the bench during basketball games, close enough to hear the coach, close enough to see the sweat on the brows of the fourteen-year-old boys in the starting lineup. I was also near enough to see the hope, the anguish, the defeat that warred on the faces of those who had yet to get into the game—the benchwarmers.

They wore the team uniform and jacket because the coach had selected them and said they were good enough to be on the team. I'd seen them running drills, just like the starting five. They practiced shooting free throws, they ran laps, but still they sat on the bench, waiting. During the game, they'd jump to their feet yelling, cheering and sometimes crying—but they didn't get on the floor. They sold candy and washed cars to raise funds for the team, but week after week, it was never their turn. "It's just not the right time. Just wait, I'm going to need you," the coach would tell them.

There's a change in my life that I've been preparing for and praying for, waiting for, and all indications are that it's coming; I just don't know when. I'm anxious, waiting to get into the game, and sometimes there are moments when I feel like going to the locker room and putting on my street clothes. That would be easier than waiting.

I think about all the preachers waiting to preach, all the practiced dancers waiting to dance, all the mothers waiting to give birth and all the brides waiting to marry. All of us waiting to get into the game.

I look up toward the heavens. "I trust You, God," I whisper. "Coach, let me in the game!"

Lord, help me to be patient until my preparation, my passion and my destiny intersect with Your divine plan.

—SHARON FOSTER

FOLLOWING JESUS

13/*THU*   THE SMALLEST THINGS CAN MAKE A DIFFERENCE

A poor widow came and put in two very small copper coins, worth only a fraction of a penny. Calling his disciples to him, Jesus said, "I tell you the truth, this poor widow has put more into the treasury than all the others."   —MARK 12:42–43 (NIV)

The tumor on the left side of my head had returned again. It caused excruciating pain, and if that wasn't enough, my thick, heavy eyeglasses dug into it, adding to the pressure. It was a constant reminder that without divine intervention, I would never know the end of pain as long as I lived.

As I got ready for my shift at the hospital, I stared into the gilded oval bathroom mirror and applied Band-Aids to all the pressure points around my left ear, positioning a thick gauze pad inside the ear piece of my glasses. That only made things worse.

Why don't you try that new optical place? an inner voice suggested. "That would do about as much good as this useless stuff," I answered out loud, tossing Band-Aids and gauze into the trash. "Nothing I do to these glasses makes one millimeter of a difference."

When my shift at work ended, I drove over to Marshall's Optical. An optician named Mark Morris was on duty, and I soon learned that he suffered from severe visual problems and had experimented with every trick in the book to make his own thick lenses more comfortable.

Immediately, Mark seemed to sense my dismay. "Sometimes the smallest adjustment can make the biggest difference," he assured me. He scrutinized my glasses from every angle, then disappeared with them into his laboratory in the back.

Mark returned, whistling, and slid the glasses onto my face. "I loosened things up about a millimeter on the right side to give you more room on the left," he explained.

They fit perfectly—and painlessly.

In Your hands, dear Jesus, a millimeter can move mountains. Help me never to discount the value of the smallest gift.

—ROBERTA MESSNER

*14/*FRI   *If ye then be risen with Christ, seek those things which are above, where Christ sitteth on the right hand of God.*   —COLOSSIANS 3:1

By the time I left Ohio and got to Princeton, New Jersey, in the early 1960s, one of its most famous citizens, Albert Einstein, was already gone. He died on April 18, 1955. But stories about the celebrated scientist were told over and over by townspeople who had seen him walk the streets (sometimes in house slippers, oblivious to his surroundings).

A trainman who served the Dinky, the Toonervillelike shuttle that runs from town to the Princeton Junction railroad station, once related a story about Einstein to me. The famous man often traveled by train to meetings in New York, Washington and points in between. It was the points in between that apparently tested his memory.

On one trip, the conductor came by collecting tickets, and Einstein couldn't find his. Recognizing the illustrious scientist, the conductor said, "That's all right, Dr. Einstein. I know you've got a ticket."

"No, it's not all right," Einstein replied. "Without it, I don't know where I'm going."

It's not forgetfulness as much as bad compasses that plague many of us today. I read in today's paper about a successful businessman who had lost his fortune and committed suicide. He didn't know where he was going. Neither did the rich young ruler who came to Christ, wondering what he needed to do to inherit eternal life. Jesus told him to sell all that he had, give the proceeds to the poor and follow him (Luke 18:18–25). But the cost was too much. It always is for people who don't know where they're going.

Teach us, Lord, to discern siren's song from angels singing,
Lest too late we learn, to wrong things we've been clinging.

—FRED BAUER

READER'S ROOM

Today I have been quite moved by Elizabeth Sherrill's devotional about "listening closely to the songs of others." I have been privileged to go on mission trips through groups sponsored by the Southern Baptist Convention to Russia, Scotland, France, Germany, Australia and Ukraine (the Odessa area, with which Mississippi Baptists are in partnership). I have felt my effectiveness, especially with children, but too often, because of interpreter problems and time in translation, I have failed to listen to the "songs" of those I try to reach. I pray God will give me opportunities this year to listen more carefully to these "other songs" in order to better share God's word. Please pray for me as I go again to Ukraine, Hong Kong and wherever else God chooses to send me.

—LILLIAN HENDERSON MILLER, GREENVILLE, MISSISSIPPI

15 / SAT

I thank my God upon every remembrance of you. —PHILIPPIANS 1:3

I'd been carrying it around with me for at least a couple of months, a smart handsome new pocket address book, all ready to replace the dilapidated one I'd clung to for several years beyond its natural lifetime. All that remained was for me to transfer the old addresses and numbers into the new book.

The book I'd used for years—a promotional freebie from an early Internet company long since defunct—was disintegrating, its cover gone, its spine reinforced by tape, and many of its crowded pages tattered and stained.

Yet the book had served me well through some very good years. It gave me a pleasant feeling to look at a name I'd scrawled into my book and to think that that person had grown, sometimes quite unexpectedly, into a friend, someone whose life was now a part of mine. Of course, there were names and numbers that were a complete mystery, as well as those I had transferred the last time I changed books and probably hadn't called or contacted once. Should I edit those people out? It was all causing me a great deal of anxiety and a bad case of procrastination.

Finally, one rainy weekend, I got down to business. It turned out to be not so bad, partly because I discovered a little trick: I said a prayer for each name as I worked, usually just a simple prayer of thanks to God for bringing that person into my life. It wasn't long before I felt the stirrings of gratitude. How blessed could a person be to have all these remarkable people in his life?

Yes, I know, I could probably do the same thing with a Palm Pilot. Maybe next time. For now I'll stick with my little address book.

Lord, from A to Z, I am profoundly blessed with friends.
—EDWARD GRINNAN

16 / SUN

Always seek to do good to one another and to all. —I THESSALONIANS 5:15 (RSV)

It was March, and I was feeling downhearted. Christine, our insurance agent, would be here Tuesday seeking eight hundred dollars for long-term-care insurance. The Internal Revenue Service was asking for an unexpected four hundred dollars in taxes. And last Monday, while I was attending a Bible study, a hit-and-run driver damaged our car. The repair costs were five hundred dollars. I felt put upon and discouraged, and I walked into church carrying my burdens.

We had a guest preacher that morning, and his message was about reaching out to others. He suggested that we should be willing to sacrifice some of our personal time to become involved in service. He called it "freedom swapping."

Then he held up a golden loaf of bread, which he called "the ministry of nourishment." "This beautiful loaf could be placed on display and admired forever," he said. "But to be useful, the bread must be cut, torn or broken to release the nourishment. We, too, must be broken before our goodness and our comforting can reach others."

Suddenly, my cloud lifted. Each of my financial obligations was for something that benefited me: The insurance lessened the worries of loved ones; taxes paid for services that protected my way of life; the car needed to be repaired if I was to get around. To meet these obligations, I was getting out and becoming more involved in the community through the work I had to do. In a way, they represented opportunities, blessings. All that remained was for me to accept them and smile.

Gracious Lord, I thank You for using Your minister to open my eyes to see. —OSCAR GREENE

17 / MON *On either side of the river, was there the tree of life . . . and the leaves of the tree were for the healing of the nations.* —REVELATION 22:2

"Collins, huh? That would be . . . English? Irish?"

It's a game we play, reckoning heritage based on the sequence of consonants and vowels in surnames, like some kind of ethnic crossword.

"Irish. Used to be O'Collins, I think."

Our answers, of course, are misleading. We're not Irish, but

Irish-American or German-American or Japanese-American. But our nation has accumulated so many, accommodated so many (or, in some cases, compelled so many), that we often drop the hyphen and cut to our roots—a sort of cultural shorthand.

We may boast of the tough alloy forged from our melting pot, but these same immigrants are the sons and daughters of long memories. Despite their allegiance to all things American, they can't easily retract their ethnic passions when troubles brew in their homeland. It's not whether you're "from Ireland," but *which part* of Ireland? Or Yugoslavia: Bosnia, Serbia, Montenegro—the homes of highly developed cultures, of musical and artistic achievement, the cradles of many diverse and colorful folk traditions. Now the only color we see is scarlet red, bled in quantity on the evening news.

Nationality is a complicated concept. Maybe that's why I like twelve-step meetings even though I don't have any addictions (that I know of). I like a roomful of strangers—first names only, please—who admit they're powerless, who admit that only a Higher Power can help. This is the country I want to live in—one nationality, the country called Hope and Salvation and Reaching Out and Reaching Up, where arms are only used for hugging. I'm no geographer, but I suspect that if God had a nationality, it would be among these folks—the tired, the poor, the wretched, all yearning to be free.

Father, let it be as John Oxenham's hymn has it: "In Christ there is no East or West, in Him no South or North, but one great fellowship of love throughout the whole wide earth."

—MARK COLLINS

18 / TUE *"But come on, all of you, try again! . . ."*
—JOB 17:10 (NIV)

I appreciated the phone call from my publisher, warning me before I opened the letter that was in the mail. Even so, the disappointing news devastated me: My most recent book was on its way out of print. A book of conversational prayers that I'd cried over, lost sleep over. My brightest and best work—or so I thought—no longer readily available in stores.

"An early retirement," my optimistic friend Anne said, as if the book had a life of its own.

"A premature death," I countered, trying to name the depths of my grief.

The loss took its toll. I removed the framed book jacket from the wall in my home office; it seemed easier to look at a bare nail than at the cover, a photo of two light-hearted women. Though I was forty pages into a new manuscript of family essays, I shut down. I'm just an editor now, not an author.

"I'm never writing again," I told Anne when she called later that week.

"Don't be so sure. Give yourself some time," she said, neither discounting my pain nor allowing me to dwell in never-never land.

A month later she asked what I was writing.

"Nothing. Not yet."

She dropped the subject, but I knew it would come up again. And sure enough, it did. "You writing yet?" she asked next time we met for doughnuts and coffee.

Her gentle persistence sparked a smile and a new answer. "Tomorrow," I said. "Tomorrow I'll try."

I wrote a paragraph. Just one at first, but it was the start of another essay that bolstered a new book proposal. And now this devotional. And even a new prayer.

God, thank You for the nudge away from "never" and toward "try again."
—EVELYN BENCE

EDITOR'S NOTE: Next month, on Good Friday, Guideposts will observe our thirty-third annual Good Friday Day of Prayer. We would be blessed to pray for your special needs at this special celebration. Send your prayer requests to Day of Prayer, PO Box 1460, Carmel, NY 10512-7960.

*19/*WED   *Do not forget the things your eyes have seen or let them slip from your heart as long as you live. Teach them to your children. . . .*   —DEUTERONOMY 4:9 (NIV)

One of the oldest Carmelite monasteries in America is not far from our former home in Maryland. A couple of years ago, the local paper ran a photo of a life-size statue the nuns had designed and had sculpted for the monastery garden. It depicts Joseph sitting on a bench in his carpenter's apron. In his right hand he grasps a tool, holding it in his lap about eye level for a very young Jesus. Joseph's left arm encircles the child, who is tucked up against his earthly father's side, learning.

The photo crystallized a moment from the week before. As our house was being restored that spring, our contractor Sid Marcus brought along his teenage son Russell and let him handle some of the tasks. With four boys in our family, whenever we had a question or request, we hollered! Not so Sid and Russell. One morning I became aware of the quiet rumble of male voices. Instead of shouting for him, Russell had left his job and hunted up his father for help. In an even, gentle tone, Sid was telling Russell what was okay and what he needed to tear up and do again. There was no rancor, only quiet encouragement.

Holding the newspaper clipping and recalling that morning, for a moment, across the centuries, I heard the murmur of another father teaching his son.

Lord, I thank You for Joseph, who taught and nurtured Jesus so wonderfully. Thank You for those who still gently mentor others today. Help me to become a wise and kind teacher of the next generation. —ROBERTA ROGERS

*20/*THU   *As the earth bringeth forth her bud, and as the garden causeth the things that are sown in it to spring forth. . . .* —ISAIAH 61:11

This is the twelfth year of our planting pansies in honor of my mother, who dearly loved them. "Look," she would tell the children, "this is the only flower with an angel on its petals. See—two wings, two flares for a skirt and there, in the center, a small golden head, or halo, if you like!"

Before she died, she asked if we'd "please keep angels" in her garden. It wasn't much of a garden, a small patch of green that led to the porch of a tiny cottage, but enough for her to putter in. That she did, with a green thumb that coaxed enormous blooms from the smallest seeds, scattered helter-skelter in the creative disorder that was her English style: larkspur, hollyhocks, tiger lilies and tulips in season. Against the fence, she planted beds of roses.

No disorder for the roses; they were carefully spaced and cultivated, each with a formal border of pansies, her angel flower. These the children learned to press in waxed paper, between the pages of a 1943 edition of *Webster's Encyclopedic Dictionary*, the thickest, heaviest volume on our shelf. Fittingly, its frontispiece shows an angel holding high the crown of knowledge over a family reading books.

Look for angels all around you. You'll find some in the pansies in your garden.

> *There are angel blessings round about us,*
> *a promise of Your constant care.*
> *Help me, dear Lord, to look and find them,*
> *Your love revealed everywhere.*

—FAY ANGUS

21 / FRI   *But the Lord has been my stronghold, And my God the rock of my refuge.*   —PSALM 94:22 (NAS)

This has been a "butterflies in the stomach" morning. After driving my thirteen-year-old daughter Jodi to school, I dropped by a bagel shop for breakfast. Sipping a hot cup of coffee, I began to read the morning paper. As I scanned article after article, I felt my anxiety level spiking.

There was news about the fight against terrorism, the spread of biological warfare and mounting tensions in the Middle East. I thought about my nineteen-year-old son Drew, and I tasted fear. Then I looked at the financial section of the paper. Like most Americans, I have seen my retirement funds shrink as our economy has plunged. And I have watched our savings for college tuition dwindle. *How am I going to put three kids through school?* I wondered.

When I arrived home, I sat wordlessly at my desk as my eyes focused on a small, round rock sitting on my bookshelf. The rock is an old stone from a river, given to me by a friend. There is a handwritten note by the rock that reads, "Sometimes we have to hold the rock of ages and have faith."

I picked up the smooth stone and cradled it in my hands. I closed my eyes and thought of all the millions of years the rock has existed. Slowly, the words of the Psalmist formed on my lips: "Lord, thou hast been our dwelling place in all generations. Before the mountains were brought forth, or ever thou hadst formed the earth and the world, even from everlasting to everlasting, thou art God" (Psalm 90:1–2). Suddenly my distress began to ease, and a quiet peace filled my heart.

Every generation faces challenges. My task is not to fear, but to be faithful; not to be swayed by the swirl of current events, but to be made strong by the age-old promises of God.

Dear Father, Thou hast been our dwelling place in all generations. Help me to rest in Thee. Amen. —SCOTT WALKER

22/SAT *All the days ordained for me were written in your book before one of them came to be.* —PSALM 139:16 (NIV)

"Mom, I'd like to celebrate my twentieth anniversary of being diagnosed a diabetic by climbing a 'fourteener,'" Derek said in a phone call from his home in Oregon to ours in Colorado. "And I'd like to invite some friends to join me."

His words triggered a memory so vivid it might have happened yesterday: a nine-year-old boy in a droopy hospital gown bravely learning to give himself daily insulin shots and finger-prick blood tests. As I watched him take on this responsibility that would be part of his life forever, I prayed that diabetes would never hold him back or change his choices in life.

"We'd love to help plan a celebration," I told him. Yet as I hung up, I wondered if he knew that the "fourteener" (a mountain at least fourteen thousand feet high—there are more than fifty of them in Colorado) would still be covered with snow in March. And surely it would be difficult to gather all the people who had meant so much to him through the years. After all, they were scattered across the country.

Over the next few weeks, Derek made plans. He invited his buddies from college, who had stood by him during some tough physical challenges. He asked his two sisters to come from California and called a few close friends from Colorado. Amazingly, they all showed up! And so it was that Derek and his wife Alexandra and the rest of us stood together at the base of a huge mountain on a bright blue-sky morning in March, ready to strap on our snowshoes and tackle the challenge.

Several hours later, Derek and his macho buddies made it to the top of the windswept mountain. (Some of us turned back at the halfway point.) Later that evening, we hosted a celebration dinner, and as we stood in a circle, holding hands to pray before eating, with sunburned faces and tired bodies, I thanked God that a little boy had grown into a young man who has not let diabetes hold him back from achieving his dreams.

Thank You, Lord, for using life's difficult challenges to shape us into the people You've created us to be.

—CAROL KUYKENDALL

23/SUN   *We are the temple of the living God. . . .*
—II CORINTHIANS 6:16 (NAS)

One Sunday in spring I walked into our little church earlier than usual and noticed something different. Dusty footprints covered the foyer rug. Crumpled bulletins lay scattered under the sanctuary pews. Hymnbooks sat askew in their racks. A deaconess who was hastily tidying up stopped to apologize. "I'm afraid there was a mix-up in the volunteer schedule, and as a result the church didn't get cleaned this past week."

"Let me help," I said as I removed my coat. Whisking our way through the sanctuary, we straightened hymnals, and I wondered, *When was the last time I spontaneously made a joyful noise unto the Lord?* We picked up stray bulletins, and I recalled how I'd been dropping quite a few quiet times lately.

Moving downstairs to the Sunday school rooms, we erased blackboards as I prayed, *Lord, I'm having a hard time wiping away a past hurt.*

We picked up scraps of paper and crayons, and I asked forgiveness for picturing a certain person in a bad light when she was only trying to do her job. We straightened chairs. *Haven't I shoved aside a good intention recently?*

Coming back upstairs, we agreed that the dusty footprints on the foyer rug would have to stay for now . . . *like that belated apology I still owe a friend.*

Tidying the church had made me aware of the clutter that had accumulated in my own inner sanctum. I had tried to dismiss each scrap of guilt with "Oh, it's nothing much." Perhaps it seemed like nothing much when taken separately, but collectively it became quite noticeable. I couldn't blame it on a mix-up in the volunteer schedule either.

More than forty years ago, I promised God I would try to keep my spiritual house in order so that nothing in my life would distract others from worshiping Him. Now it was time to ask His forgiveness for becoming a spiritual litterbug.

Lord, thank You for the privilege of worshiping in a neat, clean sanctuary that challenges me each week to tidy up my own personal walk with You.
—ALMA BARKMAN

24 / MON   *Then will . . . the mute tongue shout for joy. . . .*
—ISAIAH 35:6 (NIV)

When my mother moved into a nursing home, I said a pleasant, "Hello. How are you today?" to Mom's new roommate Jeanie, but I got no response. *She must not feel like chatting today, or perhaps she doesn't understand.* I turned my back and moved on to my visit with Mom.

Over lunch Dad told me, "Jeanie had a stroke and can't talk, but she understands clearly enough."

Feeling a bit ashamed of how I had ignored Jeanie, I decided to make a better effort at conversing with her. As I nervously entered the room, my eyes caught three or four small statues of dachshunds on the bed table. "Did you have a dachshund?" I asked.

Jeanie slowly nodded her head.

"Was it a boy?"

She shook her head.

"Was it this big?" I asked, holding my hands apart.

She shook her head and pushed my hands closer together. "Oh, she was a miniature!" I said.

We went on with our yes/no guessing-game conversation, and I discovered that she had a daughter and several grandchildren.

Before my next visit, I found a small dachshund kitchen magnet to take to Jeanie. When she pulled the little gift out of the bag, a small miracle happened. She opened her mouth, and exactly one enthusiastic word came out quite distinctly. "Baby!"

That was all she said, but it was gift enough for both of us. I squeezed her drooping shoulder. "Oh, Jeanie," I said, "how wonderful! I heard you say 'baby' loud and clear."

One of the miracles that always sent shock waves of praise and amazement through the crowds that followed Jesus was when He caused the dumb to speak. You, too, can hear a miracle happen if you listen hard enough to the silences beyond the words.

Lord, today, help me to offer my own silences wisely to bring out a word from someone who is struggling to be heard.

—KAREN BARBER

25/TUE *Charity . . . seeketh not her own. . . .*
—I CORINTHIANS 13:4–5

"No charge. The postage is on me," said the uniformed postal clerk firmly, putting the large carton on the scale.

"But . . . but," stammered my friend Judith reaching for her wallet, "I don't want you to pay. Please."

She called me that night to tell me her story. "I've never felt so touched," she said. "I went into this little post office just around the corner yesterday to buy a mailing carton. The clerk got me the right size from the back. I took it home and packed up my latest crop of sweaters." She laughed. "I had ten and felt very proud of myself." She'd been knitting for the Guideposts sweater project for a couple of years.

Arriving bright and early the next day to mail her package, Judith found the same clerk on duty. He remembered her and her box. She handed it to him and saw his eyes flicker over the address she'd written in large letters with a felt marker.

"Then he told me he knew *Guideposts* magazine and asked me if I'd mind telling him what was in the box," she continued. "I told him, 'It's sweaters. I knit them and Guideposts sends them to children who need warm clothing.' Before I knew it, I was telling this man with JOHN on his name tag about the other knitters and the crocheters, how many sweaters we had made, and the total by all the knitters combined. I can't believe how I rattled on. But there was no one else around, and John seemed such a kind man with a lovely smile.

" 'No charge,' he said again when I had finished my story. I tried to protest but he just insisted.

" 'I'll take care of the postage. Personally. It'll be my small contribution to the children. I can't quite see myself hitting the knitting pins!'

"I couldn't argue with that," she told me.

Thank You, Lord, for all those who share their talents with those in need. —BRIGITTE WEEKS

EDITOR'S NOTE: For a free copy of our sweater pattern, send a self-addressed stamped envelope to Guideposts Sweater Project, 16 E. 34th St., New York, NY 10016.

*26/*WED *Jesus saith unto him, Have I been so long time with you, and yet hast thou not known me, Philip? he that hath seen me hath seen the Father. . . .* —JOHN 14:9

Elizabeth and I were on the subway, talking. As she launched into an animated explanation of some math concept she'd recently read about, part of my brain held itself in reserve and observed my seven-year-old daughter. *She's so incredibly different from me!* I thought. *Her mind works differently, her emotional constitution is different, her social needs are different. She doesn't even look like me!*

I love my daughter passionately, yet she and I are so unlike each other that I sometimes wonder if I leave any imprint on her at all. We're not like oil and water; we're more like oil and a giraffe, a living non sequitur.

As we neared our subway stop, I asked Elizabeth to get ready to get off the train. She jumped up off her seat and swung, grinning, around the pole designed to give standing passengers something to hold on to. I gathered our belongings, and we stood by the doorway. Just as the train pulled into our stop, a man who had been sitting across from us spoke. "I have to tell you how much I enjoyed watching you and your daughter. It's amazing how much her body language and her mannerisms are like yours! And then, when she jumped up, it's as if she underwent a transformation, and it's obvious that she is also completely herself."

I smiled my confused thanks, and we stepped out onto the platform. *Elizabeth acting just like me? Really?* I had seen and sensed none of it, and yet a total stranger was able to see my reflection in her. Wonders never cease.

Lord Jesus, I am only fully myself in You. May all people see Your reflection in me. —JULIA ATTAWAY

27/THU "Do not be anxious for tomorrow; for tomorrow will care for itself..." —MATTHEW 6:34 (NAS)

I picked up the little black sedan when I was living in California after the hand-me-down family station wagon I'd driven west finally conked out. From the second I drove it off the used-car lot, I was ready for disaster. My lack of confidence, my doubts and suspicions about what life had in store for me—somehow I managed to focus all these feelings on this new car of mine. *It's probably a lemon. I bet the dealer was just waiting for a sucker like me to show up, so he could finally unload it.*

Not too long after buying the car, I decided to move back to the East Coast. *This thing's run pretty well so far*, I thought as I wedged the last overstuffed cardboard box into the trunk. *But it'll probably break down in the middle of Nebraska.*

Back east, my life, so long in disarray, slowly began to fall together. I found a job I really liked, met a woman whom I eventually married and finally settled down after years of drifting from place to place.

"You've had this car for a long time," my wife said one day. "Maybe we should think about trading it in." Before I knew it, we were signing the last of the papers on a new car.

"Better go check your old vehicle," the dealer said. "Make sure you haven't left anything in it."

I walked out to the little car that had been such a focus of my worries for so long and did a double take. It felt as if I were seeing it for the first time, and seeing it as what it always had been: the perfect car for me. How come I'd never noticed before?

When I let worry obscure my sight, I miss so much. Lord, help me to trust. —PTOLEMY TOMPKINS

28 / *FRI* *But when the first came, they supposed that they should have received more. . . .* —MATTHEW 20:10

In December, excitement rippled through our parish. Our youth, most of whom had never been east of the Mississippi, had been invited on a pilgrimage to Europe for World Youth Day activities. My daughter Trina would be beginning high school that summer and was eligible. Imagine! A spiritual journey with the youngsters I had taught in religious education classes! It was too good to be true.

The pilgrimage and call for chaperones had been announced on Sunday. The deadline was Friday. Over the next two days, I checked and double-checked my finances. We could just squeeze out the funds. Tuesday evening after choir practice, I fidgeted with excitement, eager to approach the youth leader and confirm our plans.

"Trina can go, but you can't. We don't need any more chaperones," the youth leader announced abruptly. I slapped my hymnal on a chair, snatched my purse and shoved my way out the door without even saying good-bye.

Alone under the stars, I raged at this youth leader, whom I had taught in class as a teenager! Hadn't I responded well within the time limit? Hadn't I taught religious education for twelve years and provided music for church for twenty-three years? Didn't I *deserve* to go?

For the next several months, I avoided the many fund-raisers needed for the huge undertaking. I simply couldn't bring myself to help others go on a trip that I'd been denied. Then, in early spring, while I was praying for a dear young man to be relieved of his bitterness, I thought I'd better begin praying for an end to my own.

Healing came gradually. I eased into fund-raising efforts and chaperoned a spiritual retreat, genuinely enjoying my former students. By the time the pilgrims departed, I had hugged the youth leader with genuine affection and had prayed for her ministry many times.

Trina and I may make a European pilgrimage one day. In the meantime, I've learned that you don't have to leave town to make a faith journey.

Merciful Lord, thank You for reminding me in so many ways that Your grace isn't "merit pay." —GAIL THORELL SCHILLING

*29/*SAT *The earth is the Lord's, and everything in it, the world, and all who live in it.* —PSALM 24:1 (NIV)

As I sit on my porch, the world according to the morning paper lying heavy on my lap, grim news fills me with a sense of doom. The world, I think, is spinning out of control. *Lord, where is the hope?*

Across my long porch, a male finch perches on the edge of a hanging fern, warbling his heart out. His tune, I think, also carries news. Grabbing my binoculars, I look inside the fern at the tiny nest cradling three pale blue eggs. The eggs have somehow survived cat-stalking, storms and at least one bird of prey. My newspaper slips to the floor. Through my lenses, I watch the plain, brown female pecking at the eggs. *They're hatching!*

I wait awhile, then I creep closer, climb on a railing and angle the binoculars to peek inside. The hatchlings are twined together, the size of a nickel, naked, helpless and mud brown. They cannot feed themselves and, left alone, their shallow, exuberant breathing will soon cease. But their parents are hovering nearby to nurture their brood, so they can grow up and fly and sing their song and propagate their species all over again.

Here, in this little backyard miracle, I see the hand that holds the world. An event too small, too ordinary to make the morning paper. But, light as a feather, soft as a whisper, its good news lands in my soul. God is in control.

Creator God, thank You for the works of Your hand that cry out the awesome truth of Your care for me. —SHARI SMYTH

30/SUN

"The greatest among you will be your servant. For whoever exalts himself will be humbled, and whoever humbles himself will be exalted." —MATTHEW 23:11–12 (NIV)

My wife attended a wonderful retreat last year on the Gulf Coast. "From the moment I arrived at the hotel," Rosie told me, "I could feel the presence of the Lord there." She learned later that the organizers of the retreat had been praying and occasionally fasting during the whole year leading up to it. The participants had been especially invited because, after much prayer, God had impressed their names upon the hearts of the leaders. Each of the rooms they were staying in had been prayed over as well, and Rosie said that she'd never slept so peacefully.

Eleven "angels," the ladies who were the leaders and prayer warriors of the retreat, served the thirty participants. "The love and care we received was overwhelming," Rosie said. "The 'angels' waited on us hand and foot. We weren't even allowed to carry our food trays to the tables. Each day we were given special gifts, as well as much affirmation and encouragement."

The most moving experience for Rosie was the Communion service and foot-washing ceremony. "My tears wouldn't stop flowing as those dear 'angels' washed our feet. I was so moved and humbled by their prayers and tenderness that I could almost picture Jesus washing His disciples' feet. What love and care He must have shown! What a picture of true humility! I'll never forget this living picture of how much God loves us, and how He wants to shower us with blessings."

Lord, may the example of Jesus inspire me, like Rosie's "angels," to seek opportunities to serve others. —DOLPHUS WEARY

31/MON

Pray without ceasing.

—I THESSALONIANS 5:17

I looked up at the clock on my classroom wall one more time, squinting to see the time through the glare of afternoon sun. It was one o'clock, and still no word from my son Christopher, who was taking his firefighter certification test—a challenging and competitive test that required mental and physical stamina. As a rookie firefighter, Christopher had to pass in order to continue his training. I looked up at the clock again. Only a minute had passed. My students were taking a history test; the room was quiet except for the sound of pencils scribbling furiously and the loud tick-tick-tick of the clock.

I prayed silently, as I had all morning: *Lord, bless my students and my son with a clear mind and a steady hand as they take their tests today.*

When the final bell rang to signal the end of the school day, I had still not received word from Christopher. I decided to call.

"Oh, hi, Mom," Christopher said. "Sorry I forgot to call you. I got busy here at the fire station after I found out that I'd passed my test."

I was overjoyed, but also annoyed. I had spent the day in constant prayer while waiting for a phone call that never came. Right before I was about to embark on a "Do you have any idea what my day was like waiting for your call?" lecture, I remembered the advice of a wise friend. "If a problem brings you to prayer, then it has served its purpose," she had calmly stated when offering counsel years ago.

Indeed, I had spent the day in almost continuous dialogue with God simply because I had a problem that led me to prayer. What a blessing!

Gracious and loving God, thank You for turning my problems into opportunities to become one with You in prayer.

—MELODY BONNETTE

My Daily Blessings

1 _____

2 _____

3 _____

4 _____

5 _____

6 _____

7 _____

8 _____

9 _____

10 _____

11 _____

12 _____

13 _____

14 _____

15 _____

16 _____

17 _____

18 _____

19 _____

20 _____

21 _____

22 _____

23 _____

24 _____

25 _____

26 _____

27 _____

28 _____

29 _____

30 _____

31 _____

APRIL

Blessed be the God and Father of our
Lord Jesus Christ, which according to his
abundant mercy hath begotten us again
unto a lively hope by the resurrection
of Jesus Christ from the dead. . . .
—I Peter 1:3

S	M	T	W	T	F	S
		1	2	3	4	5
6	7	8	9	10	11	12
13	14	15	16	17	18	19
20	21	22	23	24	25	26
27	28	29	30			

1/*TUE*   *Let the field be joyful, and all that is*
therein. . . .   —PSALM 96:12

I flew to Detroit a few years ago to interview a ballplayer whose team would be playing that night at grand old Tiger Stadium on the corner of Michigan and Trumbull avenues. To me, the stadium was a shrine, not just to the Tigers and to baseball played on real grass under an open sky, but to a boyhood spent living and dying by the fortunes of the hometown team. How many sultry summer nights had I lain awake listening to Ernie Harwell describe one of Rocky Colavito's late-inning blasts arcing into the upper deck in right, kicking my feet in the air as Ernie shouted, "He's done it again, folks!"?

I arrived early and decided to wait out on the field. It was a nice spring day, the late-afternoon sun still high enough in the sky to bathe the infield in sunlight. There's nothing prettier than a major league infield, the grass cut short in crosshatch style, the dirt raked smooth and immaculately free of pebbles and debris. I marveled, thinking back to all those games I'd seen and listened to. I checked the clock above the scoreboard. A few of the ushers and vendors had drifted into the stands, preparing for the night's game.

Why not? I thought. *This is my chance.* I threw off my sport coat and ran to home plate. I made a mad dash down the first-base line, my wingtips kicking up the dust, rounded the bag and chugged toward second. I touched second and headed to third, then steamed home, where I hit the dirt just under the imaginary tag. Springing breathlessly to my feet, I heard sporadic cheering and clapping from the bemused ushers. I waved heroically and pretended to tip my cap.

When I got back to the visitors' dugout, my interview subject had arrived and was giving me a perplexed look. But he just didn't understand. He got to do this every day.

Lord, on Opening Day, let me thank You again for the blessing of baseball, for boyhood dreams and lifetime memories, and for moments in the sun, however brief and breathless.

—EDWARD GRINNAN

AN EYE FOR BLESSINGS

2/WED THE WATER OF LIFE

And ye shall serve the Lord your God, and he shall bless thy bread, and thy water. . . . —EXODUS 23:25

It was April 1950, and my husband John and I were returning from Europe for the birth of our first child. Because the harbor at Cherbourg was still war-damaged, the *Queen Elizabeth* was anchored offshore. As we walked down the ramp to the launch that would ferry us out, not a ripple showed on the placid surface of the sea. But the instant my foot touched the deck, my stomach rose into my throat.

"It will be better on the big boat," John said.

It wasn't better. John helped me down several stairways and onto the lower bunk in our cabin. And there I remained for the five-and-a-half day crossing. Eating was out of the question: I couldn't bear even to hear John's enthusiastic reports from the dining room. What I remember most from that nightmare trip is the thirst. Water was all I could think of. Unable to hold down more than a teaspoon's worth, I fantasized gulping it by the tumbler, the gallon.

Dehydration finally brought on a kind of delirium. In the refrigerator of my childhood home there had always been a jar of ice water. I saw it now, suspended from the upper bunk just above me—a tall narrow bottle with a red cap. Again and again I reached for it, felt the cold moistness of the glass, unscrewed the cap. . . .

All of it came back this morning. They're working on the water main in our part of town, and when I turned on the faucet this morning, nothing happened. I stared at that dry kitchen faucet. How generously water has always come from it! Water so abundant, so readily available in our part of the world that I'd forgotten what a blessing it is simply to pour a glass and drink.

I'm learning, this year, to thank God for overlooked daily gifts. But, oh, let me not forget the everyday provision on which life itself depends!

Come to me today, Lord, as Living Water.

—ELIZABETH SHERRILL

EDITOR'S NOTE: How has God been blessing you this year? Please take a few moments to look back at what you've written in the "My Daily Blessings" journal pages, and let us know what He's been doing in your life. Send your letter to *Daily Guideposts* Reader's Room, Guideposts Books, 16 E. 34th St., New York, NY 10016. We'll share some of what you tell us in a future *Daily Guideposts.*

*3/*THU   *Do not conform any longer to the pattern of this world, but be transformed by the renewing of your mind. . . .* —ROMANS 12:2 (NIV)

The other morning as I drove to the monthly men's breakfast at church, I thought how pleased I was to be back living in sunny Southern California. Here I was, dressed in shorts and a polo shirt, going to a function at church. One of the things I like about California is the casual social climate. I could go to the worship service on Sunday morning dressed in shorts (as some in fact do) and feel perfectly at home.

But I recalled with embarrassment another church function my wife Carol and I had attended after moving from California to New Jersey more than twenty years ago. Of course, we realized the East Coast is more formal, and we dressed up for Sunday services like everyone else. But when we went to a church family retreat at a rural conference center, we wore casual clothes. Imagine our chagrin when we arrived for the Friday-night dinner to find everyone else wearing his or her Sunday best! No one commented on my sport shirt and slacks, but I was ill at ease all evening.

I guess I'm something of a conformist—I like to fit in. When we lived in Manhattan in the 1960s, I felt out of place if I left our apartment without a coat and tie. During our ten years in Hawaii I enjoyed wearing colorful aloha shirts and Carol often wore long muumuus to church. Everywhere we've lived, we adapted to local customs.

But as I got out of my car in the church parking lot and tucked my Bible under my arm, I thought how wonderful it is that God accepts me just as I am. Whether in coat and tie, or polo shirt and shorts, I am accepted by the One Who loves me unconditionally.

Lord Jesus, thank You for becoming one of us, so that we can become part of Your family.   —HAROLD HOSTETLER

4/FRI   *I have a message from God unto thee. . . .*
                                                —JUDGES 3:20

I was turning into our garage, weary from shopping, when a scrap of paper stuck in the back door caught my eye. Immediately, joy, energy and anticipation settled into my heart, and I wasn't nearly as tired. Smiling, I turned off the ignition and momentarily forgot about the groceries in the trunk and the packages on the backseat.

I stepped out of the car and reached for the note. It was scribbled on the back of an envelope in my husband Gene's familiar scrunched-up handwriting. Neither of us went anywhere without leaving a note for the other. This one said, "Hey. I've gone to the drugstore, the grocery and to feed the cows. Julie wants you to call her. Your watch is ready to be picked up. Home before six. Want to eat out?" Then came the best part: a hastily drawn heart with an arrow through it and his initials at the top and mine at the bottom. I read it twice because—well, because I adore Gene and I like being reminded that he loves me.

Once, after Gene and I'd had a pretty hefty fight, he left a note on the door that said, "Busy day. Don't know when I'll be back. Gene." I turned the paper over, searching in vain for something like, "P.S. I love you." When Gene returned, stern-faced and moving around like the Tin Man, I ran into his arms shouting, "Your note was terrible. The mailman leaves better notes than that!" He held me while I cried. Since then, Gene's notes have always contained that lopsided heart-and-arrow and our initials, a little message just for me.

Today, Father, help me to read the message You have just for me in Your Word.
                                                —MARION BOND WEST

5/SAT   *In those days a man will say to his brother,*
"You have some extra clothing, so you be our king and take care
of this mess."   —ISAIAH 3:6 (TLB)

One thing about being single and an empty-nester is that you get to
fill up all the closets. No sharing; every inch is mine. And what
happens over the years is you end up with far too many clothes. I
have clothes for every season, every reason, every style, size and
event.

I should take my cue from my stepmother Bev, who, at age seventy-
eight, always looks like she just stepped out of a fashion magazine.
When it comes to clothes, she's a minimalist. For instance, for
summer wear she has five or six really nice spotless T-shirts; I have
about thirty. Some are in the same condition as my dad's shop rags.
How can you ever get rid of the T-shirt your daughter painted in
high school? Or the one you bought at the Eiffel Tower? Or the
one your son bought you for Mother's Day fifteen years ago?

Well, I'm going to try. My goal for this year is to reduce my
clothes-chaos from three closets full to perhaps one and a half. I'm
going to try to find something that looks really good on me and
stick with that style. I'm going to give the rest away to Goodwill or
Human Concerns so that others who have little can have more. I'm
going to share a few special things with friends who, unlike me and
my dreams, have already lost the extra twenty pounds.

Yes, I am going to conquer my closets! My new mantra: Less is
more. I feel lighter already.

Jesus, thank You for keeping me well clothed. Help me to be
more like You and share my bounty with others who have less.
                                        —PATRICIA LORENZ

6/SUN   *Now there stood by the cross of Jesus his*
mother, and his mother's sister, Mary the wife of Cleophas, and
Mary Magdalene.   —JOHN 19:25

Standing in church one day, I noticed an older woman across the
way. She was around seventy years old. There were two younger
women with her—in their forties, I guessed. They seemed like
family—two sisters with their mom, or their aunt, perhaps.

It was pouring cars and boats outside, and all three women were wearing rain slickers. The older woman reached up to brush back the younger women's gleaming hoods, and as she did so, the two younger women just stood there quietly. Then she brushed back their hair, and the young women stood there obediently, like small children. I realized slowly that something was strange—the younger women were too calm. They didn't seem quite alert, quite all there.

During services, the younger women held hands, and they watched the older woman to see when to rise and when to kneel. The older woman was calm, her gestures deft. She led the two younger women gently and efficiently down the aisle and out the door when the service was over.

I sat there for a moment amazed and abashed and astounded at the strength of women, the mountains that mothers are, the way mothers carry their loads all their lives, and who knows what those loads are? For some mothers, too-placid children who will never really grow up; for another, her own son bleeding and broken above her as she stared up into His face.

Dear Lord, every one of Your children must bear his or her load, well or ill. Lend us Your sinew, Your broad shoulder, Your capacious heart, Your sudden joy. This we ask, this we beg, this we pray.
—BRIAN DOYLE

7 / MON   *Your beauty. . . . should be that of your inner self, the unfading beauty of a gentle and quiet spirit. . . .*
—I PETER 3:3–4 (NIV)

I had stopped at a local fast-food restaurant to read the newspaper and drink a cup of tea before heading into the office. As I walked toward the building, something caught my eye. The van next to me had a mini-chandelier hanging from its rearview mirror! I looked past it and saw that the whole vehicle seemed to be filled with boxes and ribbon and bright splashes of cloth. *I'd like to meet the person who drives that,* I thought.

Inside the restaurant, I spotted her. She was at the counter, ordering. She was wearing wonderfully sparkly bracelets, half a dozen on each arm. Around her neck hung an antique necklace, amber stones set in shiny black. "I like your necklace . . . and bracelets," I said.

She turned and smiled. "Thanks. I have a store in Chicago, but I'm off to Grand Rapids to give a jewelry show for a friend." I remarked that I'd wanted to meet her when I'd seen inside her van. "Want to see my stuff?" she asked. She grabbed her breakfast sandwich and coffee, and I stepped out of line.

Outside, we pawed through the back of her van. Such beautiful things! The morning sun caught green crystals, elaborate marcasite, black glass beads. I tried things on as she pulled one pretty item after another from plastic bags. We chatted about the artists who had designed the pieces and which ones were made from antique jewelry. Suddenly, she turned to me and said, "I bet you are a Christian."

I was surprised, since all we'd been talking about was jewelry. "Yes," I said, "I am."

"I knew it!" she laughed, slipping yet another bracelet on her arm. "I could just tell."

In another few minutes, we parted ways. I left with a big smile, the address of a new friend—and a really gorgeous bracelet.

Father, may Your love and gentleness be the real adornments of our lives. And may they sparkle every day!—MARY LOU CARNEY

8/TUE   *Blessed are they that mourn: for they shall be* *comforted.*   —MATTHEW 5:4

A couple of years ago, I took the training course for hospice volunteers, so I'd be able to help the terminally ill and their families. If you know about hospice care firsthand, I don't have to tell you what a fantastic service it is. Not only can volunteers be supportive of those at the end of their journey, they can also give relief to caregivers who sometimes become exhausted and ill themselves from the strain of watching over a loved one.

When the instructor asked our class why we wanted to be hospice volunteers, there was a wide variety of responses. Not surprisingly, many were church members who thought hospice work would be a way for them to be God's hands and feet. Some were people whose dying loved ones had been beneficiaries of hospice services, and they wanted to give something back. "I don't like the thought of anyone dying alone" was my answer.

Today I got a phone call from Eleanor, a member of a family I had served. Her husband had died a few months earlier, and she thanked me again for my help. In truth, I did little more than listen to her and her husband talk about their long life together. I began my writing career as a newspaperman, and one of the things interviewing people taught me was how to listen. Sometimes I had to ask a few leading questions, but the key to extracting the facts of a story is listening. Eleanor and her husband had a wonderful faith story: Both had been active Christian workers who believed they'd meet again in the hereafter.

Dying is never easy, but our faith in God will help us cope. If we listen to His still small voice, we will hear His reassuring words even when the shadows grow long and life grows short.

> *Teach me, Lord, the holy art*
> *Of hearing others with my heart.*
>
> —FRED BAUER

9/ WED   *Dearly beloved, avenge not yourselves, but rather give place unto wrath. . . .*   —ROMANS 12:19

Her husband left her twenty years ago, and she's still getting even. She's turned her son against his father. She has a permanent scowl on her face. Most of her friends have drifted away, weary of hearing her ex-husband's faults replayed over and over again. She has never remarried. The alimony she would lose is part of her revenge. Seeing my old friend makes me terribly sad, as the life she's lost is staggering.

Yes, her case is extreme. But, in truth, I don't have to look very far to find my own dark places where grudges fester, because I have refused to forgive. I avoid a co-worker who said hateful things to me when I was working for a cause I believed in. I resent a neighbor who was hostile when I stopped to ask for help. My list goes on.

Over and over, our Father practically begs us to forgive:

"Love your enemies, bless them that curse you, do good to them that hate you, and pray for them which despitefully use you" (Matthew 5:44).

"When ye stand praying, forgive" (Mark 11:25).

"Judge not" (Luke 6:37).

Could it be that our Father, Who dwells with us, simply wants to give us the best chance for a happy life?

The scenario should go something like this: I take the resentment, the hurt, the damage that's been done to me and give it straight to God. I'm free from my burden. I don't have to get even or take on the responsibility of paying someone back. I don't have to tell God how to handle my situation: I just have to let go, walk away and trust.

Free of grudges, I can even find something good about the ones who wronged me, for now they are forgiven—and I am, too.

Father, let me forgive so completely that prayers of kindness come naturally to my heart. —PAM KIDD

10/THU Anyone willing to be corrected is on the pathway to life. ... —PROVERBS 10:17 (TLB)

On our very early walks each day, my dog Shep and I eventually go to the highest point in New York City's Central Park, the Summit. There are benches there, and we sit and watch while the sun rises. Occasionally we'll see another dog-walker, and during the first week in May there are bird-watchers, but normally the place is ours.

One morning we were sitting, enjoying the swallows who pecked their way close to us, when a rugged, dour-looking man appeared. He took a seat distant from us. He didn't have a dog or evident reason to be there. "Come on," I said to Shep, and we left. The next morning he was there again. We left, a little curious about him. On the third morning he was back, and this time he lifted an arm and waved to us.

"Good morning," he said. "We seem to be on the same schedule."

"Why, yes," I replied tentatively as I waved back. Then he settled down and took out a book and started to read. "A Bible," I said. "You're reading a *Bible.*"

"Something I do every day," he said. "I think it helps me put that extra something into my work." His work, he went on to say, was a wood finisher. His present job was in the vast building in which I live, in the apartment of comedian Jerry Seinfeld. During the next few weeks, through my new friend, I learned just how extensive the apartment was.

Then one morning he said, "I've been assigned to another job.

This one is finished." He gave Shep a pat, and with a "God bless you," he went off. And I said a silent prayer for the woodworker, whatever his job, wherever he went. And a prayer for Seinfeld. Would he ever know that "extra something" that was burnished into a balustrade or honed into a kitchen cabinet? No matter. Have a happy home, and welcome, Mr. Seinfeld.

Thank You, Father, for the gift of the Woodworker.

—VAN VARNER

11 / FRI   *Call unto me, and I will answer thee, and show thee great and mighty things, which thou knowest not.*

—JEREMIAH 33:3

I arrived back at Denver International Airport on a late-night flight in a full-blown spring blizzard. Huge flakes swirled furiously around the wings as we touched down in what looked like a giant snow field. As I got off the plane to retrieve my luggage, I heard the announcement that the airport had closed down for the night.

I hurried out of the terminal but was not prepared for the world outside. Nearly a foot of snow covered the ground . . . and my open-toed shoes. My light suit coat offered no defense against the stinging cold flakes, but I hurried toward the parking lot, determined to find my car quickly. Who would have thought yesterday when I left sunny Denver that I'd return to this kind of weather? Yet these spring snowstorms are not uncommon in Colorado and are even considered adventuresome because they build what we call "Western spirit." At least that's what I was thinking until I reached the parking lot.

There I stopped in amazement. Instead of rows of parked cars, I saw what looked like a bunch of big snowballs. The cars were covered with so much snow that they all looked alike. How would I find my car?

I got to the right general area and began removing snow from cars with my bare hands. *Nope. Wrong color. Nope. Wrong again.* Just then I remembered my keys had the remote lock and unlock buttons that trigger a response from the car, along with a friendly flicker of the rear lights. I pulled out the keys and started clicking.

"Speak to me, baby," I kept saying as my nearly frozen fingers clicked the button. I saw no response from the cars. *Click.* Nothing. *Click.* Nothing. Then suddenly, down the line, I saw the faintest flicker of pink under a mound of snow. I kept clicking; it kept flickering. My car!

Quickly I ran to the car and brushed off enough snow to climb inside. Soon I was on my slow way home through the blizzard, praising God that cars are miraculously wired to respond to keys.

Thank You, Lord, for the cars that respond to keys and for the grace that makes me able to respond to You.

—CAROL KUYKENDALL

FOLLOWING JESUS

12 / SAT   A SERVANT'S HEART

After that, he poured water into a basin and began to wash his disciples' feet.... —JOHN 13:5 (NIV)

At a flea market in Columbus, Ohio, I happened upon a vintage black and white enamel stove in mint condition, perfect for my cabin. It was much too big to fit in my car, and the owners graciously agreed to cart it back home until I could rent a truck and pick it up. My father had been ill, however, and it was many months before I had a free Saturday.

On the three-hour drive to Columbus, the freedom of a day without the burden of caring for Dad got the better of me. Before long, the white pickup was piled high with things I discovered at a neighborhood yard sale: wooden shutters for a friend who crafts angels out of them, a wicker bassinet for a new grandma, a glider for my sister's porch, two ladder-back chairs for my newlywed niece. Not only was there no place left in the truck for the stove, in all the excitement, I'd failed to bring along materials to pad and secure it. I dreaded facing Lynn and Bryan, the stove's owners.

To my surprise, they gave me a conspiratorial wink, congratulated me on my finds, then disappeared inside their bungalow. They returned with bungee cords and a stack of blankets and T-shirts. "Let's see what we can do," Bryan said. "Why don't you kick your shoes off and rest a minute under that tree?" Lynn went to get me a glass of iced tea.

Lynn and Bryan loaded the heavy stove, meticulously padding every pressure point. As they fitted my finds around the stove like a giant jigsaw puzzle, my life back home seemed suddenly manageable. And if that wasn't enough, they sent me on my way with a colorful old Fiestaware ad. "Hang this over your stove and remember us," they said as I drove off.

I would do just that—after I stopped at that farmer's market on the way home to pick up some of that Amish cheese Dad loved.

Thank You, Lord, for those who show us how to serve You with joy.
—ROBERTA MESSNER

A CLOSER WALK

The events of Holy Week and Easter are the foundation of all our everyday blessings. This Holy Week, join Daniel Schantz as he helps us to reconnect history's most momentous week with the joys and sorrows of our own daily walks. —THE EDITORS

13/SUN PALM SUNDAY: THE TRIUMPHAL ENTRY
A great multitude. . . . took branches of palm trees and went out to meet Him, and cried out: "Hosanna! Blessed is He who comes in the name of the Lord! . . ." —JOHN 12:12–13 (NKJV)

When Jesus rode into Jerusalem on a donkey's colt, the whole town came out to sing His praises. After all, many of them saw Him as the liberator who would lift the foot of Rome from the neck of the world. Jesus accepted their praise, but He was wise enough to know that in a couple of days the hosannas would turn to hisses.

When I started teaching college, I was very young, which made me popular with students. One day an older teacher said to me, "Praise is like bubblegum. Chew it, but don't swallow it." I laughed, but he was right. After I issued my first grades, I fell from icon status.

The incident was sobering, and it reminds me that applause is not the best indicator of success. In fact, I've known many people who never heard the sounds of praise:

- A secretary who made her boss look good, but her boss won all the awards.
- A beautiful girl who was bypassed as homecoming queen in favor of someone with less character and charm.
- A dedicated student who could have been valedictorian if he hadn't been working two jobs to support his family and pay his tuition.
- A wife who gave body and soul to her husband, only to be abandoned.

Being praised does not always mean I am doing right, and getting "crucified" doesn't mean I have failed. My job is not to play to the crowd but to do the task God gave me and trust Him for accolades in His own good time.

Purify my motives, Lord, and help me to serve You whether I am lauded or loathed. —DANIEL SCHANTZ

14/MON MONDAY IN HOLY WEEK: MOTIVATION FOR SUFFERING

Looking unto Jesus . . . who for the joy that was set before Him, endured the cross. . . . —HEBREWS 12:2 (NKJV)

This was a blue Monday for Jesus, and I've often wondered where he found the strength to face the betrayal, the trial and the Crucifixion He knew were coming. The writer of Hebrews suggests that Jesus looked beyond the Cross to the joy that His sacrifice would bring to millions yet unborn.

When Sharon and I started our family in the sixties, we knew there would be crosses involved. For Sharon, it began with nine months of feeling ill and ugly, followed by forty-eight hours of labor with our firstborn Teresa. It cost thousands of dollars to rear our girls, and we were determined to live on my teacher's salary so Sharon could be a stay-at-home mother. Then came the turbulent teen years that kept us awake nights, and finally the letting-go process as they went to college. Yet, when I look back on it, I remember the ecstasy and have forgotten the pains.

If I can keep my focus on the value of my crosses, I think they will be easier to bear. Once, when I was weary of being a teacher, I attended a Sunday-school class taught by Rick Willis, a former student of mine. Somehow Rick's lecture was custom-fitted to my heart, as if he could read my mind. I sat there with tears in my eyes, thinking, *So this is what it's like to sit under a good teacher. I never realized how valuable a good teacher can be. If I can be this useful to my students, it'll be worth all the work.* When I went back to the classroom, it was with a different attitude.

Whether you drive a truck, manage a corporation, run a household or create software, there will be tough times, but they can be made bearable by dwelling on the joy that your work brings to others.

Help me to carry my crosses patiently, Lord, looking for the joy that will follow. —DANIEL SCHANTZ

15/TUE TUESDAY IN HOLY WEEK:
PERFECTED PRAISE
But when the chief priests and scribes saw the wonderful things that He did, and the children crying out in the temple and saying, "Hosanna to the Son of David," they were indignant and said to Him, "Do you hear what these are saying?" And Jesus said to them, "Yes. Have you never read, 'Out of the mouth of babes and nursing infants You have perfected praise'?"
—MATTHEW 21:15–16 (NKJV)

On Tuesday, the praises of Jesus continued, but this time they came from children. I suspect that these praises brought tears of joy to Jesus. After all, the praises of children are sincere, spontaneous and unsolicited. Children could plainly see what the sophisticated religious professionals could not—that Jesus was indeed the wonderful Son of God.

As an author of children's books, I have visited many elementary schools and have received hundreds of letters from little people. Lines like these are among my greatest treasures:

"Thank you for coming and shoing us how you rot your stores."

"I wish I was your son."

"You are the best arthur in the world."

The truest test of my character is what children think of me. They are hard to fool.

Once I was sitting in the waiting room at the doctor's office. A little girl sitting next to me suddenly climbed up on my lap and said, "Are you scared of the doctor?" I smiled, thinking, *I sure am. How did she know?*

Then there was the day I caught a little neighbor boy in my strawberry patch. Blushing, he looked at me and said, "I likes you pretty garden." It was the nicest thing anyone has ever said about my work.

If I want to be somebody important, I think I need to aim low, down where children live. Nothing I do for them is ever wasted.

Lord, I join the children in saying, "I likes You pretty world."
—DANIEL SCHANTZ

16/WED WEDNESDAY IN HOLY WEEK: FINAL WORDS OF COMFORT

"A little while longer and the world will see Me no more, but you will see Me. Because I live, you will live also."
—JOHN 14:19 (NKJV)

Lord, life is just one thing after another. Dad has Alzheimer's disease. Our daughter had another miscarriage. Our old friends are getting divorced, and a church member's house burned down.

"Let not your heart be troubled."

I try not to be upset, Lord, but sometimes I just don't know what to believe.

"You believe in God, believe also in Me."

I do believe, but I also doubt like Thomas. I built my whole life on You and on the hope of heaven. What if it's just a dream? What if it's not true?

"If it were not so, I would have told you."

Everything is changing down here, God. Our country is in trouble,

*friends move away. Even the church has changed so much, I don't enjoy
it as I did. Sometimes I feel so out of place, like a homeless person.*

"In my Father's house are many mansions."

*I would settle for a little farm. You know, a couple acres with a barn
and a bungalow. Maybe a pasture with a willow-lined creek running
through it. A little red pickup truck, an orchard and a pond, some chick-
ens and a big garden . . .*

"I go to prepare a place for you, and if I go, I will come
again . . . that where I am, you may be also. I will not leave you
orphans."

*I know, but I get so confused. So many voices, giving different
directions.*

"I am the way, I am the truth, I am the life. No one comes to
the Father except through Me." (Based on John 14:1–6, 16–18,
NKJV.)

***Thanks, Lord. I just needed to hear You say it. No one can settle
me down the way You can. I will keep trusting You, even
through the storms. And, Lord? Be merciful to my dad. He is
such a good man, and we all love him.*** —DANIEL SCHANTZ

17/THU MAUNDY THURSDAY: THE LAST SUPPER
*And as they were eating, Jesus took bread, blessed and broke
it. . . .* —MARK 14:22 (NKJV)

The Last Supper—what a perfect way for Jesus to say good-bye to
His friends and to institute a memorial of his life and death.

I grew up in the fifties, when families still ate together: before
drive-throughs and fast food; before dark, smoke-filled restaurants;
before mall-courts with their thousand eyes and loud rock music
"entertainment."

I remember coming home from church to sit down for a home-
cooked meal with family and friends: real china plates, piled high
with plump Kentucky Wonder beans, buttery baked potatoes and
roast beef so tender you couldn't keep it on your fork, all washed
down with sweetened tea or real lemonade. For dessert we enjoyed
fresh strawberries poured over hand-churned ice cream, served
with hot coffee.

Food was only part of dinner, however. A good meal might last two hours, with no one anxious to leave the table. Everyone had stories to tell, each one funnier than the last. At dinner we planned our careers, repented of our sins, fell in love and found courage to face hard winters. Together we solved world problems, shook our family trees, relived our childhoods and imagined what heaven was like.

When it was finally over, the men staggered to the living room to sprawl on couch and carpet, adding the bliss of sleep to the flavor of food. The ladies washed and dried the dishes and exchanged secrets for living with imperfect husbands and children.

Eating is an everyday blessing with heavenly possibilities. It's up to me to provide the sauce of friendship. What if my next meal were my last supper? How would it be different?

Thank You, Lord, for the gift of hunger, which brings us together.
—DANIEL SCHANTZ

18/FRI GOOD FRIDAY: HANDS
They pierced my hands and my feet. —PSALM 22:16 (NKJV)

Even more than the suffering described by the Psalmist, the piercing of Jesus' hands is a horrible scene. It seems to fire the imagination of artists and moviemakers like no other torment Jesus endured. I think there was something unspeakably dark about the deed, even beyond the pain. Without free hands, Jesus could not rub sweat from His eyes or shoo flies from His mouth or adjust His position. He was utterly helpless.

Furthermore, to puncture those hands was to mock His whole life. After all, those hands had healed the blind and blessed children. Those hands raised the dead, animated His talks about heaven and passed along miraculous gifts.

When I was just a boy, I attended a Christian camp where the chapel speaker described the Crucifixion in graphic detail. When he got to the part about Jesus' hands, I began to cry. I rubbed my palms and felt overwhelming gratitude for the Lord's sacrifice. Afterward, I asked my father if I could be baptized.

Hands are unique, with their amazing blend of sensitivity and strength. My mother could read one degree of fever with the back of her fingers, and she could thread a tiny needle faster than a magician. Although she complained about her tired back and tired feet, she never once mentioned tired hands.

I'm really not surprised to find that hands had something to do with our redemption. I use my hands to teach my grandson to build a birdhouse. I show my love to my wife Sharon by holding her hand. Hands seem to have infinite possibilities for good when I dedicate them to God.

My Lord and my God, when I think of Your hands, I know that You really do love me. I give You my hands to be used for good.
—DANIEL SCHANTZ

EDITOR'S NOTE: As we spend this Good Friday Day of Prayer in the shadow of the Cross, let's pause a moment to pray for all the members of our *Daily Guideposts* family.

19/SAT   HOLY SATURDAY: FORSAKEN
"My God, My God, why have You forsaken me?"
—MATTHEW 27:46 (NKJV)

It was the loneliest Saturday in history, with the Hope of the World lying in a tomb, and the disciples scattered to their hideouts in shock. Still, I am comforted to know that Jesus understood the ache of loneliness. His only question on the Cross was about why His Father had abandoned Him, just when He needed Him most.

Suffering has a unique ability to make a person feel all alone. I once heard a story that when Jesus was dying, a passerby stopped to stare at the Cross. As he watched, tears streamed down his face. Someone asked him, "Did you know this man Jesus?" The man shook his head. "Then why are you crying?" He rubbed his jaw and replied, "I'm crying because I have a terrible toothache." He had no room for anyone else's troubles.

"Laugh and the world laughs with you," Ella Wheeler Wilcox noted, and she quickly added, "weep and you weep alone." I need to think about this truism when a student calls me in the middle of the night to tell me that his girlfriend dropped him. More than wise advice, he simply needs someone to keep him company until he calms down. When my wife is wounded by careless friends, that would be a good time for me to cancel that fishing trip and stick around the house. And when my daughter is nervous about giving an important piano recital, it would be a richer experience if she could see my smiling eyes in the audience.

Lord, You promised never to forsake us, but sometimes I do feel forsaken. At such times, help me not to withdraw from You and the people who could help me. —DANIEL SCHANTZ

20/SUN EASTER SUNDAY: THERE IS ALWAYS HOPE

"But we were hoping that it was He who was going to redeem Israel. . . ." —LUKE 24:21 (NKJV)

What a joy it must have been for Jesus to appear to His friends after His Resurrection. I see this joy coming out in the covert encounter with two discouraged disciples who were shuffling their way toward Emmaus. Incognito, Jesus joins them and pretends not to know what they are talking about. "What things?" He asks, as if He didn't know. He listens sympathetically and reminds them of some Scriptures they had overlooked. When, at last, He reveals himself, their hearts once again burn with hope.

It's all too easy to lose hope in this life, I think. That dream job gets put on the back burner because you need cash now. The handsome prince you married turns out to be a toad. Someone else bought the split-level you wanted, and college plans were set aside when the children came along.

The Resurrection of Christ is a wake-up call for my sidetracked yearnings. When God is involved, there is always hope. Hope is not just a noun, it's also a verb—something I should *practice*, like Abraham, who "hoped against hope" (Romans 4:18).

Perhaps God has already set in motion forces that will even yet bring my dreams to pass. Maybe, when children are grown, college will be even sweeter. That split-level might come up for sale again, at a better time. That chubby hubby might just need time to find his princely side. And that current job might be a stepping stone to more stellar assignments.

Today, the anniversary of death's defeat, would be a good time to dust off one of those dreams and present it to the Lord of Hope.

Father, forgive me when I practice despair more than I practice hope. Help me to work toward making my dreams come true.
—DANIEL SCHANTZ

READER'S ROOM

I appreciate the beautiful Florida weather, the magnificent azure skies, the gorgeous live oaks and the walking path in the park. God has given me the ability to teach children. They share so much with me that I know God has sent each one to me. The ladies in my quilting class are each God's gift to me as we share a time of fellowship. My handbell choir sings to glorify God, and He rewards our efforts with our love for one another. We enter Holy Week knowing it's our busiest season, but what joy God gives us! And last, but not least, my family: the grandchildren who just keep on growing, the children who have accomplished so much and the husband with whom God has allowed me to share thirty years—so far! Oh my! Has God showered me with gifts, or what?

—PAT LOEK, MIAMI, FLORIDA

21/MON The Lord passed before him, and proclaimed, "The Lord, the Lord, a God merciful and gracious, slow to anger, and abounding in steadfast love and faithfulness."

—EXODUS 34:6 (RSV)

For years, I had longed to go to the Church of the Holy Sepulchre in Jerusalem, which for more than sixteen hundred years Christians have believed marks the very place where Jesus died and was buried.

The church itself is a huge, cavernous building, a combination of several churches built over the centuries. Even though hundreds of tourists were wandering through when we first entered, I experienced a hushed reverence. In various corners of the church, people were worshiping or quietly kneeling to pray. But as we climbed the narrow steps to the section built over Golgotha, the atmosphere changed completely.

The area was packed with people and tour guides chattering in many languages. People pushed and shoved to reach the front to light a candle and kiss the floor under the altar where Jesus' Cross had stood. I stared in amazement as a young woman tried to put a big stuffed teddy bear on the altar and pose next to it. Instead of scolding her, the monk tending the candles gently told her it wasn't appropriate to put her stuffed animal on the altar. He suggested she hold it for the photo and asked people to stand back for her to do so.

I continued to watch him handle the crowd. He quietly yet firmly reminded people to wait their turn and give others a chance to kneel or pray a few moments. He answered questions, patted the children's heads and gave them leftover candles to "take home for your prayers." His gentle firmness diffused the tension and frustration of the crowd; his patience brought peace.

He was a reminder: Jesus died for all of us different people, whether reverent or rude. He welcomes each of us as we are and lovingly helps us change.

Lord Jesus, in all my dealings with people today, help me to love as You love—with patience, kindness and forbearance.

—MARY BROWN

22/TUE *The flowers appear on the earth; the time of the singing of birds is come....* —SONG OF SOLOMON 2:12

My computer sits on a desk in my home office, its back to the windows that show me the view of my front lawn and the street on which we live. Below the windows are beds with green plants in them: calla lilies; a broad-leafed plant whose name I don't know; some cacti in terra-cotta bowls; and a large bird-of-paradise plant, which every spring produces exotic orange and purple blossoms.

This past spring, Perky, the little Australian shepherd mix who lives in my office because she can't get along with the other dogs, took to standing on her hind legs and looking out the window at the street. I thought she probably did it because she was lonely when I wasn't in the office with her. Then I discovered she had a friend.

I was sitting at the keyboard, typing one morning, when I saw an iridescent green hummingbird at the bird-of-paradise blossoms, wings moving impossibly fast, long beak probing for nectar in the vivid blooms. I stopped working to watch; there is something about a hummingbird that makes me marvel at creation. Perky came over to the window and stood to put her paws on the sill. I thought she would bark at the hummingbird, but she didn't, and I didn't want to shoo her away because I thought it would startle the little bird.

The hummingbird left its flower and came over to the window, hovering on the other side of the glass just beyond Perky's nose. They looked at each other for almost thirty seconds, and it was possible to imagine that they were communicating, asking how things were going, wishing each other well. The meeting done, Perky dropped back down to the rug, the hummingbird went back to breakfast, and I returned to my work, feeling privileged to have been eavesdropping on a natural scene I could never have imagined.

Thank You, God, for the glimpses You give me of the glory of Your creation. —RHODA BLECKER

23/WED "*Then his body will become as healthy as a child's. . . .*" —JOB 33:25 (TLB)

In April of 2001, my mammogram showed two spots of invasive cancer in my left breast, and I was referred to a surgeon. He verified the findings and ordered a biopsy. I was then advised that the entire breast would have to be removed.

Because my daughter and grandchildren insisted on a second opinion, I went to another surgeon. In the examination room, the nurse prepared me, then left to bring in the doctor. Before the two of them returned, I prayed, "If it is in Your will, Father, let this be just a misreading of the mammogram. But if cancer is there and the operation must be done, I know You will be with me through it all."

A deep, warm feeling of quiet submission swept over me as the second surgeon confirmed the original diagnosis. I told him to schedule the surgery, which went fine, but an infection made it necessary for me to stay in the hospital for eight days.

My daughter stayed with me as long as she could be away from her job. She hated to leave me alone, but I assured her I would not be alone. "God and I are going through this together," I told her and everyone else who questioned my staying at home alone. A dear young nurse living across the street from me came twice daily to check on me and change the infection drains I had to wear. Friends and church members took turns bringing me meals and driving me to the doctor for follow-up appointments. I was then referred to an oncologist who ordered a CAT scan of my chest and abdominal area and a bone scan of my entire body.

I was surrounded with prayer on the day the tests were performed. And then the wonderful report came: My cancer had not spread. There was no sign of cancer in my body at all! I cannot thank God enough for the blessing of this healing.

Dear loving God, help me to use this experience to help others who are facing frightening times to trust You and Your healing power. Amen. —DRUE DUKE

24/THU *Be ye kind one to another, tenderhearted, forgiving one another....* —EPHESIANS 4:32

It was a beautiful April day, and I was heading home after a business meeting. As I drove down the gradual incline into West Medford, Massachusetts, a police officer stepped out and motioned me to the curb. I was startled. What had I done?

He approached the car from the rear and stood at the door, visible only from the waist down. "You were driving thirty-four miles an hour in a twenty-mile-an-hour zone," he said. "May I see your license and your registration?"

I handed him my license and reached toward the glove compartment for my registration. "That's all right, Mr. Greene," he said. "You don't have to show your registration. I'm going to let you go with a warning this time, but I don't want to have to pull you over again. My name's LeBert!" I thanked him, but I wondered why he had let me go.

I remained puzzled until I chanced upon a Sunday school lesson book from twenty-four years earlier and glanced at the student roster. There was the police officer's name, LeBert. What had I said or done in that class that caused him to remember me? Then I read the lesson:

- Being different doesn't mean you are wrong. You will meet others who are attending a different church, who are less well-dressed and who are a different color. Treat everyone fairly.
- Love your God, home, family and school. These are your building blocks. Like alphabet blocks, stack them carefully.

- Hurtful things will happen to you. Sometimes you will feel knocked down like toy soldiers. It isn't the hurt that matters. It's what you do after you have been hurt. Remember trouble seldom circles back to hurt you. Always forgive.

As I read, Officer LeBert became my teacher, and his lesson in forgiveness taught me never to speed on High Street—or anywhere else—again!

Forgiving Lord, thank You for lessons well learned, whether early in life or much, much later. —OSCAR GREENE

25/FRI *He hath made every thing beautiful in his time: also he hath set the world in their heart.* . . .
—ECCLESIASTES 3:11

The night before my husband Robert and I left on our trip to Japan, we received a fax from the owner of Amherst House, where we were to stay during our week in Kyoto. "The weeping cherry tree in the backyard is in full bloom!" We'd tried to plan our trip to coincide with cherry blossom time, but that time varies from year to year, and the blossoms last only a very short while. So we were indeed fortunate to arrive at just this brief season of fullest blooming.

On our first day there, we walked the three-kilometer "philosopher's path" under an archway of gorgeous cherry trees, their boughs gracefully bent by hundreds of vivid pink blossoms. Everywhere we went during that week, we were awed by the beauty and lingering scent of these gorgeous flowering trees. But near the end of the week, it seemed as if the trees were raining blossoms. And by the day we left Kyoto, their branches were nearly bare. I thought, *How swiftly the pink blossoms fade into winter snow!* Suddenly, I was deeply aware of the shortness of human life, of *my* life! Then I remembered an admonition once given to me by a spiritual teacher: "What will you do with your remaining breaths?"

So what's my answer? I want to grow spiritually, enjoy my grandchildren, savor Robert's companionship. But perhaps, as much as anything, I want to appreciate the simple things: the tang of fresh Texas grapefruit at breakfast; deer tracks in the new snow of our backyard; a surprise call from my son John; the satisfaction of a clean house and the scent of dinner cooking in my warm kitchen. I want to use my remaining breaths to be fully alive in each moment.

What will you do with your remaining breaths?

How precious is this life You have given me, Lord! May gratitude grace each remaining breath. —MARILYN MORGAN KING

26/SAT And I John saw the holy city, new Jerusalem, coming down from God out of heaven, prepared as a bride adorned for her husband. —REVELATION 21:2

"It's such a *big* church, Mom," said my daughter Charlotte as we looked around St. Bartholomew's, the beautiful and spacious city church where we worship. "We'll need so many flowers—that'll be really expensive."

Weddings are like that. It's hard to keep one's mind on the holy and profound nature of the event when florists, dressmakers and caterers keep tripping across the stage in the most distracting way. And then there's money. Of course, it's not supposed to be important in approaching this sacrament, but there aren't many families who aren't concerned about the amazing expense of a simple wedding.

Charlotte is both sensible and loving. "St. Bart's is beautiful, Mom. We don't need lots of flowers," she decided briskly. "Just an arrangement on the altar. The church will do the rest by itself." And I certainly wasn't going to argue.

The big day was in April, and as we stepped out of the car in front of the church, I suddenly noticed that the cherry trees along New York's Park Avenue had flowered almost overnight. They were all covered with a glorious mass of white blossoms.

As we entered the church through the big bronze doors, I gasped. This was the Saturday after Easter; for Easter, the church had been filled with flowers, including spectacular white hydrangeas high above the nave. I had assumed that their day of glory was past and they would have been swept neatly away. But now I saw that the hydrangeas were live plants, not bouquets, and they brought the springtime into the whole church.

All I could think, as my husband and I walked carefully and

sedately down the aisle with our daughter, was that God had sent
His own florist to the city streets and to the church—especially for
Charlotte.

Lord, help me to appreciate Your divine generosity.

—BRIGITTE WEEKS

27/SUN *"How can I give you up, Ephraim? How can I
hand you over, Israel? . . ."* —HOSEA 11:8 (NIV)

My wife and I have two sons, Patrick and Ted. Patrick is my wife's
son. When I met them, Patrick was two years old. We adopted Ted
when he was seven.

Patrick, who is only eight months older than Ted, was excited
about getting a younger brother, but Ted was—and is—much taller
than Patrick. Patrick wanted someone who would obey his every
command, and Ted refused to obey any. After about two months,
Patrick came to me and announced, "It's not working out."

"What's not working out?"

"Ted. We have to get rid of him. We have to get someone
smaller. And nicer."

"When?" I asked.

"Right now!" Patrick insisted. "I mean, we don't have to find a
new brother right away. We just have to get rid of Ted."

"What if we got rid of you instead of Ted? He seems to like it
here."

"Dad, don't be stupid! Mom would never do that. Would she?"

I pretended to ponder the matter.

"I'm sure she wouldn't," Patrick said. "Trouble is, she won't get
rid of Ted either. That's why I came to you."

I had to disappoint Patrick. Despite the doubt in his mind, as a
father, I could never be persuaded to keep one son and give up the
other. God told the prophet Hosea that He could never give up on
Israel despite the peoples' sins, and it's comforting to know that
God will never give up on any of us either. He will never give up on
Ted, and He didn't give up on Patrick . . . even when he wanted to
get rid of his new brother.

*Dear God, thank You for never giving up on us, even when we
give up on each other.* —TIM WILLIAMS

28/MON   *Have mercy upon us: for we are exceedingly filled with contempt.*   —PSALM 123:3

Ten-year-old Maggie irritated me. Both of her parents worked, and she just assumed she could get off the school bus every day with my daughters. No arrangements had been made between Maggie's mom and me. Maggie just skipped down the driveway after school and plopped down her book bag in the green chair in the den right next to Jamie and Katie's, as if she belonged. *Go home*, I thought. *You don't live here. I'm tired of pretending you're one of us, Maggie.*

During the end of my third pregnancy, it became harder to be nice to Maggie. I clenched my teeth and did all the right things, but inside my resentment grew. It grew even more when Maggie showed up at our house on the day I went to the hospital to have our new baby.

Our baby boy Robbie lived only twenty-five minutes. Nine hours after Robbie was born and died, I left the hospital and came back home. Deep depression and grief consumed me. In a day or two, our den was covered with fancy flowers from friends and family, even covering the fireplace mantel. But most people stayed away; many were afraid to call.

I was resting on the sofa three days after Robbie died when I heard a familiar gentle knocking at the front door. I opened it, and Maggie tiptoed in. She held wildflowers from her yard wrapped in a wet paper towel and crunchy tinfoil. "Here, these are for you," she said. "I loved Robbie a lot. I felt like he was almost my little brother."

"Oh, Maggie, I love you, too," I said, my voice breaking as I bent down to hug her.

Oh, Father, forgive me for resenting the people You send my way. Let me love them the way You do.   —JULIE GARMON

29/TUE   *Let us run with patience the particular race that God has set before us.*   —HEBREWS 12:1 (TLB)

My young cousin Tim is a triathlete. He recently made the team for the international "Iron Man" competition. That means he has to swim 2.4 miles in the ocean, then cycle 112 miles, after which he runs a 26.2-mile marathon, all nonstop. He trains vigorously, pushing his body to its full capacity and more.

I've never had much stamina, but I could run pretty fast. During my school days, I played right wing on the field hockey team. Now, of course, a brisk walk is about all I can manage, and some days this dwindles down to a slow stroll, an amble or a dawdle. My husband says we are rapidly approaching the point when we will have to ask each other, "How about a ponder?" and simply visualize the walk without leaving our armchairs.

Spiritually, though, I'm still running on a fast track in the race that God has set before me, speaking and traveling and maintaining the priorities of family and home. On bone-weary days, I must confess I've asked the Lord to slow me down. Instead, He is training me in the art of spiritual sprinting: short bursts of high energy in a give-it-all-you've-got effort. Sometimes this involves racing through airports to get to a cross-country conference or staying up pounding a computer late into the night.

In running the particular race God has set before each of us, some, like me, are short-distance sprinters. Others, like Tim, are on an endurance track. Whatever the race, the best part is that when we give it all we've got, we're winners. We "press toward the mark for the prize of the high calling of God in Christ Jesus" (Philippians 3:14).

Holy Spirit, how grateful I am that You are the One Who walks (runs) beside me. At those exhausting times when I want to quit, energize me so I can complete the race God has set before me.

—FAY ANGUS

30/WED *In thee shall all families of the earth be blessed.* —GENESIS 12:3

When I came home from the office, the boys were already in the kitchen, William stirring something over the fire, Timothy pulling things out of the refrigerator. "What's for dinner?" I asked.

"You'll find out," Timo said.

"It's a surprise," Will added.

I went into the bedroom to change clothes. My wife Carol was lounging on the bed, reading a novel—unaccustomed leisure for 6:55 on a school night. "What are they making?" I whispered.

"Ravioli, I think. With peas and a salad."

"Nice for you to get a break from cooking."

"They won't let you wash the dishes, either."

I took off my tie and removed my heavy shoes. In the dining room, Timo was setting the table, and I could hear Will in the kitchen clanging a spoon on a pot. I thumbed through the mail and picked up a magazine. Unaccustomed leisure for me, too.

"It's done!" Will announced. "Come and get it!"

The ravioli was steamed to perfection, the peas were slathered in butter, the sauce was piping hot. My water was poured, the boys had their milk, William had lit the candles in the dining room. "Serve yourself," Timo said proudly.

I did. We all did. Then we sat down at the dining room table. "You can say grace," Will said, and we bowed our heads.

"Dear God," I prayed, "when I got married, I never could have expected that I'd be celebrating my anniversary eighteen years later with the most perfect present. Thank you for a wonderful wife and two great kids."

"Happy anniversary!" my boys exclaimed.

Thank You, Lord, for the many blessings You've given me, especially my marriage. —RICK HAMLIN

My Daily Blessings

1 _____

2 _____

3 _____

4 _____

5 _____

6 _____

7 _____

8 _____

9 _____

10 _____

11 _____

12 _____

13 _____

14 _____

15 _____

16 _____

17 _____

18 _____

19 _____

20 _____

21 _____

22 _____

23 _____

24 _____

25 _____

26 _____

27 _____

28 _____

29 _____

30 _____

MAY

Blessed are they which do hunger
and thirst after righteousness:
for they shall be filled.
—Matthew 5:6

S	M	T	W	T	F	S
				1	2	3
4	5	6	7	8	9	10
11	12	13	14	15	16	17
18	19	20	21	22	23	24
25	26	27	28	29	30	31

1/THU   *For it is written, As I live, saith the Lord, every knee shall bow to me....* —ROMANS 14:11

One of my most vivid teenage memories is of my father, a pastor, kneeling to pray beside our living room sofa. For him, respect for the majesty and authority of God meant kneeling when he came into God's presence through prayer.

I, on the other hand, have taken a more informal approach to prayer. I encouraged my own four children to pray openly and spontaneously as they were growing up, but we never knelt to pray. Our son Philip developed an especially deep and meaningful prayer life, along with a hunger to study the Bible. I often thought how that would have pleased my father, who died when Phil was just two and a half years old.

After we moved from Alaska to Minnesota, Phil, then twenty-four, came to live with us for a few months. Every day he would shut himself away for a time of prayer in our upstairs guest bedroom. One morning, after he had left the room, I noticed that the bedspread was rumpled at the foot of the bed. I walked in, and as I bent to smooth it, I saw two distinct indentations in the soft rose carpet—the impressions of my son's knees.

Almost shyly, I knelt down on the same spot and settled my own knees into the carpet. With tears of joy and gratitude, I thanked the Lord for His generosity in giving me a father and a son who loved Him in the same way—on their knees.

Lord God, on this National Day of Prayer, help me carry the blessings of prayer into my family's future. —CAROL KNAPP

AN EYE FOR BLESSINGS

2/*FRI*   SEEING THE PATTERN

"Do not destroy it, for there is a blessing in it. . . ."

—ISAIAH 65:8 (RSV)

I spilled some coffee on the kitchen counter this morning. I grabbed the sponge to wipe it up, then looked closer. The stain was shaped like a sassafras leaf! I stood for a moment, enjoying the pattern—and remembering an art exhibit.

I've always admired the work of the sculptor Henry Moore, whose giant creations enhance public spaces around the world. So I was lucky to be in Texas two years ago when the Dallas Museum of Art held a Moore retrospective. Room after room, his genius unfolded—huge, sensual, curving shapes, compelling and memorable.

Leaving the exhibit, I noticed a glass display case holding what looked like an array of rubbish awaiting the dustbin. Pebbles, broken shells, splinters of wood, bits of bone, scraps of rusting metal. Why in the world would an art museum put such worthless stuff on view?

I bent down and read the label. The objects in the case, it stated, came from Moore's studio, where they had been for him "a constant source of inspiration." All his life, the label continued, Moore had picked up such random debris, drawing from the shape and texture of the smallest, most insignificant objects, ideas for his monumental sculptures.

Worthless stuff? Not to the discerning eye of the artist. I thought of Leonardo da Vinci's famous remark that he could be inspired by "the mottled stains on an old wall." I'll never have the perception of a Moore or a da Vinci, but since that visit to Dallas I've often been aware of pattern, color, surprise harmonies, in the untidiness of daily life.

Spilled coffee—a small mess or a small blessing?

Give me an artist's eye, Lord, to see in the accidental a display case for Your wonders. —ELIZABETH SHERRILL

3 / SAT   *And he was angry, and would not go in: therefore came his father out, and entreated him.* —LUKE 15:28

First I saw an advertisement for a book called *Seabiscuit* by Laura Hillenbrand. *Nobody else will notice it,* I thought. Then a friend who knew of my fascination with horse racing called my attention to it. "Oh, that, yes," I said high-and-mightily, "I'm familiar with the story."

Familiar? Seabiscuit had been a canker in my life since 1938. Being a proper Kentuckian, I'd been brought up with a respect, and in my case a love, for the majestic beauty of thoroughbred racing. I had my equine heroes, but none surpassed War Admiral. In 1937, he was a Triple Crown winner and Horse of the Year. I adored him; I had a scrapbook of articles about him and over my desk in boarding school. I had a picture clipped from a newspaper's rotogravure section showing the "Little Admiral" flying, four hooves off the ground. He was invincible. But on November 1, 1938, in a much-heralded match race, Seabiscuit was victorious. I went into a funk, a real funk. It was a maturing moment when I realized that nothing but God was a sure thing.

Now, who would have thought that a racehorse some sixty years dead would capture the public's fancy? Laura Hillenbrand's book climbed up the best-seller charts until it was number one in *The New York Times* listing, and I received, not one, but three copies of the book as birthday presents. That's when I said, "Yes, I'll read it."

Grudgingly, reluctantly, I fell under the book's sway. I relived the times—for me, exciting times—and though the book didn't change my mind about who was the better horse, I thrilled to

Seabiscuit's courage. More than that, I felt a release from my adolescent animosity. It was time for me to let go of sixty-five years of pique. It was time for me to be glad for an old enemy.

Some resentments last a long while, Father. Let me follow Your teaching and be rid of them. —VAN VARNER

4/SUN   *And behold, there arose a great storm on the sea, so that the boat was being swamped by the waves; but he was asleep.* —MATTHEW 8:24 (RSV)

Like everyone else, I've been through a few thunderstorms in my life. The first I remember was when I was two or three years old, living near Chicago while my father attended Wheaton College. I remember the gentle touch of my grandfather's hands on my ankles as he coaxed me out from under a bed. Bundling me into something warm, he took me outdoors, sat me on his lap under the shelter of the front porch and explained how "the big clouds can't see in the night and bang into each other and yell, '*Ow!*'" Grandpa, I quickly realized, wasn't scared at all. Rather, he exulted in the fury of the skies. Soon I, too, caught his excitement and lost my fear.

Emotional storms have not been so easily resolved. While I've seen God's eventual provision and healing, I've never learned to appreciate biopsies or losing my house in the same way I do a raging wind. It's difficult to trust Jesus amid harsh emotional, physical, financial or spiritual crises. Like His disciples, I tend to panic. I ask God, "Don't You care? Don't You see?"

At least I did until Pastor Sam came to our church.

"Has it ever occurred to you," he asked us when preaching about Jesus asleep in the storm-tossed boat, "that He slept because He had no fear? And that He slept, safe, unafraid, with those He loved?"

No, it had never occurred to me.

"He does us the same honor," said Pastor Sam.

This last observation was even more revealing. And so now, when life's storms overtake me, instead of "waking Jesus up" with the same old accusation, "Don't You care if I perish?" I feel a sense of honor, not abandonment.

Lord, help me to remain unafraid. —BRENDA WILBEE

5 / MON *Consider the lilies how they grow. . . .*
—LUKE 12:27

I often see birdwatchers in my neighborhood because I live next to a bird sanctuary where there are miles of fields surrounding a big reservoir. But the woman I began to see almost every morning wasn't your typical birdwatcher. Most of them stand still, peering through binoculars. This woman had binoculars hanging by a cord around her neck, but she didn't always use them. What made her different was that she would stop and peer intently at the ground, or up at the trees on the ridge. Sometimes she just stared at the sky. She must have liked what she saw, because she was always smiling.

Since we passed each other so often, we nodded. Then we said "Hi," and finally she asked if she could say hello to my dog. My curiosity got the better of me, and I asked her what she was looking for.

"I'm interested in everything," she said. "The different grasses, the birds, the deer peeking out from the bushes." I felt a little embarrassed because I've lived here fourteen years and I've seen the same things, but they didn't stop me in my tracks. I think the woman must have read my expression because she told me she had recently moved from the city to live with her son and his wife. "It's so beautiful here!" she said, looking around.

"Didn't you like the city?" I asked.

"I loved it!" she said. "I used to walk around, just as I do here, looking in store windows and at the fronts of houses, even little alleyways, marveling at it all." She stopped to look at some geese flying toward the reservoir. Then she smiled and said, "I feel as if each day is a gift, and I get to open it."

Dear Lord Jesus, thank You for the gift of this day. Amen.
—PHYLLIS HOBE

6 / TUE *Therefore I will give thanks unto thee, O Lord . . . and I will sing praises unto thy name.* —II SAMUEL 22:50

"Hey, is anybody out there?" the coach shouted during my sons' baseball team's practice. Immediately, the kids began a noisy chorus:

"Way to go!"

"That's okay. Get him next time!"

"Good swing!"

"What was all the chattering about?" I asked the boys later. "Nobody said anything very important that I could tell."

"The important part is to know others are out there rooting for you," one of them answered.

Well, that made sense. So while waiting to drive them home, I joined in the team's chatter, no matter what sport it happened to be. In fact, I became a pretty good hollerer myself, whether my sons were up to bat, bent down on starting blocks or loping onto a football field looking like Superman in a helmet and padded shoulders.

"That's one smart coach," I told my husband one evening after hearing the trainer's usual *Hey, is anybody out there?* "Kids need to know they're appreciated."

"So do adults," my husband said.

His words hit home. It had been a long time since he'd heard my chatter of appreciation for his faithful trek to work every day. I took care of that omission right away. Not only that, I became more vocally grateful to others: the janitor who dutifully sets up chairs at each and every PTA meeting; the smiling volunteer who directs me to the correct hospital room when I'm visiting a sick friend; the young man who puts my morning paper on the porch instead of in the bushes.

Then my thoughts went higher, and I wondered, *Does God ever feel like shouting, "Hey, is anybody out there?"*

Father, I'm so sorry that I too often forget to chatter my thanks to You for Your constant care of me and my loved ones. I am truly grateful for Your love and mercy.   —ISABEL WOLSELEY

$7/$ WED   *All the assembled worshipers were praying. . . .*
—LUKE 1:10 (NIV)

Tony, a parking lot attendant, was relatively new to the ranks of practicing Christians, but his sincerity of heart left no doubt about his devotion to God. On Wednesday evenings, he was one of a sprinkling of people who faithfully gathered for prayer in our little church, and Tony had a unique, unjaded way of voicing his concerns.

"Dear Jesus," Tony prayed one night, "we've come here to make another conference call to heaven. . . ."

A "conference call to heaven"—what a good term for corporate prayer! People of like faith, at a given time, gathered by mutual consent to discuss current needs and then prayerfully approaching God for His blessings and guidance.

Tony's insight gave me a new determination to attend prayer services faithfully. In fact, if I had an answering machine, the message I would leave on my voice mail might sound something like this: "Should you wish to reach me, I am no longer available on Wednesday evenings. I am participating in a conference call to heaven on behalf of my family, my church, my community and my country. Please leave a list of any concerns you wish me to forward and God will get back to you."

Lord, thank You for being a "sovereign CEO" Who graciously takes time to hear and respond to the prayers of Your people wherever we gather in Your name.   —ALMA BARKMAN

8/THU   *The Lord will perfect that which concerneth me. . . .*   —PSALM 138:8

I sat down at my computer this morning to write an important letter, a task that I'd been procrastinating. But the words didn't come easily, so I decided to clean my keyboard instead (another procrastination technique). I got some cotton swabs from the bathroom, some cleaning solution from the kitchen, and I went to work wiping off each key.

That's when I noticed that the question mark key was much dirtier than the exclamation mark key. Had I been doing more questioning than exclaiming lately? How about since I woke up this morning? I easily remembered several questions:

Why did I eat two muffins? Why is my friend experiencing more than her fair share of difficult circumstances? Why do I still worry about our children, even though they're grown and gone? What do I really want to be when I grow up? What should I say in this letter? Why do I procrastinate so much?

How about exclamations? Had I uttered any words of conviction? My mind went totally blank. But then I spotted some, right there above my desk; a bunch of God's promises that I'd taken from the Bible and written on sticky notes so they would permeate my mind when I sat there.

I can do all things in Him who strengthens me (Philippians 4:13).

For nothing is impossible with God (Luke 1:37).

The joy of the Lord is my strength (Nehemiah 8:10).

God is with me always (Matthew 28:20).

God knows the plans He has for me . . . to give me hope and a future (Jeremiah 29:11).

Amazing how these one-line promises could become exclamation answers to most of my questions.

I looked down at my clean keyboard. *The question mark and exclamation point are at opposite ends,* I thought, *but for today, at least, I've connected them.* Now, back to that letter!

Father, may every question today lead me to an exclamation of Your promises!
—CAROL KUYKENDALL

9/ FRI   *From childhood you have known the sacred writings which are able to give you the wisdom that leads to salvation through faith which is in Christ Jesus.*
—II TIMOTHY 3:15 (NAS)

I first met Father Bill Houghton in 1958. He was a young man in his early twenties, a recent seminary graduate and a newly arrived Episcopal missionary in the Philippines. Most important, he was the new Bible teacher for my second-grade class at the Brent School.

Few second-graders liked Bible class; there was something about it that was always too serious for us. We would much rather be tormenting our reading teacher or playing. Then Father Houghton arrived. I remember what he was wearing the day I met him: khaki pants, a black clergy shirt, white clerical collar and white bucks. White bucks! That's what Elvis Presley and cool teenage boys wore; even a second-grader knew that. Suddenly, Bible class got a lot better.

Today, forty-three years later, I had lunch with Father Houghton in Waco, Texas. Now retired, Bill Houghton has stayed trim and fit. Silver and gray flecks his dark hair and his handsome face is creased with the character lines of age. I was disappointed to learn he no longer owns a pair of white bucks.

As I watched Father Houghton stir sugar into his coffee, I asked myself, *What did this man teach me about the Bible? I don't remember a single lecture, story or illustration. So what did he teach me?*

The answer came quickly. He taught a squirming second-grader two things of immeasurable value: First, the Bible is important, important enough for a young man to travel far from home to teach Bible stories. Second, and most important, he taught me that you can love the Bible and wear white bucks, too.

Dear God, thank You for all of the people who have taught me that the Bible is important, interesting and always relevant. Amen. —SCOTT WALKER

10/SAT *Be sure to use the abilities God has given you....* —I TIMOTHY 4:14 (TLB)

When I was a girl, my mom used to help curl my hair while we had one of our many "girl talks." One day, sharing my dreams, I told her about my future husband.

"I want to marry someone with a lot of money!" I said, echoing something I'd heard a friend say. Mom wasn't going to let that comment slip by.

"Well, I don't think that's so important," she said. "Besides, it doesn't matter what he has unless he's willing to share it."

Of course, she was right, and I've always remembered that bit of wisdom. I thought of it recently while attending our church's Saturday evening service. While singing the first hymn, I heard a strong soprano voice behind me. *Whoever she is, she should be in the choir,* I thought. I don't know many of the Saturday regulars since I usually attend on Sunday morning, so I decided I'd introduce myself after the service and try to recruit her. I was surprised when I later turned around to discover that this wonderful singer was a woman I knew. I had no idea she sang.

"Why aren't you in the choir?" I asked. "You have a great voice."
"Oh, I don't know," she shrugged. "I've thought about it, but I don't have time."

I couldn't imagine hiding such a great gift. But then I thought about how I had avoided teaching Sunday school for years, in spite of our church's need for teachers. Finally I gave in to my daughter's pleas and took on the task of teaching her class. I soon discovered that God had given me a gift for joyfully sharing His message with children.

Whether I'm afraid to try something new or would rather sit back and count my blessings than put them to use, Mom's words still resonate: It doesn't matter what you have unless you're willing to share it. That's certainly true of God's gifts.

God, give me the courage to share generously all that You have given me. —GINA BRIDGEMAN

11 / SUN   *My son . . . forsake not the law of thy mother.*
—PROVERBS 1:8

A few years ago, after my mother moved into a nursing home, I spent a melancholy weekend boxing up her things, trying to decide what should be saved and what should be tossed out, and resisting the urge to donate it all to Goodwill and let them deal with it.

Then, in the big bottom drawer of her old oak wardrobe, I discovered a collection of stuff in a beat-up Hudson's department store box: all the childhood gifts I'd given her for Mother's Day. I didn't know whether to cringe or cry.

There was the shamrock key chain with the illegible "Mom" I engraved on it myself, and the Jean Naté Fleur de Versailles bath set I saved my lawn-mowing money to buy at the five-and-ten. She still had the awful blue Wedgwood candy dish with the poodle head cameo in honor of Pete, our dog. There was the pot holder that said "#1 Cook" (Mom didn't really like to cook); a chintzy picture frame with my fifth-grade class shot still in it, taken the day after I got a front tooth knocked out playing tetherball; a snow globe of the Mackinac Bridge from my smart-aleck gag-gift phase (crossing that huge span always made her dizzy); and the cards with my earnest attempts to put my feelings into words. I was amazed I ever passed spelling, let alone penmanship.

Yet what I felt most keenly as I went through those Mother's Day gifts of mine was the joy with which each and every one was received, the delight Mom took in the act of giving, especially when practiced so imperfectly by a little boy. No, Mom never cringed, not even at the sight of the Wedgwood poodle dish, and sometimes, I remember, she did cry. So did I that day over the old Hudson's box. No one will ever love you like your mother, they say, and I had found proof of that.

Lord, You give us mothers for countless reasons. I think the most important is this: They teach us to love. —EDWARD GRINNAN

12/MON   *Lord, be thou my helper.*   —PSALM 30:10

"God, help me to cheer up Mrs. Menina." She was the Russian woman I was tutoring in English. I'd already gotten her a plant and some upbeat musical tapes, but she still seemed down lately. The crimson sign of a pet store lured me in; she'd once mentioned admiring some goldfish. I'd buy her a fish!

Once in the pet store, though, I had second thoughts. Never having bought fish, I wasn't sure how expensive they'd be. The clerk said, "We only sell feeder fish."

Not knowing anything about goldfish, this sounded to me like some rare exotic breed. "I haven't got much money on me," I cautioned. "And I'll need two. I wouldn't want them to be lonely." Hoping to get some sympathy for my small purse, I added, "They're for an elderly woman I volunteer with. I want something to make her smile."

An odd look. "How about if I give you two for the price of one?"

I was stunned at his generosity. "God bless you," I said. "That's so kind of you."

He went in the back and eventually came out carrying a plastic bag with two large goldfish. *Uh-oh,* I thought, *they look expensive. I'll have to charge them.* Silently the man handed the bag to me, then punched in a few numbers on the big metal cash register. I handed him my Visa. He looked me in the eye. "That'll be twenty-four cents."

I stared at him and burst out laughing, and after a moment the man joined in. "Twenty-four cents!" I said, gasping with laughter.

My prayer had been answered. I now had something to cheer up Mrs. Menina . . . the story of how I bought her the goldfish!

God, when I pray for something, let me trust that You will answer my prayer—though not always in the way I expect!

—LINDA NEUKRUG

13 / TUE   *"He will wipe every tear from their eyes. . . ."*

—REVELATION 21:4 (NIV)

Last night, while putting the kids to bed, I stopped to say a special prayer for a friend who was in the midst of a difficult labor and delivery. Moments after I asked God to keep Mary Ellen and her baby safe and healthy, my daughter Elizabeth wanted to know what could go wrong. I groaned.

Being seven months pregnant myself, I didn't want to get into a big discussion of the possible travails of childbirth. Somehow, though, we launched into a long talk. In the course of our conversation, Elizabeth grasped for the first time that some children die as infants and that others are born with physical problems. Sorrow and a sense of injustice fell deep in her heart. "It doesn't seem fair!" she sobbed. "Why does God allow that?"

Oh, dear. There's no quick answer to that question. There certainly isn't one that's easy to present to a first-grader. I talked to my grief-stricken child as best I could, knowing that even the most profound words probably meant far less than the silent reassurance of my arms wrapped about her. We sat in silence for a while; I prayed to the Holy Spirit, holding my terribly sad and bewildered six-year-old.

I suggested that Elizabeth needed to talk to God about how she felt. "Why do I need to tell Him, since He already knows what I think?" she asked. Compared with her previous question, that one was easy to handle! I gave her a kiss and left her to pray her way to sleep.

I prayed for my daughter while I washed the dishes. Then, after another quick prayer for Mary Ellen, I prayed for all those who suffer in the dark, struggling to understand the ways of God.

Lord Jesus, You answered all our unanswerable questions on the Cross. Let my heart rest there with You when I wrestle with hard questions of faith.

—JULIA ATTAWAY

14/WED   *I am the Lord thy God . . . which leadeth thee by the way that thou shouldest go.*   —ISAIAH 48:17

A neighbor of mine is a highway surveyor, and recently we were talking about one of his projects, a bypass being built around a nearby city. His assignment: to build the shortest route (for convenience and economy), the safest route (with rivers, woods and terrain some of the considerations) and the least disruptive route (avoiding business and home sites as much as possible). "And your job is to show the road builders the way," I commented.

"Yes, my associates and I are the Lewis and Clark of the moment." We laughed at the comparison, but to anyone who knows of the 1802 assignment Thomas Jefferson gave Meriweather Lewis ("Find a safe passage to the Pacific"), it was good hyperbole. Except, of course, it was nature-wise Native Americans who guided the famous expedition, not surveyors. Otherwise, Lewis and Clark would have surely failed.

All of us have had guides in our lives—parents, teachers, pastors, relatives, friends—who took us by the hand and ushered us through unknown lands. And when we became adults, it was our turn to be the "way-showers" to those who came behind, wanderers and seekers in need of direction. St. Paul showed new disciples of Christ "the way" to a God-pleasing life with his letters, one of which I'm reading now. "None of us liveth to himself, and no man dieth to himself," St. Paul states (Romans 14:7). Poet John Donne was right when he wrote that "no man is an island." We are all dependent upon God and fellow journeyers-surveyors, if you will, who help us chart our path and find the best course for our life.

Thank You, God, for Your Word and Your Son,
Guides beyond compare—bar none.

—FRED BAUER

FOLLOWING JESUS

15/THU LOVE WITHOUT PASSING JUDGMENT
"And do not judge and you will not be judged. . . ."

—LUKE 6:37 (NAS)

For years, I'd looked forward to spending a couple of days in the charming old town of Fredericksburg in the Texas hill country. But on the plane ride there, I became extremely ill and, strangely, the more medication I took for nausea and dizziness, the sicker I became.

Amid glorious fields of wildflowers, I somehow managed to locate the log cabin bed-and-breakfast pictured in my reservation packet and found the promised room key under the welcome mat. I stumbled up the loft stairs and pulled a quilt up over my head in an under-the-eaves bed that looked like something Goldilocks might have stumbled into. *Surely, with a good night's rest, I'll be fine,* I told myself.

I awoke a couple of hours later, my skin clammy and heart racing. I alternated between pacing the stone floor, taking warm baths, and lying on my back and spinning my legs like I was riding a bicycle. Nauseated, dizzy and disoriented, I took yet another dose of the prescribed medication.

When I started dodging bugs, I knew I was in trouble. I called a pharmacist friend back home in West Virginia. "You're taking the wrong medicine," she advised. "This is serious. Get to an emergency room right away."

When I arrived at the ER, my agitation escalated when I wasn't seen immediately. By the time the nurse arrived with a shot to counteract the medication error, I was sobbing and creating a terrible scene, acting like every difficult patient I'd ever cared for all rolled into one. "You must think I'm terrible," I tried to explain. "I'm sorry. I'm so scared."

The nurse cupped my face in her hands, looked into my eyes and spoke softly: "There is no judgment here, only love."

Today in my own nursing practice, I, too, sometimes encounter patients imprisoned by condemnation, either their own or that of others. The simple, freeing words of my angel-nurse—His words—guide me still: "No judgment, only love."

Use me, Lord, to speak Your words to hurting hearts.

—ROBERTA MESSNER

16/FRI   *A gift is as a precious stone. . . .*

—PROVERBS 17:8

The thought popped into my head out of nowhere: *Why, that was a gift!*

I was thinking back to a party my husband and I had attended a few nights earlier. The bandleader announced, "We have a request from David Kidd," and David led me out to the floor to dance to "our song."

How had I missed something so obvious? I couldn't count the number of times I had complained to David after some party or celebration, "We didn't dance a single dance!" Even though I like to dance, David doesn't. That special dance had been a gift of love!

Later, after delivering a belated thank-you to David, who was working in his study, I began to wonder just how many other gifts I might have missed lately.

There was the prune cake with old-fashioned caramel icing that my mother had just made for my birthday. Not just any cake, but my favorite cake—and she doesn't really like to bake! There was my son Brock's anxious call after I returned from my doctor's appointment. "Mom, are you okay?" There was my daughter Keri's unexpected visit; she'd driven three hours just to help me prepare for a big meeting at our house.

How many such gifts do you receive in a day? The paper brought up to your porch by a kindly neighbor or the morning coffee brewed by an early-rising spouse, a note of encouragement, an affectionate hug, a compliment, an article clipped from a magazine, an invitation to lunch—you can certainly make your own list!

Think back to the last love-gift you received. Look at it in your mind's eye as though it were a rare jewel. Enjoy the intricacies of its beauty. Then say a prayer of thanks for the giver. Isn't today a good day to give a gift in return?

Father, how rich my coffers become when I count each loving gesture extended to me as a jewel. Remind me daily, Father, to share my wealth.   —PAM KIDD

READER'S ROOM

God has been reaching out to me this year through my first child, Laura Therese, born January 21, 2001. My husband Mark and I have marveled at the love and support from our family and friends, and especially from our church family! My "Daily Gifts" pages record how God has reached out to us through others—from meals made to offers of help, prayer and words of encouragement.

Having a baby has expanded my capacity to love in ways I couldn't have imagined. And God has been developing my character with sleep-deprived challenges and joyous moments. I have had to rely on God more than ever before in my life. I have never felt so inept and unsure as I have being a new mom. But God has reached out to me through my supportive husband, as well as through my friendship with Adriane, another new mom. I look forward to walking this faith adventure, relying on Him!

—LISA WALKENDORF, GRAND RAPIDS, MICHIGAN

---

17 / SAT

"By this all men will know that you are My disciples, if you have love for one another." —JOHN 13:35 (NAS)

I stood there at home plate, wearing a baseball cap on my bald head and just ten years of life experience under my belt. My cancer-ridden leg had been amputated only a month before, and now I was trying to prove that a disability wouldn't hinder my life by attending a church softball game. At the encouragement of the group, I had come up to bat.

Learning to balance on one leg was hard enough, but swinging a bat without falling over was a different story. With each successive strike, the pitcher stepped up a little bit closer and tried to throw a little bit slower.

I continued to rack up strikes, and everyone from my church watched expectantly. Since I was still a little shaky on my crutches, my "runner" was positioned behind me to take off when I hit the ball.

"You can do it, Josh!" I kept hearing people yell.

Looking around the field, I could see several kids on both teams whose hair was very short. They seemed to have normal buzz cuts, but I knew they were among the twenty kids who had attended a "head-shaving party" at my house when I first lost my hair to the chemotherapy.

Another kid in the game was wearing a T-shirt that read, "Covenant Kids for Joshua." My church, Covenant Presbyterian, had designed the shirts and handed them out to fifty-four kids at Vacation Bible School. For the year I was on chemotherapy, parents allowed their children to come to church casually dressed if they were wearing that shirt.

Sometime after I had passed the ten-strikes mark, I hit a short grounder up the middle of the field. The infielders threw the ball to first base, but I had chosen a fast runner and he was safe. After a few more plays, he had rounded the bases and scored a run.

The entire church seemed to want to give me a high-five afterward, and I certainly felt victorious. But I also knew that everything —from the unlimited strikes, to my fast runner, to the bald heads and T-shirts—was from God, and was given to me through the body of Christ.

Lord, thank You for the love You give to the body of Christ.
—JOSHUA SUNDQUIST

18 / SUN   *Oh how great is thy goodness. . . .*

—PSALM 31:19

I recently met an amazing man who is a good friend of my husband Robert. Paul Tashiro was born in Japan. At the age of twelve he volunteered as a kamikaze pilot. Fortunately, World War II ended before he could take off on his one-way mission. When he returned to Tokyo after the war, he had no home, and food and jobs were scarce, so he joined a gang of young soldiers selling drugs to American GIs.

After three years of leading a gangster life, Paul was passing by a tent one night when a burly American pulled him in and planted him in the front row of a congregation of 250 people. "When I heard the minister say, 'God gave His only begotten Son for you,'" Paul said, "I was so happy to hear that someone still loved me that I began to cry. I confessed everything to Jesus that night."

Paul made another crucial decision that night: to turn his life around. He came to America and enrolled in college, eventually becoming the only Japanese-born minister in the United States at that time. He began preaching in churches in small towns around the American South.

One day at a church in Tennessee, the congregation was singing "How Great Thou Art" when a blind, one-armed man came hobbling down the aisle, weeping. The singing died down as the man said, "Brother Paul, if I had met you five years ago, I would have killed you. I lost my arm and my eyesight to a kamikaze pilot." The American veteran wrapped his arm around the Japanese minister and said, "I love you." As the two men embraced, the voice of the congregation rose again in song: "How great thou art! How great thou art!"

No one knows the truth of those transforming words more than Paul Tashiro, who now teaches at a seminary in Jackson, Mississippi.

O Lord, how great Thou art! How great Thou art!

—MARILYN MORGAN KING

19/MON   *"You shall have no other gods before me."*
—EXODUS 20:3 (RSV)

"I don't believe the doctrine of any single church," my friend Ken said. "I take part of what one group says about the Bible, part of the liturgy of another and part of the theology of yet another."

I nodded. "You seem to be convinced that you're on the right path," I said. "I'm curious about why you came to talk to me about it."

Ken looked out the window behind my chair. Then he said, "For years I've read a lot about God and various religions, and I've worshiped in at least a dozen different churches. But the truth is, I don't have a sense of being connected to God. You seem to be more grounded in your faith than I am. Can you tell me why?"

I smiled and shook my head slightly. "For me, faith in God is a personal, intimate relationship, like a marriage. You have to make a commitment.

"Ken, trying to construct an intimate relationship with God by assembling attractive pieces of different faiths is like trying to marry a composite woman. There'd be no one there to relate to."

"But what if you pick a woman to marry who turns out to have a really irritating flaw that doesn't show up at first?"

I laughed. "Oh, that *will* happen. Whoever you choose will have at least one flaw that you think will drive you crazy. So will any church. But after you make a commitment, the big question becomes, 'How can I learn how to live in this relationship?' It's only inside the relationship that you learn how to lose your self-centeredness."

"*Hmmm*, is that why God says in Exodus, 'You shall have no other gods before me'?"

"I don't know, Ken," I said with a laugh. "I just know that my relationship with God and my marriage to Andrea are bringing me more peace than I could have imagined."

Lord, thank You for the wisdom and understanding You give us through Your Holy Spirit and Your message in the Scriptures. Help and guide us on our journey to You. Amen. —KEITH MILLER

20/TUE "The Lord will fight for you while you keep silent." —EXODUS 14:14 (NAS)

I was fighting an overwhelming desire. I longed to urge my thirty-three-year-old son Jon to enter a drug rehab program. I knew he was close to making the phone call; surely there was something else I could say. But God seemed to insist, *You can't help him. Be quiet.*

As I entered our local pharmacy at five o'clock that afternoon, my eye caught a slight movement in a piece of crumpled newspaper resting against the building. The tip of a bird's tail protruded from it. Inside, I asked the cashier, "Do y'all know there's a baby bird outside?"

"Oh, my! Is it still there? It's been there since early this morning."

The temperature was in the mid-nineties and the humidity was intense. *I don't need a bird today*, I thought as I left the store. Even so, I stooped down and removed the newspaper. The little swallow didn't struggle when I cupped a hand over it and slid my other hand underneath. From the top of a building high above us, the frightened mother bird called loudly.

I gazed up at her and at the relentless May sun. *You aren't going to be able to help him, Mother Bird. You have to trust me.*

Back at home, I phoned the wildlife department at the University of Georgia. An hour and many calls later, someone on the other end of the phone asked, "Do you know about Elizabeth? I have her number somewhere."

Elizabeth confirmed that she rescued wildlife as a volunteer for the state of Georgia. But she was sorry; she couldn't help today. She was already feeding quite a few birds and she was expecting company. The birds had to be fed every forty-five minutes. Despair closed in quickly. First Jon and now this bird.

Suddenly Elizabeth said, "Listen, Marion, I'm supposed to take this bird. I don't know why."

Three long days later, Jon made that life-changing phone call.

Oh, Father, teach me when I should remain silent, so those I love can hear Your powerful voice. —MARION BOND WEST

21 / WED   *We are to grow up in every way into him who is the head, into Christ, from whom the whole body, joined and knit together by every joint with which it is supplied, when each part is working properly, makes bodily growth and upbuilds itself in love.* —EPHESIANS 4:15–16 (RSV)

Three-year-old Mary was having fun. She sped through the course at her gymnastics class: walking the balance beam, doing forward rolls, jumping on the trampoline. In her eagerness to get around the gym, she lapped the other two- and three-year-olds, her strawberry-blonde pigtails bouncing.

As I watched my little girl, my father's joy in her happiness was mixed with a little envy. I've gone through life tripping over chairs, spilling the soup, knocking over water glasses, stepping on the toes of fellow bus passengers and walking into innocent passersby on the street. As a child, I could fall down and sprain an ankle while standing still. (It happened in front of the orangutan at the Bronx Zoo.) As an adult, I managed to have my eyeglasses removed by the doors of a subway train. (I spent an hour waiting on the platform until the workmen came and retrieved them from the tracks.) Mary is very different.

We first noticed it when she was a toddler. When my wife Julia took our daughter Elizabeth and our son John to the gym, Mary would watch them through the glass wall and try to imitate what they were doing. She'd come home and practice forward rolls on the living room carpet and turn our bed into a trampoline. When we enrolled her in a class of her own, she almost burst with happiness.

Mary isn't a gymnastic prodigy; I don't expect I'll ever see her in the Olympics. She's a sturdy little girl with wonderful coordination and a simple delight in what her body can do. And she's a reminder to her clumsy father that bone and sinew, muscle and ligament can move with amazing grace.

Thank You, Lord, for athletes, big and little, who remind me of the miracle that is my body. —ANDREW ATTAWAY

22/THU *For I the Lord thy God will hold thy right hand, saying unto thee, Fear not; I will help thee.*

—ISAIAH 41:13

I had brought a troubled heart to the conference center, high in the San Bernardino Mountains of Southern California. Our son and daughter-in-law had made a serious decision: Melissa would give up her job in order to stay at home and be with their children. I was worried about the financial struggle they would be facing.

During a break in our retreat, I was sitting on a boulder, praying, when a group of girls burst into the sunshine. "Come on," they said, "we're going to give the Ropes Challenge Course a try." This was a maze of logs and ropes strung among the trees, designed to teach some important spiritual truths.

Seven of us squished together, some balancing on only one leg as we stood on a low two-foot-by-two-foot platform. "This shows the importance of compassion," the activities director explained. "You have to keep your arms around each other, or else you'll fall off."

Next we clutched an overhead rope and walked the length of a log suspended horizontally some twenty feet off the ground. "The rope is the Word of God. Keep a firm grip on it and you'll stay steady."

Last was the Leap of Faith. Supported by a strong rope, each participant was to climb a telephone pole, stand on the top and dive to catch a trapeze swinging six feet away. Only a few had the nerve to try. They missed the trapeze, but swung gently down to the ground, steadied by the director's control rope.

"Hardly anyone actually makes this one," he said. "The point is that they tried and were willing to trust me. When we face a leap of faith, we need to trust God to be our support and the safety net underneath us."

Give me the courage to follow the leading You have put in my heart, Lord, even when it takes an awesome leap of faith.

—FAY ANGUS

23/FRI   The Lord recompense thy work, and a full reward be given thee of the Lord God of Israel. . . . —RUTH 2:12

The minister who married my husband and me is a very interesting man. Not only is Jerry Lites co-minister of an active and growing little church in northern California, he's also a local law-enforcement officer and, in his spare time, he travels with a crisis team to hot spots all over the world to teach people how to deal with potential terrorist and hostage situations.

I didn't learn about Jerry's other life until after I got to know him as a caring, faith-filled minister. Frankly, it was a bit hard for me to reconcile the gentle servant of God with the vigilant cop and the cool crisis negotiator. When we walked out to the parking lot after our wedding rehearsal, Jerry told us a story that closed the gap.

He had been on patrol the night before in what was apparently a very cool unmarked car. When the youngster who had just gotten his license decided to impress his friends by trying to race the gentleman in the great car, he didn't know whom he was tangling with—until Jerry pulled him over. After admonishing, ticketing and sternly lecturing the youngster, Jerry noticed how unhappy the boy was. He put his arm around the boy's shoulders, handed him his cell phone and said, "Now, I'll stay here with you while you call your mom."

As we drove away from the church that night, I understood that Jerry was a good minister because of, and not despite, his wide range of experience. His knowledge of human nature—the good and the bad—had taught him how to nurture the one and forgive the other.

Father, help me to follow Jerry's example in all my relationships and in all my work.   —MARCI ALBORGHETTI

24/SAT   I will instruct thee and teach thee in the way which thou shalt go: I will guide thee with mine eye.
—PSALM 32:8

One Saturday morning when my son Ryan was nearing his four-teenth birthday, I realized that although all of Ryan's friends had been learning to drive for some time, I hadn't started teaching him. So I got Ryan up, and we took the car to a nearby park.

I talked to him about the mechanics of driving: how to steer, how to use the brakes and the different gears and the accelerator. When he seemed to be comfortable with the basics, I let him get behind the wheel and drive while I sat next to him. Whenever he made a mistake, he'd say, "I'm sorry, Dad. I'm sorry." I knew he was afraid and anxious to please me.

After a few lessons, Ryan's assurance grew, but I could see that my presence in the car was still making him nervous. Then one Saturday morning, when there was no one else in the park, I let him drive by himself. As he passed by me, I could see the big smile on his face. When we left the park, he couldn't seem to stop saying, "Thank you, Dad."

I grew up without a father, and I know how hard it was not to have a dad in my life. So whenever I have a Saturday free, I take Ryan to the park for a drive, and I praise God that He has blessed me with the time to be with my son.

Lord, help me to remember that every day I can be a blessing to others, especially my children. —DOLPHUS WEARY

25 / SUN   *So we, being many, are one body in Christ, and every one members one of another.* —ROMANS 12:5

As a five-year-old growing up in a small New Hampshire village, I knew exactly how a church should look: white, with a white steeple. So I felt stirrings of frustration that morning in Sunday school when I couldn't find a white crayon in the sharing box. I was too shy to ask my classmates to borrow theirs. And why bother? Since all the other five-year-olds knew that churches were white, and the coloring project was large, I would never have time to finish even if I waited for a white crayon.

So I did the next best thing: I poked around in the sharing box, found my favorite colors and concentrated on staying within the lines. After a few moments I paused to survey my church: purple roof and steeple, pink front. Why stop there? Blue side, green door, a dash of yellow on the entryway. The innovative color scheme of my church did not at all reflect the way I wanted it to be, but I had done a pretty good job, even crudely cutting the front door so that it opened. I felt strangely pleased with my colorful project. Not perfect, but the door opened. It worked.

My wise mother saved my creation.

Today I worship in a modern church of beige brick. I'm not very shy anymore and can ask for what I need, but my church still isn't all I want it to be. I try to adapt to the inconvenient schedules, the irritating personalities, the startling innovations that knock me out of my comfort zone. That's when it's good to reflect upon my yellowing pink and purple church, and remember that my congregation reflects my imperfect personality, too. My church isn't always the way I want it to be, but it works. And the door is always open.

Lord, help me to do my best and not waste energy criticizing myself or others—in and out of church. Amen.

—GAIL THORELL SCHILLING

26/MON *For thou art my lamp, O Lord: and the Lord will lighten my darkness.* —II SAMUEL 22:29

The door to the hotel bathroom crept open. Inside, I had set up a makeshift office so I could work late while the children slept. My eleven-year-old daughter Rebecca announced, "I can't sleep." I turned off my laptop computer while she sat on the edge of the tub and began to talk. She told me about her frustrations with having a younger brother, about her recent trip to Disney World and about her upcoming elementary school graduation. Suddenly, she wiggled her toes and yelped, "Ugh!"

"What?" I said.

"An ant was crawling on my toe."

We looked down at this insect, hardly big enough to see. It was climbing over mountainous tufts of fuzzy bathroom mat. After watching it struggle for a few minutes, we realized it was going in circles. So we decided to help it along its journey. We picked it up, removed the mat and placed it on the smooth tile.

"I think ants have a good sense of direction," I said hopefully. "Maybe now it can find its way home." Soon, it was crawling in circles again.

As we watched the ant, I felt as if I were watching myself. I'd been lost a few times in my life: when my parents divorced, when my father died, when I was laid off from a job. Each time, I struggled to find my own way.

Suddenly, Rebecca said, "Let's put it in the flowers." There was a vase of fresh flowers on the counter. After letting the ant crawl onto a piece of tissue paper, she gingerly placed it on an iris. "At least it will feel at home there."

I smiled at Rebecca's innocence and at her caring heart. And I said a silent prayer for the people who, each time I was lost, were there to comfort me, help pick me up and put me back on the right road.

Lord, thank You for Your guidance and the comfort You give through others. —BILLY NEWMAN

27 / TUE *Better is the end of a thing than the beginning thereof: and the patient in spirit is better than the proud in spirit.* —ECCLESIASTES 7:8

When my grandson Bob received his college degree, our family attended the graduation. After the usual round of congratulations and hugs from friends and family, we gathered at a restaurant for lunch.

We had placed our orders when I said to Bob, "We are so proud to be here to see you receive your bachelor's degree."

"Then start planning for the time when I get my master's degree, Grandmom," he said.

"And you're going to start that next fall?" I asked.

"Yes, I am." His voice was almost hard with determination. "I'll have to work to pay for it, but I already have a job here at the college."

"That's great!" I exclaimed. "What will you be doing?"

He straightened his shoulders a bit and fixed his eyes on my face as he answered, "I'll be moving furniture, emptying trash, mopping floors, painting walls and—"

I interrupted him to ask, "You'll be doing custodial work?"

"Yes. Are you ashamed of me, Grandmom?"

"Oh, no!" I reached over to clasp his hand in mine. "I'm very proud of you. Not every young man your age would be willing to do that kind of work to get his education."

Bob moved into my outstretched arms and we hugged each other, both already looking forward to that next graduation day.

Dear Lord, bless those who work hard to make the most of the gift of life. Amen. —DRUE DUKE

$28/$ WED *The Lord also will be a refuge for the oppressed, a refuge in times of trouble.* —PSALM 9:9

Rebecca and I hadn't had much trouble deciding on where we were going to spend our honeymoon. She loved Irish music and literature, while I had long wanted to visit some of the mysterious prehistoric standing stones that cover the countryside of the British Isles. Five days into our Ireland trip, a small sign on the side of the highway caught my eye: STANDING STONES NEXT RIGHT. The hotel we'd reserved for the evening was still a long drive away, but I had to take a look.

Twenty minutes of driving up a long mud road plentifully supplied with twists and potholes, I was starting to regret the idea. That's when another sign came toward us out of the mist: DONKEY SANCTUARY, 1 KILOMETER.

The stones, I decided, could wait. Minutes later, we pulled up in front of a cottage and stables that looked as if they belonged in another century. A young woman with long blonde hair and big rubber boots covered in mud came out to greet us. "You must be here for the donkeys," she said simply.

So it was that Rebecca and I were introduced to Sue, or "Sue at the Zoo," as she signs the newsletters that she still regularly sends us. Sue's sanctuary is one of a handful of places in the British Isles where sick, ill-treated or abandoned donkeys can find a secure and caring home.

Jacob, the first of Sue's donkeys we sponsored, has passed on since our visit. But Sue was quick to send us pictures of our new charge—Solomon. Like Jacob, Solomon had a long and not always happy life before coming to the sanctuary. With Sue's care, he promises to have many happy years ahead of him, which is what Rebecca and I hope for, too.

Thank You, Lord, for the unexpected people who come into my life and for the gifts they bring. —PTOLEMY TOMPKINS

29/THU

While he was blessing them, he left them and was taken up into heaven. Then they worshiped him and returned to Jerusalem with great joy. —LUKE 24:51–52 (NIV)

When our family lived in Germany, we were surprised that Ascension Thursday was a national holiday. Glad to have a break from our workday routine, we packed a picnic lunch and headed through the *wald* (the forest) to a park. There, to celebrate *Himmelfahrt* (heaven-going), a kite-flying festival was underway.

Brightly colored kites filled the sky like floating jewels, fluttering, dipping, soaring. As we strolled through the park, we found our gaze constantly turning upward. What a perfect way to celebrate the Ascension—the sky that had received Jesus was now adorned with banners of victory!

I had never thought much about the Ascension before, but I began pondering what the disciples experienced that day. How could they possibly have "returned to Jerusalem with great joy"? I think I would have felt devastated to see Jesus leave.

They must have believed His promise to be with them always and give them the power of the Holy Spirit. Perhaps the sight of Him ascending gave them a glimpse of their heavenly home with Him. Maybe they thought, *This earthly life is not all there is. Someday we will be with Him again!*

So they went to Jerusalem with joyful expectation. And God gave them His Spirit as He promised. Those who formerly had huddled fearfully in a locked room boldly proclaimed the Gospel "to the ends of the earth." Through all that assailed them, He was with them. No matter what they endured, wherever they went, they were on a journey home to be with Him.

Here in the United States, Ascension Thursday is a normal workday. Yet for me, it can be a reminder to seek renewal in the Holy Spirit and, like the disciples, find courage for my own journey.

I'll be submerged in work today, Lord, but please help me focus on You and remember that You are with me always.

—MARY BROWN

A HERITAGE OF FREEDOM

30/*FRI*   THE VIETNAM VETERANS MEMORIAL
"These stones are to be a memorial to the people of Israel forever."
—JOSHUA 4:7 (NIV)

Although I've never served in the military, like most of my generation I was deeply affected by the Vietnam War. Many of us lost our political innocence because of that war and most of us, including me, lost friends. So the Vietnam Veterans Memorial, the most visited site on the Mall since it opened, holds a special place in my heart. I visited it that first year, and I've returned every year since.

The memorial, a slash in the earth opened to receive the two arms of a wall that rise to meet in the middle, was conceived to inspire reflection and healing. On the wall are carved the names of the 58,226 men and women who died or remain missing in Vietnam.

Since it was constructed, the wall has inspired people to leave offerings of love and forgiveness at its base. Medals, helmets, dog tags and bracelets are accompanied by countless photographs and letters. Each night park rangers collect and preserve the offerings that have become a record of love and healing. Seeing those mementos through the years has helped me to deal with the sense of futility and loss I felt for the names I knew on the wall.

As the years passed, I wondered how long people would continue to leave things at the memorial. One day last year, I watched a pregnant woman leave a sonogram photo at the wall. "He would have been her grandfather," she said to her companion. Then I knew, the remembering would last for generations.

Father, let me always remember that the wounds of conflict are healed only by forgiveness and hope.   —ERIC FELLMAN

31 / SAT   *Now my days are swifter than a post. . . . They are passed away as the swift ships: as the eagle that hasteth to the prey.*   —JOB 9:25–26

Is buying a 1985 Yamaha Riva 180cc motor scooter a sure sign of male middle age?

You bet your bottom it is.

And your bottom would know. So would your spine and your brain and all your extremities, especially if they're straddling a tiny 330-pound frame rolling fifty MPH down US 30.

Some sensations simply defy description. Even if too much blues guitar had rendered you hard of hearing, you would still know you were on a motorcycle. You would know it the same way Beethoven knew his Ninth Symphony, written while he was stone deaf—yet he heard all the notes, all the voices.

Why have I, a mild-mannered suburban male with 3.0 children, a lawn and a mortgage payment, bought such a dangerous machine?

Part of the answer lies in cliché: I want to feel the thrill of speed, the wind against my face, the throttle in my right hand. Yet I know the real reason I'm riding: To ride anything with two wheels on an open road is to deliver your fate into the hands of God.

While the rest of the world drives SUVs the size of Sherman tanks, I putt along unprotected, save for a fifty-dollar helmet. I am extremely careful and extremely aware of my tiny place in this world. Bikers hardly seem like a band of believers, but as soon as I pull up on the throttle through a tight curve near the exit ramp, leaning my body ever so slightly, keeping my head up, my eyes active, I'd say that I'm as close to God right now as I am to the pavement, and I know, in the words of the hymn, that "grace will lead me home."

Father, bring everyone on the road today safely to their destinations. And give me a fresh sense of prudence to go with my old bike.   —MARK COLLINS

My Daily Blessings

1 _____

2 _____

3 _____

4 _____

5 _____

6 _____

7 _____

8 _____

9 _____

10 _____

11 _____

12 _____

13 _____

14 _____

15 _____

16 _____

17 _____

18 _____

19 _____

20 _____

21 _____

22 _____

23 _____

24 _____

25 _____

26 _____

27 _____

28 _____

29 _____

30 _____

31 _____

JUNE

Blessed are the merciful: for
they shall obtain mercy.
—Matthew 5:7

S	M	T	W	T	F	S
1	2	3	4	5	6	7
8	9	10	11	12	13	14
15	16	17	18	19	20	21
22	23	24	25	26	27	28
29	30					

1 /SUN   *The Lord preserveth the strangers. . . .*
                                        —PSALM 146:9

Years ago, when my husband Lynn and I were in Australia with
MOPS (Mothers of Preschoolers), we attended a Sunday morning
church service where I felt a bit self-conscious and out of place.
After all, we were strangers going to an unfamiliar church in a foreign country. Once inside, we saw several groups of people, talking
and laughing with one another. I looked down, avoiding
eye contact with anyone as we made our way toward the main
sanctuary.

"Would you like a lolly?" I suddenly heard a woman ask. I
looked up into the smiling face of a lady who was thrusting a gaily
decorated wicker basket toward us. Inside were assorted pieces of
candy.

"Why, thank you," I said, reaching into her basket and returning
her smile.

"Lolly lady . . . lolly lady!" two teenaged boys called as they
raced up to her to select a treat from her basket. She responded
warmly to them.

We settled into the pew, and I smiled at the stranger next to me.
"I see our Lolly Lady found you," the young woman grinned, nodding at the candy in my hand.

"She's very friendly," I replied.

"She hasn't always been. Years ago when she came to our
church, she was terribly shy and self-conscious, so the pastor suggested she carry around a basket of candy to offer to others, as a
way of connecting with them. She's been known as the 'Lolly Lady'
ever since."

I chatted on with this stranger next to me, learning, among other
things, that *lolly* means candy in Australia. Soon the church service started, and during the first prayer, I thanked God for the
Lolly Lady, a reminder of the many sweet ways that self-conscious
people can make a direct connection with others.

*Father, thank You for the reminder about overcoming
self-consciousness.*   —CAROL KUYKENDALL

AN EYE FOR BLESSINGS

2/MON   THE WORK OF OUR HANDS
Ye shall rejoice in all that ye put your hand unto. . . .
—DEUTERONOMY 12:7

Before going to a friend's house last night, I gave myself a mani-
cure. I was taking a gift, but I couldn't wrap it till the polish dried.
I couldn't get dressed, either, or work on my hair. I stood in the
bedroom, fanning my hands in the air, helpless without them.

That's why hands are the blessing I'm focusing on today. Hands,
those miraculously designed tools I used this morning for everything from hammering a picture hook into the wall to tying my
shoelaces. Sensitive, strong, flexible, adaptable, surely the human
hand is one of God's most awesome creations!

Our life stories could be told as the record of what our hands have
touched. These hands have held babies and placed my mother's urn
in its niche. They've washed dishes and worn rings, held flowers and
pencils, scrubbed floors and gripped the hands of strangers.

What if they could do none of these things? I have a paraplegic
friend whose fingers are curled against his palm. Watching him struggle just to hold a spoon or turn the page of a book, I think I'll never
again take for granted the matchless dexterity of "ordinary" hands.

But, of course, I do. Within an hour, mine are performing a
hundred needed functions quite unnoticed. Until, that is, a coat of
nail polish interrupts their activity long enough to remind me that
hands are also active when they're folded in a prayer of gratitude.

*Lord, whose Word tells us "Whatsoever thy hand findeth to do,
do it with thy might" (Ecclesiastes 9:10), show me the work You
have for my hands today.*   —ELIZABETH SHERRILL

3/TUE   *Suffer the little children to come unto me, and forbid them not....*   —MARK 10:14

My arms were filled with groceries as I entered the house. On the floor just inside the door, I spotted a piece of paper covered with what looked like a child's drawing. I put the groceries down and picked up the paper. It was an invitation, designed by our six-year-old neighbor Billy, to attend a school play at 9:30 the next morning.

Billy was in kindergarten, and he was playing the lead role in *Peter Rabbit*. I wanted to go, but June was my busiest month, and I had two appointments scheduled for the next morning. I didn't want to disappoint Billy, but I had responsibilities. Anyway, I was a little annoyed that I'd only been invited at the last moment.

The next morning, as I reached for the cereal, these words seemed to leap from the front of the box: "The greatest gift you can give a child is your time." I picked up Billy's invitation from the counter where I'd left it and then glanced back at the box. I got the message. I would reschedule my appointments and attend the play.

At 9:30, parents and children were squeezed into the hall where the kindergartners sat in a circle. Our Billy was brilliant as the naughty Peter Rabbit, who ran away from home, ate too much and suffered a terrible tummy ache, while a chorus of children admonished him, "Peter, mind your mother!"

After the play, when I shook Billy's hand and thanked him for inviting me, his face beamed with pride. And I silently thanked God for using a cereal box to nudge me to do the right thing.

Heavenly Father, thank You for Your nudges. Please keep me always willing to encourage the very young. —OSCAR GREENE

4/WED   *To him that is afflicted pity should be shown from his friend....*   —JOB 6:14

Bad days happen, and this was one. My plane ticket turned out to have the wrong return date, I lost my gloves on the way to the airport, the ATM rejected my card and it was raining hard. Worst of all, I didn't want to go on this trip to a large meeting in an unknown city. I hate flying at the best of times. My confidence was low and ebbing as the minutes passed. I felt uncertain, miserable and also quite ashamed of myself.

At the airport, I went to check-in, wondering if my electronic ticket would turn out not to exist. As I waited glumly in the line feeling as alone as one can feel in a crowded airport, arms came around me from behind and an exuberant voice said, "Oh, how great, Brigitte, you're on my flight!"

The sun came out. Eric was one of the people in my profession I had loved and admired since I met him fifteen years before. I knew he would never laugh at my fears, and I knew he'd help me get to where I was going. He did not fail me.

"We can share a cab at the other end," he said.

"That would be great. Maybe," I added, "we could sit together?"

"I'll see what I can do with my big smile," he said with a laugh.

The bad day was beginning to look like a good one.

Lord, thank You for the generous and affectionate people in my life. —BRIGITTE WEEKS

5/THU *"At that time I will change the speech of the peoples to a pure speech, that all of them may call on the name of the Lord. . . ."* —ZEPHANIAH 3:9 (RSV)

Although school was officially over, I returned the following week to begin teaching a computer class. One of the participants was the mother of one of my high school students.

"How do you think the students will react to the new uniform policy?" she asked. (Our school had been the first public high school in the district to adopt school uniforms.) Before I could answer, she continued, "Kids these days don't agree about much of anything. Don't be surprised if their personal differences become even more pronounced."

As I walked down the hall on my way out of the school that afternoon, I stopped to read a few of the colorful signs taped to the lockers. Some students had decorated their lockers with the purple and gold colors of Louisiana State. Others had used Tulane's green and white. The two schools' baseball teams were in the throes of a hard-fought, three-game series. The winner would advance to the College World Series, and fans of both teams were equally adamant about who the winner would be.

Just then I overheard a group of students talking in the room across the way. "Let's start our meeting with a prayer," one student said. "Lord," she prayed, "help the Tigers as they march to victory—"

Another girl interrupted her quickly. "God, bless the Green Wave as they beat . . ." She stopped abruptly.

At that moment, all of the kids laughed. They quickly joined hands as one boy began to pray, "Heavenly Father, watch over all of our athletes, and bless their attitudes and ours. May we have a well-played game. Amen."

Most gracious and loving God, You are the common bond that unites us in spite of our differences. Help me to remember that different attitudes can still be good attitudes.

—MELODY BONNETTE

6/FRI   *For we are God's workmanship, created in Christ Jesus to do good works, which God prepared in advance for us to do.*   —EPHESIANS 2:10 (NIV)

To dye or not to dye, that is the question. Should I get my hair cut, wrapped, braided, straightened or curled? Should I get myself tucked, stretched or tweaked?

Each morning, I play a little game with myself: I avoid looking into the mirror. *What difference does it make,* I ask myself. *Shouldn't I be beyond all that—worrying about my appearance? What does what I look like have to do with who I really am? It doesn't matter, right?*

Except that it does matter. A career change from civil servant to writer has meant TV appearances and speaking engagements. After having seen a little too much of me on a video monitor, I am now more conscientious about exercising, my diet and my wardrobe. Unfortunately, sometimes I worry that I worry too much about it all. Hence, the looking-glass game.

When I do lose the game and find myself looking into the mirror, I notice how thin my eyebrows are, that my pores could be smaller, that I have lost less weight than I had planned to lose. And each day there seems to be more and more gray hair on my head. One, two, three, ten, twenty . . . I stop counting.

I sigh. Then a thought occurs to me: *I'm perfect.* Maybe I'm not what TV or film producers think is perfect, but I am perfect. I'm exactly the right height, the right weight and the right color. I'm exactly who and what I need to be to do the work that God intends for me to do. Maybe someone I will encounter today needs some-one who looks just like me doing just what I'm doing so that he or she can be encouraged or inspired.

I look in the mirror and smile at my reflection. This time, I've really won the game.

Lord, help me to see myself with Your eyes and be grateful.

—SHARON FOSTER

$7/$ SAT   *For he is our peace, who hath made both one,*
and hath broken down the middle wall of partition between us.
—EPHESIANS 2:14

After sixteen years of marriage, Julee and I are pretty good friends. We hardly ever fight anymore. But the other night we had one of our rare blowups.

I won't go into the details because it was over something pre-dictably silly. At the time, though, we were serious. I went into my usual post-fight mode, retreating into a book, chancing an occa-sional aggrieved glare in my wife's direction while trying not to stoke the flames of the argument again. For her part, Julee clicked through the TV channels distractedly—coldly, I thought. I glanced at the clock. *Is it time to walk the dogs yet? Could I just get out of here for a few minutes?*

I was determined to let Julee make the first peace gesture. After all, she had started it. I hadn't helped, fighting right back when she lost her cool. But she shouldn't have pushed me. I'd had a lousy day, too, and I wasn't going to apologize. At least not before she did.

In the beginning of our marriage, this sort of nasty stalemate could go on for days. Back then, we didn't know how to fight. We had to learn how to have a disagreement, and accept that not every day of our lives together was going to be fair weather. Once, during one of these early matrimonial Armageddons, when Julee and I hadn't relaxed around each other for a couple of days, I impulsively ran home at lunch one noon with an inspired peace offering—tuna salad on a sesame bagel from her favorite neighborhood deli. What a miracle that simple sandwich worked!

Now I closed my book. "Tuna sandwich?" I asked. There are a lot of different ways to say you're sorry after sixteen years.

Father, You have guided me through my marriage much as a parent guides a child. Our love alone is not enough; we need Yours.
—EDWARD GRINNAN

8 / SUN   *He that believeth and is baptized shall be saved. . . .*
—MARK 16:16

On a balmy Sunday in early June, my husband Robert and I attended St. Luke's Episcopal Church, my former church home in Kearney, Nebraska, where we had the great joy of seeing my little granddaughter Saralisa baptized into the family of Christ.

As we stood at the baptismal font behind Saralisa and my daughter Karen, and heard Father Park speak those precious words, "I baptize you, Saralisa Christine, in the name of the Father and of the Son and of the Holy Spirit," tears of joy started flowing down my cheeks. Then I looked up and saw Anita, Beth and Verna, members of the prayer group I belonged to when I lived in Kearney, beaming smiles at me. We had prayed for this moment, and our prayers were now being answered in the most lovely way. How beautiful Saralisa and Karen looked, happy in their new church home.

I think I hadn't realized until that moment how valuable my membership in this church family had been to me and, yes, how much I missed my friends there. I even felt the presence of my dear friend and prayer partner Carolmae, who had died shortly before I moved away. And a deep truth rang in my heart like a bell: Those who are baptized into Christ's family can never be separated.

I will return to St. Luke's many times in the years to come, both in person and in thought. And I know, too, that Carolmae will keep her promise to "meet me at the river."

Lord Christ, thank You for this family that bears Your name, this family that is our true and lasting home.
—MARILYN MORGAN KING

9/MON   *And let us not be weary in well doing: for in due season we shall reap, if we faint not.*   —GALATIANS 6:9

Every year in June, my friend Joe invites me to a luncheon at the Rusk Institute for stroke survivors. Joe is one of them; so am I. We are both living with a communication impairment called aphasia, caused by brain damage from a stroke. Joe's stroke happened years before mine, and his condition is considerably worse, for understanding him when he speaks is far more difficult. He is an actor-director, and you will note that I say "is" because he continues as both. "How?" you might ask. I'm not sure, but through gestures, writing, facial expressions and just plain doggedness, he wins out. A play by Sam Shepard, directed by Joseph Chaikin, will be opening soon.

The luncheon was a wonderful affair. The people were as different as you could find—strokes are not choosy about whom they pick—but they were happy. They were proud of their progress, as was I, though I was in awe of what most of them had done with their affliction. I can speak, on occasion, and sometimes get my ideas across, but I am in difficulty if the idea is too complicated, and sometimes when it is simple the words will not come. Fortunately, those whom I love bear with me. And the man I have taken as a model from the beginning is Joe. His doggedness is catching.

It was good being in a crowd where everybody understood. At one point I leaned over to the white-haired lady who sat next to me and said, "How long, *eh, uh, eh*"—I just happened on a moment of frustration when the words would not congeal. "How long . . ."

The lady cheerfully took out a pencil and wrote on a convenient pad, "That's okay, my friend, don't hurry. God has time to wait."

God has, Joe has and I, thankfully, have time.

Thank You for using my aphasia, Father, to show me so many things that are more important.   —VAN VARNER

10/TUE   *A good man leaveth an inheritance to his children's children. . . .*   —PROVERBS 13:22

A lady I knew casually stopped by my office the other day. "Oh, I see you love purple! So do I!"

After she left, I looked around my office. Purple had been my mother's favorite color, but I'd never been particularly fond of it—until Mother's death. Now I surrounded myself with it. A purple vase. A picture of an iris. The lavender border on a piece of stained glass.

Loving the color purple was one way I'd become like Mother. But what else had her legacy to me included? Was I as filled with laughter as she had been, always ready with a witty comment? Was I as eager to study the Word of God as she was, rising early to spend quiet time before the day's work began?

And what about my own daughter? What would be my legacy to Amy Jo? Fast-food meals? Hurried phone calls? An inflated sense of my own importance?

Perhaps I could incorporate another "hallmark" of Mother, too. Her ability to listen. That unhurried way she would sit and listen to folks who stopped by, even though she had a stack of ironing to do or a dozen rows of corn to hoe. I'd inherited Mother's favorite color. Had I inherited her talent for listening, too?

I picked up the phone to call Amy Jo. We'd have a leisurely dinner. I'd listen to what's going on in her world. I'd work on leaving her a legacy worth inheriting.

Maybe I'd pick up some irises for her, too.

Remind me, Lord, that listening to each other is good practice for listening to You. —MARY LOU CARNEY

11 / WED *And some of the parts that seem weakest and least important are really the most necessary.*
—I CORINTHIANS 12:22 (TLB)

It was April of my freshman year at Oklahoma State University. My father had died that January, and I needed a summer job to help with next year's college expenses. But what could I do? There were no jobs available in my town of 350 people, and I didn't have a car. Then I spotted an announcement posted on the Student Union bulletin board:

Female Counselors, Red Rock Canyon Girl Scout Camp, 9-week position. Preference given to former Girl Scouts with both wilderness and traditional camping experience.

That job would be an answer to my prayers. Red Rock Canyon was only thirty miles from my home. There was only one hitch: I wasn't qualified.

My lack of experience was woefully evident during the interview. I'd never slept in a jungle hammock, much less unpacked and hung one. I'd never lashed tree branches together to make a bridge (and I couldn't imagine why we'd need a bridge in Red Rock!). My mouth went dry when Maryellen, the camp director, asked if I could remain calm around poisonous snakes. The only question I answered with an enthusiastic "Yes!" was "Do you know how to cook?"

When Maryellen called a week later, I was amazed to hear I'd landed a job. "Almost everyone had basic scouting skills," she said, "but you were the only girl who could cook. Counselors prepare meals on the wilderness trips, and they also teach campers about food preparation and safety."

That summer I skinned snakes and dried the skins with borax. I survived four-day wilderness trips without washing my hair or brushing my teeth. And, yes, I mastered the art of the jungle hammock.

It was the most valuable summer of my life, for I learned something that has helped me in every job since: God can use my everyday skills to answer my prayers and to build His kingdom on earth.

Lord, You have come to the lakeshore, looking neither for wealthy nor wise ones; You only asked me to follow humbly.

—PENNEY SCHWAB

ᘓᓂ

12/THU   *"Pour out your hearts to him, for God is our refuge."*   —PSALM 62:8 (NIV)

I've always admired people who are disciplined in prayer. But despite my best intentions to set aside a time for earnest prayer each day, it doesn't always happen.

One day as I was driving home from town I thought, *perfect time for praying.* I began to formulate a prayer, but it sounded wooden and phony. I made a few more attempts, but the words just wouldn't come.

Finally, in desperation, I gave up. "Lord Jesus, I just can't pray today," I said. "Is it okay if I just look out the window for a while and say nothing?"

As I climbed Marshall Road, I drove past a pink splash of Japanese cherries in bloom. "I like that," I said out loud. "Thanks, Lord." At one house, a neatly landscaped yard was ablaze with red azalea bushes. My heart leaped with joy. "That's neat, Lord," I exclaimed. At a roadside garden, clumps of bright yellow and red tulips swayed gently in the wind. "You did a great job when you made tulips," I said. Almost home, I crested a hill and spread out before me lay Mount Baker, its rugged snowcapped peaks mellowed by a late afternoon sun. "Wow, God!" I whispered. "You must be incredibly great to create a scene like that."

And so it went all the way home. I wasn't praying, mind you, I was merely expressing my delight in the pristine beauty I saw and telling the Person I felt was responsible for it.

When the words won't come, Lord, open my eyes to the prayer-starters You've put all around me. —HELEN GRACE LESCHEID

13 / FRI *The world and its desires pass away, but the man who does the will of God lives forever.* —I JOHN 2:17 (NIV)

My niece Meredith spoke at her recent high school graduation about the peculiar feelings of graduating seniors, stuck between two worlds. They don't feel they belong in high school, but they don't yet belong in the place they're headed: college. "We just don't fit," she said, and I understood what she meant. I sometimes feel that way about the world I live in. I don't fit into a society that so highly values material wealth and financial success and yet devalues faith and family. Many of TV's most popular shows honor cruelty in words and deeds while kindness is ridiculed. Popular magazines tout all kinds of values I'm trying *not* to teach my children. I don't fit in that world, but I don't yet fit into God's eternal world either. The reality is that even though I don't feel part of this world, whose treasures are as fleeting as the wind, I still have to live in it. So how do I fit in?

Meredith's simple message to her classmates makes sense: Where you are now is your best fit. Make it work. That means focusing on ways to make my world a place where God lives, too. I can read the Bible at least as much as I read the newspaper. Before I speak, I can determine if my words will bring God glory or shame. And when deciding where to spend my time, I can ask myself if I could proudly answer Jesus should He ask me that night, "So, what did you do today?"

I've accepted that I'm not always going to fit in with everything that's going on around me. And I've learned that if I can't change some of those things, I can consider it a victory when they don't change me.

In every choice I make, Lord, help me to remember that You are the center of my universe. —GINA BRIDGEMAN

14/SAT His banner over me is love.
—SONG OF SOLOMON 2:4 (NIV)

For my husband Bill and me, as for so many Americans, every day has become Flag Day. Our flag, a bit tattered from wild mountain winds, flies day and night at the edge of the garage. It has a special poignancy: Our youngest son David is in the Army, just back from a year in South Korea. After that, he may be sent elsewhere to fight. Our son Peter has been called from his civilian job for up to two years of active duty with the Air Force as part of Operation Enduring Freedom. He has already been to Afghanistan, and he may be sent elsewhere to fight. My mother-heart vacillates between fear and faith.

Yet in the midst of these changes and concerns, I think of another flag in my life, one flying in a refrain my boys sang as tots:

> *Joy is the flag*
> *flung high*
> *from the castle of my heart . . .*
> *when the King*
> *is in residence there!*

This chorus comes alive at Christmas when I change the small "Welcome" garden flag along our front walk to a red, green and gold one with the word *Joy* emblazoned on it. It reminds me of the kingdom yet to come, the kingdom of God, whose flag flies invisibly above my life every day and night. No matter what trials I face, no matter what troubles threaten, I am safe wrapped in the flag of my Father because "His banner over me is love."

Lord, thank You for the flag of our nation, which strives to be "under God." Thank You, too, for symbols like flags that are sweet shadows of truth. May Your love become the banner over us all. —ROBERTA ROGERS

READER'S ROOM

God is reaching out with new gifts for me this year. At my age, "new" is always amazing. But God likes to surprise us. I've had financial struggles as a self-employed senior citizen who recently had a brain tumor removed. Instead of increasing my income with more work, which would be exhausting right now, God has reduced my expenses dramatically. A delightful apartment in a retirement community opened up, reducing my rent. And this month, reaching the age of sixty-five has reduced my health insurance by two-thirds. This last week, job opportunities started coming in, some for later in the year, when I'll be feeling better.

God is good. I love His reaching out with such good surprises.

—SALLY EDWARDS CHRISTENSEN, KANSAS CITY, MISSOURI

15/SUN *A son honoureth his father . . . if then I be a father, where is mine honour? . . .* —MALACHI 1:6

My vast Irish-American clan was at the dinner table on a bright summer evening, grandparents at either end and a gaggle of sons and daughters-in-law and mobs of children in between and a baby on a lap somewhere. Hilarity and hubbub were in the air.

"Pass the ketchup."

"This is terrific pasta. Who made this pasta?"

"Who's on the dishwashing crew?"

"What time is the game tonight?"

A story started as my sister got up to get more food and my brothers were laughing and correcting one another in loud voices getting louder. My dad, down at the end of the table where the king sits, cleared his throat and started to add to the story, but no one heard him. The conversation swirled on without him, and he subsided without being able to say his piece. I noticed this when it happened, but I said nothing.

Dad leaned back in his chair and didn't say anything for a while. I realized later that something important in the family had passed at that moment, and that I wasn't brave enough to force the table to listen to the old king, and that I loved that man immensely for the king he had been—calm, generous, trustworthy, graceful.

Dear Lord, if by Your sweet will I am someday even a scant shadow of the great man my father is, I will thank You ten times a day for ten thousand years. —BRIAN DOYLE

FOLLOWING JESUS

16/MON LOOKING FOR THE BEST IN OTHERS
Wherefore, accept one another, just as Christ also accepted us to the glory of God. —ROMANS 15:7 (NAS)

Ever since the little concrete rabbit disappeared from my herb garden, I had looked at everyone with a jaundiced eye. "I'll bet it was that guy who came to fix my washing machine," I confided to a friend. "He kept going on about my yard, and he sure took his time leaving. Or maybe it was that kid selling candy. She was carrying an awfully big tote bag."

Then one morning a rosemary topiary appeared on my doorstep wrapped in shiny green cellophane. I searched for a gift tag, but there was none. When I waved at my neighbor who was getting her mail, she seemed especially friendly. *I'll bet it was her*, I decided, and took an extra few minutes to ask if her husband was feeling better.

At work, two young women in my office stopped talking when I approached the coffee pot. *Must have been them.* I lingered and inquired about their kids.

Then I ran into an old friend at the grocery store. "Why don't we go to the open house they're having at that new herb farm?" she suggested. *Well, she sure let the cat out of the bag. And all this time, I thought she'd forgotten me.* But I later learned she'd been out of town when the topiary mysteriously appeared on my doorstep, so she couldn't have been the one who left it.

Over the next week or so, I must have imagined a dozen scenarios pointing to the likely source of the topiary that spread its fragrance in my home and in my heart. I found myself listening to a new voice, ignoring the negative thoughts within; a voice that nudged me to accept others at face value and expect the best.

And that silly concrete rabbit someone took from my herb garden? How could I dwell on that when I had a date with an old friend to visit that new herb farm?

Help me, Lord, to accept others as You accept me.

—ROBERTA MESSNER

17/TUE *"'Well done, my good servant!' his master replied. 'Because you have been trustworthy in a very small matter, take charge of ten cities.'"* —LUKE 19:17 (NIV)

Dripping with sweat, I finished a brisk thirty-minute walk around our neighborhood and dropped to a slower pace to cool down. My new discipline was finally paying off. I'd come to look forward to these regular early morning walks as a time not only to exercise but also to talk with God. This morning, however, my prayers were more like complaints.

When I retired from my editorial position in New York City and my wife Carol and I moved to Southern California, our income dropped by more than half. I intended to supplement that by writing. But without the daily routine of going to the office, I lost the structured life I'd had. I slept late. I got involved in church activities. I surfed the Internet. Writing often took a backseat. Although I did make sales, they were insufficient.

Lord, inspire me, I prayed. *Provide for our needs.* I removed my baseball cap and wiped the sweat from my forehead. As I strolled along, the sun filtered through the palm, carrotwood and jacaranda trees so common in our community. Suddenly, a glint of copper caught my eye. I stooped and picked up a penny. *It's worth so little,* I thought. *Why even bother?*

The following morning, I found not one, but two pennies on the pavement. This time as I picked them up, I wondered if they had some significance. Abruptly I stopped. In my mind I heard the words, *Be faithful in little things, and greater things will come to you.*

In those coins I felt God's gentle rebuke. I'd already disciplined myself to walk each morning. Right then I promised to set another goal: to write something every day, too. If I kept at it, I sensed, God *would* inspire me. And who knows what might result?

Father, help me to be faithful in little things, so that with Your help I might accomplish greater things. —HAROLD HOSTETLER

---

18 / WED   *For now we see through a glass, darkly. . . .*
—I CORINTHIANS 13:12

When people ask me how I am feeling these days, there is only one response: big. With four weeks of pregnancy left to go, I have all the usual discomforts and a few special ones besides. But big pretty much sums up how I feel.

What I don't feel is prepared. I'm vaguely aware that sometime soon I ought to get out the baby clothes and buy some diapers. I ought to at least try to remember some of the details of what life with a newborn is like so that being roused at 2:00 A.M. is the only rude awakening I'm in for.

Yet my mellowness about the impending arrival of baby number four is mostly because I've realized that the practicalities have very little to do with preparing for *who* this baby is. I've lived with this new life for eight months now; I know her or him better than anyone else on the face of this earth. And though I already know that this baby is a wiggle worm and hiccups a lot and is awake often, my knowledge will take on a whole new dimension the moment I meet my daughter in the flesh or see my son's face for the first time.

I'm a physical being, and I understand most things through my senses. When I meet someone about whom I already know something, I think, *Oh, why of course!* Or, *She isn't at all what I expected!*

So this is what I know about my baby: that I don't know him or her fully yet, and that I won't begin to until the day my child is in my arms. In some senses, that's true of my relationship with God, too. I know Him, I love Him, and I strive to serve Him. But, oh, how small that knowledge is compared with what I will know on the day I finally meet Him face to face! That heavenly birthday is going to be grand.

Heavenly Father, fix my eyes on You always so that I may know You as fully as my heart is able. —JULIA ATTAWAY

19/THU "This . . . is how you should pray. . . ."
—MATTHEW 6:9 (NIV)

My friend Elton Trueblood once wrote a book about the humor of Christ, which showed that Jesus on occasion engaged in wit, irony and satire. Sometimes it seems to me that Christians take themselves too seriously and miss the immeasurable blessing of laughter.

Recently, I heard a funny story about two pastors conducting a funeral. One of them, Tom, agreed to handle the preliminaries, and the other, Orville, the eulogy for the deceased. While Tom was praying just before the eulogy, Orville realized that he had left his notes in the church study. Slipping up behind Tom, Orville whispered, "Keep praying until I get back."

Tom, who was about finished, didn't understand why, but he struggled on, thanking God for everything from the pews and the ushers to the newly paved parking lot. His last prayer was a silent one: that his colleague would be back when he opened his eyes. And he was—breathless, but with sermon in hand.

The story got me to thinking about my prayers. Sometimes I forget to include the Almighty in my plans and try going it alone. I need to remind myself that I'm the principal benefactor of prayer, and that I need to thank my heavenly Father for His grace, mercy and blessings, and ask for His guidance every day of my life. Jesus left us much the same message as Orville gave Tom: "Keep praying until I get back."

> *Remind me, Lord,*
> *When I forget to laugh, and fret and stew*
> *That I'm just a tourist passing through.*
>
> —FRED BAUER

20/FRI **Please the Lord and honor him, so that you will always be doing good, kind things for others. . . .**
—COLOSSIANS 1:10 (TLB)

My cousin's flight back to Australia from her California visit included a week in Hawaii, and my husband John and I decided to join her. As luck would have it, I came down with bronchitis. Antibiotics helped, but didn't cure it. By the time for our flight home, I had a bad case of the grumps for my part of a vacation gone wrong.

The airport in Honolulu has winding walkways through a garden of ferns and flora. As we passed through the many stalls offering leis, I pulled on John's jacket. "Let's get some leis to take home."

I approached a stall where a couple were laughing, kissing and exchanging leis. *Honeymooners,* I thought, *so much in love!* The young man reached for a lei thick with plumeria and orchids entwined with ferns. "This?" he questioned, and the young woman nodded yes.

"Oh," I whispered, "that's the most beautiful lei I've ever seen!"

The young man smiled. "For my mom. She's the best!"

"Your mother is blessed to have a son like you," I said. "I have a son like that, too. If he were here, he'd be doing the same thing for me."

As the saleswoman gave the young man his change, I told her, "I'd like one of those, too."

"Sorry," she said, "that's the last we've got. No more till tomorrow."

Disappointed, I walked slowly away. Suddenly, I felt hands on my shoulders turning me around, then that most beautiful lei slipping over my head. "Here, this is for you," the young man said. "We want you to have it!"

"Oh, I couldn't," I gasped. "This one's for your mother!"

He shook his head, "We'll find her another lei. This is for you."

I reached for my purse. He put his hand on mine, "No! It's from the son who would buy it for you if he were here. *Aloha!*"

Bronchitis and all, that sweet surprise made our week in Hawaii forever treasured in my heart.

Aloha!

Thank You, Lord, for the unexpected blessing of Aloha *(love).*
—FAY ANGUS

21 / SAT   *"As a mother comforts her child, so will I comfort you. . . ."*
—ISAIAH 66:13 (NIV)

When Leah, our daughter-in-law-to-be, told me of plans for the wedding reception, she mentioned there would be a special time when, as the mother of the groom, I would dance with our son Jeff while Leah danced with her father. At first I thought, *Oh, no, me out there on the dance floor with everyone watching!*

But, as the time approached, I began to look forward to the dance. How special to have a few minutes with Jeff at the reception, perhaps the last few moments I'd get to spend with him before they left on their honeymoon and settled into their home in Colorado. I imagined the profound and wonderful things I might say to Jeff during those moments.

The wedding festivities went by in a blur, and finally the time came for our dance. As I reached up to my son's tall shoulder and he grasped my right hand, all of the things I'd planned to say to him evaporated from my mind. Instead, I found myself asking with concern, "I noticed you've been so busy you haven't eaten. Aren't you hungry?"

"I haven't eaten all day," he admitted, "but it's okay. They're putting together a basket of food from the reception for us to take in the car with us."

Looking down at his rented shoes I asked, "Do your feet hurt?"

"No, they're fine," he answered.

Soon the dance was over, and my friend Charlene was eager to know what Jeff and I had said. When I repeated the conversation,

I laughed. Out there on the dance floor, I had asked my twenty-three-year-old son, who was an Air Force officer and a brand-new husband, if he was hungry or if his feet hurt!

I sat down and took off my own too-tight shoes, then reconsidered my seemingly wasted opportunity. Perhaps it had been just right after all. During that dance, I had unconsciously performed my last act of mothering by revisiting my first. When our children are newborns, our questions are always, "Are they hungry? Are they hurt?" And as they grow, these questions grow into prayers that fit each new stage of their lives: "God, fill them and comfort them."

I put my shoes back on and made sure the basket of food was tucked into the backseat of Jeff and Leah's car before Jeff's college buddies started "decorating" it with plastic wrap. I was the one who borrowed the scissors from the receptionist so Jeff and Leah could cut the wrap to open the car door. After all, the need for parenting never really ends, not even with a final dance.

Dear Heavenly Father, thank You for the generous hearts of mothers. And give me also a heart of love for all who are hungry and hurt.
                                                          —KAREN BARBER

22/SUN

simplicity. . . .

He that giveth, let him do it with
                                        —ROMANS 12:8

Carmen is what Victorian novelists would call simple. She can barely read, she's not very good at remembering names, and her conversation doesn't go much beyond "How are you today?" Sixty years old now, she still lives with her mother, and when she comes to church and sits in the pew, there's something of an eight-year-old about her. She alternates between rapt attention and fidgeting, her head swirling to the back of the sanctuary to see who's there, her feet swinging from the pew.

And yet, Carmen has an intuitive sense about people. When new people come to church, she makes a beeline for them at the coffee hour, grabs them by the hand and leads them to meet people. When a parishioner has been away for a long time, she goes up to that person with a big smile and puts out her hand. When a name has been read from the pulpit with a request for prayers, she'll give whoever it is a hug later in the back of the church. I remember her best at our wedding, when she appeared at church in her prettiest party dress and shiny Mary Janes, wreathed in smiles as she celebrated our happiness.

Some people are a gift by their presence: the calming influence at a contentious meeting at work; the good listener who makes you feel better just by hearing your concerns; the enthusiast who adds energy to a room the moment she walks in the door. What is comforting about Carmen is her goodness. Her kindness arrives unedited, disarming everyone she meets. She brings out the best in people through simple warmth. That's her gift.

What can I give You, Lord? I give You my heart.

—RICK HAMLIN

23/MON *And the earth brought forth grass, and herb yielding seed after his kind, and the tree yielding fruit, whose seed was in itself, after his kind: and God saw that it was good.*
—GENESIS 1:12

I'm conducting a campaign to keep my lawn free of dandelions. Now this is not an easy task on my street, which could be renamed Dandelion Lane without anyone wondering why. Lawns across the street and on both sides of us are alternately speckled in yellow and then white and then yellow again, and the breeze carries seeds from their dandelions onto our thick green grass.

I haven't had time to root out every one, so my campaign is limited to picking every yellow flower and bud I can find on my way to the car in the morning or from the car in the afternoon. (I don't care about the backyard; it belongs to the dogs). I've been winning. Every yellow bloom that sticks its head up on my lawn or my next-door neighbor's driveway gets plucked and tossed away.

Recently, though, I've reached the conclusion that God wants me to have flowers on my lawn, even if they're not the all-pervasive dandelions. Down among the blades of green grass, nearly but not entirely hidden, are patches of other flowers, white and yellow, much tinier and less obtrusive than the dandelions, and also much less likely to be plucked out by someone with limited time, like me.

I'm starting to think they look kind of nice, splashes of color in the green. I'll admit that God knows best about that. But I still think dandelions look better on the other lawns.

Dear God, thank You for green lawns and for wildflowers and even for weeds, dandelions included. —RHODA BLECKER

$24/$ TUE *But blessed are your eyes, for they see. . . .*
—MATTHEW 13:16

When my son was preparing for his driver's test, I knew I had to convince him that driving on the busy, eight-lane interstate system of Milwaukee, Wisconsin, was different from navigating the two-lane streets in Oak Creek. One day on the interstate, I got a brainstorm.

"Andrew, time me for one minute while I say aloud every single thing I'm thinking. Here goes.

"I'm looking in my rearview mirror, glancing at my side mirror. The guy in front of me is slowing down, the man in front of him has his blinker on to change lanes. I look in the rearview mirror again. The semi behind me is swerving into the left lane as we go around the curve and he's picking up speed. I look in my rearview mirror again and in the side mirror to my right. An older car is speeding up behind me in the far right lane with five teens in it. They pull into the middle lane behind me, in front of the semi, trying to pass me. I maintain my speed, giving them a chance to pass on the left. I glance into the rearview mirror. A police car's speeding up in the left lane. The speeders pass me. I see an open spot in the far right lane and signal to enter that lane just as the police lights go on behind the speeders."

I paused for a breath.

"Mom, that was only forty-two seconds."

"Well, do you get my point? So much is happening out here every single second, and you have to be aware of all of it!"

A few weeks later, Andrew got his license. In the meantime I started paying closer attention, not just while driving, but to everything around me. While riding my bike on the county's new bike trail, I memorized every scene: How the trail winds back and forth as if the designer was an artist. The wildflowers growing in bunches as large as living rooms. The *clank, clank, thump, thump* of the new two-by-fours on the footbridge. . . .

Lord, help me to notice as much as I can of Your world and then remember to thank You for it during my evening prayers.
—PATRICIA LORENZ

℮

25/WED *Pure and undefiled religion in the sight of our God and Father, to visit orphans and widows in their distress, and to keep oneself unstained by the world.* —JAMES 1:27 (NAS)

It's amazing how something as simple as an old-fashioned tea cake can mean so much and be so encouraging. My wife Rosie loves to visit the elderly, and she uses tea cakes as a means of ministry to them. They look forward to her dropping by and sharing those tasty delicacies with them—and some prayers, too.

One morning, Rosie met an elderly lady at the grocery store and started a conversation with her. Sobbing intensely, the lady (we'll call her Mrs. Johnson) told Rosie that she had a serious illness and was afraid of dying. Rosie walked Mrs. Johnson to her car, and somehow the conversation got around to the subject of tea cakes. Mrs. Johnson loved tea cakes, but she was unable to bake, and it had been quite awhile since she had had any. She perked up when Rosie promised that she would drive the thirty-five miles to Mrs. Johnson's house to bring her some.

My wife now takes tea cakes to that dear lady regularly. On days when Mrs. Johnson is at the doctor's office, Rosie will open the screen door of her house and put a bag of tea cakes between the doors. Mrs. Johnson says she often goes to her front door and looks down, hoping that Rosie has left more tea cakes.

It's amazing how things that may seem insignificant to us can be a special blessing for others. A smile and a friendly greeting can bring comfort to a lonely heart—and so can a plate of tea cakes.

Lord, every day, help me to use the gifts and abilities You've given me to be a blessing to others.
—DOLPHUS WEARY

26/THU   *The love of God has been poured out within our hearts through the Holy Spirit who was given to us.*
—ROMANS 5:5 (NAS)

As I sat in the hospital room with my ninety-two-year-old mother, I longed to be comforted. She was so very sick and weak that I knew without being told that the prognosis wasn't good. I'd done everything I could think of to comfort her.

The nurses shut the door each time they left our room. I felt closed in and alone, and I longed for someone—anyone—to come through the door.

I was staring at the door when it opened and a tiny, well-dressed, young woman came in. She smiled and offered her hand. "Hi, I'm Brenda," she said.

Reluctantly, I shook her hand. "Can I do anything for you?" she asked.

"No, thank you," I said, eyeing her neat little CHAPLAIN pin.

"May I pray with you?"

I looked into her eyes. "How will you pray?" I asked bluntly. I didn't want a canned prayer or a memorized one. I didn't want this efficient young thing just to mumble something and then check us off on her list.

She looked at me silently for a moment. Her face glowed. "I'll pray as the Holy Spirit leads—unless you'd rather I didn't."

Suddenly, I knew there were four of us in the room. "Oh, please do pray. Thank you, Brenda," I managed.

Brenda prayed powerfully, concluding with Romans 8:38–39: "For I am persuaded, that neither death, nor life, nor angels, nor principalities, nor powers, nor things present, nor things to come, Nor height, nor depth, nor any other creature, shall be able to separate us from the love of God, which is in Christ Jesus our Lord."

She couldn't have known it was my mother's favorite Scripture.

Holy Spirit, the way You suddenly bind believers together remains a marvelous mystery!   —MARION BOND WEST

27/FRI   *"He who brings thanksgiving as his sacrifice honors me. . . ."*   —PSALM 50:23 (RSV)

Kathy's been coming in for kidney dialysis for thirteen years, always with a smile and a warm "How do you do?" One evening I asked her how she maintained her buoyant attitude.

"I keep a grateful journal!"

"What's that?"

"Every day I write down five things I'm grateful for."

"What kinds of things?"

"Oh, like the sun coming out." In the Pacific Northwest this is unusual and merits attention! "Or like the man who let me merge in front of him," she went on, "when I was getting on the freeway tonight. You'd be surprised how finding just five things a day changes your whole outlook."

I decided to try it. My first entry, of course, was *I am grateful not to be on kidney dialysis.* But I quickly made more positive notations: details about my children for which I was grateful; new insights I happened to have; art projects that brought me satisfaction. Pretty soon I noticed that I was recording conversations I had with people, sometimes complete strangers who took time out of their day to be pleasant: the carpenter dressed in overalls who poured my coffee in the convenience store; the old widower at the sauna who detected I was a Canadian; a store clerk who remembered I ski and asked about this year's snow.

It didn't take long to realize Kathy was right—but not in the way I'd expected. True, the very act of looking for daily blessings did encourage me to see things that had gone unnoticed before. But more importantly, I discovered myself recreating these little "people moments" for someone else. What made me feel recognized and human, I started passing on. A student's "Nice boots, teach!" became my "Danny, you're looking on top of the world! What's up?" A stranger's "Would you like the Colombian or French Roast coffee this morning?" became my "Cheryl, can I grab you a cup of coffee while I'm at the cafeteria?"

I still write in my grateful journal, but not for myself anymore. I write because the kindness of other people keeps me supplied with ideas on how to spice up someone else's otherwise unnotable day.

Thank You, Lord, for Kathy's grateful journal. May I increasingly give thanks and be found giving those around me something for which to be grateful. —BRENDA WILBEE

28/SAT The fruit of the Spirit is love, joy, peace. . . .
—GALATIANS 5:22

One summer day, my Aunt Eunice and her husband George gave a family picnic. Eunice had worked for days making sure that everyone's favorite dish was waiting. She had even set a place underneath a leafy tree for our dog Bandit: A blanket folded into a bed and a big bowl of cool water welcomed him with love.

"Vintage Eunice," my husband David said after he told that story from the pulpit of the First United Methodist Church in Florence, Alabama. David's funeral sermon was filled with lovely stories of Eunice's life, but it was the story of the dog that brought tears of knowing to the congregation's eyes.

Ever since I first got to know Eunice, after my mother married Eunice's brother Herb Hester, I saw her as the kind of person I'd like to become. Now David's words helped me to see what that would be like.

How many times have I worked myself silly, cleaning everything in sight, so my guests would admire my housekeeping? To become like Eunice, I'd have to pay less attention to dust bunnies and cobwebs and concentrate on creating a place of warmth and welcome for my friends.

How many times have I monopolized conversations with stories of "me"? To become like Eunice, I'd have to take the time to listen, holding on to each word as if it were the finest ever spoken.

How many times have I gloated over my possessions? To become like Eunice, I'd have to take more pleasure in giving away my treasures than in keeping them.

The truth is, by living the way she lived, Eunice offered me a choice: I can either spend my days concentrating on what makes me look good, or I can work to create situations that make others feel good.

Father, when You show me the fruits of the Spirit in another's eyes, help me not only to admire but to emulate. —PAM KIDD

29/SUN When [Peter] saw the wind, he was afraid and, beginning to sink, cried out, "Lord, save me!" Immediately Jesus reached out his hand and caught him. . . .

—MATTHEW 14:30–31 (NIV)

Some years ago, I took my family to visit Hersheypark, the amusement park in Hershey, Pennsylvania. Our older sons Ryan and Joel went off in search of the most challenging rides, while my wife Kathy and I took ten-year-old Kyle to sample the gentler ones, like the merry-go-round.

But Kyle was unhappy. "These rides aren't exciting enough," he said. "Let's try that one over there."

It was called The Rotor, and it was a cylinder of sorts. Inside, it looked like an empty soup can with padded walls. We stood in a circle against the walls as a voice came over the loudspeaker and said, "Welcome to The Rotor. This will be a ride you'll never, ever forget."

Suddenly, we began to spin around. *No big deal,* I thought. Then we began to spin a little faster. Pretty soon we were spinning yet faster. My shoulders were thrust up against the wall and I couldn't move. The voice came back over the loudspeaker and said, "Now experience The Rotor!" All at once, the floor dropped completely out from under us and we hung suspended.

I began to try to think of some faith-building Scripture, but all I could think of was the simple prayer of Peter as he sank into the sea: "Lord, save me!"

At last the floor came back up, and the ride began to slow down. My stomach was churning, my legs were like jelly, and my thoughts were in total confusion. Weak and wobbling, Kathy and I managed to walk out and find a place to sit down. Kyle ran out, overflowing with enthusiasm. "That was great, Dad!" he said.

If you should ever go to Hersheypark for an outing on some summer afternoon, beware of the "exciting" rides. But if you want to test your faith, step aboard one.

Lord, when the bottom falls out of life, help me to pray, believe in You and keep a positive attitude. —TED NACE

30/MON ... *Bringing into captivity every thought to the obedience of Christ.* —II CORINTHIANS 10:5

If he doesn't fix that dryer, I don't think I'll be able to stand it. Our clothes dryer worked just fine, but it made a persistent, high-pitched squeaking sound that was driving me crazy. My mechanically minded husband Rick pulled the dryer away from the wall, spread out his tools and tried to locate the problem.

"I think it just needs a bushing," he said finally.

"Well, how do you get one of those?" I asked.

"Oh, I'll look around when I get a chance and buy one."

"When?" I asked anxiously, thinking about his already full schedule. Rick works twelve-hour days; at night he cuts our grass and does other chores, and this week he'd be busy building the concession stand at our daughter's high-school softball field.

"Soon as I can get the part, I'll fix it." He left the dryer jutting out in the middle of the laundry room.

When people called to talk to me, they could hear the dryer screeching in the background. Wearily, I explained the irritating sound and added a few tart sentences about my annoyance with my husband. Every night I bellowed down the basement steps or out the back door, "Please fix the dryer! I can't stand that horrible sound!"

One day, my mom called from the hospital, where she'd been staying with her mother. I'd visited my grandmother a few times lately, but my mom rarely left her side. She'd heard all about my dryer frustrations.

"Oh, Julie," she, crying softly, "the sound of your dryer . . . everything sounds so . . . *normal* in your house. Will it ever be normal here?" I began to cry with her.

"Mom," I said, "I'm so sorry things are hard for you right now. Everything is normal here. I just haven't realized it lately." The sound of the dryer in the background suddenly sounded like a melody.

Lord, help me to stop letting the tiny negatives drown out all the positives in my life.
—JULIE GARMON

My Daily Blessings

1 _____

2 _____

3 _____

4 _____

5 _____

6 _____

7 _____

8 _____

9 _____

10 _____

11 _____

12 _____

13 _____

14 _____

15 _____

16 _____

17 _____

18 _____

19 _____

20 _____

21 _____

22 _____

23 _____

24 _____

25 _____

26 _____

27 _____

28 _____

29 _____

30 _____

JULY

Blessed is the people that know the joyful
sound: they shall walk, O Lord, in
the light of thy countenance.
—Psalm 89:15

S	M	T	W	T	F	S
		1	2	3	4	5
6	7	8	9	10	11	12
13	14	15	16	17	18	19
20	21	22	23	24	25	26
27	28	29	30	31		

AN EYE FOR BLESSINGS

1/TUE   HUNGER FOR THE WORD
Seek and read from the book of the Lord. . . .

—ISAIAH 34:16 (RSV)

Before leaving the house this morning I picked up my grocery list and glanced at the calendar: "11:30, dentist." Better stick a paperback in my purse—there's always a wait. Better look up the phone number of that lampshade place, too.

An ordinary day . . . with an extraordinary gift in constant use. The gift of reading. So much a part of daily life, I usually accept it without thinking. But because this morning's newspaper had featured a story on illiteracy around the world, I found myself aware all day of this taken-for-granted skill: the street signs as I drove, the flyer of specials at the grocery store, the letters I scooped from the mailbox on my return, the e-mail waiting on my screen.

Reading is an essential component of daily existence, but also my daily joy! A morning without *Daily Guideposts* is an impoverished one, bedtime without a book unthinkable. Once my husband and I spent a week in a house where there was not a single book or magazine, not even a seed catalogue, though the family were farmers. So starved were we for anything in print, we found ourselves opening the kitchen cupboard and reading the labels on the cans.

Literacy—how much of the world is still without it! I remembered the day I brought a stack of nutrition leaflets to the school where I taught in Uganda. "Take them home to your parents," I urged the students. Next day the leaflets were still there; the kids explained with embarrassment that their parents could not read.

What does the gift of reading bestow? Information, ease of communication, the past and the present at the turning of a page, the knowledge of God. From the Jews comes our heritage of Holy Scripture—sacred writing, the Bible passages with which I begin each day. But sacred reading, too, without which even the greatest book of all is only little black marks on a page.

Lord Jesus, Who asked so often, "Have you not read?" guide my reading today. —ELIZABETH SHERRILL

*2/*WED *Watch and pray, that ye enter not into temptation: the spirit indeed is willing, but the flesh is weak.*
—MATTHEW 26:41

In the spring and summer, I often take the kids out into the courtyard garden of our apartment building while we're waiting for our laundry to dry. They play in a little house there while I weed. It's a pleasant way to pass the time, even when you're very pregnant and bending over is awkward.

A few weeks ago I noticed a rash on my wrist one evening after doing some gardening. I didn't think much about it until it began to worsen the next day. Then reality hit: poison ivy.

Our doctor suggested a few simple remedies; the blisters spread anyway. They itched ferociously. We entered into a major battle of wills, that poison ivy and I. During the day I was obsessed with not scratching it; at night I was awakened by the intensity of its itchiness. Rarely in my life have I been beset with such a clear and obvious temptation.

Oh, how I wanted to scratch! I wanted to scratch and scratch and scratch, to the point where I joked to a friend that if I ever let myself start, I'd end up scratching the baby right out of my belly. For by now my stomach, thighs and arms were bubbling with fierce, red patches of poison.

One night while I was up applying ice packs to some of the worse spots, it struck me that an obvious temptation, while intense, is in some ways easier to deal with than a subtle one. At least you can focus your attention on it, direct your will toward fighting it. I wondered how many temptations I succumb to simply because I don't recognize them as temptations. Probably a lot.

Yesterday I went to a dermatologist and got a prescription ointment. I'm seeing signs of improvement already. With two weeks to go until my due date, I continue to pray that the poison ivy will be gone before my baby is born. But I also have found a new topic that I need to pray about, now and always.

Dear Lord, open my eyes to the temptations that beset me. May I turn my face against them. —JULIA ATTAWAY

3/THU   *Verily, verily, I say unto you, If a man keep my saying, he shall never see death.* —JOHN 8:51

A friend who works in the movie industry called one day and asked if I would like two tickets for a preview of a film called *Death and Denial*. It doesn't take me long to accept anything for free, and Antonio, an artist, popped into my mind as someone who might like to see what was probably a serious foreign film. We met, went to the screening room and were in for a surprise. I hadn't heard correctly. It wasn't *Death and Denial*, but *Death on the Nile*, a Hercule Poirot mystery! We laughed and enjoyed the show anyhow.

Later, during dinner, Antonio was ruminating. "Suppose it had been *Death and Denial*? What do you think we would have seen?"

"An Italian film. Probably exploring some dour secret of eternal life," I quipped.

"Eternal life." The words seemed to spark an idea in him. "How wonderful it would be to have all that time! I'd paint and paint until I was really good at it." Then he turned very solemn. "I wonder," he said, eyes looking beyond me, "I wonder about eternity."

That was prophetic: Antonio Acosta died shortly after that. He was fifteen years younger than I—too young. In the ten years since his death, he has proven to be a "really good" painter; his pictures have sold well (I have several of them and can attest to their luminous cheerfulness). They will go on bringing pleasure to people after we are gone, which is eternal life on this earth. The real eternity, however, Antonio has found, I am sure, and it is beautiful.

Yes, Lord, eternity must be just that, a place that any painter would cherish. —VAN VARNER

A HERITAGE OF FREEDOM

4/FRI   THE JEFFERSON MEMORIAL
In you our fathers put their trust; they trusted and you delivered them.   —PSALM 22:4 (NIV)

One of the most difficult things I've faced living in Washington, D.C., these last few years has been being labeled a "religious" person. Somehow the "freedom of religion" that the framers of our Constitution wanted to preserve has evolved into a "freedom from religion" that leads to the exclusion of most things spiritual from all things governmental.

Among the words of Thomas Jefferson inscribed on the walls of the Jefferson Memorial are these: "God who gave us life gave us liberty. Can the liberties of a nation be secure when we have removed a conviction that those liberties are the gift of God?" As the author of the Declaration of Independence, with its appeal to the Creator as the ultimate source of human rights, Jefferson—perhaps in spite of himself—endowed our national beginnings with the idea that faith and freedom are inseparable partners.

In the wake of September 11, 2001, "God Bless America" was spontaneously sung at meetings and sporting events and even played at the end of some newscasts. It was as if our nation was awakening from the sleep of indifference and complacency into which our material success had lulled us. I wanted to be a part of it.

My chance came quickly. I was asked to lead in prayer before a breakfast meeting where prayer was, to say the least, unusual. One person present objected, and a growing murmur spread around the room. I simply quoted Jefferson and asked that we follow his example by acknowledging our liberty as a gift from God. The murmurs died, the prayer was said, and we continued in a recollected spirit.

Father, thank You for preserving this nation, and let us be united in honoring You through our love and respect for each other.
—ERIC FELLMAN

5/SAT   *Shall I come to you with a rod, or with love in a spirit of gentleness?*   —I CORINTHIANS 4:21 (RSV)

We were visiting my husband Paul's parents in Ohio, and Grandma thought we'd enjoy watching the Fourth of July parade in a neighboring town. But when we arrived, the main street was empty. She had misread the time of the parade in the newspaper, and we had missed it. All we could do was turn around and head home. My daughter Maria, who'd been jabbering to her brother like a typical six-year-old, didn't realize what had happened until Grandpa turned the car onto their street.

"We're going home?" Maria asked. "But what about the parade?"

"I goofed," Grandma answered, sounding sad and a little embarrassed. Nobody said anything. I knew that whatever happened next to fill the silence would set the mood for the entire day. *Help me say the right thing,* I prayed. Then an idea that didn't even take the time to pop into my head first popped out of my mouth: "Let's have our own parade."

Everyone jumped on the idea. "I'll drive the lawn mower, with Maria in the cart in back," said my twelve-year-old son Ross, running off. "I'll push Dan," Paul said, helping his big brother out of the car and into his wheelchair. "We need music," Paul's brother Tom said, heading to the garage and returning with an old plastic horn, a metal bucket and some sticks. "I'll get the camera," Grandpa said, while Grandma ran into the house and returned with a toy piano and a huge smile. Tom's wife Ann brought their dog Randy out on a leash, and I grabbed the big American flag from the front porch to carry myself. We marched our horn-blowing, bucket-banging parade around the neighborhood, laughing and waving, bringing neighbors out to cheer and laugh with us.

Later, I wondered how many of those decisive moments I have faced unawares, especially when someone's feelings were involved. I can't always control what happens, but I can control how I react when things don't turn out right. By bringing love instead of scorn, and with the help of God's joyful Spirit, I can do more than make the best of it—I can have a parade.

Lord, help me to think first, then speak with Your wisdom, Your joy and Your love. —GINA BRIDGEMAN

6/SUN *"For it shall be given you in that hour what you are to speak."* —MATTHEW 10:19 (NAS)

It certainly wasn't much by American standards, but for these poor kids from the slums of Mexico City, it was a treat! Four days at a luxury resort, every day packed with games, plenty of food, a swimming pool and Bible teaching.

I helped at the camp as a part of a summer missions trip to Mexico with my church. A girl my own age named Nora and I had quickly developed a friendship. One hot, sticky evening as the campers were preparing for bed, Nora approached me with our team's translator. For a while, we just talked about the camp, but then Nora turned serious and said she was "different from the other kids." Unsure exactly how to respond to such an unusual statement, I waited for her to continue.

Nora said something in Spanish that made her and the translator begin to cry.

"Last year, I was raped," the translator finally said. "I became pregnant, but four months later the baby died."

At a total loss for words, I just sat there and looked at her. After some time, the translator said, "She wants you to tell her what you think."

This comment hit me like a ton of bricks. I was just an average teenager from America. What advice could I possibly offer?

I excused myself to the cabin, where my dad, who was also on my team, was reading the Bible. I explained the situation to him and told him how utterly helpless I felt. "We need to pray," he said, so together we asked God to give me the words to say, the words Nora needed to hear.

A few minutes later I emerged and sat back down with Nora and the translator. "I can't understand how hard this is for you," I said. I told her that no matter what happened, God would still love her. I told her God still thought she was beautiful no matter what had happened.

Looking back, I'll never really know if my words helped Nora, but I will always remember how much God helped me.

Lord, thank You for giving me the words to say when I need to say them. —JOSHUA SUNDQUIST

$7/$MON   *Be content with such things as ye have. . . .*
—HEBREWS 13:5

I grew up with dogs, lots of dogs. My father was a hunter and liked to keep several hunting companions, especially beagles. He often bred them and sold the puppies, sometimes keeping the pick of the litter for himself. His favorite, Cyclone, had just given birth, and the puppies were beautiful: big, healthy, playful and keen on sniffing out everything in their paths.

"Time to sell these," Daddy said to me one night as I poured fresh water into their bowls. "We need to put an ad in the paper."

"I'll write it!" I volunteered. I had dreams of being published someday, and the classifieds seemed a good place to start. I wrote several drafts of the ad; the final version went to great lengths expounding on the virtues of the pups, predicting what fine hunting dogs they would become and even mentioning how happy they would make their future owner.

When I had finished the ad and read it aloud to Daddy, he was quiet for a long time. Then he looked at me and, with perfect sincerity, said, "Tear up that ad, Mary Lou. I've wanted dogs like that all my life!"

O God, You are the giver of every perfect gift. Open our eyes to the wonders and riches in our lives that we may have overlooked. —MARY LOU CARNEY

8/TUE   *"His lamp shone over my head, And by His light I walked through darkness."*   —JOB 29:3 (NAS)

TOUR A COAL MINE! The billboard fairly shouted as we drove along Canada's east coast. "Can we, Mom? Can we?" The two youngest kids, ages nine and ten at the time, were game to do anything that held even a hint of adventure.

"Oh, I suppose we could," I replied without really thinking about it.

The grizzled old coal miner who acted as our guide that day handed each tourist a waterproof cape and helped us adjust the lights on our miners' helmets. As we rattled down underground in the steel cage of an elevator, the guide proceeded to fill us in on the gory details of every disaster that had ever occurred in this particular mine. I was already shuddering when the elevator cage jolted to a stop at the bottom of the shaft. "Okay, everybody, turn the lights out on your helmets, so you can experience how dark a coal mine really is!"

The darkness was impenetrable. "Gee, Mom, I can't even tell if my eyes are open or not!" our son exclaimed. Nor could I. We stood for a moment experiencing the absolute absence of all light: pitch blackness. Scary, real scary. And cold, clammy cold.

"Okay, you can turn your lights on now and come this way." As I squinted into the shadows, the beam of light from my miner's helmet caught the fluorescent heels of the running shoes worn by the tall tourist ahead of me. By bending my head just so, I could follow in his steps, while he, in turn, focused on the guide. Playing "follow the leader" spared me from succumbing to my absolute worst fear—being left alone in the twists and turns of that pitch-dark mine shaft.

The tour over, we squeezed back into the elevator cage. I held my breath as it creaked and groaned its way to the surface.

"That was neat, huh, Mom?" exclaimed our son. "What did you like best?"

"The fellow's shoes who walked ahead of me," I replied.

Father God, thank You for those whose lives are so focused on You that I can safely follow in their steps. And thank You for offering to be the guiding light to us all.   —ALMA BARKMAN

*9/*WED   *Incline thine ear unto wisdom, and apply thine heart to understanding.*   —PROVERBS 2:2

I am devoted to a form of aerobic insanity known as spinning, a heart-pounding, leg-pumping, sweat-drenched stationary bike workout set to loud, thumping music. I take a class a day, as many as four hundred spin hours a year. Some people jog, some people stretch, some people walk the mall. I spin.

The other night I rushed from the office and slipped into a popular spin room at my gym to stake out a good bike before I changed into my biking gear. I heard some people in the back of the spin room giggle, and I thought I heard the name Mark or Clark. I tied my towel to the handle bars of the bike I favored, dashed into the locker room to change clothes and raced back into class just as the instructor was cranking up the music. Before long I was huffing and puffing and groaning, pedaling up simulated mountain terrain, doing sprints and jumps and surges, pushing my heart rate to ninety percent of maximum.

Afterward, I stopped by the juice bar for a bottle of water. Again the giggles started. *What's up with these people?* I wondered.

Finally a woman spoke. "Know what your nickname is?" she asked.

"I didn't know I had one," I said, fighting off embarrassment.

"You run in there in your suit and tie and glasses, then reappear a minute later and ride your bike like Superman or something. We always say, 'Look out, here comes Clark Kent!'"

All right, I had to laugh. In fact, we all had a pretty good laugh.

Maybe I am a little serious about my exercise, and I guess it shows sometimes by the way I behave. But I don't really think of myself as Clark Kent, and I know I'm no Superman. I can get carried away with my spinning, though. It's probably not a good idea to be so overwhelmingly focused on something. I'm going to remember that, thanks to my spinning friends.

Lord, let me remember where the real focus must always remain—on You.   —EDWARD GRINNAN

10/THU

He who loves money shall never have enough. The foolishness of thinking that wealth brings happiness!
—ECCLESIASTES 5:10 (TLB)

After I quit my job at the radio station in 1992 to work at home full-time as a freelance writer, a number of people suggested that I get a real job when times got tough financially for me.

"You should be a salesperson. You've got the personality for it. And think of the money you could make!" one friend suggested. "Why don't you consider teaching? Or, at the very least, you could be a substitute teacher. They make good money," another offered.

All good suggestions, but I've learned that the paycheck isn't nearly as important as the satisfaction I get from doing my work and living my life. My daily commute takes me approximately twenty seconds, from my bedroom to my office downstairs. No traffic to fight. No stress. If I feel like going for a bike ride at eleven o'clock in the morning, I go. If a friend stops by for tea, I'm thrilled with the company, knowing I can catch up on my work later. If I feel like sitting on the deck for an hour in the middle of the day with a good book, I do it. If I want to spend an extra twenty minutes pondering a perplexing Proverb, nobody's there to insist I "get back to work."

I'll probably never make enough money to be called rich. But I hope to have had a happy, content and fulfilling life with plenty of time for the important stuff.

Tea, anyone?

Lord, thank You for this simple life of great abundance. A plethora of friends, time to enjoy them, no stress and a career I love. Help me to hang on to this simple, happy lifestyle.
—PATRICIA LORENZ

11/FRI

And He said to them, "Come away by your-selves to a lonely place and rest a while." . . . .—MARK 6:31 (NAS)

I wonder if youngsters still have "hidey-holes" as my friends and I did when we were growing up. A hidey-hole, of course, was a spot that was yours alone.

My hidey-hole was an opening—the size of a coat closet but only half as high—left in a thick hedge where a small juniper had died. It was furnished with a chair (the dead juniper's stump), a table (an upside-down apple crate) and a cupboard (another apple crate, this one stood on end). It was my own secret spot, a place to retreat to when I felt sorry for myself, a place to dream of a handsome prince on a white horse who'd carry me to his castle.

When I outgrew the hedge cranny, my hidey-hole changed. One year, it was my bedroom. Another year, it was my folks' car; I'd hop in and drive to a quiet destination. Each provided solace when I worried about upcoming tests or a fuss with a boyfriend or the reason for my existence on this planet.

It makes me wonder if anyone else remembers a favorite hidey-hole—a spot to be alone or to share with a special friend; a place to think, to read, to nap, where no one sees you. It also makes me wonder if Jesus had a particular hidey-hole in mind when He invited His disciples to come with Him to a secluded place. Probably they—like me—often felt the pressure of their daily duties, or suffocated by the presence of too many people, or overwhelmed by financial burdens. Probably they—like all of us—needed a quiet place to pray.

Dear Lord, will You join me in my hidey-hole? I feel the need to be alone with You. —ISABEL WOLSELEY

*12/*SAT *The lines are fallen unto me in pleasant places; yea, I have a goodly heritage.* —PSALM 16:6

Last summer I spent two nights in Red Wing, Minnesota, the sleepy Midwestern town where my mother grew up in the 1920s and '30s. My room in the historic St. James Hotel overlooked Levee Park, which hugs a bend in the Mississippi River.

My mother had often talked about her grandmother's visits to Red Wing. Grandmother Helene would sit for hours near the river's edge in Levee Park, staring across the water. She had emigrated from Norway's breathtaking fjord country to the prairie of South Dakota, and I suppose she never lost her longing for the sparkle and dance of water.

On my last morning in Red Wing, I was able to sit down on a bench in Levee Park, Bible in hand, for some solitary reflection. A young man approached me and asked if he could play his trumpet at a nearby picnic table. "Fine with me," I told him, "if you'll play a tune for me." Perhaps he had noticed my open Bible, because as the rich round notes rolled from his horn and sailed out across the water, I heard the old hymn "Blessed Assurance."

The young trumpeter knew nothing about my Great-Grandmother Helene or her faith in Christ. But his song evoked for me the image of a short, plump lady, her hair caught in a neat white bun, with a faraway look in her eyes as she gazed at the river in this very place, and offered her prayers to the Lord.

I felt a deep peace. "Blessed assurance, Jesus is mine." My Great-Grandmother Helene knew it to be true and, some seventy years later, so did I.

Loving God, may the praises of my Savior come through me to my children's children's children. —CAROL KNAPP

13/SUN *If ye have faith as a grain of mustard seed ... nothing shall be impossible unto you.* —MATTHEW 17:20

During the summer, wild mustard grows freely along the roadsides in Wyoming. Narrow pale green foliage and dainty yellow flowers give it an airy, delicate appearance. Even by late July, when many other species have shriveled and died, the mustard continues to thrive in broiling heat and sandy soil. Sometimes it even sprouts from cracks in the pavement.

After sidestepping a particularly dense mustard plant that was crowding me off the sidewalk one summer evening, I remembered the necklace I had worn as a child: a spherical glass pendant that encased a tiny mustard seed. It had fascinated me, and I decided to share the miracle of the mustard seed with my fifth-grade religious education students. All I needed was a Bible and a box from my spice cabinet.

Once my class was settled, I gave each child a mustard seed and listened.

"What is it?"

"I think it's from a pickle jar."

"What does it do?"

One student dropped the seed on the floor and rooted around searching for it. Another bit into the seed with eye-watering results.

After a few minutes I asked the children to look up Matthew 17:20, the memory verse for the week. We opened our Bibles and read aloud. Somewhere a brain-bulb flashed on.

"Hey! It's a mustard seed!"

"Mustard hasn't got seeds!"

"Sure is little."

I pointed out that the bushy mustard plants in the nearby pasture had grown from seeds like these. "Hold your mustard seed. Look at it again, boys and girls. This is all the faith you need to move mountains."

There was silence. The clock ticked and ticked.

Someone whispered, "Wow!"

"That's all? Just that much?"

"Totally awesome."

Totally awesome, indeed.

Lord of Creation, thank You for giving me little things to help me understand the big ones. —GAIL THORELL SCHILLING

14/MON   *O Lord my God, in thee do I put my trust. . . .*
—PSALM 7:1

My friend Toni Eames is blind, and she gets around very well with the aid of her guide dog Escort, a handsome golden retriever. Last summer they were in Philadelphia for a conference, so we made a date for lunch.

I met them at their hotel room, where I had a chance to play with Escort for a few minutes. But as soon as Toni put his harness on, he was all business. "Find the elevator," Toni said as she opened the door to the hallway. Without hesitation, Escort led us to the elevator and lifted his head up to the buttons so that Toni could press the correct one.

Outside, in the busiest part of the city, the sun was shining and the sidewalks were filled with people. As we passed under a long arcade connecting the buildings on two streets, I saw that some construction work was in progress. A long hose zigzagged along the sidewalk and huge trash bins were everywhere. Toni walked comfortably alongside Escort and talked as she went, but I became concerned for her safety. I wondered how Escort could possibly guide her through such an obstacle course.

"Toni," I said, slowing down, "do you want to take my arm? There are a lot of things in our way."

Toni stopped and smiled at me. "No, I'll be fine. Escort knows what to do. Besides, I never tell him which way to go. I trust him to make the right decision."

And he certainly did. He guided Toni away from the trash bins and alerted her to the hose so that she could step over it. As Toni went on talking, I began to calm down and depend on Escort, too, and it was a very comfortable feeling. In the midst of so many cars and people going every which way, we were being safely led.

No matter where I am, Lord, I know that You are always with me. All I need to do is follow You.   —PHYLLIS HOBE

FOLLOWING JESUS

15/TUE SPEAKING THE SPECIAL LANGUAGE OF THE HEART

"The good man out of the good treasure of his heart brings forth what is good . . . for his mouth speaks from that which fills his heart."   —LUKE 6:45 (NAS)

A friend had died and I'd gone to the funeral home to pay my respects. In a corner, I noticed a boy sitting all alone. "That's the son of the man who died," I heard someone say. "He's deaf. He's taking his daddy's death harder than anyone."

My heart broke for the boy, all lost in a world of his own. I walked over to him and took his hand, hoping he could read my lips as I tried to tell him how very sorry I was. He nodded politely, but I knew I hadn't really reached him.

Then as I was leaving, an elderly gentleman entered the room, and as he walked toward him, the boy's face lit up in recognition. Immediately, the two began communicating in sign language. The boy's hands flew, unable to get the words out fast enough, as if he were tripping over them at the joy of having someone who at long last truly understood him.

Thinking back, I recalled seeing the gentleman at a church I once visited where he heads a ministry for the deaf. I had observed him translating a sermon, but I'd never had the chance to watch him one-on-one, speaking the very language of a grieving boy's heart and turning isolation and pain into love and belonging.

Jesus, help me to speak Your language of love.

—ROBERTA MESSNER

READER'S ROOM

Being a flutist is great fun, and so is going up to the nearby Tule Reservation with the Mobil Aglow Lighthouse. The Tule hold the drum and its beat in high regard; it accompanies their traditional chants and dances. On one of my visits, a Native American picked up a rawhide-covered drum and a fleece-covered mallet, and started drumming a beat. Intrigued, I picked up my flute (and later my piccolo!) and started to play notes around her beat. The dancing notes and the resounding drumbeats intertwined, becoming a lively song. One aglow lady started to dance, and the rest of our friends listened with enjoyment. At that moment we became one in the Spirit—two cultures meeting together in the song.

—REBECCA ANN MURRAY, PORTERVILLE, CALIFORNIA

16/ WED *He will turn again, he will have compassion upon us . . . and thou wilt cast all their sins into the depths of the sea.* —MICAH 7:19

I am on the beach in Avalon, New Jersey, trying to tune in my new hand-cranked radio. It's a gorgeous day, the kind you pray for the week before vacation. My kids are in the surf—a distracting little fact for a man trying to tune a radio.

"Daddy, c'mon in," Faith says.

"In a minute," I call to her. I find that if I hold my finger to the dial I can hear bits of Bonnie Raitt.

"Dad, are you coming?" Hope calls.

"In a minute, okay?" I call back, sounding cross. Bonnie comes and goes, replaced by the news, fading in and out, like a shorthand telegram: *Middle East . . . Jerusalem . . . trouble. . . .*

"Daddy . . ." Grace starts.

"In a minute, I said!"

And that, ladies and gentlemen, sums up my relationship with the Almighty. I can't seem to tune in God. I have been given vast gifts—wonderful, curious children; a job that allows vacations; and this earth, "our island home," as *The Book of Common Prayer* says. And my reply to these divine gifts is consternation. Instead of enjoying what's in front of me, I try to find God the way I try to find a radio station, wondering how to make sense of the voices coming in from thin air. Meanwhile, the inquisitive, playful voices of my own children—my own hymns from heaven—go unheeded.

I'm sure there's more to this metaphor—something about gratitude, I'll bet, and something about spiritual recognition along the lines of the disciples on the road to Emmaus, unable to recognize Jesus—but you'll have to excuse me. I'm wanted elsewhere—no doubt for a frantic game of Dunk Daddy, who very much needs to be re-baptized in this ancient, eternal, endless sea.

Lord, on the days when my spirit can only hear static, help me hold on to the clear signals of Your presence. —MARK COLLINS

17 / THU *Tell them how great things the Lord hath done for thee. . . .* —MARK 5:19

My friend Cheri and I do walk-talks together five mornings a week. It provides us both with the regular exercise we need and a chance to share whatever is going on in our lives. Almost every time, our shared processing of life events brings insight, and we both leave feeling a little wiser than before. But early last week, I was in one of those everything's-going-wrong moods, so Cheri let me talk. I ended up listing all my problems and complaining about them.

I follow our walks with my morning prayer time, so when I got home, I sat in my blue prayer chair by the window and opened a little book titled *Safe within Your Love* by Hannah W. Smith. My reading ended with this prayer:

My Father, help me to notice what I say to others about the challenges spread before me. Do I tell them, "I have such great problems"? Or do I say, despite my problems, "I know a great God"?

Suddenly, all of those problems that my mind had magnified clicked into proper perspective as I offered them to my all-powerful heavenly Father. After prayer time, I called Cheri and apologized for my problem-listing monologue. Then I said, "It's been awhile since we've talked about our relationship with God. Let's put that on the agenda for tomorrow!" It's been the subject of our walk-talks all week, and we're both feeling enriched.

Loving Father, let my problems be reminders that now *is the perfect time to tell a friend, "I know a great God."*

—MARILYN MORGAN KING

18/FRI   It is not good to have zeal without knowledge, nor to be hasty and miss the way.   —PROVERBS 19:2 (NIV)

The office phone had rung at 11:30 that morning. "Honey," my wife Julia had said, "I think you'd better come home. My water just broke." Now, after a half-hour cab ride, I was at our apartment in upper Manhattan.

"Julia, I'm home!" I called as I unlocked the door. There was no answer.

Maybe she went to the hospital, I thought. *But where are the kids?* Julia had told me she was calling our friend Loretta to come and stay with them while we were at the hospital, but there was no sign of Loretta either.

She wouldn't have gone without leaving me a note. But there was no note on the dining room table or on the refrigerator. My puzzlement was turning into worry. *What if something went wrong?*

I sat down and tried to think. *Julia said she'd ask one of the neighbors to keep the kids if she had to leave in a hurry. Now which one was it?* I wasn't having any luck remembering. Worry was threatening to turn into panic when the apartment door opened.

There were Julia, Elizabeth, John and Mary. "Hi, honey," Julia said. "How did you get home so fast?"

"I took a cab," I answered. "Where have you been? Why didn't you tell me you were going out?"

"We were across the street at school lunch when my water broke. I took the kids back there. They hadn't eaten their lunch yet."

"But why didn't you leave me a note?"

"I didn't expect you home so soon. I thought you'd be taking the subway."

"But—but—the baby—your water—" I gave up, astonished that my practical wife couldn't imagine me rushing home in a cab to be at her side.

Loretta arrived a few minutes later, and Julia and I walked—her idea—the mile to the hospital. The baby was in no hurry to be born, so it wasn't until eleven that night that we finally got to meet Maggie, our nine pound, one ounce beautiful Margaret Therese.

Lord, when I jump to conclusions, please break my fall. And thank You for nervous fathers and levelheaded moms and children who eat their lunches, and especially for new babies.

—ANDREW ATTAWAY

19/SAT   *Cast thy burden upon the Lord, and he shall sustain thee....*   —PSALM 55:22

Our youngest son Daniel's latest conquest was a triathlon. Two years before, he had completed the New York City Marathon, and he trained just as long and as hard for this competition. But unlike a marathon, which is running more than 26 miles, a triathlon requires athletes to swim 1.2 miles, bicycle 56 miles and run 13 miles in succession.

"How in the world can you complete the course with no rest between races?" I asked Daniel.

"You just focus on one thing at a time," he replied. "Don't think about bicycling while you're swimming, or running while you're bicycling." His strategy apparently worked, because he finished the race in less than six hours, midway in a field of more than six hundred competitors.

Daniel's comment about taking things one event at a time reminded me that we all have our limits. When we try to do more than our minds or bodies can tolerate, we suffer the consequences. Fortunately, we don't have to run, swim and bike through life all by ourselves. As the old hymn assures us, "He will make a way for you and will lead you safely through."

Lord, when in Your name we bite off more than we can chew,
Give us strength to go on and the wisdom to lean on You.

—FRED BAUER

20/SUN *And God saw every thing that he had made,*
and, behold, it was very good. . . . —GENESIS 1:31

One summer Sunday morning I took my Sunday school class of first- and second-graders to our church's spectacular flower garden. Tucked away behind the church, the garden has fragrant roses, marigolds, petunias, zinnias, nasturtiums and lavender. We trudged across a carpet of grass to a picnic table under an old shade tree. I handed the two boys and six girls paper and pencil.

"I want you to go into the garden with a partner and choose a flower. Write something about it. What is its shape? Is it tall or short? What is its smell? What does it remind you of? Then come back and we'll compare what you've found." My aim was to spark a wonder in them at the variety and beauty of God's creation.

The girls spread out into the flowers like butterflies, giggling and comparing. The boys, Turner and Gregory, got no farther than the grass. I watched them plop down just out of earshot and talk as if they were in a two-man huddle. Knowing their penchant for sports, I was sure that baseball, not flowers, was their topic.

After the allotted time was up, I summoned them back to the picnic table. "I think we'll let Turner and Gregory go first," I said.

"We picked a clover flower," Gregory said. *A clover!* It never occurred to me to call such a lost-in-the-grass thing a flower.

"What did you write about it?" I asked.

"We thought it looked like a ballerina," Turner said.

"The wind is its music," added Gregory.

Creator God, help me to stop underestimating Your children and
the other works of Your hands. —SHARI SMYTH

THE WALLS OF CUMBRIA

John Sherrill and his wife Tib recently spent a week in England's Lake District, known for its sheep-covered hills, its daffodils celebrated by William Wordsworth, its picture-book villages like Hawkshead, setting for Beatrix Potter's Peter Rabbit stories. What most interested John, however, were the walls. From the first day of their visit, John was captivated by the stone walls that enclosed every field, lined every roadway and public footpath. Soon, John says, the walls began to speak to him. . . .

—THE EDITORS

21/MON   DAY ONE: MR. TOWNSEND
For the Lord seeth not as man seeth. . . .   —I SAMUEL 16:7

Every morning the "breakfast" part of our bed-and-breakfast here in the Lake District consists of a rasher of bacon, two fried eggs, fried toast, a rack of dry toast, butter, orange marmalade, beans, mushrooms, a broiled tomato and coffee. And every morning, in repentance, Tib and I walk to the village of Hawkshead, some forty-five minutes away.

We follow public footpaths that wander down lanes and cross farmers' fields. Most of the way, the footpaths are hedged with stone walls. My mind struggles to imagine the work involved, each rock rooted out of the fields, hauled to the fence line, hoisted into place. When I mentioned the walls to our B&B landlady, she said, "Then you'll want to meet Mr. Townsend. He's patching a wall just down the road."

Next morning, as Tib and I followed a chest-high wall, we heard the unmistakable *tap-tap* of a mason's hammer on the other side.

After a moment, a dust-covered cap appeared, then a pair of blue eyes and then the torso of a wizened man covered with stone dust. Mr. Townsend seemed pleased to be asked about his trade. "I've been building walls since I was a lad," he said. "Helped Dad clear the pastures." As a teenager he was apprenticed to a mason. Most walls were built by local farmers, Mr. Townsend said, though they usually needed help from real wall-men like himself. "Not everybody gets to work on walls all year round like I do," he said. "For a farmer, walls are winter work."

After a quarter of an hour, Mr. Townsend signaled that he had to get back to work by bending (straight-backed, I noticed) to pick up a large fieldstone. As he did so, he said something that has changed the way I look at the "stones" in my own work—interruptions, time pressure, an aging body.

"Our fields are full of rocks," he said, gesturing toward the pasture behind him. "But . . ."—and here Mr. Townsend settled the huge fieldstone into place—"the good Lord helps us turn these stones into something useful, doesn't He!"

Father, help me to see the obstacles in my life as building material. —JOHN SHERRILL

22/TUE DAY TWO: THROUGH STONES

For [Jesus] was in all points tempted like as we are, yet without sin. —HEBREWS 4:15

Today, Tib and I found Mr. Townsend pouring a cup of tea from his Thermos. It takes a farmer an entire day, he told us between sips, to build three feet of waist-high wall. The problem is, he must use the material at hand: small stones, large stones, round stones, flat stones, gravel from some ancient river.

I looked more closely at the wall Mr. Townsend was working on, noticing a single course of flat stones about halfway up. Thicker than the rest, they stuck out a couple of inches from the face of the wall.

"Come round here," Mr. Townsend invited when I asked about them. I stepped through the gap he was repairing and saw that the large stones went all the way through the wall.

"Those are *tra*verse stones," Mr. Townsend said, stressing the first syllable. He explained that stone fences were often built by first constructing two thin parallel walls with space between to act as a bin for disposing of pebbles and rock fragments collected from the fields. These aggregate-filled fences did not have the strength of walls made entirely of large rock.

"That's where traverse stones are needed," said Mr. Townsend. "They reach right through the small rocks all the way to the other side. The pebbles lean on the traverse stones, not just on each other, and the wall stands."

You build Your church, Father, not only with rocklike saints but with the men and women at hand—the pebbles of Your world. When stresses come, help me lean on the traverse stone of Jesus.
—JOHN SHERRILL

23/WED   DAY THREE: WALLFLOWERS
They answered, "We have only five loaves of bread and two fish. . . ."   —LUKE 9:13 (NIV)

Today, our walk took us past a sunlit wall that made us stop, delighted, every few feet. Growing between the somber stones was a profusion of delicate flowering plants: tiny hanging bouquets, clinging to the walls with blossoms smaller than my little fingernail, a lavish display of purple, yellow, orange, blue.

Even bending close, I couldn't detect the soil in which the plants had taken root. Infinitesimal specks of dust must have blown into crevices, to be seized on by wind-sowed seeds. A dot of soil, a drop of dew in the morning, was enough for these splendid creations to unfold their beauty.

Our walk this morning was no way to work off an English breakfast, but it did teach me something about provision. How often I worry that my talent or time or money is too little for the job at hand, when God has provided just what I need.

Never let me underestimate, Father, the resources of Your unfailing grace.
—JOHN SHERRILL

24/*THU* DAY FOUR: LICHEN

We have different gifts, according to the grace given us. . . .

—ROMANS 12:6 (NIV)

Today, Tib and I stopped to admire a garden very different from
the wildflower bouquets we enjoyed yesterday. On the gray stones
in front of us was a flat patchwork of subtle color—gold, gray,
black, white, rust, chartreuse.

"Lichen!" I said to myself.

When I was a boy, we kids called lichen "rock fuzz." Later on, in
college, I gained a lot of respect for this humble-looking life form.
I learned that lichen is not a single organism but a mutually dependent relationship between two totally unrelated living things, fungus
and algae. The fungus establishes the secure foothold that the algae
require and hoards the needed moisture. The algae convert the
sun's energy into food for them both. Together they colonized the
barren rocks of the early earth, life's first beachhead on land,
preparing the way for all that followed.

Interdependence. I looked at the wall before us, the hard,
unyielding stones, and then at this hardy pioneer, linking very different needs and abilities to do the impossible. And I thought I had
a glimpse of the body of Christ at work, each member depending
on others with different contributions, each an image of the one
Lord.

*Father, help me to rejoice in our differences. Those most unlike
me may be the ones I need most.* —JOHN SHERRILL

25/*FRI* DAY FIVE: WEEP HOLES

Jesus wept. —JOHN 11:35

Most of the walls we saw on our morning walks were constructed
of fieldstone, left in its original raw condition. But for some reason
lost in history, one tall wall outside the village had been made differently. Cement had been troweled between the stones, and the
hole had been plastered over to present a smooth white surface.
Here and there small holes appeared in the elegant wall, their
regular pattern testifying to the fact that they were left there on
purpose.

"Weep holes," said Mr. Townsend when I saw him next, putting down his mallet. "Water collects behind the plaster. If it weren't for them holes, the water would sit there out of sight, building up pressure until it'd just burst through. Ruins everything."

Weep holes. One of the surprises of becoming a Christian is that it's okay to cry. Tears, I have found, were one of God's most valuable gifts. He knows my tendency to plaster over sadness until the built-up pressure causes me to explode. But to this day the gift of weeping allows me to release the pent-up strain before it does damage.

Father, Jesus' own tears give us the model we can follow to show honestly just how we feel. —JOHN SHERRILL

26/*SAT* Day Six: Step Stones
Jesus withdrew. . . . —MARK 3:7

Talking with Mr. Townsend on our last day in the Lake District, I remembered a boyhood disaster.

We lived in the humid Ohio River Valley, where summer temperatures hover in the high nineties and air conditioning was still in the future. Hot though my father's study was, when he worked on a book, he couldn't use a fan or even open the window very wide because his research was organized on scraps of paper spread neatly over several tables.

One breezy afternoon I burst into his office without thinking. The open door created a cross draft that sent every slip of paper flying. I will never forget the dismay on my father's face as he looked at the weeks of work undone in a careless second. That day a handwritten note went up on his door: "Come in . . . but knock first."

Lake District farmers do a similar thing. Their stone drywalls, the heavy work of weeks or months, are surprisingly fragile. The law allows hikers to cross farmers' fields using designated public footpaths, but climbing walls can knock stones loose, destroying the wall.

For centuries, walkers and landowners have coexisted peacefully because the farmer has learned to build four or five extra rocks into his wall at crossing points. Jutting out just enough, they create a stone staircase on either side of the wall.

"Those are our step stones," said Mr. Townsend. "They're a farmer's way of saying, 'You are welcome, but do respect my wall.'"

How often in my own life do I find a tension between my need for private space and the desire to be hospitable. Step stones echo the lesson of my childhood: my needs and other people's are both valid, both worth protecting.

Teach me, Father, to build step stones into my day.

—JOHN SHERRILL

27/SUN *And they continued stedfastly in the apostles' doctrine and fellowship, and in breaking of bread, and in prayers.* —ACTS 2:42

For as long as I can remember, I've gone to church on Sunday mornings. As a little girl, I enjoyed sitting in the small Methodist church in Iowa (and later in Michigan) where my father was the pastor, hearing his gentle voice recount the stories of the Bible to the congregation. I'd listen to him say the Lord's Prayer as I sat between my brother and my mother. Every now and then, I'd wiggle in the pew as children often do, until my mother's soft hand would tap my knee and my father's tender glance would come my way from his big pulpit. I loved sitting with my family, looking up at the stained-glass windows and listening to the hymns. Church was the cornerstone of our family and our faith.

Then, in college, I met Norman Vincent Peale. For three years, while we dated, I spent a lot of time in church, and it didn't let up after we were married either—after all, he did have to be in church every Sunday to preach!

Norman and I had the great joy of raising our three children with a deep respect and appreciation for the church. They, in turn, have raised their children to recognize that regular worship services and fellowship are staples of positive, fruitful living. And now, in my nineties, church is still a vital part of my life.

Why not look for new ways to get involved in your church's outreach? And if you don't currently have a church home, look for one where you'll be comfortable, where you can be surrounded by other believers looking for a deeper spiritual life and where you can serve your community. You'll find it makes a great difference in your life and in the lives of those around you.

Lord, thank You for the rich gifts You have given me as I have come to worship You, Sunday after Sunday.

—RUTH STAFFORD PEALE

28/MON

O death, where is thy sting? O grave, where is thy victory?

—I CORINTHIANS 15:55

My mother died on the sixth floor of the hospital early on a July morning. Her death wasn't an easy one, and as my husband Gene and I left the hospital, an old saying invaded my mind: "Death makes amateurs of us all."

Maybe so, I thought, *but doesn't the Bible promise victory for believers?*

When our minister and his wife came to visit shortly after Mother's death, their seven-year-old daughter Bethany, who had been in my Sunday school class, chose to come along with them. When I stooped down to hug Bethany and take the sympathy card she had painted for me, a thought occurred to me. "I have all my mother's jewelry out in the garage," I told her. "Would you like to look through it and select some things?"

Bethany nodded, and soon she was settled down on the cement floor of the garage, carefully sorting through the big box of necklaces and earrings. "May I have some for Avie, too?" she asked. Avie, Bethany's best friend, had also been in my Sunday school class.

"Sure," I said. Bethany left that day clutching a large plastic storage bag full of Mother's things.

I was surprised but overjoyed to see both Avie and Bethany at Mother's funeral with their parents. Dressed in their Sunday clothes, they both gave me long hugs. As I stooped down, Bethany's mother leaned over and whispered, "Check out the earrings, Marion." Both girls proudly pulled back their long hair, and there, dangling at eye level, were two pairs of Mother's earrings! "Ear bobs," she'd called them.

"We thought it would be special, and that your mother would have liked us to wear these," Avie whispered.

I smiled—a huge, victorious smile!

Father, You show up and do the most astonishing things just when I need You the most! —MARION BOND WEST

29/TUE *And we urge you, brothers, warn those who are idle, encourage the timid, help the weak, be patient with everyone.* —I THESSALONIANS 5:14 (NIV)

This morning I was working, racing to beat the clock of a self-imposed deadline. I had just poured a cup of hot tea when the telephone rang. Knowing my tea would grow cold and my concentration be broken by the interruption, I impatiently grabbed the receiver and barked a gruff hello. Stifling a groan, I recognized who was calling me: a long-winded and cranky old widow, living alone, desperate to talk to someone.

At first I did not listen to her due to my own irritation. Professional courtesy kept me in line, but my heart was not in the conversation. Slowly, however, I got beyond the word of idle talk—mostly about flowers and the need for rain—and started listening to her voice. Her voice told a different story: a tale of loneliness and isolation and grief.

God's Spirit began to nudge me. *Listening for a few minutes is more important than your own agenda,* the Spirit urged. *You can brew another pot of tea, and your work can wait.* It was true. What was most important was a narrow window of time when a soul was exposed and a tongue held captive by grief was ready to talk.

Dear God, I am not a patient person. Give me Your gentle compassion this day. Amen. —SCOTT WALKER

30/WED *And let them have dominion . . . over every creeping thing that creepeth upon the earth.* —GENESIS 1:26

"Your dog has bone cancer in his right front leg," the vet told us gently as we stood together in a small examining room, stroking our seven-year-old golden retriever Boaz. "His best chance for survival is to amputate the leg."

There it was: the news we'd been dreading. And now we faced a difficult choice that I also dreaded. As I wiped tears from my eyes, I pictured Boaz running through the fields near our house where we went on our evening walks, a routine that's as much a part of my day as his.

"We have to give him a chance," I said to my husband Lynn. "He's part of our family." Lynn agreed, and so we left Boaz there for the operation early the next morning. Two days later, we picked up our precious tripod dog, who came hopping out, wagging his tail and wearing a colorful T-shirt that covered up his scar.

That was seven months ago. Boaz has healed pretty well, and though he can't run the way he could before, we're making the most of our time together. Still, we get mixed reactions, especially when we go on our walks. "What happened to his leg?" people ask. Most of the time, I simply say, "He had bone cancer." I can tell from their faces whether they think we did the right thing.

But while walking through the field on a recent summer evening, an elderly gentleman put things into perspective when Boaz hopped over to him, wagging his tail. "What happened, buster?" the man asked gently, reaching down to stroke Boaz with a weathered hand.

I told him and added, "We don't know what's ahead, but I do know he's having a doggone good summer."

"I'm sure you are, too," the man said with a kindly smile. "And I reckon that's what matters most to both of you."

Lord, thank You for nudges of the heart that help us make choices for the precious animals that You place in our care.
—CAROL KUYKENDALL

31 / THU   *Here am I; send me.*   —ISAIAH 6:8

The early morning light fell softly on the streets of downtown Harare. I breathed deeply. The smell of burning coal oil reminded me that even though it was midsummer back home in Tennessee, it was winter here in Zimbabwe.

A few months back I had received a letter from a Presbyterian missionary: "We're praying that you will come and write about the street-children of Africa." At first I had tossed the letter aside. I was knee-deep in our daughter Keri's wedding and had no time for such faraway fantasies. But the letter gnawed at me and, finally, I gave in.

Since arriving in Africa, I had seen homeless children sifting through garbage bins for morsels of food. I had seen them in the back streets where they sleep at night in shelters of cardboard and rags. And now I stood amid a great crowd of children gathered along a low-slung rock wall near the center of town. I focused on a half-starved girl huddling with her baby brother in a single patch of sun.

As I stood there, the girl's gaunt face brightened. "Mabawe!" she called. Others joined in, "Mabawe is coming! Mabawe!" It was a name I'd heard over and over as I talked to street children: "Mabawe—the lady who gives us tea and bread."

A rattletrap of a car rounded the corner and stopped. A middle-aged woman tugged a huge pot from the trunk. I stood in the shadow of an acacia tree and shivered. *Where are You, God?* I prayed.

I was stunned when He answered, *Here I am. Look into My face.*

I raised my head and found myself toe-to-toe with Mabawe, a simple woman in frumpy clothes, her hair pulled back in a bun. Yet it was clear that God was in her. She was changing the world for these children.

And, finally, I understood: It's through plain people like Mabawe, like you, like me, that God gets His best work done. We just have to say yes.

God, whatever the need where I am, use me to bring Your presence to it.
—PAM KIDD

My Daily Blessings

1 _____

2 _____

3 _____

4 _____

5 _____

6 _____

7 _____

8 _____

9 _____

10 _____

11 _____

12 _____

13 _____

14 _____

15 _____

16 _____

17 _____

18 _____

19 _____

20 _____

21 _____

22 _____

23 _____

24 _____

25 _____

26 _____

27 _____

28 _____

29 _____

30 _____

31 _____

AUGUST

Blessed are the pure in heart: for
they shall see God.
—Matthew 5:8

S	M	T	W	T	F	S
					1	2
3	4	5	6	7	8	9
10	11	12	13	14	15	16
17	18	19	20	21	22	23
24	25	26	27	28	29	30
31						

AN EYE FOR BLESSINGS

1/FRI　　THE OPEN DOOR
"Knock and the door will be opened to you." —LUKE 11:9 (NIV)

Opening the front door this morning, I remembered a conversation I had with my daughter-in-law eleven years ago.

Two months after Hurricane Andrew left its trail of devastation across Florida in August 1992, my husband and I flew down to visit our son and his family in Miami. Though the palm trees in their yard were stripped of their fronds, repairs to the house were well along. The roof had been patched, water-damaged furniture replaced and a handsome new front door installed in place of the one the storm had blown in.

"I like it even better than the old door," I told Lorraine.

Lorraine shook her head. "It's so unfriendly!" she said.

Unfriendly?

The requirement for front doors post-Andrew, she explained, was that they open outward to offer better resistance to hurricane-force winds. "It's so unwelcoming," she went on. "When someone rings the bell, the first thing you have to do is push them away."

Her words came back to me this morning, as I pulled my own front door inward. It was a postman with a registered letter this time, but as I signed for it, I was remembering the thousands of times in the forty-four years we've lived here that our "friendly" door has ushered in family and guests.

Afterward, I walked through the house. Each door—to the basement, the porch, the dining room, my office, every door at which people knock—opens inward. Even when I forget to, the motion itself says, "I'm glad you've come!"

Thank You, Father, that when You tell us to knock, it's at a door that opens into Your kingdom.
　　　　　　　　　　　　　　　　—ELIZABETH SHERRILL

2 / SAT   *"Who am I, O Lord God, and what is my house, that thou hast brought me thus far?"*   —II SAMUEL 7:18 (RSV)

When I look at my kitchen, I don't see the spotless counters, the crumb-free toaster, the scrubbed stovetop. I don't notice the sparkling sink, the smudgeless dishwasher, the streak-free refrigerator. I don't observe the clean floor tiles, the carefully stacked cookbooks, the immaculate pottery. And, I'm ashamed to say, I barely note the metal sculpture depicting Jesus at the Last Supper. What I see is one doorless cabinet. The gaping cabinet. The cabinet with the dishes, glasses, serving bowls and measuring cup sitting there in plain sight. My plain sight.

I'm obsessed with this open cabinet. The hinges broke months ago, no hardware store seems to have them, and I can't locate the original builder to find out where to order them. And since we're renting, it doesn't make sense to replace all the other cabinets, which work just fine. And so I daily mull over alternatives.

What about draping a curtain over the cabinet? A decorative towel? Could I somehow lean the door against the opening? Perhaps I should just empty out the entire cabinet and simply stare at the bare space?

Today my friend Lori came over to visit. She had never seen our place before and was full of compliments. I was chewing on the inside of my mouth when I showed her the kitchen. "It's perfect," she exclaimed enthusiastically.

"Perfect?" I groaned. "Yeah, sure, if you ignore the gaping cabinet!"

"Mmm," she said, glancing at it briefly, "I hadn't even noticed it. But this Last Supper sculpture is really great!"

It's a good thing God is more like Lori than like me.

Lord, thank You for the grace that forgives my faults and renews me in Your likeness.
                                                        —MARCI ALBORGHETTI

3 / SUN   *Ask the Lord for rain ... and he will answer with lightning and showers. Every field will become a lush pasture.*
                                                        —ZECHARIAH 10:1 (TLB)

It had been an extremely hot summer with practically no rainfall.

Backyard gardens lay parched, and daily the produce offerings of grocery stores and markets grew smaller and smaller.

At the morning worship service on Sunday, the pastor said, "I'm sorry that the church is not cool today. We have some paper fans in the pews, but not enough for everyone. So if you find one, please share it with those near you."

He cut the service short that morning and asked the congregation to join him in prayer. It was a beautiful prayer, thanking God for His many blessings. He finished with these words, "And please, Lord, send us rain. Rain, now, would *really* be a shower of blessings."

That night I was tempted to skip church, but my conscience wouldn't let me. So I was there when, just as we had begun to sing the first hymn, the pastor raised his right hand high in the air. "Listen!" he exclaimed loudly.

The organist stopped playing, and we all heard the wonderful music of rain pounding on the roof and beating against the windows of the church. You can imagine the happiness, the gratitude and the praise expressed throughout the rest of the service.

As my friend Lita and I were leaving, a little girl joined us at the doorway, which was blocked by the downpour. In her hand, she carried a small red umbrella, the only one I saw anywhere in the church. "I see you brought your umbrella," Lita said to her.

"Of course," she replied with a big smile. "I knew I'd need it. We prayed this morning for rain."

Oh, Father, grant me the faith of a little child. Amen.

—DRUE DUKE

4 / MON   *And let us consider one another to provoke unto love and to good works.*   —HEBREWS 10:24

It was a one hundred degree August afternoon, the day before the Wichita County Fair—a hectic time at my son Patrick's house. Ryan, ten, and David, eight, were brushing their steers, getting them clean for the next morning's 4-H competition. Their mother Patricia helped Mark, four, wash a bucket calf; Mark was finally old enough to show in the "pee-wee" competition. When the calf was rinsed, Patricia went to turn off the faucet, then let out a piercing yell: "Snake! Snake!"

For most Kansans, the cry of "Snake!" means you have spotted a harmless green garden snake.

Country dwellers usually appreciate the work snakes do in keeping down rats, mice and bugs. But Pat and Patricia live in rattlesnake country. Pat found a baby rattler in the kitchen soon after they moved in. Another time, Patricia was on the mower and saw a snake half-coiled by the fence post. Ryan walked right up to it before pronouncing it a medium-size diamondback.

This time, Patricia recognized her adversary as a nonpoisonous bull snake, nearly four feet long. She prodded it with a stick, hoping to move it far enough so that she could reach the faucet handle. The snake, enjoying the cool, damp ground, stayed put. Patricia prodded it again and again, each time a little harder. The snake started to coil, and she backed off. Eventually Pat maneuvered the snake into a large shovel and carried it to the pasture.

"I don't know why it got so mad," Patricia said. "I didn't hurt it. I just wanted it to move!"

"You were poking it with a stick!" Pat answered, laughing. "Wouldn't you get mad if someone did that to you?"

The Bible uses the word *provoke* when it instructs us not to verbally poke and prod one another. Colossians 3:21 reminds parents to "provoke not your children to anger, lest they become discouraged." Jeremiah 25:6 contains one of many warnings not to provoke God: "Provoke me not to anger." But poking and prodding can be used in a good way, too, as in the passage from Hebrews.

The question is this: Today, which way will I seek to provoke my family, friends and colleagues? To anger? Or to love and good works?

Lord God, help me learn from the coiling of a bull snake how much my actions affect the responses and choices of others.

—PENNEY SCHWAB

5 / *TUE*　　*This is the day which the Lord hath made; we will rejoice and be glad in it.*　　—PSALM 118:24

My name is Shep, though Van Varner, my owner, often calls me Clay, the name of a dog predecessor. I am a Belgian shepherd; they say that I'm bred to corral sheep, but I consider this as questionable as the name of the place we wander to in Central Park, the Sheep Meadow. It's a meadow all right, but there are no sheep.

I can't speak in your way, so I do a lot of communicating through my wagging tail, my supplicating eyes and a modulation of sounds from a bark to a whine. Some dogs growl; I haven't done so because it hasn't been necessary. Anyway, I'm satisfied with my "speech" because, forgive me, humans talk too much. Gossip, for example, and politics. *Bah.*

While on the subject of human behavior, it has always troubled me that when people are late for an appointment, they're often met with a kind of irritation, rather than the joy of seeing them. I'm so relieved at Van's arrival, no matter how long I've waited, that I bark and run in circles, and get my latest rubber toy to shake in an enthusiastic hurrah. Why aren't you as grateful at the sight of a loved one?

I want to tell you about Ted and Uta. Ted is a Labrador and Uta is a dachshund, two playmates in the park. Ted has only three legs, but he chases and bounds about gleefully, all sunniness and no vanity whatsoever. Uta has a more serious affliction with her two hind feet, but her friend fixed up a dolly with wheels for her lower limbs and she gets along merrily. They're happy to be living. I don't feel it's the same with many of you. Misfortunes come to everyone, but why can't you savor life and be glad the Ted-and-Uta way? I've tried to get my philosophy across to Van, and sometimes I think I've succeeded by simply showing him my love.

Forgive me, Lord, if I have said too much. —VAN VARNER

6 / WED   *Do not deceive with your lips.*
—PROVERBS 24:28 (RSV)

I was about to go camping through northern California with two former college friends and catch up on one another's lives. Sharise was a high school teacher, soon to be a department chairman, and Anna was an actuary with her own secretary. And I was working in a bookstore for little above minimum wage. I liked my work, but it was not exactly a career I was eager to share with my more successful friends.

So I began practicing how to present my job to them. *God, help me find a way to . . . well, not lie exactly, but make it sound like I'm doing better than I am.* There was a lull in the line at the registers, so I mentally practiced. *I'm in retail.* Nah, true but too vague. *I'm in management.* (Well, I did manage the carts of books to be shelved!)

Suddenly, I was interrupted by two customers. Behind the cash register was a very expensive boxed Batman set that attracted a lot of attention from collectors. So when the boy, about ten years old, asked what was in it, I handed it over gingerly and warned, "Be careful. It's a collector's item: an action figure and a graphic novel."

He opened the box and immediately his freckled face fell. "Oh," he said, "it's just a doll and a comic book."

I had to laugh. The child had cut right to the chase. Call it what you will, it was a doll and a comic book. And call me what you will, I was a bookseller. My friends had liked me in college for myself, not for my grades or career plans. And they would like me now, whether I was president of the company or president of nothing!

God, if there is something in my life I've been "fancifying," then for today, teach me not to turn a comic book—or bookseller— into something that it's not. Let me enjoy and be proud of who I am in Your eyes.
—LINDA NEUKRUG

7 / THU   *Lo, children are an heritage of the Lord. . . .*
—PSALM 127:3

I'm sitting in my yard early on a summer morning, sipping coffee with a fresh newspaper and a sleepy son draped one over the other on my lap, and as I hear the new young crows croaking and bleating at their parents, I have to grin, even as I want to snarl at them to stop their incessant blubbering.

I've heard that same relentless moaning and whining from my own children, and I have lurched around the house at night goggle-eyed and gibbering just like the crow mothers and fathers blearily hopping along the fence in front of me, complaining quietly to themselves in crow-speak. I mutter insults at the noisy young crows, in utter sympathy with their exhausted parents.

All creatures are thrown headlong into raising their young without the slightest training or semblance of an organized system. It's astonishingly exhausting, and it never ends, as far as I can tell, until you do, and it's the greatest thing that ever happened to me.

Despite the lines cut into my face by those bleary nights, and the worry lines cut around the tired lines, there are also laugh lines that otherwise wouldn't be there. And I'm not tired enough to think that this exhaustion and this joy and these children aren't extraordinary miracles from the Maker of all things, moaning new crows included.

Dear Lord, You have given me riches beyond imagination or measurement, for which I am speechless in gratitude. Could You maybe do me one more favor and let the children learn how to sleep through the night? —BRIAN DOYLE

8/ FRI   *"The one sitting on the throne will shelter them . . . and they will be fully protected from the scorching noontime heat."* —REVELATION 7:15–16 (TLB)

In June 2001, I bought an old car for my son Andrew, a student at Arizona State University. My brother Joe generously volunteered to help me drive the 1986 gray beast cross-country from my home in Oak Creek, Wisconsin, to Phoenix. I say "generously" because the car had no air conditioning, and we had to drive across the hottest part of the country in the middle of the summer.

As sweat poured down our faces and the scorching one hundred-degree sun beat down on the car, Joe and I took turns driving across Kansas, through the corners of Oklahoma and Texas, and across the entire southern part of New Mexico in the worst heat we'd ever experienced. To take our minds off the mind-numbing temperature, we punctuated the adventure by taking in some sights, including an airplane museum with an air-conditioned lobby, the world's largest pallasite meteorite housed inside an air-conditioned gift shop and the world's largest hand-dug well—thirty-two feet in diameter and 109 feet deep—into which we climbed with glee, basking in the coolness at the bottom. I tried to talk Joe into visiting the world's largest ball of string, but he vetoed the idea. "It's outdoors. No air conditioning."

Our trip across America taught me that although it's easy to complain on a long, hot trip, it's a lot more pleasant to find humor, adventure and even a few learning opportunities along the way.

The day I left Phoenix for my return to Milwaukee it was 116 degrees. Did I mention that the plane I flew home in was air-conditioned?

Father, today's "temperature-controlled" everything has me spoiled. Thank You for opportunities to feel and see the real world, so I can truly appreciate the comforts in my life.

—PATRICIA LORENZ

9/SAT *The Lord thy God will make thee plenteous in every work of thine hand, in the fruit of thy body. . . .*

—DEUTERONOMY 30:9

When our friends Scott and Katie showed us the house they had bought, my wife and I were quietly appalled. The old Victorian dowager might have been grand once, but now it was in terrible condition: plaster flaking off ceilings, windows missing panes, hardwood floors that reeked of an incontinent cat. To describe it as a fixer-upper would be generous. No matter how long I stared at the details that enchanted the new buyers—the stone fireplace, the bow windows, the leaded glass—I couldn't see how the place could be made livable.

But over time our friends succeeded mightily. They redid walls, ceilings and floors, put in a new bathroom downstairs, fixed windows, sanded, painted, hung wallpaper. Seeing the work step by step made me appreciate how talented they were. *I would never have thought of that,* I'd say to myself when I saw how they opened up a room or covered up a wall. It was a kind of stewardship I could appreciate, especially since the gifts involved were foreign to me.

And then one day, when the old dowager looked completely restored, they announced to us, "We're going to move the kitchen to the other side." Both my wife and I were appalled—until we thought of what the house had first looked like.

It's a vision thing, no less essential than what it takes for a composer to write a symphony, a minister to build a church, a teacher to transform a student. They held that vision in their head as they applied their gifts to it, and when it seemed done, they were still open to a new idea. But it all had to start with a vision: to see what wasn't there. That's how it happens with the worthiest endeavors.

Lord, help me realize the visions that You put before me. Amen.

—RICK HAMLIN

10 / SUN   *And unto one he gave five talents, to another two, and to another one; to every man according to his several ability....* —MATTHEW 25:15

In our church, Sunday morning worship means music—lots of it! From the one hundred-voice choir to the electric guitars, from the grand piano and electric keyboard to the full set of drums, it's a wonderfully loud, joyful sound.

One morning I noticed an addition to this menagerie of instruments. My friend Ashley stood in the far back corner, almost obscured by the gaggle of guitars in front of her. I knew she was a talented musician; what would she play this morning? A saxophone with its rich, mellow sound? Maybe a trumpet, whose bright, high-stepping notes would fill the sanctuary? But as the music began, she held up a tambourine.

A tambourine? How could anyone appreciate her talent when all she was holding was a tiny circle of silver slivers? The bigger, noisier instruments were certain to drown her out. The scores of voices would obliterate her efforts for sure.

But as the song progressed, an amazing thing happened. Above the rhythmic pounding of the drums, the pulsing strumming of guitars, the ripple of piano keys, the heavy harmony of voices came a sweet, simple, happy sound. The jingle of the silver circles in my friend's hand, a sound of joy that I knew came not just from her wrist but from her heart. I smiled and added my only slightly flat alto to the voices around me.

Remind me, God, that when it's lifted to You, no talent or effort is ever too small. —MARY LOU CARNEY

11 / MON   *Consider your ways.* —HAGGAI 1:5

Every August I have my annual physical examination. This year, I was feeling fine, and I was looking forward to a busy round of activities. The doctor weighed me, and then he took my blood pressure, not once, but three times. *What's wrong?* I thought. *My pressure has always been normal.*

The doctor paused and said, "Your pressure is two hundred over ninety-six, and I don't know why. You'll have to take medication, and you'll have to rest."

I gasped. I'd have to miss my sixtieth high school reunion and cancel the class I'd promised to teach at the State of Maine Writers Conference. But what was worse, after twenty-three years, I wouldn't be able to prepare my beloved Trash and Treasure tables for our church fair. How I loved the people and the challenge!

I wrote to the fair chairperson to tell her that I wouldn't be doing Trash and Treasure. A few days later, she came up to me after church and said, "Oscar, I'd like to talk with you." Over a cup of coffee, she said, "I got your letter, and I sensed that you're feeling guilty about Trash and Treasure. Please don't feel that way. For some time I've been wanting to tell you that you don't always have to be in charge. Just do as much as you can. We'd be glad to have you as a team member."

I appreciated her gracious response, but I still felt uneasy about the situation, and I wondered why. Slowly, I began to see that "being in charge" was a big part of the reason Trash and Treasure was so important to me. It had become *my* activity instead of the church's. It was hard, but I stepped away from it, and my replacement did a wonderful job. Not only could I follow my doctor's advice and walk more easily through each day, but letting go also meant creating room for others to serve.

Father, thank You for showing me that to change my direction,
sometimes I have to slow down.   —OSCAR GREENE

12/TUE   *Cause me to hear thy lovingkindness in the morning; for in thee do I trust. . . .*   —PSALM 143:8

I've been a bit out of sorts the past couple of days from lack of sleep. It's not that I can't get to sleep, but that I wake early in the morning, no matter how late I get to bed.

This morning, for example, I found myself wide awake at about 4:30, following a late night. After lying in bed for an hour, tossing and turning and hoping to go back to sleep, I finally decided to get up. I thought of reading or writing in my journal or answering mail, but none of those things had a strong appeal for me at 5:30 A.M. So instead, I chose a CD of lovely, ethereal music, put on the headphones so I wouldn't wake my husband, and kicked back in the recliner that faces the east living-room window.

The silence of the starry sky felt like the expectant hush that comes over a theater when the lights have dimmed, just before the curtain rises. I felt a sense of great anticipation as the sky turned, ever so gradually, from diamonds on black velvet to an etching of evergreens on parchment, then to a soft, candle-glow gold as the morning sun rose over Mount Dewey. Something inside of me knelt, and I found my soul at prayer. Could it be that God had been waking me in the early morning so I could experience the wonder of His presence in the light of the dawning day? I believe so! And there was a bonus. My husband said he noticed right away that I was in good spirits!

On those days when I find myself unable to sleep in the early morning hours, I hope I can remember that Someone is waiting for me—Someone with a gift beyond words.

Creator of all that is, how many times must You call before I answer? When I waken early, let me recognize Your call and rise to meet You at the edge of the dawn. —MARILYN MORGAN KING

13/WED   The Lord will guide you always. . . .
—ISAIAH 58:11 (NIV)

The most amazing experience my wife Joy and I had last year was visiting the mountain gorillas in Rwanda's Virunga National Park. Because of the fragility of the gorilla population and the danger involved, only two families of gorillas are visited, and only eight visitors are allowed to see each family each day. As we began the hike to their habitat, we were handed twenty-eight rules for visiting the gorillas. Here are my favorites:

- All visitors should stay together in a tight group. Please stay behind the guide at all times.
- Keep your voice down at all times. If you are stung by nettles or ants, please try not to cry out!
- If a gorilla charges you, please follow the guide's example. Crouch down slowly and wait for the animal to pass. Do not attempt to take a picture at this time, and do not run away.
- Do not attempt to touch the gorillas.

When we reached the family of eleven, led by a three hundred-pound silverback male, I was trying hard to remember all the rules.

Do they really think I'm going to crouch down and not scream if that big fella charges? Joy, who knows no fear, was enthralled by the baby, who didn't know the rules and tried to touch her. I was about to panic when the guide reached through the bamboo undergrowth and gently pulled Joy behind him.

I watched the two guides closely as they kept themselves between us and danger. It was a wonderful picture of the way Jesus leads me through life if I let Him. He leads me up the mountain, knows the location and nature of the dangers, stays between me and them, and then always leads me safely home.

Jesus, thank You for being the shepherd and guide for all Your followers. Help me learn to stay behind You and follow Your example in all we do.   —ERIC FELLMAN

14/THU   The Lord . . . is thy life, and the length of thy days. . . .   —DEUTERONOMY 30:20

My friends sometimes accuse me of being morbid because I make a point of reading the obituary page of the newspaper. I try to read a couple of daily papers, but even on days when I'm pressed for time, I read the obits no matter what.

It helps that my local paper, *The New York Times*, has perhaps the finest obituary page in the world. You will learn about some of the most fascinating people by turning to it, people you might never have known about otherwise. One of my favorites was an Englishwoman named Megan Boyd, who tied beautiful fishing flies with the workmanship of a fine jeweler. Her fame among fishermen was unsurpassed, yet she never charged more than a dollar for her masterpieces and never in her life went fishing. Prince Charles was a regular customer, and once, when the queen summoned her to Buckingham Palace to receive an award, she declined because she had no one to care for her dog that day. The queen said she understood completely.

Obviously there are *Times* obituaries for the famous—Tom Dooley, Winston Churchill, Jackie Kennedy, Mother Teresa, even the racehorse Secretariat—and the semifamous: writers I'd never have read, musicians whose work I'd never have listened to, athletes whose accomplishments I'd have forgotten, scientists and philosophers whose ideas I'd never have known about without the help of the obituary page. But the obituaries I most appreciate are the inspiring stories of ordinary people overcoming incredible hardships or turning their lives around after disastrous personal or professional misfortune. Day in and day out, reading the obituary page makes me feel better about the world and the people in it.

"Why do you want to know who died?" friends will ask. I tell them that's not the point. I'm finding out who lived.

God, Giver of life, let me give back to You by the way I live.
—EDWARD GRINNAN

FOLLOWING JESUS

15/*FRI*   OFFERING A FORETASTE OF THE ABUNDANT LIFE CHRIST PROMISED

"I came that they might have life, and might have it abundantly."   —JOHN 10:10 (NAS)

Our dog Sterling loved nothing more than to go for a ride in the car. But one afternoon when we stopped to run a quick errand in a neighboring town, she got loose, hightailed it down a busy street on the trail of another barking dog and didn't find her way back.

We were heartsick, but despite days of searching for her and the ads we placed in local newspapers, she was never found. Then one day we got a telephone call. "I think I may have your dog. Terrier-poodle mix? Gray? Bark bigger than her bite?"

"Yes. Yes. Yes."

"When I found her, she must have been in the wild for a while," the lady said, "all tangled up with a mess of briers. But she's sitting pretty here on the sofa with the rest of my brood now. You can come and take a look."

It was indeed Sterling. But not the Sterling that had flown out of our car that afternoon and in a mad dash for freedom lost her way. This Sterling had little pink bows in her hair, and her nails were painted a matching pink. She sat poised like a queen on the lady's best furniture, an esteemed member of the family.

Days before, Sterling had been a common stray. But her kind benefactor had treated her to an appointment with the groomer and lavished her with love—the abundant life. Just as Jesus offers us when we lose our way.

Some folks are so generous, Lord, that they point me back to You. Help me to bask in Your abundant life and freely share it with others.
—ROBERTA MESSNER

READER'S ROOM

It wasn't until this year that I learned the power of prayer—prayer and absolute trust in God. I'm not saying that everything is fine now; it's only the beginning of a beautiful friendship with my Lord Jesus Christ, and I'm not about to let go of Him, even when things seem to be going well. I've learned that it's then that I need to pray all the harder and hold on all the tighter.

God has brought my daughter out of a harmful relationship and sent her home to heal; He's brought my husband and me back together to love and help one another, instead of fighting each other; and He's changed my work environment from hostility to enjoyment. God has given me courage and strength I did not know I could ever possess during these difficult times. And He has had many people praying for us, people I will never know.

Every day, the dear Lord shows me something about myself that needs work, and I pray every day that I hear Him.
—FRAN BARKER, FAIRFAX, VIRGINIA

16/SAT   *The light that shines through the darkness—
and the darkness can never extinguish it.*   —JOHN 1:5 (TLB)

The lure of the Blue Ridge Mountain breezes was just too tempting, so instead of heading for bed as midnight approached, I let myself out onto the long gray deck and sank into a plastic Adirondack chair. Slowly my eyes adjusted and the stars above me became clear and clearer. For often-hazy August, the sky was unusually dark and the stars unusually bright. I sighed in pure pleasure: After years of living in dense Maryland woods, the open sky here in Virginia is a new joy for me.

Like a child discovering the stars for the first time, I began to play with ideas: *Gee, what if all that is really a great black velvet drape and the stars are pinholes where heaven shines through!*

Suddenly, out of the corner of my eye, I became aware of a flickering. Somewhere beyond the black mound of Massanutten Mountain was a thunderstorm. I watched the flashes and flickers silhouetting the ridge for quite a while, but heard no thunder. *Strange, I watched the TV forecast at eleven o'clock and there were no storms.*

Curious, I crossed the deck, entered my office and called up the Virginia weather radar on my computer. There was only one storm anywhere in the three-state area, a large red-orange blob covering Cape Charles—the point where Chesapeake Bay meets the sea at Hampton Roads—a five-hour drive away from us. The night was so clear that the darkness could not hold back the lightning; it bridged the ridges and lit up my deck 170 miles away.

As I called Bill to come see the silent display, I thought of how many times the Lord's light had bridged the dark valleys in my life to bring His peace and His presence. Watching lightning moving out to sea—beyond two mountain ranges, the long Piedmont and the Tidewater—I knew I was seeing a parable in action: Darkness cannot extinguish light.

Lord, bring Your light over the ridges and into the valleys of my life.
                                                    —ROBERTA ROGERS

17/SUN   *And the Lord said unto him, What is that in*
thine hand? And he said, A rod.   —EXODUS 4:2

"What's that in your hand?"

The pastor kept asking this question in his sermon this morning. His text was Exodus 4:2 on God's question to Moses, who held a staff in his hands. And his message was about giving God whatever we hold in our hands, because God uses what we offer to help us change and grow—and to help others through our offerings.

The pastor's question reminded me of a game we often play with children. We put a piece of candy in one hand, and nothing in the other, and then offer both closed hands to the child, asking, "What's in my hand?" And we push the candy hand out a little and pull the empty hand back, because we're eager to give the child what's in the candy hand.

I sometimes play the same game with God. I eagerly offer Him what I want to give out of my fullness: the little envelope of money I brought to church for the offering, or my free hour once a week, or the abilities I think of as my strengths. But what about the things in my "empty hand": the weaknesses I'd rather hide, or my fears or recent mistakes. They need to be offered to God for His use as well.

When the offering plate came by, I opened both hands, and along with my little envelope of money, I gave some offerings out of my emptiness—my pride, impatience, my struggle with quick criticism—with this prayer:

Lord, I pray You will use the offerings from both my hands, out of my fullness and my emptiness, to change me and to change others for Your glory.   —CAROL KUYKENDALL

18/MON   *And I will come down and talk with thee there*
. . . and they shall bear the burden of the people with thee, that
thou bear it not thyself alone.   —NUMBERS 11:17

When my mother died on July 28, 2001, the whole family hoped and prayed that my son Jon would stay put at Dunklin Memorial Camp in Florida. He had been there for not quite three months of the ten-month drug rehab program. He was getting his life back on track, being set free from his addictions and learning to listen to God.

The camp permitted men to leave for family funerals, but we hoped that Jon would choose to remain. He wasn't allowed to make or receive phone calls; he had been told about his grandmother's death by a counselor. As my husband Gene and I drove to Elberton, Georgia, to make funeral arrangements, praying about Jon and his decision, my cell phone rang. It was Jon.

"Hi, Mom. They let me use the phone. Are you okay? I'm okay. I have to tell you what happened this morning during my prayer time. I was sitting out under the pavilion alone, praying and journaling, at seven-thirty. The biggest dove I've ever seen flew down and sat right by me on the picnic table. He didn't seem afraid of me at all. He just watched me as I wrote out my prayers for each family member. I knew something was going on, and I felt like it was with Grandma. So when I got the news that she'd left this life, I was prepared. I could even rejoice. And God spoke clearly to me. He said I should stay here and not make the trip home for the funeral."

"Oh, Jon," I said, "you were praying for her—for us—at the exact time she died!"

"Really, Mom? Isn't that just like God to send me a dove."

Father, thank You for the dove and for all the gentle ways You come to us.   —MARION BOND WEST

19/ TUE   *"Come to me, all who are weary and burdened, and I will give you rest."*   —MATTHEW 11:28 (NIV)

Behavior around here has taken a nosedive, and I'm struggling to right the plane. Yesterday was meltdown day. First it was Elizabeth, then John, then Elizabeth again. Mary mostly whined and tried out new methods of being two years old; Maggie, our baby, was satisfied with spitting up and incessant crying. By the time we were walking home from the older kids' drawing class at the end of the day, I knew that I was next in line for emotional collapse. I decided to try something new.

"Kids," I announced, surprisingly calm, "Mom needs some time out. I'm out of patience, and I need some quiet. I don't want any of you to talk to me or touch me until we get home." They scanned my face, assessing my seriousness. I was serious. They skipped ahead, leaving me in peace. So far so good. I thought. *But now what am I supposed to do? How am I going to recover my sanity in three blocks?*

Pray. *Okay, I'll pray.* I prayed. It didn't help much; I still felt lousy and on edge. Week five of having a newborn in the house is always my point of utter exhaustion, and I think the kids must be pretty stressed, too. I know that their poor behavior is a temporary stage. I know, too, that I can't give in to it, or it will become permanent. But, oh, it takes such energy to respond to them instead of to react; to be consistent and firm yet not angry and bossy. It's so hard to remember that *discipline* is from the same root as *disciple*, and that discipleship begins with love.

I sighed and prayed some more. Instead of asking for the miraculous (four perfect kids with impeccable manners and admirable behavior), this time I asked for the obvious: a few drops of grace to illumine my weary soul, and the wherewithal to let that grace shine through to my children.

Jesus, there were times You wanted to go to a lonely place, but the crowd would not leave You alone. Remind me that the Cross is a lonely place, too, so that I may take mine up gladly and follow You.   —JULIA ATTAWAY

INTO THE WILDERNESS

Last summer, Mary Brown headed from Michigan to the wilderness of northern Minnesota for a fiftieth-birthday canoe trip in the Boundary Waters Canoe Wilderness Area with her younger sisters and teenage daughter Elizabeth. "It was my lifelong

dream to camp in this pristine paddle-only area with no noise of boat motors and no planes allowed to fly overhead—only the peaceful sounds of water lapping, birds calling and trees rustling." While Mary's husband Alex held down the fort at her sister Sue's cabin on nearby Crane Lake with their son Mark and cousin Michael, the ladies ventured into the wilderness. As with any expedition, the trip was laden with challenges and lessons. Over the next three days, Mary invites us to share it with her.

—THE EDITORS

20/ WED   DAY ONE: BACK ROADS

Love does not insist on its own way. . . .

—I CORINTHIANS 13:5 (RSV)

I stepped off the ferry, bristling with eagerness to get to Crane Lake. While riding across Lake Michigan, I had hatched a plan: We'd drive top-speed across Wisconsin to Duluth, Minnesota, spend the night there, shop for supplies, then make a beeline to the cabin.

My husband Alex, however, was in a totally different mode. He'd also planned a route. "Let's take back roads up to Bayfield, then travel along Lake Superior the next day."

"Bayfield?" I almost shrieked. "But that's so far out of the way! I want to get to Duluth today."

"We'll never make it that far today. And why should we rush and race? There's beautiful scenery to see along the way."

I wanted to protest. *This is my big birthday trip. I want to get right to the cabin and start packing for the canoe trip!* But as Alex told the kids about the lovely old town and a bed-and-breakfast right on Lake Superior, I had to give in. *Well, I guess it's his vacation, too.*

That evening, as we strolled around Bayfield admiring the Victorian houses and the gardens brimming with flowers, then ate dinner on our balcony overlooking the lake, I began to unwind. Leaving Bayfield the next day, Alex drove along Lake Superior and stopped for "just one more look at the lake." Walking a forest path to the lake, listening to the lapping waves, and breathing the fragrance of lake and woods, I swallowed my pride and turned to Alex. "You were right, this was the best way to come." As he squeezed my hand, I was so glad I hadn't insisted on my high-pressured travel plan, and so grateful for my husband, who slowed me down to savor the scenic route.

Lord, after all these years I still struggle to have my own way and rush through life. Please show me today if I'm resisting Your will. —MARY BROWN

21 / THU   DAY TWO: CATCHING UP
My flesh and my heart may fail, but God is the strength of my heart and my portion forever. —PSALM 73:26 (NIV)

I plodded up the steep portage trail, stopping often to catch my breath. "Are you coming, Mary?" my sisters shouted from up ahead.

"Yes," I called back with feigned enthusiasm. I adjusted my backpack and forced one foot in front of the other, growing increasingly discouraged. How had I ever thought I could keep up with my younger sisters?

I'd always thought age is only an attitude—just think young and you'll stay young. But lately my body has begun telling me loudly and clearly how many years I've lived. Without my reading glasses, I couldn't read the map. While paddling yesterday, I kept finding excuses to rest, exclaiming, "Look at that shoreline! Aren't those trees beautiful?" Now on this hill, I simply had to catch my breath. Plopping down on a rock, I decided to enjoy the peace of the forest.

Eventually I pushed myself back into motion. I soon felt winded, yet I faced another hill ahead, even rockier and steeper. *Lord, please help me catch up.* I'd been praying that prayer often on this trip. Then an encouraging idea flashed across my mind: *As the body gets weaker, the spirit can grow stronger.* The inevitable slowing down in this time of my life could bring me to rely on God in new ways, to pause, to ponder and to experience His presence with me.

When I returned home and went to the doctor to check on a nagging cough, I learned that I'd probably had "walking pneumonia" during the trip. It was a relief to learn that my lack of stamina and shortness of breath were not just a consequence of turning fifty, but I do hope I can remember the lesson I learned through whatever the years ahead bring.

Dear God, please help me turn to You more often and grow more fully alive in spirit in each phase of my life. —MARY BROWN

22/FRI   DAY THREE: IN THE BUBBLE
No evil shall befall you, no scourge come near your tent.
—PSALM 91:10 (RSV)

As my sister Sue, my daughter Elizabeth and I snuggled in our sleeping bags, reading by flashlights, my sister Sarah looked out the tent at the lake, smooth as glass. "Wow!" she exclaimed. "There's some heavy lightning in the southeastern sky."

"Do you think we'll get a thunderstorm here?" Elizabeth asked anxiously.

"I don't think so," said Sue. "Storms usually come from the west up here." What she left unsaid for Elizabeth's benefit was that when they do come from the east, they're usually fierce.

Soon thunder began rumbling closer. Sarah dashed out to batten down the campsite. She ducked back in just as lightning crackled behind her and thunder roared. Rain slashed against the dome tent, now shaking from the swirling winds.

"Good thing we all weigh a lot," said Sue, laughing. "If we weren't in this tent, the wind would pick it right up."

Elizabeth trembled. "Could it blow away with us in it?"

"No, no, we're perfectly safe," we all reassured her.

But inside, I was trembling, too—remembering that people have been killed by thunderstorms in the Boundary Waters. Lightning traveling through tree roots has electrocuted sleeping campers. The old jack pines, barely anchored on this rocky site, could easily topple onto our tent. *Oh, Lord, save us and protect us!* Elizabeth began voicing similar fears. *Lord, help me calm her.*

Suddenly, I remembered Marion Bond West's image of "staying in the bubble." When her husband was ill, God gave her an image of being in Jesus as if she were in a bubble, carried through the storms of anxiety and grief. As I shared this, Sue said, "Well, this dome tent is a perfect reminder. We'll picture it as a bubble of God's protection around us."

We heard a loud cracking and a tree came crashing down nearby. *Thank You, Lord, that we are safe.* Picturing God's protection around us, we eventually dozed off to the sounds of wind and rain.

Dear God, help me remember in all the storms to come that You are my Guide and Protector.
—MARY BROWN

23/SAT *Rejoice with the wife of thy youth.*
—PROVERBS 5:18

August 23, 1953. That was the day—a sweltering hot Sunday afternoon—on which Shirley and I tied the knot. The place was Bryan, Ohio, in what is now the Faith United Methodist Church.

So today we'll be celebrating our golden anniversary, if the good Lord's willin' and the creek don't rise. I add that proviso because four or five years ago I wouldn't have bet a wooden nickel on my chances of reaching fifty years with Shirley. A bout with non-Hodgkin's lymphoma made it seem unlikely, but I prayed the only prayer I knew how to pray when storm clouds gather: "Thy will be done." That's not to say I didn't add, "Of course, I hope to be healed, God, but You already know that, and You know that I trust You the same now as when times were peachy."

The Lord guided me to some wonderful doctors and nurses, and I got some magnificent care (though I didn't call it that when I was going through a wrenching three-week chemo and stem-cell transplant procedure at the University of Pennsylvania Hospital in Philadelphia). What sustained me, in addition to thousands of prayers and the support of family and friends, was Shirley's unflinching faith.

When I got the good news that my cancer was in remission, Shirley looked at me with the same smile that had melted my heart and caused me to fall in love with her a million full moons ago. "I knew you'd make it," she whispered as she brushed my cheek with a kiss.

When I asked her how she could be so absolutely sure, she said, "Remember when we flew back from the Mayo Clinic, and you were going downhill like a toboggan? I looked out the window as we were landing and saw a double rainbow amid the clouds. I took it as God's sign that you'd recover."

That's the gal I married fifty years ago today.

Thank You, Lord, for a special, one-of-a-kind wife
To heighten the ups and lighten the downs of my life.
—FRED BAUER

24/sun   *"Now then, stand still and see this great thing the Lord is about to do before your eyes!"*

—1 SAMUEL 12:16 (NIV)

When I found out that our daughter in New York City was expecting our first grandchild, I began to notice babies everywhere I went. At church, I watched blissfully when the little ones toddled up the aisle for children's church. At times I was overwhelmed with baby fever, especially because our daughter lived so far away.

The following Sunday, our church was recruiting new Sunday school teachers, and I volunteered right away. *I'll teach the three-year-olds*, I reasoned. *What better way to fulfill my need to nurture a grandchild?*

That evening, the Sunday school coordinator called me. "Thanks for offering to teach Sunday school. Would you mind teaching a first-grade class? That's where we really need the help."

"Oh, sure," I replied quickly. I turned to my husband Roy. "I'll be teaching first graders."

The look of surprise on his face at my calm and quick acceptance of this turn of events started me thinking. What a different response I would have had in the past! I might have grudgingly agreed to teach the first graders even though I had my heart set on the younger children. Or I might have turned down the request and not taught at all because it wasn't what I had expected.

Why was I able to accept this change of events so readily? My faith had grown; I knew that God was placing me exactly where He wanted me. Years ago, I wouldn't have figured that out until the end of the school year. Then I'd have looked around at all the children and seen how much richer my life was because of each of them, selected by God to bring me a special gift. This time, I'll know all that going in.

Help me, God, always to rely on my faith in You to accept the unexpected blessings in my life.   —MELODY BONNETTE

25/MON *Refrain from anger, and forsake wrath! Fret not yourself; it tends only to evil.* —PSALM 37:8 (RSV)

My dog Perky doesn't like screens. They clearly irritate her because when windows are open, there are wonderful things outside to bark at and try to leap for, like squirrels, passersby and mail carriers. Last year, when I opened my office window and left the room for a few hours, the screen developed a number of large holes.

I don't yell at Perky because she doesn't really know which of her many foibles—knocking over the wastepaper basket, turning off the computer's surge protector, pulling everything off my desk—is triggering the loud voice. I calmly closed the window, which meant nose prints on the glass but forestalled an invasion of gnats, bees, flies or other insects.

I sweltered for a while, because the cool outside breeze could not reach my hot face through a closed window. And I simmered at how my ongoing love of a dog was making me so uncomfortable because I couldn't afford to get the screen replaced, and patching it with something I couldn't see through would waste the window.

As the summer wore on, it occurred to me that I wasn't approaching this problem in an effective way, that I was brooding over it as I'd brooded over other problems in the past when I hadn't allowed myself to relax and let the answer in. I put the torn screen out of my mind for a while, and when it came, the answer was simple: I covered the holes with clear packing tape. I could see out, the pests could not get in, and I could open the window just enough to get the breeze in—and keep Perky's paws out.

Dear God, thank You for helping me to see that so much of my stress is self-created, and that if I relax, I can usually see my way clear. —RHODA BLECKER

26/TUE *Yet it is I who taught Ephraim to walk, I took them in My arms. . . .* —HOSEA 11:3 (NAS)

One steamy summer day, I hurried down to our neighborhood pool in a tizzy. Things seemed to be going the wrong way in our family. "God, why won't You change things?" I prayed. "I'm tired of all these problems. Nothing I do seems to matter, and I'm working so hard. Where are You?"

I pushed through the metal gate at the pool and ran over to thank my neighbor Mary Ann for watching Thomas, my nine-year-old son. Mary Ann is Megan's mom, and Megan is very special to me, as she's my four-year-old goddaughter. Born with a heart problem, Megan has gone through three heart surgeries and had her gall bladder removed, but she has amazed everyone with her determination and spunk.

Thomas and Megan were sitting cross-legged on a striped beach towel at the edge of the pool, drinking juice boxes and sharing some goldfish crackers. Mary Ann called me aside to whisper, "I've got to tell you what Thomas did. All the big kids were hurrying to the other side of the pool to eat a snack. Megan didn't have her flip-flops, and the pavement was burning her feet. Thomas gave her his flip-flops. He dipped his feet into the water to cool them off while he waited for her to walk. Megan was thrilled to be wearing big-boy shoes, but she couldn't walk very fast, and she kept tripping. So Thomas took off his towel and wrapped her up. Then he picked her up and carried her, letting her wear his shoes the whole way. He walked barefoot. Julie, you should have seen him."

Lord, You want to pick me up and carry me, but I try to run alone, burning my feet and stumbling along. Help me trust You to carry me.   —JULIE GARMON

27/ WED   *Praise his name in the dance. . . .*
—PSALM 149:3

It was a paralyzing moment: A skunk had walked in through the patio door and was ambling its way across the kitchen. "Don't move," our daughter Katrelya whispered. "Stay quiet." I blanched, petrified at the thought of how we would cope if it let loose with its spray.

Slowly moving with the grace of a shadow, Katrelya went through the patio door, raced around the side of the house, then opened the back door so the skunk would have an exit. Sure enough, after crunching a dish of cat chow, Mr. Skunk raised his head, sniffed the air and lumbered out.

A family of skunks is raising their young in the woodpile across our fence, under a large Chinese elm in our neighbor's yard. We are becoming wise in the ways of skunks and are constantly amazed by their intelligence and amused by their unusual antics.

"Turn out the lights," I said to Katrelya on a late summer night as she came to the dining table to join me in a bedtime cup of tea. "Look—what's that moving about the bushes?" We both crept outside and peered into the darkness.

"It's skunks," she said. "Two huge skunks with their tails up and spread out like fans." Mesmerized, we watched. They were dancing, tumbling and chasing each other in what was probably a mating ritual as beautiful as an orchestrated ballet. Within moments they were gone, out of our range of vision.

"Wow," I mused, "I never thought skunks could be so graceful and lovely."

"Not only that," our daughter answered, "they make sweet pets, too."

"Don't even think about it!" I gasped.

"De-scented?" she asked.

"Never!" I said.

In all our forty years of living in the foothills, close to wildlife, we had never seen the likes of this: skunks, the much maligned, dancing in the moonlight.

For the blessings of "all creatures, great and small," I give You thanks, dear Lord.   —FAY ANGUS

28/THU   *"For if you forgive men their trespasses, your heavenly Father also will forgive you."* —MATTHEW 6:14 (RSV)

I was looking into the eyes of a young Christian, a client named Bill. He had been confessing his sins to me, but his face was a pretzel of anguish.

"Why can't I *feel* forgiven? I confess one particular sin every day, and I haven't committed it again since I first brought it to the Lord. What's the matter with me? Am I too awful a person to be forgiven? Maybe I'm not confessing in the right way."

I was sad about Bill's frustration. I remembered being in the same boat, and I told him about my struggle with not feeling forgiven.

"Bill," I said, "I'd always thought God forgives our sins if we confess them. But Jesus didn't say that. What He actually said is that we're not ready to receive forgiveness from God until we've forgiven the people who have sinned against us."

Bill looked thoughtful. Then suddenly he said, "My gosh, it's my brother Jimmy! He felt I'd deserted him when I became a Christian last summer. He made fun of me, and he burned my New Testament in the campfire when the two of us went camping. He said he was sorry, but I just got up and went home. And I never forgave him!"

"There's one other thing Jesus said about this forgiveness process, Bill."

"What's that?"

"He said that if you're ready to pray and you remember that your brother has something against you, go and be reconciled to your brother, then work things out with God."

A few days later, Bill told me how he'd asked Jimmy, face to face, to forgive him for anything he had done to hurt him. "Finally, although I didn't want to, I told Jimmy that I forgave him for burning my New Testament."

"How do you feel now, Bill?"

"Very different, about Jimmy—and about me, much better!"

Dear Lord, thank You for the gift of forgiveness. Amen.

—KEITH MILLER

29/FRI   *Humility comes before honor.*

—PROVERBS 15:33 (NIV)

Occasionally, I feel as if I'm in—or from—outer space. I just can't keep up with the new language, symbols, machines. Like the evening when a girlfriend and I tried a new restaurant. "That moon place," I said tentatively.

"The Luna Grill?"

That was it. Walk in and you can't miss the space theme. A heavenly mural spans the main wall. From the center, a big, bright sun face smiles down on the diners. From the sun's forehead, cheeks and chin flow light-rays that tint the plaster yellow, all the way to the ends of the "horizon."

We sat near a pillar painted like the night sky. From the star-spangled menu, we ordered the special. After coffee I excused myself.

"The ladies' room?" I asked the waitress.

She pointed me toward a back hallway, where I found two closed doors, each painted with a planet. One door said MARS, the other, VENUS.

I knew Mars and Venus were popular gender labels, as if men and women came from different planets. But when faced with the prospect of walking into the wrong restroom, I was uncertain: *Men from Mars? Women from Mars? Women from Venus?*

I looked for more clues. I saw only one: those gender symbols made from circles with stick-lines. *Arrow or cross? Which is which? Which is mine?* I suddenly couldn't figure that out either.

I swallowed my pride, found the waitress and admitted my ignorance. "Mars or Venus?" I asked, feeling as helpless as an alien who can't read the local language.

"Venus," she said, assuring me I hadn't been the first to admit I needed help to discern the signs. "Remember, M—Men and Mars."

"Got it. Thanks." I confidently knocked on the right door—marked with a cross, not an arrow.

Lord, when I'm not clear on the meaning of the signs or directions, help me to humbly admit my bewilderment and ask for help—from someone nearby or directly from You.

—EVELYN BENCE

$30/$SAT   *When I was brought low, he saved me.*
—PSALM 116:6 (RSV)

All summer, my girlfriend Donna had been pestering me about visiting the big amusement park that had recently opened in the southern part of our state. "We're too old for amusement parks," I told her. But Donna was insistent.

Finally, I gave in. I swung by her house early one morning and found her waiting out front, all dressed up for our big adventure. She even had on her favorite pair of gold earrings.

"We're not visiting royalty, you know."

"Oh, cheer up. You're going to have a good time today, you just don't know it."

By our second hour at the park, I felt like a ten-year-old. "Let's go on the loop-the-loop," I said.

"Oh, no, I hate roller coasters."

"Hey, you were the one who wanted to come, remember?"

Finally, I cajoled Donna into line. She screamed louder than anyone I'd ever heard as the car rushed through a 360-degree loop, plastering us to our seats.

On the drive home, Donna reached up and touched her left ear. "Oh, no! My earring! I must have lost it on that roller coaster." I felt terrible. Not only had I been a grouch about going to the park, but I'd also pressured Donna into going on the roller coaster.

Just then, I felt something funny in my breast pocket. I reached in—and pulled out Donna's earring.

The rest of the way home, we tried to figure out how that earring had made its way into my pocket. Finally, we decided it must have dropped from Donna's ear on the loop-the-loop, just as she'd thought. Then, against more odds than we could even imagine, it had fallen straight into my pocket as we swooped back down.

It's been twenty years since that day at the amusement park. But to this day, whenever I find myself in a fix I can't see my way out of, I stop and remember the feel of that earring brushing my fingertips as I reached into my pocket.

Thank You, Lord, for the assurance that whatever happens, You will get me through. —PTOLEMY TOMPKINS

31 / SUN "I tell you the truth, anyone who will not receive the kingdom of God like a little child will never enter it." —LUKE 18:17 (NIV)

A few years ago, I traveled to Greensboro, Alabama, to help rebuild the Rising Star Baptist Church, which had burned to the ground. I'm a builder. When I stepped onto the red clay of the building site, I felt that I had entered the kingdom of God.

Everyone on my volunteer crew was unskilled but highly motivated. By the end of the week, I could trust each worker to mark and cut lumber accurately. Each worker, that is, except Ian.

Members of the church, including parents with their children, came by the building site each day to help with the work. Ian peeled off his nail belt the moment he saw the kids and went over to play with them. Some of my other workers grumbled about Ian's work habits; I couldn't blame them. I planned to talk to Ian on Sunday evening about how he was affecting the morale of the crew.

On Sunday afternoon, the congregation of Rising Star served us a huge meal at the building site. I looked forward to fielding questions about the dimensions and design of the new church. I was also prepared to point out how hard everyone had worked all week—everyone except Ian.

The church members were kind to me and my crew, but they had no questions for any of us—any of us, that is, except Ian. All afternoon, parents thanked him for being so good to their kids.

I still planned to talk to Ian that evening. After all, I needed to thank him, too—for reminding me about the real kingdom of God. My crew and I thought we were in Greensboro to rebuild a church. None of us thought we could rebuild the broken hearts of its people. None of us, that is, except Ian.

Thank You, God, for giving me something to contribute to building Your kingdom.
—TIM WILLIAMS

My Daily Blessings

1 _____

2 _____

3 _____

4 _____

5 _____

AUGUST 2003

6 _____

7 _____

8 _____

9 _____

10 _____

11 _____

12 _____

13 _____

14 _____

15 _____

16 _____

17 _____

18 _____

19 _____

20 _____

21 _____

22 _____

23 _____

24 _____

25 _____

26 _____

27 _____

28 _____

29 _____

30 _____

31 _____

SEPTEMBER

Blessed are the peacemakers: for
they shall be called the children of God.
—Matthew 5:9

S	M	T	W	T	F	S
	1	2	3	4	5	6
7	8	9	10	11	12	13
14	15	16	17	18	19	20
21	22	23	24	25	26	27
28	29	30				

1 / MON   *There is nothing better for a man than . . .
that he should make his soul enjoy good in his labour. . . .*
—ECCLESIASTES 2:24

Down the hill from our house lies a stretch of track that carries trains from Nashville to Memphis. Since our move here three years ago, my husband David and I have come to love the sound of the trains that pass at intervals throughout the day and night. Each comes with its own distinct sound, a personality lent by the engineer who sounds the whistle.

We've named my favorite "Soul Man." He nurses the whistle like a man coaxing the blues from a horn on Beale Street. David favors "Puff Daddy," an engineer who pulls the whistle in quick, short shouts that sing a happy song as he moves down the track.

But beyond the poetry and the pure enjoyment of living near the rails, David and I have gleaned another lesson from our engineers: There's nothing better than to find something to enjoy in whatever work you happen to be doing.

Cooking a meal, washing clothes, cleaning a house matter to those we serve in this way. Waiting tables in a restaurant, cleaning rooms in a hotel, pressing clothes in a laundry matter just as much. Take any job, and chances are that the bottom line will be one person serving the needs of another. As a child and adolescent therapist, our daughter Keri is helping others to have better lives. Despite some of the preconceived notions of what a financial adviser does, it's clear that our son Brock is working to help people achieve financial security and have better lives, too.

Dig down through the layers of your job until you get to the ultimate truth that what you do matters. Then find the glory in your job. Blow your whistle, toot your horn, enjoy the good in your labor. There's nothing better than this!

Father, let me see my work as worthwhile and let me enjoy the good that my work generates.   —PAM KIDD

AN EYE FOR BLESSINGS

2/TUE   TIME OUT
My times are in thy hand....   —PSALM 31:15

I stopped at the foot of the stairs and set down the vacuum. I'd been running up and down, getting a bedroom ready for guests. The phone had rung nonstop, the breakfast dishes were still on the table and none of this was getting that writing assignment done.

It was time for a minute vacation. I stuck a CD into the player, dropped into a chair, put my head back and let Gregorian chant transport me for a moment to an unhurried world.

I discovered the wisdom of these brief getaways when my husband and I were on an actual vacation. In the Florida panhandle, we had stopped for the night at a motel set in a grove of ancient live oaks. Printed on the breakfast menu of the adjoining restaurant we noticed "The Oaks Prayer for Today":

> Slow me down, Lord. Ease the pounding of my heart by the quieting of my mind. . . . Teach me the art of taking minute vacations: of slowing down to look at seashells, to chat with a friend, to pet a dog. . . . Let me look up into the towering oaks and know they grew great and strong because they grew slowly and well.

Minute vacations—could I really recapture, in the workaday world, the release of pressure we felt on that rambling, no-special-destination car trip? For a few days we really were stopping to look at seashells and make friends with playful dogs. I copied down the prayer and, back home, set out to experiment. A two-minute stretching exercise turned out to be a quick way to relax. So did a stroll around the yard. Or a few minutes with a crossword puzzle.

I developed a score of instant escapes, like preparing a cup of Lapsang Souchong tea with my best china, or opening a photo album and spending a moment in another time and place.

It isn't only the minute vacation, I'm finding, that's different. To stop, to step aside, to lay down—even for a moment—the pressures to achieve is to see all the other minutes in a new way, to receive time itself as a daily blessing.

Lord, teach me to walk today in Your unhurried steps.

—ELIZABETH SHERRILL

*3/*WED   *On this wise ye shall bless the children of Israel, saying unto them, The Lord bless thee, and keep thee.*

—NUMBERS 6:23-24

All summer long we had been talking and praying about where our son Ryan would go to high school. He had been going to private schools since his first preschool at age three, but now he pleaded with us to let him attend a public high school. He had a number of reasons for wanting to go, some good (a wider range of courses to choose from, better sports and activity programs, a more diverse student body) and some not so good (he'd never had the privilege of riding a school bus).

After carefully considering the pluses and minuses, my wife Rosie and I decided to listen to Ryan. But I was still uneasy.

On the morning of the first day of school, I went into Ryan's room full of concerns about this new chapter in his life. He and I prayed that he would be successful, both academically and personally, that he would make good friends, and that he would grow in character and in his walk with the Lord. I opened my heart and fears to God, acknowledging that I couldn't go to the school and protect him from all that he would encounter.

By the time Ryan left, I was able to relax. Although a new environment, new challenges and new temptations awaited him, he was in God's hands.

Ryan came home excited about his first day in public school. He talked about the bus ride, the other students, his new teachers and what a good day it had been. I guess as a father, I'll always be anxious about my children, but each day I'm learning a little more about how to let go and trust God.

Lord, thank You for the blessing of Ryan's first day in high school. Help me to deepen my prayer for him and my trust in You. —DOLPHUS WEARY

$4/_{THU}$ *Wherefore comfort yourselves together, and edify one another. . . .* —I THESSALONIANS 5:11

A few weeks ago a young couple called and asked Lynn and me to be their "marriage mentors." I felt flattered, but even before hanging up the phone, I could think of lots of reasons why we couldn't. First of all, "marriage mentors" sounds like know-it-all people who have all the answers about how to maintain a meaningful, sizzling marriage, and the track record to prove they're doing it. Although Lynn and I have been married thirty-three years, we don't have any formulas about what makes a marriage work, and I know I don't always love him as well as I should.

"Maybe they just want us to be their friends," Lynn suggested.

That sounded a lot less intimidating, so we invited them over for dinner and sat on the patio together, eating chicken enchiladas and talking about their three young children and how the responsibilities of being mom and dad change the husband-and-wife part of marriage. We talked about struggles with finances and grandparents and priorities. Lynn and I spent lots of time listening and laughing as we remembered our own bungling journey through some of those challenges in the early years of our marriage.

At the end of the evening, the couple said they'd like to get together like this, once a month, "just to talk." Later, as I marked that next date on our calendar, I realized that mentoring isn't about having the right answers or being perfect examples. It's about listening and sharing our own stories, especially our mistakes. It's about being friends at different places of the same life journey. It's about letting these young people see that we have survived the struggles they are facing.

Father, please help me always to be willing to encourage those who are coming along behind me. —CAROL KUYKENDALL

5 / FRI   *Our mouths were filled with laughter. . . .*
—PSALM 126:2 (NIV)

For several years I taught a workshop called "Clutter Be Gone." I was embarrassed at first because I came to do it almost by accident. After all, I was no expert, just someone who'd struggled with the problem herself. But when I spoke honestly about having hidden piles of papers in the bathtub one night and my students responded with similar tales, I knew I had something to offer them. Still, I struggled with shame around the topic. "God," I pleaded one night, "help me help these students."

A few days later my mother sent me a clipping in the mail about "National Clutter Awareness Week." (I think it's in November, but I misplaced the clipping, of course). Mentioning that curious fact to my friend Louise, I said, "Can you believe it? There's a holiday just for clutter. How are we supposed to celebrate? By cleaning the refrigerator?"

"Now if I ever cleaned out my refrigerator, that *would* be a holiday!" Louise quipped.

Continuing along that silly vein, I said, "I wonder if they'll close the banks and schools?"

"They would," said Louise, "except nobody who celebrates the day can remember where they put the keys."

As we chuckled, I realized that I wasn't feeling quite so gloomy over the piles of laundry in my room or the mail I hadn't sorted yet. That was the answer to my question: *Use humor in your class. Making light of the subject doesn't mean that it's not a serious problem, it just means that you can have fun while working on it.*

Thank You, God, for showing me that laughing at a problem doesn't mean that I'm taking it lightly.   —LINDA NEUKRUG

6 / SAT   *For we are members of his body, of his flesh, and of his bones.*
—EPHESIANS 5:30

Over the years, I've worshiped in many different kinds of churches: formal and informal, conservative and liberal, emotional and reserved, warm and very cold. I was in a chilly church once where the ushers wore gloves—in the summer—but I was never in a church like the one reputed to be so cold that the ushers wore ice skates. Beyond worship style, however, I have another criterion for evaluating a church: How serious are its members about reaching out beyond their church's doors?

The Pennsylvania church that my wife Shirley and I attend during the summer has impressed us with its missions, one of which is a shoe bank for families on a tight budget. Many of us take a pair of shoes for granted, but if the head of the house is out of work or ill or earning the minimum wage, finding money for shoes for four or five kids can be overwhelming. That's where our church comes in. With the help of a local store, the church purchases new sneakers at discount and dispenses them free to needy youngsters.

Recently, Shirley and I helped one Saturday just before the start of school. For better than three hours, we, along with several others, scurried around nonstop on our hands and knees, fitting kids with shoes. All told, we passed out more than 125 pairs. Our reward was the beaming smiles of grateful boys and girls. One little towheaded boy with bright sky-blue eyes was so overjoyed with his new sneakers that he gave me a big hug before skipping out of the room.

When the last of the crowd had departed and the workers sat down exhausted, I brushed the dirt off the knees of my tan chinos. "They look as if you've been working in a coal mine," Shirley observed with a grin.

"No, I've been praying," I answered. And in a way, I had.

> *Teach us, God, to make our lives a prayer,*
> *So that our acts reflect You everywhere.*
>
> —FRED BAUER

7/SUN   *Give, and it shall be given unto you; good measure, pressed down, and shaken together, and running over. . . .*   —LUKE 6:38

I woke up this morning feeling that all I wanted to do was to stay in bed and cry. I really had no reason to feel sad: I love my life, my husband and my children; this little village we live in; our spiritual community. In fact, I had no excuse at all for feeling tearful and wanting to stay in bed.

Today is Sunday. Robert and I attend church on weekdays so that we can stay with Belva, our hospice patient, on Sundays, and give her husband an opportunity to go to church. It was a great effort for me to drag myself out of bed, get dressed, fix breakfast and drive the five miles to Belva's house. But when we walked in the door, something unusual happened: Belva smiled and said "Hello"—quite an amazing thing for this end-stage Alzheimer's patient, who is usually mute and sleeps most of the time.

After her husband left, I began feeding Belva, and she eagerly opened her mouth to receive each bite of cereal and spoonful of juice. And when she had her breakfast, she looked right at me and smiled again! I felt my heart open, and my early-morning sadness left as mysteriously as it had come.

Sometimes I wonder which of us is nourished most by this Sunday morning ritual, Belva or I. But I do know that it's quite impossible to help someone else without having my own soul fed in the process.

When I'm feeling down, Holy One, please lead me to someone I can help, so I may know the grace of both giving and receiving.
—MARILYN MORGAN KING

8/ MON   *"Whoever humbles himself like this child is the greatest in the kingdom of heaven."* —MATTHEW 18:4 (NIV)

I have a friend named Venus who sometimes braids my hair. She's a very serious woman, and most of her time is devoted to Bible study, to being a good wife and to raising her two children Cameron and Marian.

"She doesn't talk much when others are around," Venus said of her daughter Marian. "But when we're alone, she dances, spins and leaps all over the place. She seems to have difficulty sitting still. Marian loves music, and she wants to sing all the time. She even wants to sing her prayers."

Venus has worked hard to help her daughter grow into a responsible adult. Yet Marian seemed so different from her logical, level-headed mother.

When Marian turned five, she announced that she wanted a butterfly birthday party. Her cake was to be shaped like a butterfly. She wanted butterfly clothes and butterfly food, and she would be the "butterfly queen." Venus fretted over every detail, searching craft stores for touches that would make the party perfect.

When the big day arrived, each girl who came to the party was given a wraparound skirt of magenta or turquoise tulle and a makeshift crown of the same color. Each boy was given a cardboard crown and a royal robe made of *kente* cloth. Each child received a large jeweled plastic ring.

The mothers who came to the party flushed and giggled. Some of them—including Venus and me—joined in the dress-up. The fathers took videos of the party and seemed to be making an effort to speak in especially deep voices.

The most beautiful moment was the butterfly dance. In a white lace dress, ballet slippers, tiara and what looked like gossamer wings, Marian was the queen. The butterfly queen's eyes, however, stayed glued to her mother.

Arms over her head, her eyes closed, Venus led the dance. On her tiptoes, she twirled and sashayed in just the way I'd often seen Marian perform.

Lord, help me to find and reclaim the gifts of childhood I've left behind. —SHARON FOSTER

9/ TUE   *And fear not them which kill the body, but are not able to kill the soul. . . .*   —MATTHEW 10:28

This noon I went to say good-bye to an old friend. She was now known as *Norway*, but to many of us she would always be *France*. I'd sailed on her four times—three times across the Atlantic in the 1960s, when she was a true ocean liner, and once in the mid-1990s when she had been turned into a cruise ship.

I was part of a privileged group of ship-lovers who went aboard for what was billed as a final visit. There was a brief speech from the captain and a display of objects relating to the ship's history, and then we were free to join a guided tour. I preferred to wander alone.

I saw the old leisurely veranda deck, which was now a slicked-up Fifth Avenue, with different shops opening along the way. The first-class smoking room, now the Club Internationale, was still handsome, though I missed the huge windows that looked out gloriously to sea. I entered the dining room by the grand staircase, where women, as they made their way down, vied to outdo each other in elegance. Then I saw that a favorite little dining room I was lucky enough to know about, La Louisiane, was no more. Little things, perhaps, but they troubled me.

Suddenly, I caught myself. What was I doing, trying to conjure up the past to make me doubly sad? This was a farewell visit, so why not bid it good-bye and think of the improvements that cruise ships have that ocean liners did not.

Old salts and lovers of the sea say ships have souls. If they do, then they, too, will not die. And so it is, I am sure, with *France.*

Good-bye, old girl, good-bye.

There are lots of good ships to sail on, Father. Let me stop living in the past.
—VAN VARNER

10/WED *My letters have been straightforward and sincere; nothing is written between the lines!*
—II CORINTHIANS 1:13 (TLB)

I remember vividly one of the few times my second husband came to me for advice. As a high school principal, he'd written a letter to send to the students' parents, and he asked me to comment on it. I read the entire two pages, then took a deep breath. As gently as I could, I explained that the sentences were too long and hard to understand, the words were too big, and the tone was too academic. Most of what he was trying to say was in the last two paragraphs—and those were very good.

I asked him to tell me what he was trying to say. It was wonderful, interesting, appropriate and poignant—and I simply wrote it down almost exactly the way he said it. The final version of that letter, shortened to less than one page, was something I'm sure the parents enjoyed reading.

All of us are sometimes guilty of "puffing up" our words on paper. A doctor once wrote on a chart, "negative patient-care outcome." Why didn't he just write that the patient died?

My Uncle Ralph told me that when he was a young military cadet he was expected to salute his superior officer at the end of each meal and say, "Sir, my gastronomical satiety admonishes me that I have reached that state of deglutition consistent with dietetic integrity." In other words, "I'm full."

Today, Lord, and every day, whether I'm writing a letter to a friend, an office memo or a simple note to my children, keep me from trying to impress others with my vocabulary and wordiness. Instead, help me say what I want to say clearly and stop when I've said it. —PATRICIA LORENZ

11 / THU   *From everlasting to everlasting you are God.*
—PSALM 90:2 (NIV)

September 11, 2001: the day the World Trade Center and the Pentagon were targeted by terrorists. The day death and tragedy swept over our country like a dark plague. At work, we all bent toward the small radio that kept giving us the too-terrible-to-be-true news. But it was true. As the editor of two Web sites—one for kids and one for teens—I longed to meet—quickly—the challenge of helping young people cope with this horror.

Like everyone else in the office, I went home at noon. And if the radio reports were bad, the TV images were unthinkable. Finally, late in the day, I went for a walk along the shores of Lake Michigan. I had decided to write an open letter to our young Web visitors, but what could I say? I could make no sense of it all; how could I help the kids?

The sun was just setting, a huge, perfect ball, red as a ripe tomato. Magnificent in every way, it sank slowly, purple clouds easing it into the horizon. My heart still heavy, I turned back toward my car. That's when I saw them: two teenaged girls sitting in the sand, playing guitars. Their heads were bent forward as their fingers strummed and their voices blended in harmony. As I got closer, I heard the song:

> *Our God is an awesome God,*
> *He reigns from heaven above,*
> *With wisdom, power and love,*
> *Our God is an awesome God.*

And suddenly I knew what to say in my open letter: *God is still in control. God doesn't want you to be afraid.* I turned back for a last look at the sunset-streaked sky. *And He will be near you—in ways more awesome than you can imagine!*

When the foundations of the earth shake, God, You are our rock and our salvation!
—MARY LOU CARNEY

12 / FRI   *In humility consider others better than your-selves. Each of you should look not only to your own interests, but also to the interests of others.* —PHILIPPIANS 2:3-4 (NIV)

There were just two ladies ahead of me that day at the supermarket checkout aisle. The first had a shopping cart loaded top to bottom with groceries and household cleaning supplies.

Must have a family, I speculated as I watched her unload. (It's a mental game I often play in lineups.) *Big box of detergent—active outdoor kids. Prepackaged puddings, small boxes of juice, crackers and cheese—kids take lunches to school. A wide variety of salad makings—Mom diets. Choice cuts of beef—Dad barbecues. Tins of dog food—pampered pooch.*

The old lady ahead of me was also watching the succession of boxes and cartons and bags that passed over the scanner. The total appeared, and the well-dressed young woman reached into her leather handbag and took out her debit card. Meanwhile, the old woman was fumbling in her own purse for a crumpled slip of paper, which she smoothed out on the counter. I recognized it instantly as a coupon redeemable for ten percent off any grocery order over one hundred dollars. "Wait a minute!" she said to the woman who was about to pay. "I clipped this out of the weekly sale bill. Go ahead and use it. It could save you about fifteen dollars."

"Why, uh, thank you. Thank you for your . . . uh . . . generosity," the recipient stammered.

"You're most welcome," the old woman replied cheerfully. "I pass on those coupons to other folks as often as I can." Then placing a head of cabbage, three potatoes and a small bottle of cola on the checkout counter, she greeted the cashier brightly. "Hello there, sonny! I guess you better run a subtotal before you ring up that pop. I might just be a little short today."

Father in heaven, even though I may be "a little short today," help me to maintain a generous spirit. —ALMA BARKMAN

*13/*SAT *And there I will meet with thee, and I will commune with thee from above the mercy seat. . . .*
—EXODUS 25:22

My son Jon, his twin brother Jeremy, his sisters Julie and Jennifer, his stepfather Gene and I were crowded together in Room 48 of the small motel at Dunklin Memorial Camp in Florida—a city of refuge where men like Jon are set free from all kinds of addictions.

We all knew that Jon was learning how to communicate effectively with God, and today he shared his prayer journal with us.

"Father, thank You for getting them all here safely. Thank You for hearing my prayers, and being attentive to my heart and to my family's hearts this morning. Thank You also for knowing exactly how to work in each of their lives and for preparing a place in eternity for each of us. Father, speak to me about the worry I had yesterday and about my forgetting You."

"They all see a little more of My Son in you. Know that your struggles have purpose, and trust that I am capable. My spirit, the Spirit of Jehovah, lives in you. Now you cannot forget for long that you are Mine and that I shape every detail of your life. I want you to know that you are accepting responsibility for your actions. There is no one to blame but yourself for your chemical addiction, and I have taken the blame and thrown it away. I cannot even see your sin. All I see is that you are My son for eternity. How can anything I have chosen run from Me? I gave it the ability to run and the will to run. Surely I can call it back. I hear every prayer from your family and anoint the answer with My testimony."

We all wept openly together. We had never been so close as a family.

Holy Father, starting today, teach me to commune with You through prayer and journaling as my son does.
—MARION BOND WEST

*14/SUN   How excellent is thy lovingkindness, O God!
therefore the children of men put their trust under the shadow of
thy wings.*   —PSALM 36:7

It was a Wednesday in September. Our daughter Tamara was
stranded in Anchorage, Alaska, with a newborn and toddlers
Zachary and Hannah, while her husband trained at the police acad-
emy. I had come to rescue her.

This day, sunny and mellow and smelling of changing birch
leaves, I took Zachary and Hannah to play in the park. Soon an
older woman meandered by with a young child in tow. She nodded
and smiled, but didn't seem inclined to chat. Her little charge toddled off across the grass with Hannah.

Zachary and I teeter-tottered while the girls sailed down a small
slide beneath the watchful eye of the unknown woman. When I
twirled my grandchildren on the tire swing, the other child wanted
to swing, too, and the woman came over to help. Haltingly she told
me she was from Russia, visiting her daughter and granddaughter
Nicole.

"Oh," I exclaimed, "you're a *babushka!*"

She laughed, nodding yes.

I pointed to myself. "Me, too," I said.

When Zachary tired of the swing, I went off with him to play in
the sand, leaving the Russian grandmother still twirling the girls.
Somehow Hannah slipped off the tire and fell backward onto the
ground. The Russian grandmother was bending down anxiously
over her when I scooped Hannah into my arms.

"It's all right," I said. "She's not hurt."

That's when the thought hit me: *Here we are, two grandmothers
from countries that used to be enemies, playing in the park with our
grandchildren, teaching them to get along and watching out for them
with equal concern.*

The two of us left the park, taking our grandchildren in opposite
directions. We had met only briefly, but it was long enough for me
to gain new understanding of a grandmother's mission: to help
shape our world's future by sowing seeds of consideration and
respect—starting in the park.

*Heavenly Father, with my grandchildren in tow, lead me in Your
path of loving-kindness.*
                                           —CAROL KNAPP

FOLLOWING JESUS

15/MON LIGHTENING OUR LOAD

Bear one another's burdens, and thus fulfill the law of Christ.

—GALATIANS 6:2 (NAS)

When my sister Rebekkah bought her first home, I noticed that she was dragging her feet in getting everything fixed up. Her air-conditioning was on the blink, and her curtains lay limp and wrinkled in a laundry hamper. With their intricate crocheted-edge ruffles, I imagined them starched to crisp perfection in all the windows. But when I asked Rebekkah about it, she threw up her hands at all the boxes not yet unpacked and said, "I don't know how to start."

At first, her procrastination annoyed me. And then a memory surfaced: I was twenty years old and had just moved into my first apartment. All the windows were bare. For years I'd dreamed of having a place of my own with white crisscrossed curtains with big ruffles like the ones my friend Sue Sowards had. I ordered a pair of them for my living room window from the JCPenney catalog. But how did you press those ruffles just so? And how did you fashion the tiebacks like a bow on a little girl's party dress? In a word, how did you ever start? When I'd telephoned Sue with my dilemma, she was at my unair-conditioned apartment in a flash with her trusty iron and blue liquid starch.

Now, faster than you can say "spray starch," I was plotting my strategy. While Rebekkah worked the evening shift, I would make fast work of her curtains. After midnight, when Rebekkah pulled into her dark driveway, hospitality lights glowed at each window, illuminating the soft ruffles framing grapevine wreaths, each tied up with a homespun bow.

I watched from behind the curtains as Rebekkah nearly went to the wrong house. "I can't believe you did this for me," she gushed.

"There's someone else you need to thank," I told her. "You see, I have this friend who once got me started."

Today, Lord, help me lighten another's load in Your name.

—ROBERTA MESSNER

READER'S ROOM

At the age of forty-eight, after fifteen years at the same job, the Lord opened doors for me to go back to college. When I'm finished, I'll be embarking on a new career as an occupational therapist assistant.

Being a student again is exciting, as I discover how much fun it is to study and learn and meet new people in my new "mission field." God gave me four tools for evangelizing at college: I am to be myself; to love people by getting to know them; to talk about my relationship with Him whenever possible, so people get used to hearing it; and to keep my ears open to Him at all times so He can supply my words if necessary.

I know that this new chapter in my life is a joint project with God, and I am excited by the countless ways I'll be able to serve Him when I'm finished.

—MARTHA A. SUTER, SOUTH BEND, INDIANA

16/TUE   *"So I say to you: Ask and it will be given to you. . . ."*
—LUKE 11:9 (NIV)

"When you go to the men's Bible study tonight," Carol was saying, "please, *please* ask someone to recommend a plumber."

I nodded, wincing at my wife's plaintive tone. The drip in our shower had been going on for months, maybe a year. I had replaced the washers, but the hot water kept dripping. When I shone a flashlight in, I saw that the valve seat was corroded. Trying to save money, I checked my home-repair manual, bought an inexpensive valve-seat grinder and smoothed it down. The drip soon recurred. I ground some more, but the fix lasted only days. Now it was so bad that no matter how hard we turned off the handle, the faucet dispensed a constant dribble.

I feared a huge expense. "I've ground as much as I dare," I explained. "A plumber may need to replace the pipes. To get to them, he'd have to remove the prefab tub enclosure . . ."

"Whatever it costs," Carol said, "it needs to be fixed. Think of the cost of the water we're wasting."

That night at the conclusion of Bible study, I leaned over and asked one of the men, "Do you know anything about plumbing?"

"A little," he replied. "What do you want to know?"

I explained my predicament. To my amazement, my friend pulled out a sheet of paper and began sketching. "The valve seat screws in here, like this," he said, demonstrating with his hand. "It requires a special valve-seat tool."

"That's all?" I asked. He nodded. The manual hadn't explained that the valve seat was a separate piece that could be replaced.

The next day I drove to the plumbing supply store, bought a new valve seat and the tool, and replaced the corroded part. The dripping ceased. Best of all, it cost me less than six dollars, including the tool! I could have saved myself months of aggravation if only I'd asked.

Lord, remind me to ask questions when I lack knowledge.

—HAROLD HOSTETLER

17/WED   *And above all these put on love, which binds them everything together in perfect harmony.*

—COLOSSIANS 3:14 (RSV)

"Mary, are you dressed?" I hardly know why I bother to ask. If I hear the toilet flush, I know I have to go hunt down my two-year-old and put her clothes back on. If she spills a bit of water on her dress, next thing I know she's taken it off. If she were given a choice (which she isn't), she'd scamper about nude all day long.

Mary delights in being in her birthday suit, and at her age my talks about modesty don't mean a thing. I was halfway through my morning prayers today when Mary streaked by on her way to the kids' room. I sighed and debated whether to finish my devotions or get up and pursue her. Glancing at my book, I chuckled to see that the reading for the morning began with nothing other than Colossians 3:12–13 (RSV). "Put on then, as God's chosen ones, holy beloved, compassion, kindness, lowliness, meekness, patience, forbearing one another and, if one has a complaint against another, forgiving each other; as the Lord has forgiven you, so you also must forgive."

Put on. How many times a day do I tell my daughter to put on something? And how many times do I groan at how much I have to put up with? With a wry grin I put down my book and walked after my impish daughter. There was no point in being irritated with her: If I'm to put on love, then I must begin with Paul's long list of smaller things. I can put on Mary's shirt with a prayer that I may be kinder. I can put on her pants while praying for patience. Every day I can put on her clothes (and mine) with prayers for compassion and lowliness and meekness. Think how naked my life would be without these virtues. It would be downright indecent!

Lord Jesus, You clothed me with the robe of salvation; clothe my soul in holiness today. —JULIA ATTAWAY

18/THU   *"As you wish that men would do to you, do so to them."* —LUKE 6:31 (RSV)

When I was in junior high school, I was painfully, embarrassingly bashful. So I'd spend recess time off by myself in a corner of the school yard, pretending not to care I wasn't part of the group sharing in friendly chatter. *Just why do they enjoy such camaraderie with one another?* I wondered.

That's when I noticed a pattern: My classmates almost always greeted each other by name, then mentioned subjects they were interested in. "Hey, Bill, you heading for football practice?" "Hi, Mary. What did you think of that test?"

Say, that's what I can do, I thought. *I'll memorize everybody's name and their interests. What a job! There are a hundred kids in all my junior high classes.* But when you're desperate enough, you can do anything. And I was that desperate. It took me a couple of months, but I stuck to it.

Then I noticed something else: I forgot my fright when I became intent on remembering the other children's names and interests. I'd wasted years wanting others to pay attention to *me* rather than being concerned about *them*.

Well, it wasn't long before others saw a "new" Isabel.

Father, now I know why You gave us the Golden Rule. If we treat others the way we want to be treated, things seem to fall into place.
—ISABEL WOLSELEY

*19/*FRI   *"For the Lamb in the midst of the throne will be their shepherd, and he will guide them to springs of living water. . . ."* —REVELATION 7:17 (RSV)

I grew up as a city kid. I played with my friends on concrete sidewalks, and if we wanted to see a tree, we had to take a bus to a city park. For some reason, I used to dream about living in the country, although the only time I saw the country was when my parents' friends who lived outside the city limits invited us to a picnic.

When I grew up, I moved to the suburbs and became a commuter. There was a lot to do, I had many friends and excitement was in the air. But I just wasn't comfortable. I didn't feel I belonged there.

Then one day I got lost taking a detour, and I ended up on a lovely country road . . . and I fell in love! This was where I wanted to live. In time, I found a house I could afford and began packing.

Frankly, I was scared on the day I moved. Sure, there were trees and fields and hills all around my new little home. But would I miss the conveniences of city life, the multitude of people all around me, the excitement?

"Hey, this is nice!" one of the movers said as he climbed out of the van.

"If you like quiet," said the other.

After they left, I was too tired to begin unpacking, so I found some sheets, made my bed and climbed into it.

No light came into the room from outside because there were no streetlights. There were no sounds. Only silence. But I didn't feel the least bit lonely or isolated. Instead, I felt something I had never known before: I was home.

As I lay in the darkness, I began to pray. I wanted to thank God for paying attention to the dream I had as a child. Somehow, even then, I knew where I belonged—and with God's help, I finally got there.

Dear Father, thank You for the guidance You send to us in the dreams of our childhood. Amen. —PHYLLIS HOBE

20/SAT *A man that hath friends must show himself friendly: and there is a friend that sticketh closer than a brother.* —PROVERBS 18:24

It was a lazy Saturday morning, and I had stopped at a doughnut shop for coffee and a sweet roll. Relishing a day without schedule or agenda, I leaned back in my chair and breathed the sweet aroma of fresh pastries and brewing coffee. It was good to be alive.

That was when I heard an elderly woman's voice laugh and cackle, "Well, Maude, I can even remember when I could chew gum." Suppressing a chuckle, I turned to see four elderly ladies sitting at a corner table, giggling and carrying on like schoolgirls.

The waitress came to take my order, saw me quietly laughing and said, "They come here every morning, sure as the sun rises. Drink a gallon of coffee together and have a good time. They're a sight!"

As I sipped my coffee and listened to their chatter, I reflected that friendship and laughter are gifts to be cherished, the best fruits of a lifetime. The surest investment for future happiness is not in money but in relationships.

Dear God, thank You for special folks who refresh my soul and make me glad. May I cherish and nurture my friendships this day. Amen. —SCOTT WALKER

21/SUN *"I will set in the desert the cypress tree and the pine And the box tree together, That they may see and know . . . That the hand of the Lord has done this. . . ."* —ISAIAH 41:19–20 (NKJV)

My Irish bride of forty years has soft, busy eyes, framed with delicate freckles. Yet, without the blessing of eyeglasses she could not tell me from a tree. Severe astigmatism is complicated with so many retinal "floaters" that her eyes are like little goldfish bowls full of fish. "I wish I could see better," she says a hundred times a week, but I know few people who see as well as she does. She is like a detective in one of her beloved mystery novels and seldom misses a clue. There's more to vision than good eyes, and she knows the secret.

We can be out for a Sunday drive, passing by a drab soybean farm, and Sharon will keep up a constant prattle of appreciation. "Oh, look at all the billy goats! Isn't that interesting?" It's her favorite expression.

Our teenaged daughters used to mock her fascination with simple things. Natalie: "Oh, look at the pretty yellow centerlines on the road!" Teresa: "My, my, isn't that a pine tree? What a find!"

"All right, you guys," I fired back. "You should be more like your mother instead of so cynical and hard-to-please."

I have good eyes, but my mind drifts into never-never land and I miss a lot. Oh sure, I see the eighteen-wheeler that crashed and burned in the ditch and the crop duster that landed on the highway in front of me, but I missed the old man out picking wildflowers with his granddaughter.

From Sharon I have learned that vision is less about having good eyes and more about being interested in the beautiful world around me.

Isn't she interesting?

Lord, I wish I could see better.   —DANIEL SCHANTZ

22/MON *And the fruit of righteousness is sown in peace of them that make peace.*   —JAMES 3:18

Here's the story of a September morning not too long ago. Daylight was misty until the sun burned off the fog and awoke Americans everywhere, including sleepy New Yorkers. But the sky was soon rent by explosions and smoke and seemingly endless agony. By the end of the day, 3,500 people lay dead, and not just New Yorkers. Thousands more were wounded, many of them mortally; and thousands more were missing.

Five days later the President saw an opportunity in this tragedy, a chance to bring the nation together. He spoke boldly of freedom and the cost of freedom, of the value inherent in the country's founding, and how Americans would not be in bondage to their fear. In fact, he said, no American would be in bondage, period.

And so it was on September 22, 1862—141 years ago today—Abraham Lincoln signed the Emancipation Proclamation, freeing Southern slaves from the most horrid of human institutions.

The Union "victory"—if, indeed, it was a victory—that had emboldened Lincoln was the battle at Antietam Creek in Maryland. The 51st New York fought that day—September 17, 1862—as did Georgians and Texans, blue Americans vs. gray Americans from everywhere. It was the single bloodiest day in our history, one of the largest losses of life in a one-day conflict on American soil ever—until another, more recent September day.

I tell this story for one reason: Somehow we all survived. Somehow we outlasted a war of brother against brother, and we will outlast the next horror. We will survive our own insanity until the bright day we are all called home. And I believe, childlike, that heaven really is in the sky, and we'll look down on earth and see what astronauts see: that our little space island isn't blue vs. gray, but blue *and* gray, with room for the entire family.

Lord, may Your kingdom come, Your will be done, on earth as it is in heaven.   —MARK COLLINS

23/TUE   *Judge not, that ye be not judged.*
—MATTHEW 7:1

Every autumn, I get aggravated all over again. Each day on my walk, I pass a yard with a beautiful little pear tree. It's the only tree in the whole front yard, all the more noticeable for its loneliness. No taller than an average man, this little tree is literally bent over with the weight of luscious, shining fruit. Every day I walk by, hoping to see its owners gathering this bounty, taking advantage of the wondrous resource God has given them right in their own front yard. And every year, the fruit ripens, falls and rots on the grass.

I'd be satisfied if the owners would hang a sign on the tree saying, "Please Help Yourself" to hungry passersby. At least that way there wouldn't be all that waste, and the poor little pear tree wouldn't labor all year for naught.

One day last week I went walking by the tree, fuming at its inconsiderate, wasteful owners, when I had one of those lightbulb-over-the-head moments. *What am I so angry about?* I thought. *I've allowed my anger to spoil one of the most beautiful parts of my walk. I'm so annoyed with the homeowners for wasting the resources God gave them, that I'm wasting those He's given me!*

Maybe I was the one who needed to wear a sign around my neck saying, "Please Help Yourself." Just as a reminder.

Father, help me be less critical of others and more aware of my own need to change. —MARCI ALBORGHETTI

$\mathcal{C}$

$24/_{WED}$ *"I know you well; you aren't strong, but you have tried to obey. . . . I have opened a door to you that no one can shut."* —REVELATION 3:8 (TLB)

I had just completed my call and put my cell phone back in my purse when I saw my husband John's sly grin. "Don't even think about it!" I said. Trouble was, we were sitting in the same restaurant, about the same time of the evening as we were when it happened, back when everyone used public phones. . . .

People waved and smiled at me as I walked, beet-red with embarrassment, into the main dining room of the restaurant. Many of them had seen me outside as I gestured frantically to them from the small telephone booth adjacent to the parking lot. I had made my call and wanted to get out, but the more I wiggled the door, the more it resisted—I was stuck! As people went by, I signaled to them, pointing to the door, pointing to myself, pointing to the way out. They smiled and waved and moved along. I grimaced and mouthed the words, "I can't get out!" People either looked strangely at me or continued to smile and pass me by. It was getting late and soon most of the diners had gone inside. In desperation, I threw my whole weight against the door—it still wouldn't budge. "What can I do, dear Lord?" I prayed. "Please help me!"

Suddenly, as I twisted about, my shoulder caught an outside edge of the door and it folded inward. I was free!

"What took you so long?" my husband asked.

"You're not going to believe it!" I said sheepishly as I slid into my seat and told him my story. "Can you imagine, that door simply folded inward, and all that time I was pushing it outward!"

When I'm stuck in a tight place and pushing the wrong way, thank You, Lord, for hearing my cry and showing me the way out. —FAY ANGUS

25/THU *We know not what we should pray for as we ought: but the Spirit itself maketh intercession for us. . . .*
—ROMANS 8:26

I awoke at 4:15 this morning praying urgently to the sound of screeching rubber, crashing metal and shattering glass. I was completely alert, anxious even. I'd been praying when I woke up, a split-second before I heard the skidding tires. *Lord, help those people in the accident. Be with them. Comfort them.*

This is New York; I'm used to being awakened at all hours by the city that never sleeps (and sometimes won't let you, either). Still, I couldn't remember ever waking up actually praying. Even now, I didn't want to stop.

There was an all-night newsstand on the corner; they would surely call the police. Beat by beat my heart rate decelerated from a gallop to a canter. My wife Julee slumbered peacefully beside me, her slow breathing mingling in the dark with the dogs' tranquil snores. Finally, I drifted back to sleep to the sound of voices and approaching sirens.

A few hours later, I was buying my morning paper on my way to the office. "What on earth happened out here last night?" I asked Hassan, the newsdealer.

He paused, then nodded. "Oh, yes, that. Just a little fender bender. Nothing to worry about."

I strode across the intersection, now clogged with commuter traffic. My eye caught a few shards of a brake light glittering in the morning sun, the only evidence of any kind of mishap. I found myself resenting having being awakened so dramatically for a mere fender bender.

Yet the urgency of that prayer still echoed. I'd awoken an instant *before* I heard the screeching tires, and I was already praying. What did it mean?

I reached the other side of the intersection. Maybe I wasn't meant to know. The accident certainly sounded as if someone could have been hurt. What I knew for sure was that I felt as if I'd been shaken awake and told, "I need you."

God, thank You for those extraordinary moments when You use me to help others. Let me always be ready, even in the dead of night. —EDWARD GRINNAN

26/FRI *"I will not sacrifice to the Lord my God burnt offerings that cost me nothing."* —II SAMUEL 24:24 (NIV)

On Christmas night 2000, a food-processing plant in Garden City, Kansas, burned, leaving 2,300 people without jobs. United Methodist Mexican-American Ministries, where I work, together with other agencies and the entire community, assisted former employees with rent, utilities, clothing, food and other necessities for several months.

Then, in September, a seriously ill mother whose husband was still without work requested school clothes for her size five son and size seven daughter. The children literally had nothing that fit except pajamas. Our clothing room, though abundantly stocked, had no size fives and no size sevens. Nothing.

Dorothy, our emergency coordinator, immediately purchased an inexpensive outfit for each child and began hunting for additional items. Boys' clothes were easy: Dorothy's youngest son and two of my grandsons wore size five and had plenty of clothes to share. But where would we get girls' things? No one I knew had girls that size.

"I could ask my friend Sherry," our daughter Rebecca offered. "She may have clothes her girls have outgrown. You could pick them up on your way to work tomorrow."

A couple of hours later Rebecca called to report that Sherry had delivered a huge box full of size seven jeans, shoes, blouses, coats and dresses. "And that's not all!" Rebecca said. "There's a sack of candy for each child, a treasured teddy bear and even a favorite bright red sweater! Sherry says thanks—thanks for the opportunity to help someone in need, and thanks for the opportunity to help her daughters learn that a true gift is something we love."

A treasured teddy and a favorite red sweater—reminders to me that true gifts often involve sacrifice.

Giver of all good gifts, help us experience the joy of giving from the heart. —PENNEY SCHWAB

27/SAT *Know ye not that your body is the temple of the Holy Ghost which is in you, which ye have of God, and ye are not your own?* —I CORINTHIANS 6:19

"So, brown with a few highlights as usual?" asked Roxanne, the tall hairdresser with auburn curls. She had been coloring my hair regularly for a good many years.

"I think her hair is dyed, don't you?" was not a compliment in the small English village where I grew up. Sensible women simply didn't dye their hair. Years have passed and times have changed. Now almost every woman past her forties whom I know colors her hair as a matter of routine.

"Roxanne, I've been thinking that I should stop coloring my hair," I said rather tentatively.

"Why ever would you do that?" she replied. "It looks great."

"It's hard to explain," I said. "Don't you think it's, well, unnatural, now that I'm older?"

"As unnatural as wearing clothes or using lipstick," said Roxanne in her down-to-earth, cheerful manner.

As usual, she made sense. She began briskly to spread dark brown goo over my head. As she worked, I watched this strange operation in the mirror. *Why is it,* I wondered, *that I do this so faithfully and expensively every six weeks? Why am I not content with the gray hair that the years have sent me? Isn't it supposed to be a symbol of wisdom and maturity? Am I horribly vain?*

Roxanne finished her goo-spreading, set a timer and moved on to another client. I felt like a cookie browning in the oven. The timer ticked.

How I would look with white or gray hair? I wondered. How would family, friends and colleagues react?

Roxanne returned to check on her handiwork and, to my surprise, settled my unspoken debate: "Anyway, if the hairs on your head are all numbered," she said, "isn't it up to you to take good care of each of them?" The timer pinged.

Lord, help me to take good care of the body You have given me, for it is Your temple. —BRIGITTE WEEKS

28/SUN **And he shall turn the heart of the fathers to the children, and the heart of the children to their fathers. . . .**
—MALACHI 4:6

The flight was wonderful. My son William and I were traveling back to Atlanta from Connecticut where we had spent the weekend with my daughter Rebecca. Crammed into two coach-class seats, we colored and solved puzzles in his Mickey Mouse activity book. William gazed out the window, "Where are the birds?" he asked. "Can we sit on that cloud?"

Then he instructed me in the art of playing with Beanie Babies: "Keep your hand on the Beanie Baby. Don't talk like Daddy." I tried to keep his feet off the seats and his voice down as his play grew intense. Finally, he vigorously twirled his stuffed animal, accidentally flinging it into the air. It landed in the lap of a startled woman four rows away. I tried to read an article on wide-format inkjet printers, and I tried to work on my laptop computer, but William allowed none of that. We played during the entire flight.

As our plane descended into Atlanta, he paused to gaze out the window. The setting sun peered out from behind a cloud, and golden rays fanned all around. Suddenly, William exclaimed, "Daddy, I see God!"

"William, we can't see God," I told him.

"Why?" he asked. "Where is God?"

Looking into his deep blue eyes and watching the yellowing sunlight reflected in his hair, I said, "I'm not sure, but I can feel Him in my heart."

Thank You, Lord, for the times when a father and son can become a boy and his dad. —BILLY NEWMAN

29/MON   *The heart of the prudent getteth knowledge; and the ear of the wise seeketh knowledge.*   —PROVERBS 18:15

A smile crossed my face that September morning when my supervisor said, "Oscar, you've been tapped to learn the automatic boring mill and to teach others." The mill was intimidating: new gunmetal-gray and larger than a tank. I would be taught how to program the mill to produce machine parts automatically that we'd previously done by hand. It was a chance to learn a new craft, and I was excited to have the opportunity.

For seven weeks, I watched, learned and operated the mill. Then one Friday, the instructor said, "Oscar, I feel you know the machine pretty well. It was a pleasure working with you." We shook hands, and he was gone. I couldn't wait until Monday morning, when my new skills would be on display.

On Monday, my co-workers gathered to watch the magic machine perform. I pressed the start button . . . and nothing happened. My co-workers giggled, and one said, "Maybe it's out of gas. Have you put a nickel in it?" I blushed.

For hours, our chief electrician tried to solve the problem without success. We called the manufacturer, and within hours a youthful expert arrived. He smiled, pressed the start button and the machine roared into action. He turned the machine off and on several times, and then he said, "I think I know your problem."

With his left hand, he reached under a cover and pushed two matchsticklike switches in opposite directions. Then he pressed the start button. "These are safety switches," he said. "They must be reversed, or the machine won't start." During my seven-week training, I hadn't seen the instructor touch those switches, and he hadn't mentioned them.

I did teach others to use the machine. But I never forgot God's lesson for me. Those two little switches moved me from pride to humiliation to humility. And in doing so, they made me a better teacher.

Thank You, Father, for teaching me that knowledge should be shared with simplicity and sincerity.   —OSCAR GREENE

30/*TUE*   *"He is . . . like the brightness after rain. . . ."*
—II SAMUEL 23:4 (NIV)

To counteract the rainy, gloomy afternoon, I put on my red blazer to meet an architect friend, Jeff Wierenga, for lunch. As we sat near a window at the mall entrance, I watched damp shoppers scurrying in. "What awful weather," I said.

Jeff, who is an award-winning photographer, replied, "When I was traveling, I used to be disappointed when I reached a great spot to take pictures and the weather was bad. Then one day I saw a photographer in England standing in the pouring rain without an umbrella.

"I had to ask him why he was shooting in such a downpour. He said, 'Look at the shine on those slate roofs. It will make beautiful photos, the kind visitors to England want to buy.'

"After that," Jeff told me, "I didn't complain again about bad weather on my trips because I found I could get really good photos on rainy days. Sometimes they were better than the ones I took when the sun was so bright it washed everything out."

"What does the camera capture that we don't ordinarily see?" I asked.

"In the rain," he explained, "colors are more saturated. The best time to photograph brilliant fall foliage is on an overcast day because the colors stand out so much better. I've found that flowers are better to photograph on a rainy day. You just have to turn your lens wide open."

I looked out over the shoppers emerging from the mall into the grayness, and I was suddenly startled to see what Jeff meant. The little girl wearing the bright orange sweatshirt seemed to glow like a torch; the lady carrying the yellow, red, green and blue umbrella looked like a walking carousel. The gloomy landscape had become a neutral canvas that made colors come alive.

I looked down at the red jacket I was wearing. Funny, I had put it on in an attempt to brighten up a gloomy day. Now I saw that it was really the gloominess of the day that had brightened my jacket.

Father, open wide the lens of my spirit to see the beauty brought by the rain.
—KAREN BARBER

My Daily Blessings

1 _____

2 _____

3 _____

4 _____

5 _____

6 _____

7 _____

8 _____

9 _____

10 _____

11 _____

12 _____

13 _____

14 _____

15 _____

16 _____

17 _____

18 _____

19 _____

20 _____

21 _____

22 _____

23 _____

24 _____

25 _____

26 _____

27 _____

28 _____

29 _____

30 _____

OCTOBER

Blessed are they which are
persecuted for righteousness' sake: for
theirs is the kingdom of heaven.
—Matthew 5:10

S	M	T	W	T	F	S
			1	2	3	4
5	6	7	8	9	10	11
12	13	14	15	16	17	18
19	20	21	22	23	24	25
26	27	28	29	30	31	

AN EYE FOR BLESSINGS

1/*WED* COMING TO OUR SENSES
O taste and see that the Lord is good. . . . —PSALM 34:8

I knew I was over the flu yesterday when I could smell the coffee brewing. I lingered at the coffeemaker, inhaling that heady aroma. The sense of smell—how rarely I stopped to appreciate it!

I poured the coffee and sat down on a kitchen stool, hands wrapped around the warmth of the mug. Touch—another dimension I seldom gave conscious thought to. And taste! How often I ate mechanically, my mind elsewhere.

On hearing and sight I gave myself better marks: I'd often been grateful for those. I had seen my grandfather's face when he got his first hearing aid. "I can hear a clock ticking!" he said. And my father-in-law, who was blind by the time I entered the family, had said about the weeks of failing vision, "I'd never looked so keenly at things! Seeing everything for the last time, each object had an intense beauty."

But why had I never thanked God for the other three senses? Surely these were blessings, too!

I roamed through the house with broader awareness, delighting in the smooth curve of wooden chair back, the coldness of a window pane, the nubbly wool of my sweater. I peeled an orange, enjoying the sharp whiff of rind; sniffed the potted chrysanthemum on the windowsill; opened a dresser drawer to breathe in the balsam sachet.

My devotional life, I realized as I sat with a second mug of coffee, savoring each sip, has always been centered on the mind—on words and concepts. But worship in the Bible includes so much more! The joy of dance and song. The perfume of incense. The delights of food and drink. The involvement of all the senses.

"O taste and see that the Lord is good," sang the psalmist. A drop of honey is still placed on the page as a Jewish child begins the study of the Torah, signaling that the senses, too, are doorways to God.

Help me worship You today, Lord, with my whole being.
—ELIZABETH SHERRILL

2/THU   *"He must wash his clothes, and he will be clean."*   —LEVITICUS 13:34 (NIV)

New Market, Virginia, has its own fall festival days. Our first year here, I was delighted to find that I could set up a table on Congress Street and sell things; it was a wonderful way to meet new people.

One woman introduced herself as Jane DePreiter, the president of the Chamber of Commerce. She pulled up the extra chair I'd put out for visitors, and we began to chat. I told her that although I loved our new home and our new town, some unexpected circumstances in my life were creating a very difficult time. "New learning is coming slowly to me. I feel so frustrated and inadequate. I wish I would hurry up and get changed—I'm driving *me* crazy!" I said with a laugh.

Jane commiserated. "That reminds me of something I learned not long ago when I was upset about a situation in my own life. I couldn't seem to get a handle on what was happening to me and why I felt so irritable and out of control. Then one day I was leaning over my washer, shoving the last of the clothes in as the cycle began, and it was as if the Lord spoke to me. I suddenly realized that, like my clothes, sometimes I have to get agitated to get cleaned!"

Lord, when I'm in one of those frustrating, irritating, nerve-wracking times, help me remember that the end result will be a much-needed cleansing and fresh breezes blowing through my life.
—ROBERTA ROGERS

3/FRI   *And God said, Let the earth bring forth the living creature after his kind . . . and it was so.*   —GENESIS 1:24

What does an old, gun-shy hunting dog have to do with me? There, in front of the pictures of people I love that pack my living room table, is a silver-framed snapshot of a battered old dog. His name was Cricket. He was a pointer, and of all the dogs we had—three or four or five at a time, from a snippy Scottie named Lassie to an ugly mutt we called Spareribs—Cricket was the most loved, and still is, now more than ever.

On Valentine's Day 1930, we three brothers came home from school to terrible news. Cricket had been run over by a car. He was alive, a quivering, suffering mass on the kitchen floor, a pathetic, begging look in his eyes. Already a veterinarian had recommended putting him down, but my mother refused. Others urged her to do the same, but Mother was adamant.

We three boys prayed with her that Cricket would recover. For the next year we were on hand to feed him and take him out, lifting him up steps, until old Spareribs took over, literally teaching Cricket to run with his lame right hind foot. The two of them became a pair. Cricket outlived all the dogs, Spareribs included, until he died peacefully at the age of thirteen.

In October 1995, I had a stroke. For a month I was in a hospital, and for several years I was in intensive therapy. Who was on my mind as I went through my days with the therapists? You guessed it: Cricket. My memories of him, struggling yet happy, were with me while I worked on a damaged right side and tried to get my speech back. Like Cricket, I'm not perfectly recovered, but I am content.

No wonder You brought forth the animals before You created us, Father. Thank You for them—and for Cricket in particular.

—VAN VARNER

---

4 / SAT   *The Lord said to Moses, "Speak to the people of Israel, and bid them to make tassels on the corners of their garments throughout their generations, and to put upon the tassel of each corner a cord of blue; and it shall be to you a tassel to look upon and remember all the commandments of the Lord. . . ."*   —NUMBERS 15:37–39 (RSV)

In my congregation, a number of us women decided to make our own *talesim*. A *tallit* is the shawl that a Jew wears during prayer, and recently women have begun wearing them as well as men, who always did. The traditional tallit is blue and white or black and white. It has specially knotted fringes at its four corners and stripes on its sides, above the spots where the fringes are anchored.

My nun friend Mother Miriam sent me balls of wool she had sheared, carded and spun from the sheep on her monastery land, and I found a weaver to weave me the tallit body. The weaver used some darker wool to suggest stripes.

My friend Carla used pink fabric for her tallit body and stitched the stripes in bargello embroidery ranging from pale pink through dark shades into purple.

Barbara used white linen, but made her stripes an arching rainbow, and stitched doves of peace above the anchors for the fringes.

Evelynn thought carefully about it, and put two stripes on each side of her shawl, embroidered out of the names of her four grandsons, two of whom had not lived very long. "That way I'll always have them near me when I pray," she said. "I'll wrap myself in my grandsons, both the ones I lost and the ones I still have."

Each of us has things that make prayer more meaningful, and the objects of prayer more precious. In my case, the tallit is more of a treasure because of Mother Miriam's loving contribution. In Evelynn's, it's because of four lives as important to her as her own.

O God, thank You for the special things—a Bible, a candle, a tallit—that center my heart in prayer. —RHODA BLECKER

5/*SUN* *Then he took the cup, gave thanks and offered it to them....* —MARK 14:23 (NIV)

Holy Communion has always been a mystery to me. Probably because it *is* a mystery! Since childhood I've partaken in many different churches in a variety of ways: kneeling at the altar and dipping a wafer into a chalice of wine; or sitting in the pew and receiving spongy pieces of bread and little plastic cups of grape juice. As I child I would roll my tongue through the empty cup after drinking the grape juice so as not to miss a drop. It appalled the adults, but it satisfied a need in me to get it all.

Now, as an adult, I find a need to drain every drop of meaning from this sacred ritual. As I sit in the pew on our one communion Sunday a month, I must make myself fully present to this mystery, no matter how tired or distracted I am. For whether I know it or not, I'm hungry and need to be fed. And in front of me is the Food.

I look at the plain wooden table set with linen, the chalice, the plate. Gathered round are the ministers and elders. I listen to the words of invitation as I heard them in childhood, in simple faith, a child at the table with the family of God.

Jesus is the head of the family and is also the sustenance. Somehow, by receiving Him in this manner, my hunger is filled. I am being nourished, both body and soul, in a way nothing else could. I know it by faith. I know it because Jesus commanded it.

Jesus, thank You for feeding me at this table and making me whole. —SHARI SMYTH

6/MON You have made known to me the path of life; you will fill me with joy in your presence, with eternal pleasures at your right hand. —PSALM 16:11 (NIV)

After reading Psalm 16 last fall, I wrote in my journal, "What does it mean to be filled with joy in God's presence?" My answer came two weeks later when I stopped by the convenience store for my usual coffee. Absentmindedly, I'd set my mug on a crack, so when I began to pour, it teeter-tottered, spilling coffee over the counter.

"Oh, Laurie," I exclaimed when the clerk arrived with a sponge, "you should have seen the teeter-totter my father made for my sisters and me when we were kids! We lived in the woods, and he built one that went up and down on a stump—*and* around and around."

Memories of our backyard in Port Coquitlam, British Columbia, flooded my mind. "And he made us a real merry-go-round, too," I told her, "using one side of an old telephone-cable spool and a car axle." I told her how we could pile three or four kids onto that thing and how, because the merry-go-round sat at a tilt, we could spin ourselves dizzy. "Finally, we'd fly off, right into the grass. We'd lie in a pile, shrieking with sheer joy."

By the time I got home, coffee in hand, that memory of my father's love had filled me with incredible joy.

That evening when I pulled out my journal, I realized that God had answered my two-week-old prayer: Joy rises out of triggered memories. I immediately started a new list of memories, recalling the many creative gestures of love my doting heavenly Father had given me over the years. The "emerald" ring I'd lost in the grass at James Park Elementary, but which God had led me to find, despite many warnings that I'd never find it. And the sunsets when I was seventeen, sitting on the beach and watching the last ferry chug away from Thetis Island each night at 10:10, *knowing* God was God. The list continues, and so does the joy.

Thank You, God, for answering my prayer so quickly, and for filling me with joy in Your presence. —BRENDA WILBEE

7 / TUE   *I will put in the wilderness the cedar, the acacia, the myrtle, and the olive; I will set in the desert the cypress, the plane and the pine together; that men may see and know, may consider and understand together, that the hand of the Lord has done this, the Holy One of Israel has created it.*

—ISAIAH 41:19–20 (RSV)

Poking into the reasons that leaves turn colors in the fall, I discover that they don't turn colors at all—they lose the green that comes from being flooded with chlorophyll in spring, and reveal their true colors, which are, depending on the species, flaming orange, stunning purple, shouting red, searing yellow.

I didn't know that. It's sleight of leaf, as it were, a deft trick by the tree, which senses the seasonal shift in amounts of light and water and pulls back the green force for a season.

I sit and ponder trees for a minute, and begin to see them as perhaps God and children do—really tall plants, *verrrrry* slow acrobats, enormous stiff brown fingers, patient and wonderfully sensitive woody creatures who eat sunlight, drink rain, totally understand soil chemistry and house animals ranging in size from bacteria to boys.

Dear God, thanks for trees. Nice job of creation there, for without them, we would be desert dwellers always and, all told, there's a lot to be said for treedom. —BRIAN DOYLE

OUT OF THE SHADOWS

There are times in all our lives when troubles come, and the blessings around us are hard to see. Libbie Adams experienced such a time awhile ago; a time when anxiety and depression cast dark shadows over her life and threatened to rob her of joy. Over the next seven days, Libbie will show you how faith in God and the help of an extraordinary Christian therapist led her back into the sunshine. —THE EDITORS

8/WED   DAY ONE: FINDING THE WAY
To whom will ye flee for help? . . .   —ISAIAH 10:3

The sun shone golden across the front yard, and the spring birds chattered to each other from the trees. It was a beautiful spring morning, but I felt lonely and isolated. As I lowered the blades on the riding mower and started the motor, I could feel the sting of the tears that had come so often of late. *Why am I feeling this way when I have so much to be thankful for?* I searched my mind, trying to uncover anything that could have caused my melancholy. *Maybe I need to try harder to control my thoughts. Surely I can conquer this thing, if only I'm diligent enough!*

I had finished cutting the grass in the front yard when my husband Larry brought me a cold drink. He went to his workshop, and I sat down on the porch and let the tears fall freely, wondering all the while what I was crying about. *God,* I prayed, *I don't know what else to do. I can't keep feeling this way. Please help me understand.* I walked inside, savoring the cool air on my skin. I knew I should finish cutting the grass before it got hot, but I longed to go to sleep. Lately that was the only way I could find peace.

Absentmindedly, I lifted my Bible from the dining room table. I had turned to it so often for answers, and yet none seemed forthcoming. Now, riffling through its pages, my eyes settled on Exodus 18:18–19: "Thou wilt surely wear away . . . for this thing is too heavy for thee; thou art not able to perform it thyself alone. Hearken now unto my voice, I will give thee counsel. . . ."

The answer was clear: I must give up trying to manage this illness on my own and make arrangements to see a therapist. It was time to heed God's counsel.

Thank You, Lord, for answers that appear at just the right time.
—LIBBIE ADAMS

9/THU   DAY TWO: THE FIRST VISIT
He healeth the broken in heart, and bindeth up their wounds.
—PSALM 147:3

I gave my name to the receptionist and took my seat with the other patients in the therapist's office. For months now, I had felt oddly removed from my surroundings, as if I were encased in an invisible bubble. My enthusiasm for the things I usually found enjoyable had flagged, and although I hadn't yet put a name to my malady, I could sense that I needed more help than a change of scenery could provide me.

"Mrs. Adams?" I looked toward the voice that called my name and saw the therapist I had been referred to. Judith Kettner was an attractive woman in her late fifties, with an easy, welcoming smile and eyes that held no judgment. "Come right in," she said, holding the door for me.

I followed her down the long hallway and into the little office that would become so familiar to me in the months to come. For a moment, I couldn't believe I was there, ready to reveal to a stranger things that I had kept so private in my life. For some reason I had always felt that if I were strong enough spiritually, believed fully and prayed often, I wouldn't experience depression. Yet I had slowly sunk into an abyss of despair.

Now I had come to confess that I felt like a failure, spiritually, emotionally and intellectually. I knew it wouldn't be easy. But coming unbidden to reassure me was the familiar voice that often whispers in the silent recesses of my soul. And I knew, without a doubt, that this therapist was the one I had asked God to send me.

I was yet to learn that she was a devout Christian, the wife of a minister. But I felt a peaceful energy emanating from her that poured over my ragged spirit, giving me the first hope of healing that I'd experienced in months.

Thank You, Father, for loving professionals who serve others, and for Your divine presence that works its miracles through them. —LIBBIE ADAMS

10/FRI   DAY THREE: JUST AS I AM
If God be for us, who can be against us?   —ROMANS 8:31

It was Tuesday morning again, and I sat on the now-familiar couch in Judy's office, gazing out the window at the rain. This was my second month of therapy, and I had gotten to know my therapist better than I had expected.

To my surprise, she had shared her own life experiences with me. Her candid approach had made it easier for me to open up and be candid in return. And yet, even though I had given her a pretty clear picture of my life, I had not been able to isolate the things that were giving me the most trouble.

Judy sat across from me with her clipboard on her lap. "I know that I have to become more specific about what's really bothering me," I began. "It's difficult to admit, but I know that I'm responsible for most of the stumbling blocks in my life. I've struggled with doubts about my self-worth, and I've allowed those doubts to cripple me. It's been a problem since childhood, and still plagues me."

Judy smiled. "You know, Libbie, there are three keys to acquiring an unshakable sense of self-worth. The first is to live up to the ideals you set for yourself by never betraying yourself or your beliefs. The second is learning to accept validation from people you love, trust and respect. And the third, the most important, is to realize that God loves and accepts you just the way you are, imperfections and all."

I sat silently as the warm spring rain streamed down the narrow windowpanes beside me. Suddenly, I remembered a Bible verse my mother had written in my sister's autograph book years before: "If God be for us, who can be against us?" Despite my fears, God had always been for me. In His love, He had never questioned my worth, and I shouldn't question it either.

I'd taken a small step, but one I felt I could build on in the months to come.

Lord, please help me to experience Your love and acceptance.

—LIBBIE ADAMS

11 / SAT   DAY FOUR: LETTING GO
He restoreth my soul. . . .   —PSALM 23:3

It was a Friday in the middle of June. I'd been in therapy for three months now, and I'd been making good progress. After a thorough review of my life and my family history, Judy determined that I'd been suffering from depression and suggested medication for me. It hadn't been quite six weeks yet, but with the medication I finally felt that I was in control of my emotions again. The compulsive need to be busy, to take care of everything and everyone, had diminished, and I could allow myself the freedom just to be.

I remembered an afternoon a few months earlier, when I'd come face to face with the consequences of my obsession to take responsibility for everything. I had spent several hours working in my yard in the hot sun and was about to put the mower away, when I noticed Gina's lawn across the street. The grass hadn't been cut in a while, and it looked shabby. Impulsively, I steered my mower across the road, knocked on Gina's door and asked if I could mow her lawn for her. She seemed puzzled and surprised, and mumbled something about getting to it when it was cooler. I quickly assured her that I didn't mind at all, that I was mowing anyway and I'd be happy to do her lawn, too.

By the time I finished Gina's yard, it was growing late, and I was tired and dirty. I needed to get to the bank for an appointment, and I had no time to shower and change. I'd have to meet the banker wearing my grubby work clothes. I was embarrassed and resentful.

Now, with Judy's guidance, I was learning not to allow my compulsive nature to rule me but to wait for God's prompting. And to my relief, I discovered the work He gives me fills me with a sense of accomplishment and peace.

Father, please keep my feet steady on the path to recovery.

—LIBBIE ADAMS

12/ SUN DAY FIVE: AN ANCHOR IN THE STORM

Which . . . we have as an anchor of the soul, both sure and steadfast. . . . —HEBREWS 6:19

I parked in an empty space in front of Judy's office building, dreading my weekly appointment. This was my fourth month of therapy, but something in me still fought the idea of revealing myself to my counselor, even though I knew that Judy would not judge me. Closing my eyes for a moment, I recalled a sign I'd seen in front of a church on my way here: IN THE STRESS OF THE STORM, LEARN THE STRENGTH OF THE ANCHOR.

A long ninety minutes later, I walked back to the parking lot, relieved that another session was behind me, yet grateful for my capable therapist. Today we had discussed my need for perfection. I needed to have the stools in my kitchen aligned precisely with each other and the placemats on the dining room table positioned squarely with the chairs in front of them. It was the same with the pillows on the sofa and the books on the shelf. My world had to be symmetrical.

Judy was able to put a name to my problem immediately: obsessive-compulsive personality. It's a less severe form of the obsessive-compulsive disorder that forces many people to wash their hands repeatedly throughout the day or check the burners on the stove over and over again. Both impairments are anxiety-related and can be treated successfully with medication. How freeing finally to have that knowledge at my command!

I was learning that perfection was an illusion—only God is perfect, and He offers us His forgiveness because He knows that we are not. I thought again of the sign I had read in front of the church that morning, and an old hymn came to mind:

> *We have an anchor that keeps the soul*
> *steadfast and sure while the billows roll.*

There would be more to learn on my path of self-discovery. But the Perfect One Himself was my anchor, and I was finding Him sufficient indeed!

You are my anchor, Lord, one I can depend on during the harshest storms of life. —LIBBIE ADAMS

13/MON DAY SIX: REDISCOVERING JOY

For I will restore health unto thee, and I will heal thee of thy wounds.... —JEREMIAH 30:17

As I drove home down Fire Tower Road, I mused over the changes that had taken place within me in the past few months. It was September now, and the first signs of autumn were beginning to appear: soft yellow tints and deep scarlet reds on the maple trees, blending with the rich velvety green around the wood line. It had been misting on my way to therapy, as the remnants of Hurricane Dennis clung to the coast of North Carolina. But now the sun was peeking through, and I felt as light as a bubble.

Then I noticed movement in the ditch alongside the road. Slowing down, I spotted two little black puppies scurrying into the weeds. There were no houses around; someone had abandoned these pups to fend for themselves.

Stopping the truck, I got out and crossed the road. The bolder of the two came running as soon as I bent down and called to him. I picked him up and put him in the back of the truck, dismayed to find that he was dirty, wet and shivering. The other pup, a female, was a little more timid, but she finally came, too, and I lifted her into the truck with her brother.

When I reached home, I dried off the pups and fed them all they could eat. Then I remembered that my niece Miranda had lost her dog a few days earlier, and her children Kaleb and Kameron were anxious to have another one. I called Miranda, and an hour later I was waving good-bye to two happy children, each holding a warm, wiggling puppy.

I stood in the drive, watching Miranda's car disappear over the hill. Tending to a job that had actually been mine to do had brought me a great sense of peace and fulfillment. God's answer to a need sometimes *is* me, and, faithfully, He was restoring me to health.

Father, what more can I say than thank You? —LIBBIE ADAMS

14/*TUE* DAY SEVEN: MOVING FORWARD

If any man be in Christ, he is a new creature: old things are passed away; behold, all things are become new.

—II CORINTHIANS 5:17

October 19 was my last day of therapy. For several weeks now, I had suspected that my time with Judy was drawing to a close. I felt strong again, and capable, and ready to get on with my life.

Judy came to the door of the waiting room, as she had done every week. I picked up my photo albums and followed her down the long hallway for the last time. I had brought along the albums because I wanted Judy to see the faces of all the people in my life whom I'd talked about these past seven months. I also had my camera to snap a picture of Judy to add to the faces in my album.

It was hard to say good-bye when my time was up. Judy had become my trusted confidante, my adviser and my spiritual support, and I felt a lingering sadness that therapy was ending. Tuesdays would seem a little empty without our weekly sessions.

I gave Judy a good-bye hug, and as a memento of our time together, a copy of *Daily Guideposts*.

A few days later Judy sent me a letter. "I read the devotional for January 2 by Elizabeth Sherrill," she wrote, "about breaking molds, and that the pain of rupture must happen before new growth can come. We know a lot about breaking molds, the pain of rupture and new growth, don't we? Thank you for letting me share in your journey."

These last several months, so awful at the beginning, had taught me to press on through the difficult times, in expectation of better things to come. As the old saying has it, "Every breakdown is a breakthrough." Every day now, I'm reaping the benefits of that lesson.

Father, my tomorrows are all known to You. You will lead me all the way!

—LIBBIE ADAMS

FOLLOWING JESUS

15 / WED — FAITHFUL IN SMALL THINGS

"Well done, good and faithful servant! You have been faithful with a few things; I will put you in charge of many things. Come and share your master's happiness!" —MATTHEW 25:21 (NIV)

I was shopping at an antiques sale in Nashville, Tennessee, and had just purchased a sampler to add to my collection. A little needlework girl shared a bouquet of daisies with a neighbor over a picket fence. Below was an old saying: "Actions speak louder than words."

At the final booth, the elderly proprietor overheard me say that I was leaving and freeing up a parking space nearby. He was short-winded, battling emphysema and cancer, he explained, and his wife had just learned she had lung cancer. They had traveled all the way from Maine. "This will be our last show," he said, shaking his head at his charmingly displayed inventory.

With the chance to have my choice parking spot, the frail man followed me out to the lot to move his vehicle. I started my car and waited, but he never came. *Probably changed his mind and is just going to leave me hanging. I'll give him five more minutes.*

Then I spotted him in the rearview mirror, struggling on his cane as he huffed and puffed his way to my car window. "Found an even closer spot, young lady," he said. "One with plenty of room for the wife's wheelchair when we pack up." He pointed to an area nearly a block away, a huge distance for someone in his weak condition. "I wanted to let you know and to thank you again for your kind offer."

This gracious, true-to-his-word man had many excuses not to

walk that extra distance. It was, after all, a small thing. Yet it had been important to him to treat someone he would never see again the way he would want to be treated.

Actions speak louder than words. I'd heard that maxim all my life. But now I'd seen it lived.

Father, help me to be faithful in the small things, even when it's difficult.　　　　　　　　　　　　　—ROBERTA MESSNER

16/THU "*Beware of practicing your piety before men in order to be seen by them. . . .*"　　—MATTHEW 6:1 (RSV)

Our church was looking for a new pastor. A group of us were meeting to discuss what kind of person we wanted. "Don't ask him. We sure don't want a glory hog," someone said.

"What do you mean?" another member asked.

"You know, someone who wants to take credit for everything that happens."

As I listened to the discussion, I wondered if they would classify me as a "glory hog." At home, if my wife doesn't notice that I've done the dishes or a load of laundry, I can't resist telling her. I try to be subtle and mumble something like, "I knew you'd be tired when you came in, so I did the dishes."

Then there are the times when someone else is given credit for something I had said or written. And when I'm giving money to a ministry or a charity, I sometimes want to be sure that the treasurer or the pastor knows I'm the donor, even when I say humbly, "We want this to be anonymous."

Just then, my thoughts were interrupted by someone calling my name. "Keith, what do you think about—?" He named a particular candidate. "Do you think he's really a glory hog?"

I laughed. "You know, I sure like to get credit for what I do. How about you? Do any of you get upset when you don't get credit?"

Everyone was quiet for a few seconds. Then one man laughed and said that he, too, had a bit of "glory hog" in his genes. In the next few minutes, we all admitted that sometimes we do care who gets the credit.

"So what are we going to do about evaluating applicants?" our leader asked. After a little looking at the floor and shuffling of feet, someone suggested, "Maybe we should try to find someone like us—who's only a 'glory piglet.'"

Thank You, Lord, for showing me the beam in my own eye through the mote in another's. Amen. —KEITH MILLER

READER'S ROOM

As a senior citizen in the inner city, my days are filled with tutoring at the church I attend, taking educational trips with children and enjoying the stories in *Daily Guideposts* each day. God has led me to visit and give Communion to the shut-ins from my church and write friendly notes to those we miss.

May I reach out to Van Varner and say "thanks"? He writes about many things I can relate to, and it warms my heart. —AMY A. DUNLAP, BALTIMORE, MARYLAND

---

17 / FRI

My voice shalt thou hear in the morning, O Lord. . . . —PSALM 5:3

It was 5:00 A.M. and all was quiet as I walked upstairs with my steamy cup of tea. I sat down in my chair in the study, flipped on the tiny lamp, opened my Bible and began to read. My daily routine had been the same for months: tea, chair, lamp, Bible.

This morning, though, was different. My cat Smudge jumped into my lap and nudged my hand. When I didn't stop to pet her, she climbed on top of my Bible.

"Smudge!" I exclaimed. "No! I'm reading." I pushed her off my lap, but she refused to give up. She jumped back on my lap again and again.

"Okay, Smudge, you win," I said with a sigh. I put down my Bible and began petting her as I prayed.

In church that Sunday, my pastor shared a story. When he was a child, he had a good friend with whom he played soldiers and raced toy cars. When they grew into teenagers, they played the same sports. But after high school, they lost touch. Just recently they had run into each other at a restaurant. It was an awkward meeting; so much time had passed that they didn't have much to say to each other.

"We don't want our relationship with God to end up the same way," our pastor cautioned. "Prayer every day keeps us close to and in touch with God."

As I listened to the sermon, something clicked: I'd been so focused on reading my Bible that I'd been cutting my prayer time short! I wasn't taking the time to listen to what God was saying to me through His Word.

The next morning, after reading my Bible, I welcomed Smudge onto my lap while I prayed. Thanks to a persistent cat and a timely story from my minister, those wee hours of the morning have a new routine: tea, chair, lamp, Bible—and prayer.

Remind me, gracious God, that knowing You is more than just reading about You. —MELODY BONNETTE

18/SAT God will redeem my soul from the power of the grave: for he shall receive me. . . . —PSALM 49:15

That fall morning it was brisk outside, the first really cold day of the season. I glanced at the thermometer in the window: thirty-nine degrees. I turned to the newspaper for the forecast: it wouldn't even get up to fifty. Time for the winter wardrobe. I searched the back of the closet for my tweed jacket. Brown with autumnal high-lights of gold and red, it was the perfect thing for an October day.

As I walked to the train, I took a look at the garden in front of our apartment. The hydrangeas were turning copper, the mums a brave yellow and the little Japanese maple at the end of the drive had already blushed red. Soon there would be no flowers, no leaves, and the only bit of color would be the big red bow on the wreaths put up at Christmastime. I found myself yearning for spring.

I put my hands in my jacket. When did I last wear it? Probably last winter or on one of the cold days of early spring. But what a difference there is between a cold October day, when the summer is past, and a day in March, when spring is just around the bend.

There's something sad about saying good-bye to those vibrant colors when they won't be back for six months.

Then I felt something in my pocket and took it out. A dried palm branch woven in the shape of a cross. I suddenly remembered the last time I wore this jacket: Palm Sunday. That day in church, as I listened to the extraordinary story of Christ's suffering, I wove this cross from a green palm frond. Then Easter came with its bright promise of everlasting life, and soon spring followed. I put the cross back in my jacket and kept it there. Easter has a message I need all year long.

Lord, I turn to You for the promise of new life. —RICK HAMLIN

19/SUN *O give thanks unto the Lord; call upon his name: make known his deeds among the people.*

—PSALM 105:1

My son John came down with the "ghastly stomach virus" the other day. It's a particularly nasty one that attacks our family a couple of times a year, knocking us over like so many dominoes. It's not the kind of illness you care to have around with a new baby in the house. I said a fervent prayer, asking that no one else would get it.

But in all honesty, I was skeptical. This particular virus is so wildly contagious it seemed to be asking a lot to expect God to alter its path. I washed my hands frequently and resigned myself to the possibility—no, probability—that I was going to be tending to sick children for several days and nights.

The next morning John awoke with twice his usual five-year-old energy, ready to make up for having slept through most of the previous day. I was happy to have my boy back, but wondered who would be the next to go. We had a special seventy-sixth birthday party to attend on Sunday afternoon, and the guest of honor would be greatly disappointed if the kids couldn't come.

The day went fine. No one got sick. And the next day everyone was healthy. Sunday finally dawned, and we all seemed to be in good shape. I still half-expected someone to become sick before it was time to go to church. But a corner of my heart was turning cartwheels, wondering if maybe we were going to make it after all. *Maybe John's illness was a fluke. Maybe it was something he ate!* I thought. *How can it be that kids who shared a water bottle don't all have the same sickness?*

Then I stopped myself. I had prayed to God to keep the rest of us healthy, hadn't I? And all of us were healthy. Why was I being so quick to attribute the fact that the virus didn't spread to a quirk of fate, rather than to a "yes" to my prayer? Oh, fool that I am! Give thanks where thanks are due!

All praise to You, Lord God, for the prayers You answer faithfully, even when I'm not faithful in my thankfulness.

—JULIA ATTAWAY

20/MON   *"But you, are you seeking great things for yourself? . . ."*   —JEREMIAH 45:5 (NAS)

Deciding to join a gym at almost forty years old was pretty easy. Walking through the big glass doors for the first time was the hard part.

Everyone will be watching, I thought. *What will they think of me? I don't have many cute outfits; I'm not in great shape. What if I get out of breath or fall on the floor during a class? I bet everyone will be better than I. It'll be hard getting to know new people. I'll just focus on my workouts . . . increasing my strength . . . adding to my treadmill time each week. I'll be sure to carry a water bottle around, so I'll look like I know what I'm doing.*

Nervously, I entered the spacious room and looked around at all the equipment and the sweating people. One of the managers showed me how to use the weight machines, and I carefully jotted down notes so I could remember the amount of weight for the next time. Then I walked around the track, watching other people work out.

After my workout, I went to take a shower. There was another woman in the dressing room. As she dried her hair, she began to cry. I walked over and stood next to her, awkwardly putting my bag on the counter beside hers. Our eyes met in the mirror.

"Are you okay?" I asked as I turned to face her.

"Oh, hi," she said. "Thanks for noticing. My teenage son ran away two weeks ago, and I'm terrified. I love him so much. I want him back." Stiffly, I put my arms around her and held her. Her body softened, and she hugged me back.

A friendship began that day, and many other unexpected friendships followed. The key to my worries was to forget about myself and choose to focus on those around me.

Father, forgive me for thinking life is all about me. Only when I forget myself can You work through me. —JULIE GARMON

21 / TUE   *He is able also to save them to the uttermost that come unto God by him, seeing he ever liveth to make intercession for them.* —HEBREWS 7:25

Samson the bear is a typical Californian: He likes avocados and hot tubs. He is an old bear, sporting many scars on the bridge of his nose and ground-down teeth. Like the bear in the song, he "came over the mountain to see what he could see." He was pleased with what he saw and took up residency in the wildlife corridor along our Sierra Madre foothills. Then he found a family in the neighboring city of Monrovia who had it all. He would feast on avocados from their tree, then lumber into their swimming pool and hot tub for an early-morning frolic and a long blissful soak. Trouble was, Samson wouldn't budge.

"He's old and people-friendly," officials from the Department of Fish and Game decreed. "We can't release him back into the mountains. He just wouldn't make it. He'll have to be put down."

Samson was in a desperate situation, unable to help himself and completely dependent upon caring advocates willing to intercede on his behalf. A hue and cry was heard around the California southland. Schoolchildren became his most enthusiastic advocates. They wrote hundreds of letters to the governor and collected thousands of signatures on petitions to save Samson. Posters of this huge, amiable bear lolling in the Jacuzzi appeared in stores throughout the area. Then Samson appeared on TV and soon captured the imagination of the world. Letters and donations flooded in, some from children as far away as Paris.

The governor of California signed a reprieve. Samson was spared. With more than ten thousand dollars in donations, a three-thousand-square-foot habitat was built for him in the Orange County Zoo, complete with his own small pool and waterfall. He is living out his years with California style and pizzazz—a tribute to the intercessory power of people who cared.

Blessed Jesus, thank You for always interceding for me at the point of my need. —FAY ANGUS

22/WED   *Be devoted to one another in brotherly love. . . .* —ROMANS 12:10 (NIV)

I saw him in a stairwell on the way to my fourth-period class.

"Hey, Brett, I'm speaking tonight at a café for teens. Wanna come?"

To my surprise, he seemed really excited. "I'd love to," he said.

I'd seen him at school, usually standing alone or eating lunch by himself, and I'd said hi to him in the halls once or twice, but that was about it. I really didn't know him. For some reason, though, I had a feeling that I should invite him to this event. So that evening, I picked him up and took him to the café. We arrived early, so Brett and I walked down to the basement for a few games of pool.

We were terrible at pool, but we joked around and made it fun. It felt as if we had been friends forever. While scraping chalk onto the tip of his stick, Brett said, "If you ever do anything else like this, I'd love to come."

"Okay," I replied.

That night, I gave my testimony to about thirty teenagers gathered in the dimly lit booths upstairs. I talked about what God had done in my life and what it meant to be sure of eternal life.

Over the next two years, Brett and I continued our friendship, often going mountain biking or watching movies together. He even started coming to church and youth group.

Then one Sunday night, Brett stood up in front of about thirty teenagers gathered in a corridor at my church for youth group. "When I was a freshman, I thought that no one even knew I existed," he began. "One day, I became so depressed that I decided to kill myself after school. But that morning, someone I didn't even know invited me to hear him give his testimony. I changed my mind about suicide and went with him. That night, I gave my life to Jesus."

Lord, help me to show Your love to everyone I meet, because only You can see what's happening in their hearts.

—JOSHUA SUNDQUIST

23/ THU *Be of the same mind one toward another. . . .*

—ROMANS 12:16

While my wife Ruby was recovering from surgery in October, I enjoyed rustling up the meals, carrying trays and struggling with the housework. When she smiled and her eyes sparkled, it warmed me to the tip of my toes.

Then a neighbor called. "Is there any washing I can do?" she asked.

"No, thanks," I answered, "I've just finished the last load."

Another neighbor called. "Do you need anything from the store?"

"No, thank you," I replied. "I'm going out to shop later."

The next day, I rushed to the library and hurried past my favorite librarian's desk. Breathlessly, I searched for a book as she stepped forward to help. I shook my head and asked her to point me in the direction of the book. She remembered the volume and started to give me some additional information. I held up my hand; there wasn't time to listen. I had to get back to Ruby. "I'm here to help you, Mr. Greene," the librarian said. I looked up and saw the hurt in her eyes.

That night, I thought about my encounter with the librarian. How many others had offered me help only to be refused? What about the two neighbors who'd called the day before? I enjoyed doing things for others, but I didn't know how to let them do things for me. I enjoyed the comfortable feeling of standing on my feet and pulling my own weight. Deep down, I was too proud to accept kindness and too fearful it would make me appear subservient.

It was important to me to be a giver, but I'd forgotten that giving also means being willing to give myself in gratitude, opening my heart and my hand to accept the gifts of others. Tomorrow I would go back to the library and apologize to the librarian. Immediately, I picked up the phone to call my neighbors.

Dear Lord, help me to see the gift I give in receiving graciously.
—OSCAR GREENE

24 / FRI   *Be of one mind, live in peace; and the God of love and peace shall be with you.*   —II CORINTHIANS 13:11

My father works quite a bit with the St. Peter Indian Mission School at the Gila River Indian Community south of Phoenix, Arizona. One day when my dad was planning to take down a load of donated books, I decided to go, too, and take along our then-four-year-old daughter Maria. But that morning, Maria came to me with a worried face.

"Mommy, I don't want to go see the Indians," she said. "I'm scared." I knew what was going through her mind: stereotypical images of fierce Indians from television and movies.

"Oh, you'll like them," I told her. "They're just kids like you and your friends."

But she wasn't sure, and didn't say much in the car on the ride down. When we arrived at the mission, the kids swarmed around my dad. We had walked only a few steps from our car when they spotted Maria, and a curious group gathered around us.

"What's her name?" a girl asked shyly, and when I told her, several kids responded by saying, "Hi, Maria. How are you?" Maria clung to me tightly, unsure of how to react.

"Her hair is so pretty," said a girl with long, shiny black hair. "Can I touch it?"

"Sure. She'd probably like to touch your hair, too," I said, and the little girl reached out to stroke Maria's sandy-blond head. They both smiled.

"She's like a little doll," another girl said, and they all giggled.

Later that day Maria danced and played a game with them, then we all ate lunch together. On the ride home I asked Maria what she thought of the children. "I like them," she said. "Can we go see them again?"

I'm thinking of this today because it's United Nations Day, a day to celebrate the idea that if even the most diverse of God's people can meet face to face, they can't deny their similarities. Their swords become plowshares, as their fear becomes understanding, love and, naturally, peace.

Dear God, help me to bring Your peace everywhere I go.

—GINA BRIDGEMAN

25/SAT *Then you will understand what is right and just and fair—every good path. For wisdom will enter your heart, and knowledge will be pleasant to your soul.*

—PROVERBS 2:9–10 (NIV)

We have two sons, Ted and Patrick. They let us know—daily, hourly, if necessary—that we as parents were complete and utter failures in terms of doing what was right and just and fair.

According to Ted and Patrick, I was so careless as I measured out dessert portions on their plates that one child was literally bathed in love while the other one, neglected and abused, could only stare at his slightly smaller dessert and cry, "That's not fair!"

Moments later, if the loved son—the preferred son—was asked to take his plate to the kitchen while his forlorn brother, whom we had obviously reviled only moments ago, was allowed to linger at the table, the newly detested son would cry, "That's not fair!"

I had to explain to my sons that *fair* and *equal* were not synonyms; they would nod, and it would appear that wisdom had entered their hearts. Then I'd casually suggest that one son should take a shower and get ready for bed, so the other son could then do likewise. Oh, what a hopeless dreamer I was! The son who had to shower first would fall to the ground upon hearing his sentence, so stunned that he was almost mute. I say "almost," because a mute son would not be able to cry, "That's not fair!"

I heard the dreaded three-word phrase so often that I finally snapped. I impulsively announced, "That does it! For one week, I will be completely fair!" When Patrick had homework, Ted had to do the same assignment. When Ted cleaned his rabbit cages, Patrick had to reclean them. Ted caught a cold later that week, so I took his temperature and put him to bed. I took Patrick's temperature and put him to bed, too.

The permanent loss of "That's not fair!" from my sons' vocabulary was pleasant to my soul.

Dear God, when I'm feeling that I'm not getting my due, let me think before I shout, "That's not fair!" —TIM WILLIAMS

$$\mathcal{C}\!\!\sim$$

26/SUN *My soul thirsteth after thee, as a thirsty land. . . .* —PSALM 143:6

On an October day, I walked down the road that leads to our family cabin. It had been months since our last visit. And the last few days before we finally loaded the car for the three-hour trip were especially full. A heavy rain had fallen for most of the week, and there was no chance to go on our usual morning walks. My prayer time suffered.

At the lake near our cabin, the water was receding from the shoreline as it does every fall, and the blue herons were keeping their distance. The sky was that vibrant blue that follows a good cleansing rain. Up ahead, the road was littered with fat, ripe persimmons fallen from a tree.

I stopped to take in the day, and a warm longing filled me. Without thinking, I said out loud, "There's a place in the human heart that will always be lonely without You, God." I should know. There have been times in my life when I thought a snazzy car would fill it or really cool clothes or love. Nothing works. We are built thirsty, hungry, lonely—for God.

Weekly worship is an obvious place to begin to satisfy my need for God, but often I never really get around to the worshiping part. There are all those committees and causes and projects and stimulating conversations, and before you know it, it's time to leave. To make my Sundays fruitful, every day should be a day of worship.

From scheduled daily prayers to quick pauses to thank God for the moment or to admire His work or just to tell Him that I love Him, I can continually invite God into that space only He can fill.

Father, walk with me, talk with me, stay with me day and night.
—PAM KIDD

A HERITAGE OF FREEDOM

$27/$*MON* THE THEODORE ROOSEVELT MEMORIAL
Since my youth, O God, you have taught me. . . .
—PSALM 71:17 (NIV)

My favorite among the memorials of Washington, D.C., isn't located on the National Mall. It's the Theodore Roosevelt Memorial, located on Roosevelt Island in the Potomac River. It's probably the least visited memorial; you can only get there by driving north on the George Washington Parkway, taking the memorial exit and parking in one of only about seventy-five spaces provided. There's about a half-mile walk over a bridge and through the wooded island to the memorial.

At one end of the memorial is a statue of Roosevelt looking out over a bubbling fountain encircled by a doughnut-shaped pool that is supposed to represent a flowing stream. Surrounding the pool are great granite panels on which are inscribed quotes from the first President Roosevelt.

Roosevelt loved the outdoors, and during his presidency the drive to set aside national parks and preserves was revved into high gear and assured that future generations would enjoy the unspoiled wonders of Yellowstone, the Grand Canyon, Yosemite and other fantastic places across America. His real gift, however, was his ability to inspire youth. So during that period of time when my sons decided I was too out-of-date to be trusted, I took them to listen to recordings of Roosevelt. Since they, too, loved the wild spaces he had preserved, I hoped they would listen. Here are my favorites among the things he said to America's youth:

"Courage, hard work, self mastery and intelligent effort are all essential to the successful life. Alike for the nation and the individual, the indispensable requisite is character."

"If I must choose between righteousness and peace, I choose righteousness."

Perhaps you've noticed, as I have, that this advice applies to all youngsters, from nine to ninety.

Father, thank You for the vision of those who have gone before us. —ERIC FELLMAN

EDITOR'S NOTE: Four weeks from today, on Monday, November 24, we will observe the tenth annual Guideposts Thanksgiving Day of Prayer. We want you to join us as we pray together as a family. Please send your prayer requests (and a picture, if you can) to Guideposts Prayer Fellowship, PO Box 1460, Carmel, NY 10512-7960.

28/TUE *Let us encourage one another. . . .*
—HEBREWS 10:25 (NIV)

My mammogram had revealed a "suspicious" area. "It could be a tumor," the doctor said. Memories of the last time I'd heard those words came rushing back. It had been ten years, and—supported by prayer from friends and family—things had turned out fine. But that seemed no comfort as I pulled my hospital gown closer to my body.

Three more mammograms and a sonogram followed. I was referred to a special hospital in Indianapolis. No one had said the "C word," but fear began to suffocate me. Breast cancer? Could it be? Even the prayers I knew were being offered on my behalf brought me no comfort.

Then, the day before I was to go to the clinic, a letter arrived. It was thick and had a return address I didn't recognize. When I opened the envelope, out fell a beautiful, hand-stitched bookmark. Rendered in fine black thread and bordered by flowers and hearts was Psalm 56:3: "What time I am afraid, I will trust in thee." It was from a *Daily Guideposts* reader in faraway Oregon. She thought that this verse, which I had used for one of my devotionals, would make a good bookmark. "As I was working on it," she wrote, "I felt I wanted to send it to you. It's been in my workbasket for a couple of months, waiting to be sent!" I fingered the finely crafted words. "What time I am afraid . . ."

A few days later, when I got an "all-clear" report on my mammogram, I knew that one of the first people I wanted to tell was a lady I'd never met, a lady with needlepoint talent . . . and pinpoint timing.

Thank You, Father, for using us to encourage each other. Keep me ready to use my talents—whatever they are—for You.

—MARY LOU CARNEY

29/WED *And Hezekiah spoke encouragingly to all the Levites who showed good skill in the service of the Lord. . . .*
—II CHRONICLES 30:22 (RSV)

Promptly at 6:00 A.M., our hungry children stampeded into the hotel restaurant, then-five-year-old Elizabeth skipping with excitement and Mark toddling to catch up with her. Their shrieking drew head-turning from our fellow diners.

"*Shh! Shh!* Inside voices," we hushed. But the children were pumped with excitement for our big airplane trip home. We constantly reminded them to lower their voices. I began to lose patience, barking at Elizabeth to sit still and shouting as Mark sent a fistful of pancakes flying to the floor.

Business people surrounded us, conducting meetings before catching their planes, and constantly glanced over at our rambunctious, noisy table. Finally Alex led the children out. Kneeling by the high chair, picking up pieces of strawberries and pancakes, exhaustion overcame me. I felt like a failure as a mother and dreaded trying to control the kids on the long flight ahead.

Rising, I found a silver-haired man in a navy blue suit standing before me. *Oh, no, he's going to chastise me for the kids' noise!* Instead, he smiled. "I just wanted to tell you how I enjoyed watching you young folks with your children. It's so refreshing to see parents who care so much."

Amazed, I stammered, "Thank you."

Somehow this man had seen love coming through our dealings with our children, even through our mistakes, and made a point to tell me. As I walked to our room, I felt invigorated, ready to tackle the challenges ahead that day. And during the coming days, as I attempted to teach and discipline the children, his words stayed with me, reminding me to be "a parent who cares so much."

Lord, thank You for the power of encouraging words. Show me today someone who needs to hear them from me.

—MARY BROWN

$30/$THU   *Your faith should not stand in the wisdom of men, but in the power of God.*   —I CORINTHIANS 2:5

Did you remember your vitamins today? I did—a whole fistful of them. I use a multi, extra supplements of C, E, beta carotene and a time-released B-complex. But that's not all. I take gingko biloba capsules and DHA for my mind, DHEA for my muscles, garlic for my blood.

I dump a heaping scoop of swamp-green powder in my morning juice containing, among other things, spirulina, seaweed, soy lecithin, more beta carotene, blue algae, green algae, beet powder, bee pollen, royal jelly—don't ask me what any of this stuff actually does—ginger root, ginseng, propolis, astralagus, echinacea, oat bran and celery root. I make absolutely sure everything I take is chelated, but I couldn't begin to tell you what that means. When I dutifully apprise my doctor of my daily intake, he shakes his head and mutters, "It's your money. Just call me if you turn orange."

The other day I was feeding the dogs when my wife Julee caught me slipping in some canine vitamins containing glucosamine, reputedly beneficial to their aging joints. "You put too much faith in all that stuff," she snorted.

I was about to mount my usual protest whenever anyone mocks my vitamin mania but that one word stopped me cold: *faith*.

Was I actually putting faith into ginseng and oat bran? I considered it: It drives me crazy all day if I forget to take one of my supplements. I'm forever replenishing my stash at the health-food store, and it isn't cheap. The green powder is wretched-tasting and ruins a perfectly delicious glass of juice. My regimen probably has little provable benefit to my health, yet I persist in it, almost out of superstition.

Julee might be onto something. And she did remind me of one thing that's easy for me to overlook when I'm gobbling vitamins: where my true well-being and wholeness come from.

It's on You, God, that I ultimately depend for my health and all good things. Don't let me forget my daily dose of faith.

—EDWARD GRINNAN

31 / FRI   *For without me ye can do nothing.*
—JOHN 15:5

For years after our marriage in 1958, my husband Jerry and I argued about breakfast. He came from a family of big-breakfast eaters. I'd never eaten breakfast and would do about anything to get out of making it, even after we had children.

Fourteen years into our marriage, I had an extraordinary experience with God. He began making changes in my life, and I sensed Him speaking to my heart about all sorts of things. One night, just before I fell asleep, I was certain He whispered to me, *Marion, I want you to make breakfast for Jerry and the children tomorrow.*

As the light of dawn crept into our bedroom, I stormed downstairs and began slinging pots and pans around furiously. "I'm being obedient, Lord," I insisted grimly. *I can help you*, said the incredibly gentle Voice. But I shrugged Him off. Surely *I* could make breakfast! But, of course, I couldn't. As I thrust the food at my family, resenting everything I was doing, I sensed my failure. Blinking hard and fast to keep from crying, I asked myself, "Who cries over making breakfast?"

When Jerry and the children left, I sat down at the cluttered table, defeated. The Voice was comforting, not accusing at all: *You're going to have to ask for My help in everything you do. I love helping you.*

The next morning I asked for God's help with my scrambled eggs—and with my attitude.

Lord, when I think I'm self-sufficient, show me how needy I really am.

—MARION BOND WEST

My Daily Blessings

1 _____

2 _____

3 _____

4 _____

5 _____

6 _____

7 _____

8 _____

9 _____

10 _____

11 _____

12 _____

13 _____

14 _____

15 _____

16 _____

17 _____

18 _____

19 _____

20 _____

21 _____

22 _____

23 _____

24 _____

25 _____

26 _____

27 _____

28 _____

29 _____

30 _____

31 _____

NOVEMBER

Blessed is the nation whose
God is the Lord. . . .
—Psalm 33:12

S	M	T	W	T	F	S
						1
2	3	4	5	6	7	8
9	10	11	12	13	14	15
16	17	18	19	20	21	22
23	24	25	26	27	28	29
30						

1 / SAT   *We are surrounded by such a great cloud of witnesses. . . .*   —HEBREWS 12:1 (NIV)

"Give me *libbaty* or give me death!" crowed Mary's little voice. I tried to keep a straight face, but I had a hard time restraining a giggle as she added confidentially, "I'm being *Patwick Henwy*."

I've occasionally wondered if Mary gets shortchanged educationally because I don't have as much one-on-one time with her as I had with my older children. My memory tells me that I used to read a certain ABC book at least fifty-seven times an hour to Elizabeth, yet Mary gets only a handful of read-alouds a day.

But gradually I'm recognizing that Mary learns so much from her brother John and her sister Elizabeth that she's not missing a thing. Mary is the one who (because her big sister likes geometry) stops in the middle of a Magic Schoolbus book and says, "Hey, look! Ms. Frizzle has polyhedra on her shoes!" And it's Mary who, because her big brother is obsessed with the American Revolution, parades around the house pretending to be Martha Washington, telling her friends at the playground that they can be Hessians.

Being an oldest child myself, I never quite realized how much one picks up by osmosis from older siblings. It can be a significant advantage to be able to observe those who have gone before. Which, I suppose, is one reason why God has given us the examples of Christians through the ages to learn from. In a very real sense they are our brothers and sisters, branches of the vine that unite us across all time. Perhaps they can teach us something worthwhile about how to lead holy lives or how to pray better or how to endure suffering. It's certainly worth finding out.

Father of all, help me to run the race set out before me, encouraged by the cheers and the examples of the faithful who have gone before.   —JULIA ATTAWAY

2/ SUN   *Train up a child in the way he should go: and when he is old, he will not depart from it.* —PROVERBS 22:6

The organist had begun to play the opening notes of the first hymn of the morning worship service when I heard an unfamiliar couple and a small boy enter the pew behind mine. I turned to smile and handed them an opened hymnal. During the service, I became aware of the father holding a small white pad in his hands and writing or drawing something to entertain the child.

I must tell them about our children's programs, I thought. *A child that age should be in a class with other children.*

When the service was over, I turned, hand extended, to introduce myself and welcome them to our church. The man shook my hand, introduced himself and his wife and said, "I hope we didn't make any noise or disturb you during the service."

"Oh, no," I assured him.

"Daddy was drawing this for me," the little boy said, proudly handing the pad to me. The crude sketching I saw seemed to represent a person. There was a small circle for the head and a larger one for the body, with two long lines extending downward from it for legs. On each side of the body was a short line representing an arm. From each of these fanned five smaller lines.

"Oh?" I said, studying the sketch. Then, pointing to one group of the smallest lines, I asked, "And what are these?"

The child's face broke into a broad grin. "You don't recognize them?" he asked. "That's a drawing of Jesus and those are the fingers on His hands. Daddy says Jesus is always reaching His hands out to us."

I could find no words to speak. I simply handed him his drawing, put my arms around his shoulders and gave him a big hug.

Dear Lord, bless all the parents who make sure their children know about Your Son. May I never forget what my daddy taught me about Him. Amen. —DRUE DUKE

AN EYE FOR BLESSINGS

3/MON   SAYING "THANK YOU"
And be ye thankful.   —COLOSSIANS 3:15

What amazing months these have been, since January, learning to count my everyday blessings! God's gifts have turned out to be so abundant that I've found myself breathing little prayers of thanks all through the day. That's the blessing I'm grateful for today—the boon of thanksgiving itself.

I wouldn't know that thankfulness—to God, to other people— was a gift, if I hadn't known a woman named Bella. Bella was a Polish Jewish refugee whose entire family perished in the Holocaust. This and her own experiences in the Warsaw ghetto had so seared her that in self-defense she closed down all her emotions, not only grief and fear, but joy, hope, love.

In the 1950s, Bella, crippled with arthritis and living on a tiny pension, was a neighbor of ours in Mt. Kisco, New York. With others in the neighborhood, we saw to it that she was supplied with food, clothing, transportation and small gifts of cash. Over the several years that these efforts continued, to the day of her death, no one ever heard a word of thanks from Bella—or even an acknowledgement that any of it was needed.

"Gratitude," said G. K. Chesterton, "is happiness doubled by wonder." A cruel history denied this happiness to Bella, who had already lost so much. But the gift is mine, not just on Thanksgiving Day, but whenever I know that a good not of my own making has come my way.

Thank You, Lord, that I can thank You. —ELIZABETH SHERRILL

4 / TUE   *When the cares of my heart are many, thy consolations cheer my soul.*   —PSALM 94:19 (RSV)

It was Election Day 2001, and I was heading across the street to vote at P.S. 187 on my way to the office. The last time I had been in the building was for the primary on September 11, just as the hijacked airliners were crashing into the World Trade Center.

I was jittery as I walked up the steps. I hadn't been sleeping well over the last couple of months; I was easily startled awake by sirens or loud noises, and grateful if the interruption was our baby Maggie's crying.

In the hallway, I looked at the map to find where my election district was to vote and walked into the lunchroom where the machines were set up and the election inspectors sat at their tables. It took me awhile to find the right line: There were two for each district, one to sign in and the other to vote. At one table, the line snaked toward the door—the machine was out of order, and people were voting with paper ballots. At our table, the inspectors were trying to soothe a very angry lady who had waited for half an hour in the wrong line and was worried she'd be late for work. In front of me, people pored over sample ballots, trying at the last minute to figure out the proposed amendments to the city charter before it was their turn to vote. This, at least, was normal: a typical election day in New York City.

When my turn came, I stepped into the booth, closed the curtain, and made my choices for the new mayor and city council person our term-limit laws had mandated. By the time I walked out of the school building and toward the subway, I felt calmer. Despite the terror and our fears, we were having our election on schedule and according to law. And whatever else might befall us, we New Yorkers would muddle through.

Lord, thank You for the consolation of business as usual.

                                        —ANDREW ATTAWAY

5 / WED   *Wherever your treasure is, there your heart and thoughts will also be.*   —LUKE 12:34 (TLB)

In my bedroom I have two wooden plaques, a hand mirror and a small box, all etched with a wood-burning tool and hand-painted by my grandmother in the early 1900s. Minta Pearl Barclay Knapp was a college physics and math professor during a time when most women didn't even finish high school. She died in 1932, long before I was born. In spite of her amazing educational success, it's the objects she crafted in her spare time with her own hands that are her legacy to me.

I, too, have taken up a craft hobby in the past years with the hope that I can pass a bit of my creative self on to my children, grandchildren and friends. I save glass jars, the kind pickles, olives, bouillon cubes and mustard come in, and paint them with puffy fabric paint. They're colorful, fun to hold because of the puffy texture and quite lovely, if I do say so myself. I've filled my puffy paint jars with tea, candy, paper clips, cotton swabs or loose change, and given more than five hundred of them away to relatives, close friends and acquaintances.

Friends ask, "Why don't you sell them at craft fairs?"

I answer, "Because I'd never get back the value of my time. Besides, they're meant for people I love . . . people to whom I want to give the gift of my time and creativity."

Of course, I have to admit that I hope a few of my jars stand the test of time as my grandmother's wooden objects did, so that someday in the 2100s someone will say, "Mommy, where did this colorful jar come from?"

Heavenly Father, thank You for the fun of being creative, but most of all thank You for the loved ones who accept my simple handmade gifts with such enthusiasm. —PATRICIA LORENZ

READER'S ROOM

As I look back on my journal entries and reflect on what has happened to me, one entry stands out. I had prayed that God would help me to be Christ-absorbed and not self-absorbed. What a difference that makes—when I focus not on myself or my problems, but on Christ and His strength! My heart is taken from the things of this world and placed in heaven with my Father Who loves me. He gives me a new perspective and helps me to see other people's needs. Mine often pale in comparison. —DEBBIE STANLEY, GRAND HAVEN, MICHIGAN

6/THU

I am weary with my sighing. . . .
—PSALM 6:6 (NAS)

Sometimes a disappointment comes along that knocks me for a loop. It's been that kind of week: disappointment in a loss; disappointment in a dashed opportunity. Such experiences leave me depressed, angry and sad, in the depths of an emotional ditch.

Today, I am trying to decide whether or not I will crawl out of that ditch. Somewhere from childhood I hear my mother's voice: "Scott, you cannot always control your circumstances, but you can control your attitude." I bet she heard those words from her mother, too.

Old saw or not, it's true: I do have some control over how I will feel and act today. I can decide to crawl out of my ditch of despair or lie in my pain awhile longer. I do have choices.

Granted, I have learned over the years that grief can only be healed by expressing my emotions and feeling my pain. I also know that I cannot rush this process. But there comes a time to get on with life and enter a bright new day.

Today, I'm going to find ways to clamber out of my ditch. I'll take a brisk walk, have lunch with a buddy and clean off my messy desk. And if I have time, I'm going to do something good for somebody floundering in a ditch deeper than my own.

These are all things I can do today. Tomorrow will take care of itself.

Dear Father, give me the courage to make decisions. And grant me the strength to climb out of the ditch. Amen.
—SCOTT WALKER

7/FRI

One woe is past; and, behold, there come two woes more hereafter.
—REVELATION 9:12

There's one good thing to be said for getting old: never having to repeat certain pains of childhood.

I had three childhood pains in particular. The first was long underwear. I hated it! But parents back then were sure their offspring would develop consumption (a form of tuberculosis) if this detested garment wasn't worn all winter. It was made of wool, and it itched. Scratching, however, gave us kids something to giggle about during a long sermon at church.

The second of my three woes? Ribbed stockings, which you pulled on over the first woe. You had to fold over the longies' leg openings, then ease the hose over the flap so there wouldn't be a ridge at the ankle. It never worked. My legs always looked like they were screwed in. To hold up the socks, a sort of harness hung from my waist or shoulders with four dangling garters, two to snap on each sock. Thus their tops gaped for icy wind to whistle in. Whoever invented pantyhose should have been knighted.

My third woe was medicine. Grandma figured any kid as skinny as I surely must have worms. Probably the stuff she spooned into me was one of those "snake oil" remedies that could clean paint specks off windows and do away with dandelions.

Whenever I protested wearing long johns and ribbed stockings and taking my medicine, Mom and Dad always answered, "Children, obey your parents" (Colossians 3:20). It's the same verse I used for my children, grandchildren and now for my great-grandson. Obeying my parents concerning childhood woes was always beneficial. And always will be. At least, I've never had consumption, I am no longer skinny, and my doctor confirms I don't have worms.

Lord, because I was taught to obey my earthly parents, it is easier to obey You, my heavenly Father. —ISABEL WOLSELEY

8/SAT *The Lord will be your everlasting light, and your God will be your glory.* —ISAIAH 60:19 (RSV)

Whether we get our biblically allotted three score and ten or a few years more or less, we're constantly reminded of our mortality.

Last year, in November, North America was a prime viewing area for the Leonid meteor shower, dust particles from the comet Tempel-Tuttle that orbits the sun once every thirty-three years. To see this heavenly show, my wife Shirley and I set our alarm clock for 4:30 A.M. and went out on the dark Gulf of Mexico beach behind our house in Florida. There, under a breathtaking, starlit sky, we *ooh*ed and *aah*ed as countless meteors, like diamonds on a string, flashed by in every direction. I'd never seen anything like it.

One father was reported to have told his young son, "The stars are so happy, they're dancing." So it seemed.

Is it presumptuous of me to say that many of us who saw this meteor display will not be around for the next one in 2034? I think not. For those who believe that God made the heavens and earth and everything therein, that is not a troubling thought. His Word promises another life to follow. And just maybe those who aren't here to watch the next Leonid meteor shower will have an even better view from above.

> Remind me, Lord,
> As your child, the best is yet to be,
> In a heavenly promise named Eternity.

—FRED BAUER

9/SUN   *If we have food and clothing, we will be content with that.*   —I TIMOTHY 6:8 (NIV)

Visiting family in western New York, I anticipated a big dinner at my sister's. Because Mother was frail, I agreed to bake the ham and devil two dozen eggs—on her behalf, in her kitchen.

But it was a bad cooking day. The eggs were so peel-resistant that it took ninety minutes to shell them; the whites were so gouged, we should have made egg salad. And the ham—before taking an afternoon nap, I turned Mother's oven way up instead of way down. The smoke alarm jolted us. The outer half-inch of the shank was charred black. As for the pan juices, I figured we'd have to throw away the roaster.

If I'd been in my kitchen, I might have thrown it all away and bought better at the deli. But this wasn't my house. "We'll make do," Mom said, repeating a phrase that had gotten her and Dad through the Depression and the war rationing and us seven kids through college wearing hand-me-downs.

"Okay," I said, which meant we propped the mangled egg halves against each other, trimmed the ham, soaked the pot and loaded the food into the car.

At my sister's, the family gathered in, four generations around the table. I sat next to five-year-old Kurtis. Despite my second-rate eggs and ham, the table was generously laden. Kurtis was the first to spoon up mashed potatoes. He nudged me. "Pass the gravy. Please." It was more a demand than a request.

Gravy. Gravy. I brought the meat. Never even thought of gravy. Child, are you kidding? Gravy? All that quickly went through my head, but I had the good sense to smile and model mother's "make-do" way.

"There's no gravy, Kurtis," I said quickly. "Today is a butter day."

I handed him the butter plate. He cut off a slab and shrugged as if to say, *Okay, butter will do.*

"Pass it along," I urged.

Lord, teach me the lessons of contentment that come with knowing when and how to "make do."   —EVELYN BENCE

10/MON   *Now faith is the substance of things hoped for, the evidence of things not seen.*   —HEBREWS 11:1

There were six or eight of us on the playground that day, and we decided we wanted to organize a game of football. The only problem was the football itself—we didn't have one. "I know," one of us said, "let's just pretend we do."

The game worked pretty well for a while. The quarterback would wind up, pretend to throw and at the other end of the field one of us would jump up, pretend to make a catch and dance around victoriously. Then, inevitably, arguments started up.

"Hey, you don't have the ball. I do."

"No you don't. I intercepted it!"

"Did not!"

"Did, too!"

Even at age nine, my friends and I were discovering that our imagination, which up till then had made the world such a magical and obliging place, was starting to let us down. Little did any of us know just how much worse it was going to get—that in adult life, wishing a thing were so won't work for even a second, much less the space of a few football plays.

Of course, I also didn't know then that when God brings us out of the innocence of childhood, He also gives us gifts to make up for what He takes away. I think the reason that moment on the playground still stays so fresh in my mind is that the faith I hold as an adult is both so like and so unlike that invisible football. For though faith can't be seen, and others may even doubt its existence altogether, it is in truth the most real and lasting thing I carry with me.

Dear God, help me remember that my faith rests on the rock of Your faithfulness. —PTOLEMY TOMPKINS

A HERITAGE OF FREEDOM

11 / *TUE* THE KOREAN WAR VETERANS MEMORIAL
With a great sum obtained I this freedom. . . . —ACTS 22:28

The newest memorial on the National Mall is the Korean War Veterans Memorial. At the junction of the two walls of the memorial are these words, inlaid in silver: FREEDOM IS NOT FREE. As I read those words, I recalled the day when I first learned the meaning of that statement.

When I was eight years old, I joined a program for boys at my church. It was like scouting; the men of the church led the boys in activities and outings. There was a spiritual component as well, and I earned badges for memorizing Scripture, as well as for building campfires and model airplanes. When I walked into the first session, I was assigned to a table where we were to make birdhouses with the help of an adult. Sitting at my table was a man I'd seen before but had never approached. He had no fingers on either hand, only palms, and my father told me he also had artificial legs attached to stumps that ended above each knee.

Deftly pressing a hammer between his palms, the man smiled at me and said, "You'll have to hold the nails." Swallowing my childhood fear, I stepped up and followed his directions. Later, he spoke quietly to all the boys about how he had been wounded in Korea, left for dead and then crawled back to safety over frozen ground, losing his fingers and legs to frostbite. "Never forget," he told us, "that the freedom we have to live in peace and worship God in our own way is not free. Throughout our history soldiers have paid a high price for it."

Thank You, Lord, for those who sacrificed so that the rest of us might know a life of freedom. —ERIC FELLMAN

12 / WED   *Blessed are all they that wait for him.*
—ISAIAH 30:18

Good morning, Father.

Today, I have come perfectly prepared to spell out the needs of my friends and family—a young mother fighting depression, a challenging decision for Brock, traveling mercies for Keri, David's concern over our savings balance—and to give You some suggestions about how to answer those needs.

But now, considering just Who I stand before—the Great I AM, for Whom no words exist, the Creator Who spun our world into being, and spread universes beyond universes in space—I step back in awe. It's time to abandon my "here's how You can best answer my prayers" instruction sheet.

Remember how, as a child, I always had my Christmas letter written and ready to go by the first of November? Inside the envelope was a carefully printed list of all the things I wanted. I'd walk out to the mailbox, slip the letter inside, put up the red flag, and that was that. Ahead was the anticipation of waiting until Christmas morning. I didn't worry a minute until then. Because, always, under the tree in the living room, the answer waited. Never exactly what I listed in the letter—always better.

I'm not going to worry today, Father, about the long list of concerns and hopes and needs I had planned to recite. You have already read them on my heart. So I let them go, send them straight to You. For once, they come with no instructions. Because today I'm going to trust. Today, I'm going to take great pleasure in the anticipation of Your answers to my requests—never exactly what I include on my list—always better.

Amen. —PAM KIDD

13/THU   *Therefore, as God's chosen people, holy and dearly loved, clothe yourselves with compassion, kindness, humility, gentleness and patience.* —COLOSSIANS 3:12 (NIV)

So many children; so great a need! Those words were in my mind from the moment I stepped off the plane in El Salvador a couple of months ago. *So many children; so great a need!* My husband Lynn and I had traveled to this country to see how Compassion International helps lift children out of poverty, by connecting them to sponsors around the world. That's a huge undertaking because more than a billion children are in great need.

For three days, we toured the rural areas outside the capital city, San Salvador, and saw the children everywhere, leaning over chain-link fences, jammed into the backs of open pickups, playing together in barren, dusty lots near the huts that are their homes. So many children, some smiling, some with sad faces and some with blank, empty stares.

We visited some homes where Compassion-sponsored children live. In one home, we met Oscarito, a five-year-old I will never forget. Months earlier, following a devastating earthquake, Oscarito darted out into the street and was hit by a huge relief truck that had come to his little village. He was dragged for several blocks and left in critical condition. Because he is a sponsored child, there was no question about his care. He was taken to a hospital, where he remained in a coma for weeks, but he survived, and was now back home in his little hut with his mother, brother and sister. Oscarito needs rehabilitation to learn to walk again, but he has a future that's filled with hope.

When I boarded the plane to come back to Colorado, I carried the images of all these children in my heart. *How, in a world filled with so many overwhelming needs, can one person make a difference,* I wondered. And then I thought of Oscarito. No, I can't change the whole world, but I have so many opportunities to change the world for just one child like Oscarito, that makes all the difference in the world.

Father, when the needs I see seem overwhelming, remind me that small things can still make a big difference.

—CAROL KUYKENDALL

14 / FRI   *My times are in thy hand.* .... —PSALM 31:15

Twenty-six years ago, when still a student, I spent an unexpected tax refund on a really good watch. For twenty-six years I never took off that watch. Waterproof, shockproof, shatterproof, it went with me everywhere. With it, I could keep a constant check on the time: sneaking a glance at my watch during meetings at work; stretching my arm surreptitiously at church just to clock the sermon; holding the luminous dial up to my eye at the movies to see if a film was finishing up.

Then, on a sultry summer day at the beach, I took a wave badly in rough surf and tumbled headfirst into the sand. The watch—this reliable companion—slipped off my wrist as I was tossed in the turbulence. I swam after it, but another wave was on top of me. I stood up in the water, trying to catch the watch in the sand with my toe. *It's got to be here someplace,* I thought. I marked the spot, thinking that when the tide went out I'd come back to look. But whom was I kidding? With these waves, the sand was always moving. In another hour, my watch could be halfway out to sea. In a day, it could be a mile down the beach.

"I lost my watch," I sputtered to the lifeguard.

He shrugged, his way of stating the obvious: It was long gone. Ten years from now, some beachcomber with a metal detector would discover it, polished rough like sea glass. With any luck, it'd still work. As for me, I determined to do without a watch for a while. "The good Lord giveth and the good Lord taketh away," I told myself with an attempt at detachment.

For three months now I've been without a watch. Truth to tell, I haven't missed it. I've discovered that when I need to know what time it is, there are lots of clocks around. And there are times during a sermon, during a movie, during a meeting when it's just as well not to be staring at a watch. I keep thinking of a sign my seventh-grade French teacher had posted next to the clock: TIME WILL PASS. WILL YOU? I'm learning how to pay more attention to what's going on around me than on the passing time.

Lord, help me make the most of the passing years.

—RICK HAMLIN

FOLLOWING JESUS

15/SAT PROTECTING THE VULNERABLE
"Whoever lives by the truth comes into the light. . . ."
—JOHN 3:21 (NIV)

On my own for the first time in more than two decades, I waited for a serviceman to come to my house to look at my car. The thought of dealing with another problem alone overwhelmed me. I'd recently hired both a plumber and a painter who'd taken advantage of my lack of expertise. And now this chip in my windshield obscured my field of vision and seemed to grow bigger every day.

That frosty winter morning, I watched from my living room window as the mechanic grabbed a red rag from his back pocket, sprayed the windshield with something from a white can and rubbed it with the rag. *Wonder how much this will set me back?* I thought. In a second, the man appeared at my door with a wide grin, proclaiming, "All taken care of."

Checkbook in hand, I followed him out to my car to have a look. Sure enough, the magic solution had filled in the chip in my windshield. But the man waved off my check with a chuckle. "Don't owe me a thing," he said, unfolding the rag. "Just a bug on your windshield."

As he drove away, I jotted his company's name in my repairs log. There really were some honest people out there. And as soon as I got over feeling like the world's biggest fool, I'd be spreading the word about the honest man I'd just discovered.

Lord, give me the strength to live by Your truth, even when others would never know the difference. —ROBERTA MESSNER

16 / SUN   *"For I am the Lord, your God, who takes hold
of your right hand and says to you, Do not fear; I will help you."*
                                                —ISAIAH 41:13 (NIV)

I woke up early one Sunday in November 1998. I was nervous,
and perhaps even a little scared. I was scheduled to preach at the
morning service at a large Southern Baptist church, and I would be
the first African American minister ever to occupy that pulpit.

I was going through my notes when, all of a sudden, I began to
cry uncontrollably. How could I, a black man, say these things to
an all-white congregation? With all of the negative history extending back from that Sunday morning, how could I challenge my listeners to build bridges of reconciliation?

In the midst of my tears, God reached out to me and reminded
me that the message I was to deliver was not supposed to be about
me—it was about Him. I was just a vessel He was using on this
particular day to share His Word with this one congregation of His
people. I was to walk into that pulpit with boldness. The preacher
that morning was not just Dolphus Weary, an African American,
sharing his own thoughts on his own behalf, but Dolphus Weary, a
child of the King, who was representing the King and bringing His
message.

*Lord, help me to remember that whenever I think I am bearing
the load alone, You are always reaching out and helping me.*
                                                —DOLPHUS WEARY

17 / MON   *"Stay in the city until you have been clothed
with power from on high."*   —LUKE 24:49 (NIV)

A friend had been going through a difficult time after the breakup
of a relationship. Then she lost her job. I sat in her living room on
a Sunday afternoon visit, feeling powerless to help.

Then on Monday morning I received an e-mail from a *Daily
Guideposts* reader named Jo Biggers. A devotional I had written
about a bib worn by my mother, who is a stroke victim, prompted
her to write: "I work in the laundry at Life Care Center in
Washington. It's my passion. I love my job and the residents."

She went on to say that one of her favorite times of the day was when she delivered the huge bibs (fabric protectors, she called them) to the dining room. "When I place them around the necks of the residents, I tell them that I can turn it around so they can be Superman! The residents love it when I bring them up right from the dryer. They comment about how warm the bibs feel against them and how clean they smell. It makes my job worth everything to me."

All at once I understood: As Jo made her rounds among the health center residents, she could do nothing to remedy their disabilities. Yet the bibs she brought them could be Superman capes, with supernatural powers radiating from the warm, fragrant fabric. For she was not just putting on bibs; she was clothing the residents with the helping power of her love and kindness.

I'd thought I had nothing to offer my friend because I hadn't been able to change her difficult situation. But now I saw that it wasn't so much what I said that mattered, but rather what I did: faithfully coming to visit her, even when I had no answers.

Dear Lord, today let the patient love of the Holy Spirit work through me until I clothe someone with Your power.

—KAREN BARBER

18/TUE   *Bear with each other and forgive whatever grievances you may have against one another....*
—COLOSSIANS 3:13 (NIV)

My wife and I are in the middle of a fight. (*Middle* means she has yet to admit she's wrong.) Any couple that's been married for a while won't be surprised that we're "having a discussion," as my sainted mother used to say.

I speak to you as a happily married man. (I can't speak for Sandee, because she's not speaking.) By every measure, my wife and I are good friends, compatible, in love. But at times like these, we have trouble being in the same zip code, let alone the same house.

But this fight is different. It's our first argument since September 11, 2001. As angry as I am, as convinced as I am that I'm right, I can't help but feel a little foolish.

I have a wife to argue with. There's a widow somewhere who would love one more chance to talk to her spouse.

And it's different to fight about . . . whatever it is that I'm right about, when a real fight is going on, with bullets and "collateral damage." I know it's inevitable, I know every couple does it, but in the back of my mind is the memory of those twin towers. I still see them standing there, wedded together, solid and sound, then suddenly it's raining debris, nothing left but smoke and orphans. Maybe we took the skyline for granted, thinking that nothing could put those two asunder, and then there you are, speechless in front of your children, trying to explain this new, unplanned topography, the one with the crater where the people used to be.

And I remember sensing that crater as I pulled Sandee close and prayed, prayed, prayed for all the long nights and hard questions that couples require, prayed into the autumn darkness for just one more chance to say, *I'm sorry, I'm sorry, I was so wrong.*

Lord, bind up the wounds in my marriage and in our world.

—MARK COLLINS

SUN, MOON AND STARS

The Bible says, "The heavens declare the glory of God; and the firmament showeth his handiwork. Day unto day uttereth speech, and night unto night showeth knowledge" (Psalm 19:1–2). Is this language also personal? "I believe it is," says Carol Knapp, "and I've tried to listen hard for God's voice in His created Word, the world around me." Over the next three days, Carol will share some of God's "sun, moon and stars talk," as she has understood it in her life. —THE EDITORS

19/WED THE SUN

There is one glory of the sun. . . . —I CORINTHIANS 15:41

I was married on an autumn afternoon in a little A-frame church overlooking Kalispell Bay on Priest Lake in north Idaho. I remember kneeling at the altar, feeling the sun streaming through the glass and warming my back and shoulders. Several years ago, when my husband and I went through a shaky period in our marriage, I sometimes thought about the feel of the sun on my back that day, as if God's touch had rested there. And in that remembered moment I could hear Him encouraging me: *Steady on, girl, steady on.* I did hold steady, and the problems eventually disappeared.

Two winters ago, on our first morning in our new home in Minnesota, I woke at dawn to sit by the bedroom window and give thanks to God. I felt grateful for the freedom our house and acreage afforded after cramped townhouse living. But I felt doubt, too. The house had cost more to build than we'd expected, and there were other expenses still ahead. *Have we acted impulsively?* I wondered.

Suddenly, at the horizon, a huge red sun seemed to surge up out of the ground beside a stand of oaks, just beyond a small hill. I started to cry at the unexpected beauty. As it rose higher, I felt a deep conviction that we were doing the right thing by investing in this house and land, to enjoy it and use it for whatever God had planned. His voice was there in that awesome sunrise, giving me hope and saying, *Welcome, neighbor!*

Lord, I wait eagerly for the sound of Your voice in sunrises and sunsets yet to be. —CAROL KNAPP

20/THU THE MOON

And another glory of the moon. . . . —I CORINTHIANS 15:41

Four children in as many years had transformed our house into a neighborhood zoo. But whenever the moon shone on a summer evening, God wooed us outside for an hour of "hush." We'd sit on our kitchen chairs and make up songs about the beautiful things He has made. Sometimes we danced slow twirls across the lawn. Our zoo became a peaceful little backyard chapel.

Years later, after we'd moved to Alaska, I was driving my teenage daughter Kelly home from volleyball practice down a deserted country road. We were both tired, but the bright moon lulled me to a stop along the roadside, and I switched off the van's headlights. Out of the stillness, Kelly quietly recited a line from Alfred Noyes's "The Highwayman," a poem she'd memorized in sixth grade: "The road was a ribbon of moonlight over the purple moor. . . ."

I was amazed Kelly still remembered the poem and that our wayside pause had prompted her to recite it. Complete contentment filled me. All that the moon meant to me—peacefulness, mystery, purity, loveliness—was present there. It was our backyard chapel all over again. The yard was bigger, and mother and daughter were older, but the God Who had spoken His serenity to me then still sounded exactly the same.

At day's end, Lord, when my soul needs quieting, You whisper Your peace by the light of the moon. —CAROL KNAPP

21/*FRI* THE STARS

And another glory of the stars: for one star differeth from another star in glory. —I CORINTHIANS 15:41

On our first Christmas Eve in Alaska, our family staged an impromptu talent show in our living room. Our eight-year-old son was supposed to shine a flashlight on his younger sister, the "star" of the moment, but he misunderstood and aimed it instead at the tinseled star atop our Christmas tree. We all shared a good laugh and felt our spirits rise. His mistake got us looking up, when loneliness in a new place had pulled us down.

That's what the stars do for me—get me looking up. I remember a glittering March night outside a remote cabin in Alaska, when hundreds of stars loomed so near that it seemed I could pick them from the sky like apples and load my pockets. We were on a last outing with our youngest daughter, soon to graduate from high school. God spoke joy to me in those stars that night—a grand finale in the heavens to our wonderful at-home years with our daughter.

On Thanksgiving morning three years ago, I blinked awake to find the planet Venus, the morning star, peering at me through a crack in the blinds. My husband and I had just moved to Minnesota, and none of our family were with us in our new locale.

The morning star drew me to the window, and looking up at

that star outshining all the others, I felt God's joy seep into me with the brightening sky. The morning star faded that day, as it must. But it got me to look up from my empty nest—to Jesus, the Bright Morning Star, now and forever.

The multitude of stars, Lord, proclaims Your joy—if only I will hear. —CAROL KNAPP

22/SAT *A faithful man will be richly blessed....*
—PROVERBS 28:20 (NIV)

There were times when I wondered if I was slowing down. Or was it the fact that, in the three years since joining the Medicare generation, I just wanted to "take it easy"? I knew I needed exercise, but I'd fallen out of the habit, often putting it off as too strenuous or boring. No wonder I could no longer walk two miles in thirty minutes as I had before retiring.

I knew something had to be done, so I vowed to walk at least five times a week, early in the day, before the sun heated up our Southern California neighborhood. I measured off a two-mile course. Each morning I donned my shorts and walking shoes, set my wristwatch to tick off the seconds, and strode off. I warmed up for five minutes, walked for thirty, then cooled down for five minutes more.

As the weeks passed, I began to thank and praise God as I walked. I enjoyed smelling flowers, saying hello to neighbors and other walkers, watching commuters leave for work and seeing children head off to school. Gradually I came closer to my goal of two miles in thirty minutes. Eventually I reached it.

Then one morning my pace seemed faster. A couple jogging by called out, "Hey, you're really moving!" Me? A fortyish woman walking in the opposite direction eyed me and commented, "I guess I'd better speed up!" And she did.

When I crossed the two-mile mark, I looked at my watch and did a double take. I'd made a quantum leap in speed: twenty-eight minutes! So it wasn't my age slowing me down; it was my attitude. And that's something I could change. I continued walking for two more minutes, exhilarated. And feeling younger than I had in years.

Thank You, Lord, for the blessings of health. Help me to be faithful in all areas of my life. —HAROLD HOSTETLER

23 / SUN   *For whatever was written in earlier times was written for our instruction....*   —ROMANS 15:4 (NAS)

Back in 1975, our family vacationed in Daytona Beach, Florida. I stretched out by the pool, anticipating a few days of total relaxation with no responsibilities.

Our thirteen-year-old daughter Jennifer suddenly whispered, "Mama, look at that girl!" I sat up, adjusted my sunglasses and saw a beautiful young woman in a skimpy bathing suit serving drinks to some folks at the pool.

I quickly shut my eyes, got comfortable again and announced, "We're on vacation. She's not my problem." But when I saw a small airplane overhead trailing an advertising sign, I suddenly sat up again. The sign seemed to say, MARION, TELL THAT GIRL I LOVE HER.

Thirty stubborn minutes later, I put on my robe and marched over to the bar. "Look," I said to the young barmaid, "I know you're not interested in what I have to say, but God seems to want me to tell you that He loves you."

As I turned to go, I felt a slight tug on my arm. Behind her heavy blue eye shadow, the girl fought back tears. "Are you sure, lady?" she said. "Me? He loves me?"

Esther and I struck up a friendship. When she wasn't working, we spent hours talking about God. As we sat on the beach, I showed her my Bible, all marked up with the discoveries I'd made in the four years I'd been a Christian.

On our last day at the beach, I invited Esther to our room while I packed. I gave her a cup of orange juice, a ten-dollar bill and a big hug. Then God seemed to say, *Now give her your Bible, Marion.*

A long minute passed. Finally I managed to stammer, "Here. I . . . I—want you—to have this."

As our family headed back to Georgia, we got a final glimpse of Esther. She sat at the bar bent over her Bible, sharing it with two customers.

Today, Father, I suddenly remember the song I sang in Vacation Bible School: "The B-I-B-L-E, that's the book for me."

—MARION BOND WEST

24/MON   Without ceasing I make mention of you always in my prayers.   —ROMANS 1:9

Forty-seven, forty-eight, forty-nine. . . . Sheep are woolly but somewhat boring—black noses, white fleece. As I counted them endlessly going through the gate in the time-honored method of getting to sleep, my mind wandered. I'd counted sixty-two sheep, and I still couldn't sleep. *How will I get up in time for work tomorrow?*

The sheep ceased going through the gate. I tried praying. Prayers are more powerful than sheep. *A is for Africa, for the fight against starvation and disease. B, ah, that's easy. B is for bread, our daily bread. C is for Charlotte, my lovely grown daughter. D is for Daniel, my youngest. E is for Ecuador, the troubled country where Daniel was born.* This was much more rewarding than counting those fluffy sheep.

"Praying the alphabet" my friend called it when she told me how she dealt with insomnia. This simple pathway brings all kinds of people, events, joys and sorrows to mind that I might never have thought of including in my prayers.

I made this journey for several nights, even getting as far as *N* for Nina, my good friend suffering from Parkinson's disease. Then *O* for overjoyed, as I was when our Guideposts sweater project passed 150,000 garments. Then it occurred to me that *P* was as far as I could remember ever getting, and that only once. Sleep came softly as I prayed. *But what about all those Ys and Zs left prayerless?* I wondered the next morning.

So I resolved to pray the alphabet backward the next time insomnia twisted my brain in knots. *Only fair,* I thought. *Z is for, Z is for* . . . *zoologists? Do I know any who need my prayers? Not a one. Maybe I can skip Z, but then there are X and Y. What can I think of for X?* . . .

Dear God, on this Thanksgiving Day of Prayer, help me to remember that there are no limits to prayer, only limits to my horizons.   —BRIGITTE WEEKS

25/TUE *For he performeth the thing that is appointed for me. . . .* —JOB 23:14

When my husband Robert was asked to lead a "Spiritual Journey" workshop at St. Andrew's Episcopal Cathedral in Jackson, Mississippi, he suggested that I lead it with him. The planners were happy to accept that offer, but I was panicked.

There was a time when I did a lot of traveling around the Midwest, leading prayer workshops and retreats for church groups. But it had been at least ten years since I'd accepted an engagement like that, and I had some serious doubts. Was I still capable, at this stage of my life, of leading a successful workshop? My deepest concern, though, was my fear of disappointing my husband. I really wanted to do this with Robert, but I was torn.

Then I remembered the advice of my eighty-year-old soul friend Anna, who said to me one day before an important talk, "Remember, Marilyn, you don't have to be capable of doing this. It's not up to you. Just keep reminding yourself of Job 23:14: 'He performeth the thing that is appointed for me.' "

During the time of preparation and on the day of the workshop, I often repeated those words, trusting in them. I'm glad to tell you that the workshop went very smoothly and that many people expressed appreciation for what we had brought them. At the end of the day, Robert hugged me and said, "I think we make a great team!" And surprise! I loved every moment of it and would even enjoy doing it again!

Whenever I'm unsure of myself, Father, let me trust You to "perform the task appointed for me."—MARILYN MORGAN KING

26/WED *I have given you an example. . . .* —JOHN 13:15

My mother stoked up the fire in the kitchen stove with the wood she had carried in herself. She washed dishes with the water she had pumped from the well in the front yard. On wash day she scrubbed the family's overalls and hung them over the page-wire fence to dry. For meals she cooked countless variations of salt pork and potatoes, and people knew they would always be received with a warm welcome into her drafty old house on the Canadian prairie.

The linoleum was worn through where a welcome mat should have been—a silent testimony to the countless visitors who dropped in for food, friendship and fun. They never seemed to mind her threadbare sofa and mismatched dishes. They pulled the odd assortment of old wooden chairs up around the table at mealtime and enjoyed the hospitality as if they were members of the family.

I thought of her today as I fussed with Thanksgiving preparations. Would these dishes match that tablecloth? What could I use as a centerpiece? Supposing more company came than I expected, would there be enough turkey and cranberries and pumpkin pie? And I really should have cleaned the rug and freshened up the kitchen curtains and. . . .

In my mind's eye I could see my mother in her bib apron welcoming people through that scarred old kitchen door. I picked up the phone and dialed our son's number. "Hello, Lyle. Is there anyone you know who's alone for Thanksgiving? There might be? Well, bring them along for supper! See you all later!"

And then I began to peel a few more potatoes.

Thank You, God, for a mother who valued people instead of things. —ALMA BARKMAN

$27/$_THU_   *We give thanks to you, O God. . . .*
—PSALM 75:1 (NIV)

Okay, I admit it: I don't like Thanksgiving. It's not that I have anything against gratitude; what I don't like is all the eating and the patting of bellies and then more eating. But my family loves Thanksgiving. Last year, my daughter Amy Jo suggested a progressive dinner, where we go from house to house for different courses of the meal. "And you might want to give Grandma a break this year and cook the main part of the meal." Forget the fact that I haven't really cooked in . . . well, a long time.

My husband Gary and I went out to dinner the night before my cooking adventure was set to begin. As we were driving home, we saw a young man, barely visible in the darkness, waving frantically. Gary guided our car across three lanes of traffic and stopped. Instantly, the young man was at our window. "Wow, thanks, man," he said. "Broken down car. Been driving for twenty-four hours. Trying to get home."

We invited the young man and his buddy into our backseat and let them use our cell phone. After calling a tow truck, the boy's buddy tried to reach his dad. Finally, after talking to another relative, he handed us the phone. "My grandma . . . she had a heart attack. Everyone is at the hospital."

We were silent for a moment. Then, thinking of the long day ahead of me in the kitchen, I asked. "What's her name?"

"Emily," he said.

"Would it be all right if I prayed for her?"

Even in the darkness, I could see his shoulders sag a little less. "Yeah, that would be great."

So all day long, as I prepared for the big meal, I prayed for Emily, for her health, her family, their holiday. Thanksgiving dinner turned out great. My family had fun going from house to house all day. And I didn't mind the overeating quite so much. I kept thinking about Emily and how God had given me the blessing of praying for her. Which gave me just one more reason to give thanks.

Thank You, God, for giving us the things we truly need.

—MARY LOU CARNEY

28/*FRI* "A new command I give you: Love one another. As I have loved you, so you must love one another."

—JOHN 13:34 (NIV)

My father was born and raised in East Texas. For special occasions—holidays, weddings, funerals and the like—our family of five would make the trek from Illinois, where we lived, to visit our Texas family and friends.

What I remember most about those trips is visiting my great-aunt's house. Aunt Ara Sherman was my paternal grandfather's sister. She was about five feet tall and heavy-set, with a very ample bosom. A widow with too many grandchildren to number, her voice was soft, with a shaky tremor. She never spoke harshly— except to the baseball umpires on television who, she was convinced, were trying to keep her favorite team from winning. Her house was the family gathering place, always full of smells that said, "Come on in, grab a plate and fork, and pull up a chair."

The loudest sound in Aunt Ara's house was laughter. My family is fully capable of starting and sustaining some pretty good arguments, but differences and disagreements melted away in Aunt Ara's presence. At her house, the cousin who just got out of jail sat shoulder to shoulder with the cousin who just earned an advanced degree. In-laws and outlaws alike were all beautiful in Aunt Ara's eyes, and she let us all know that we were loved.

Her love enfolded us, uplifted us and knit us together. A house filled with too many chairs, pots full of food and her enormous warm smile said she'd thought about our coming and she wanted us there.

Lord, help me to love sincerely and deeply, and in a way that draws, touches and encourages everyone I meet.

—SHARON FOSTER

29/SAT Forbearing one another, and forgiving one another.... —COLOSSIANS 3:13

By temperament my husband is much like Winston Churchill: a brilliant wit, stubbornly persistent, impatient—and grouchy in the morning. Churchill once confessed that he had to give up having breakfast with his wife because he was "just too out of sorts" early in the morning. Same here.

John takes the newspaper and his coffee to his special den upstairs, where he can rant and rave and *harrumph* at all the goings-on in the sports section without disturbing my own peace and morning tranquility.

Churchill was devoted to his beloved "Clemmie," and John has never given me cause to doubt his love. Nevertheless, the Churchills had their quarrels, and we Anguses have ours. Not that it's ever my fault, you understand. John says, "She's too proud to say she's sorry, and I never have reason to!" Ha.

Once at a dinner party, Churchill kept walking his fingers, knuckles bent, across the tablecloth toward Lady Churchill.

Distracted and curious, her dinner partner asked what on earth Sir Winston was doing. She replied that they had had a quarrel before leaving the house, and he was acknowledging that it was all his fault. He was on "bended knees" to ask her forgiveness.

A friend of mine has another solution to the apology problem. "When my husband told me, 'The trouble with you is that you're never willing to say I'm sorry,' I fixed it. I wrote 'I'm sorry' umpteen times on a piece of paper, then cut it into strips. I put them in a tumbler on the dining room table and told him, 'There, when you need one, take one!'"

I use "sorry slips" in a tumbler, and John uses Churchill's "bended knee." When he pulls out one of my slips, or when he creeps his knuckles at me, it works. Now if only we'd learn to do this early on, we'd avoid most quarrels in the first place!

Enlarge my understanding and compassion, Lord. Help me to forbear and, most important, to forgive. —FAY ANGUS

A LIGHT FROM THE MANGER

"Many years ago," writes Shari Smyth, "a fierce storm blasted our house. The power went out and stayed out for several days. One night, as our daughter Laura sat in her chair, peering into a book with a flashlight, she asked, 'Mommy, when will the real light come on?' At Christmas, God slipped through the back door of His creation and began turning on the real light." This Advent, come with Shari as she joins the lights of the first Christmas with a few lights from her own life, praying that through these stories, the Light will shine in a new place for you.
—THE EDITORS

30/ SUN THE FIRST SUNDAY IN ADVENT

"The virgin will be with child and will give birth to a son, and they will call him Immanuel"—which means, "God with us."

—MATTHEW 1:23(NIV)

It was a Wednesday night in early December. I was downstairs in church preparing for the weekly children's story hour. At home I'd left boxes of unpacked Christmas decorations and mounds of greenery on the floor. The annual struggle to get my house just right had started, and the tension was building. Christmas brings it out in me: I scrub, I bake, I clean, I decorate, I sigh.

Now, getting ready for the children, I pulled out a large laminated picture of a white, steepled church, which had been our theme for the last few weeks. As I turned it in the light, I gasped. There was the Christ Child in the stained glass window! *Why have I never seen Him there before?* I wondered.

When the children came in, I held up the picture. "Do you see who's looking at you from this window?" I asked.

They looked blank. "We don't see anything, Miss Shari."

The culprit was the glare on the laminating. When I shielded the picture from the light, they spotted Baby Jesus right away. "He's in there. He's looking at me," a boy said. "And I never even noticed."

When the story hour was over, I returned home to the holiday tension, carrying a larger truth. In our Christmas celebrations, Christ was beckoning to me. But He was hidden by the glare of my pride—the pride that wanted a beautiful, flawless house; the pride that was desperate to impress my guests; the pride that feared I'd never be good enough.

Now, driving through the darkness, I heard Christ whisper, *Let go of your pride, your need to hide behind perfection, and let Me shine in your imperfect house—and in you.*

Lord, may all those who come through my door this Christmas know Your presence.   —SHARI SMYTH

My Daily Blessings

1 _____

2 _____

3 _____

4 _____

5 _____

6 _____

7 _____

8 _____

9 _____

10 _____

11 _____

12 _____

13 _____

14 _____

15 _____

16 _____

17 _____

18 _____

19 _____

20 _____

21 _____

22 _____

23 _____

24 _____

25 _____

26 _____

27 _____

28 _____

29 _____

30 _____

DECEMBER

Blessed be the Lord God of Israel; for
he hath visited and redeemed his people.
—Luke 1:68

S	M	T	W	T	F	S
	1	2	3	4	5	6
7	8	9	10	11	12	13
14	15	16	17	18	19	20
21	22	23	24	25	26	27
28	29	30	31			

AN EYE FOR BLESSINGS

1/ MON   A GIVING HEART
It is more blessed to give than to receive.   —ACTS 20:35

Last month I thought about the everyday joy of thankfulness; today I've been reminded of the daily privilege of giving.

It's a blessing I can lose sight of in December, with crowded stores and lines at the post office. What reminded me was a little girl, perhaps three years old, wandering among the tables in the shopping mall this morning, passing out wooden coffee stirrers from the service counter, eyes aglow with the delight of bestowing bounty.

Beside my chair she paused, selected one of the slender sticks with great deliberation and placed it carefully beside my napkin. "This is for you," she said. In her eagerness to bring riches to the next table, she didn't wait for my thanks.

Giving must satisfy a basic need. I see it every Christmas morning, as packages are opened. Instead of watching the one receiving the gift, I always keep my eyes on the face of the gift-giver as the carefully wrapped present is unveiled. In the intent expression, I see the trips to the store, the breathless hope that the choice was just right, the happiness of creating happiness.

And the best thing about giving is that I don't have to wait for Christmas. I can give myself this happiness over and over, every day. I could do it right there at the mall, surrendering my table in the busy food court to a group of four; at the exit where a Salvation Army bell rang; in the parking lot where a woman struggled with car keys and heavy packages. Tiny things, unimportant things— except for the lift they give the day.

This year, as I've focused on everyday blessings, I understand a little better the need to give. We give because we receive—day in, day out—"good measure, pressed down, and shaken together, and running over" (Luke 6:38).

This month, Lord, as we celebrate the greatest Gift of all, let me listen for the angels who tell me, "This is for you."

—ELIZABETH SHERRILL

2 / TUE

The blessings of your father are mighty beyond the blessings of the eternal mountains, the bounties of the everlasting hills. . . . —GENESIS 49:26 (RSV)

Holding the sleeping infant, I compose a silent speech to him, trying to impart some important matters by osmosis:

Listen, son, above all things, be straightforward with your love. Tend to the generous; admire mettle in the small; try to be awake to miracles, whether they are rivers or lovers or beggars. There is more beauty in this world than we can handle.

Tell the truth. Be gentle. Be open. Work hard. Choose joyful work, which is better than money. In games, find joy and milk it. Praise light, as it comes from the Maker, like truth and music.

Savor the old, as they have lived furiously and helped make your world. Pay them with love, and bring your children to them to bless and be blessed, as children are pure, closest to the light, freshly made.

Know that God has the same face everywhere, if not the same name. The search for what is true and kind will lead to God.

Touch what you love, your mother's face, your father's beard, and never be shy with a kiss. Listen: Time eats everything, so hold your family close to heart and hand, while heart and hand you have, and time to sing.

Dear Lord, for this sleeping miracle, and all miracles, which is to say every second and every breath, thanks. —BRIAN DOYLE

3/ WED   *"Blessed are those who mourn, for they shall*
be comforted."   —MATTHEW 5:4 (RSV)

Marc-James Manor Bed and Breakfast here in Bellingham, Washington, has an antique china collection boasting 323 teapots that date back as far as 1740, and more than 1,400 teacups and saucers, salt boxes, coffee "cans" and pieces of table decor. Two of the sets absorbed my attention: They were completely black. "See how elaborately they're decorated?" Marc pointed out. "The mother and child, the shrouded windows—they're for mourning."

Mourning tea sets, I thought. *How wonderful it would be to live in a culture that allowed sadness without spiritual or psychological condemnation.* When my fifteen-year-old brother snapped his neck and was paralyzed, I was told to stop grieving; this was God's will. When my grandmother died, I was told to stop weeping; she was in heaven. When I broke into tears while telling of my sister's death several years earlier, I was told to get over it; let the dead bury the dead. It isn't "Christian" to lament. Lamentation reveals a bankrupt faith.

Over the years, though, I've not been good at hiding my grief and, after seeing Marc's collection, I confessed my struggle to my youngest child, then twenty. Blake challenged me to find a scriptural basis for tears and weakness, futility and dependency. "Culturally, we give no value to the sick and poor and the bereaved," he explained, "and so our Christianity mirrors the same sorry mistake. Yet didn't Jesus preach, 'Blessed are those who mourn'?"

So I spent the year getting reacquainted with David, Jeremiah, Isaiah and Job—men who wept and wailed, who dressed in sackcloth and sat in ashes and denied themselves food whenever they found themselves dismayed by turmoil, torn apart by grief or terrified out of their minds. Even Jesus wept. Reading on, I realized that their tears were not a sign of a bankrupt faith, but the prism through which they saw clearly. Jeremiah saw his mandate, Job his confusion, David his fear, Jesus His sorrow. And in seeing, they found comfort.

We have a shop in town that lets you paint and fire your own tea sets. This Christmas, I'd like to make a mourning set.

Dear Lord, thank You for tears. They open my eyes to what I need the most, and in You I find the comfort I need.

—BRENDA WILBEE

4/ THU   *Then Joshua built an altar in Mount Ebal to the Lord, the God of Israel.* —JOSHUA 8:30 (RSV)

When my wife Shirley and I were in Israel a few years ago, we participated in an archaeological dig on what was believed to be the site of Joshua's altar. The field on top of Mt. Ebal, above Shechem, was strewn with pottery shards from the Bronze Age, around 1200 B.C. Most of the pieces of brown clay had no value, but we were still fascinated to hold in our hands artifacts that dated from biblical times. As mementos, we brought a few of the shards home with us.

For a long time they remained in the attic. Then one day we showed them to our son Christopher, and his artistic mind went to work. The next Christmas he gave us a beautiful vase he had decorated with the clay pieces. It now sits on a living room shelf, a reminder of our Israeli experience and of Joshua, who led the Israelites into Canaan after Moses' death.

Joshua is a fascinating character. His name, given to him by Moses, means "God saves," and God's hand protected this military genius through many a trial, including the conquest of Jericho. It must have been daunting to take Moses' place, but Joshua heard God's voice saying, "Be strong and of good courage; be not frightened, neither be dismayed; for the Lord your God is with you wherever you go" (Joshua 1:9, RSV).

Somewhere, sometime, all of us will be faced with a task that seems completely beyond us. Death, divorce, illness, rejection, loneliness, a lost job, financial hardship are just some of the trials that can leave us distraught and spiritually shaken. But like Joshua, we have nothing to fear; we are not alone; God is with us wherever we go. I'm reminded of the truth whenever I look at my keepsake vase made beautiful by broken shards from Joshua's altar.

Lord, to help us cross our Jordans, give us strength,
No matter their depth, their width, their length.
—FRED BAUER

5/FRI   *My soul yearns for you in the night; in the morning my spirit longs for you. . . .* —ISAIAH 26:9 (NIV)

"Will you pray with me?" an attractive young woman asked timidly during a break at a women's retreat where we'd been talking about turning our "I can'ts" into "I cans." We found a quiet corner, and her words tumbled out, describing a life filled with difficulties. She was a single mom with four children, working full-time at a job with some pressing problems, and the man in her life had just broken their engagement. "I can't figure out what to do," she admitted, wiping away tears. "I feel so lonely and overwhelmed."

My heart ached for her, and we spent the next several minutes praying together, asking God to show us some "I cans" in the midst of her "I can'ts." When we finished, I took out a piece of paper, wrote "I CAN" across the top and handed it to her. "Let's think together," I suggested, and soon she had these ideas written down on the paper:

Three things only I CAN do:
Take responsibility for my self-care.
Let my needs be known to those who can help.
Ask for help.

Three ways I CAN ask another person to help me:
Spend time with me.
Spend time with my children.
Pray for me.

Three people I CAN ask for help:
Mom
Sandy
Cindy

Three ways I CAN have fun:
Go to the movies.
Go out to eat.
Attend special events.

As she tucked her "I CAN" list into her Bible, I prayed . . .

Lord, with You, we can turn our "I CAN'TS" into "I CANS!"
Thank You.   —CAROL KUYKENDALL

*6/*SAT *Say to those with fearful hearts, "Be strong, do*
not fear. . . ." —ISAIAH 35:4 (NIV)

At work, when they needed someone to dress up as a bear for
Saturday story time, guess who volunteered? Yes, anything to distract me from the phone call I knew I had to make to apologize to
a friend for an unsolicited criticism. While I struggled to don the
heavy fake-fur costume, the long feet—that is, paws—and the hairy
hands with four-inch nails, I had visions of how happy the children
would be to see me.

While I yanked and pulled on the enormous head, I glowed.
Maybe some kids would even ask for my "paw-tograph"! Plus, I'd
be postponing that dreaded call!

As I lumbered through the store, I could see that out of the
twenty or so children who were there, only two or three appeared
actually happy to see me. The others? They scattered in terror.
Some cried. Some wailed. Some leapt into their parents' arms for
safety. I guess a six-foot-tall bear was five more feet than they'd
bargained for.

Since bears aren't supposed to speak, I could only watch silently
and couldn't say what I wanted to: "I came to make you happy! I
won't hurt! Come up to me, please!" But even if I could have given
voice to my words, they wouldn't have been heard over the shrieks
and tears.

Inside my hot furry cage, I had to laugh, although ruefully.
Wasn't I that way too many times with God? A difficult phone call
to mend a friendship, my former fear of driving—maybe God was
handing me those challenges as loving gifts. And there I was
screaming, "No! Go away!"

As I made my way to the back room to pull off my furry head,
I knew that as soon as I yanked off my paws, I'd be dialing my
friend's phone number to make that overdue apology.

*Thank You, God, for putting loving challenges in my life. Help
me not to run from them screaming!* —LINDA NEUKRUG

A LIGHT FROM THE MANGER

7/SUN   THE SECOND SUNDAY IN ADVENT
*Then they opened their treasures and presented him with gifts of
gold and of incense and of myrrh.* —MATTHEW 2:11 (NIV)

The Magi swept into the glittering halls of Herod's palace, splendid
gifts for the newborn King in tow. But when the star they were following led them away from the glamour of the court to the back-
water town of Bethlehem and rested over a humble house with a
dirt floor, they were not disappointed. Faith gave them eyes to see:
They worshiped the young Child, opened their treasures and gave.

One Sunday a woman named Claire and her husband Arthur
stopped by our small, struggling church in South Salem, New York.
Claire had a gift for teaching, so she started an adult Sunday
school class. It seemed a thankless task, a waste of her talent.
Besides Claire and Arthur, only three or four of us came. Yet week
after week, Claire gave us her best, pouring herself into the lessons.
"Don't you know," she said one week, gesturing over the all-but-
empty sanctuary, "that God and His saints and angels fill this
place?" Her eyes sparkling mischief, she added, "It should feel
crowded in here."

Then, after many months, Arthur's job took them to another
state, and we lost touch. One night, a few years later, I received a
phone call from a friend: Claire had died after a short battle with
cancer. Numb, I walked out on my deck under the winter stars. A
soft moon raised sparkles from the frosty grass. I could still see
Claire standing before our little class, short, dark-haired, plump
and glowing with faith as she spoke. "In sending Jesus, God
brought us into His presence," she'd said one Advent Sunday.
"There is no greater honor."

Claire now enjoys the fullness of that presence, with all the saints and angels she saw in our humble sanctuary. And her gift lives on in us.

Jesus, help me to follow and pour out my best for You, wherever You lead.
—SHARI SMYTH

❧

8/MON   "*Let the beloved of the Lord rest secure in him, for he shields him all day long. . . .*"
—DEUTERONOMY 33:12 (NIV)

Alone. Sad. Tired. And now lost. I gritted my teeth as the empty trailer banged along behind my van and strained to read the next street sign.

I hadn't wanted my daughter and grandbaby to move in the first place. Last week I had boxed up much of their apartment, yesterday I had loaded the trailer, and early this morning I had driven one hundred and fifty miles and unloaded much of the cargo. Now I had wasted an entire hour driving around Casper, Wyoming, trying to find the drop-off point for the rented trailer.

I pulled into a convenience store lot to ask directions. Before I reached the door, I noticed an elderly rancher wearing a white cowboy hat and a denim jacket. The silver badge he wore suggested he worked as a night watchman. The slow smile spreading under his white mustache prompted me to ask for directions.

"You're only two blocks from the street you need and about seven blocks from the drop-off," he said. Following his blue pickup truck, I edged into traffic and turned left as he had directed. He seemed to be going the same way.

Within a few moments, I found the trailer place. My newfound navigator pulled in ahead of me, hopped out of his vehicle to direct me as I backed in the trailer, then quickly unhitched it and set it down.

"Now, if you want to follow me, I'll get you on your highway home." I thanked him over and over. He merely tilted his hat brim. Then, with his dog's long ears flapping out of his pickup's cab window, he piloted me to Route 26, waved vigorously and disappeared. I felt so relaxed that I sang all the way home.

Later that night I awoke and smiled, recalling lettering on his silver badge: SECURITY.

Lord of comfort, thank You for caring for us through the kindness of strangers. —GAIL THORELL SCHILLING

9/TUE *I watch, and am as a sparrow alone upon the house top.* —PSALM 102:7

Andrew is sick. My husband has been laid flat on his back by a nasty (but, thankfully, curable) infection for the past five days. So for five days I've been on my own with parenting, cleaning, grocery shopping with four children in tow and everything else that goes with family life. By the time everyone is in bed and the dishes are done, it's at least 10:00 P.M. and I am exhausted.

It isn't the work that wears on me, though; it's something else that I remember well from the years when I was single. Back when I was in my twenties and an aspiring career woman, I worked eighty hours a week for fifty weeks and then traveled abroad for two. I went to Spain one year and England the next; I flew to the Caribbean to go scuba diving. It was wonderful to see the world, but eventually I stopped going. It wasn't until the year that I vacationed with my folks in Belize that I was able to articulate why. "The hardest thing about traveling alone," I told them, "isn't having to do it all yourself. It's that there's no one to share your joys with."

That's what's hard about having Andrew so sick. If Mary does something particularly impish or John suddenly chooses to be delightful, if Elizabeth grins with pride at mastering something new on the violin or Maggie makes an enchanting baby sound, I want to share it. It may not be earth-shattering news, but little things like that are the everyday stuff out of which we weave our lives. Even small joys are bigger than we are: They need to spill over somewhere; they demand to be told. When I can't share them, it's lonely.

There's one thing, though, that sometimes helps. If God is the fount of all joy, then one reason joy overflows is to make it obvious (even to me) that I'm wading in reasons to give thanks. So even when I'm alone, I can offer what has been given back to the Giver, and share the joy with Him.

Jesus, You are Lord, even of my loneliness.   —JULIA ATTAWAY

*10/*WED   *For to be sure, he was crucified in weakness, yet he lives by God's power. Likewise, we are weak in him, yet by God's power we will live with him. . . .*
—II CORINTHIANS 13:4 (NIV)

There were about ten of us, mostly couples, gathered for the first time in a small discussion group at church. We had been talking about ourselves, sharing childhood memories and positive feelings about our marriages. We knew we were being less than honest with each other, and that our latest attempt at creating a Christian community was a miserable failure.

Then a woman, about thirty years old, interrupted. "Wait a minute," she said. "I've been sitting here feeling awful. You talk about happy marriages. Ours has been touch-and-go at best, and often terrible. And my first childhood memory is of my mother screaming at my father to 'get out of our lives and stay out!' He left and never came back.

"But I do remember one Christmas Eve when my younger sister and I were little girls. We didn't expect anything much for Christmas because we were very poor. But that night the two of us came home late. It was miserably cold and had just gotten dark. The door was locked, and we had to climb in through a window from the front porch. I pushed back the shade, and there, in the corner of the living room, was a Christmas tree with only a few scraggly lights on it—the only lights in the room. In the soft glow of those lights, I saw two doll bassinets, and in each a beautiful baby doll covered with a pink blanket. We couldn't imagine where Mother had gotten the money for such presents."

The woman's voice had become soft, like a child's. She stopped talking. Then she looked at us and raised her eyebrows. "And that was the happiest moment in my life."

As I looked around the group in the stunned silence that followed, I knew that this young woman had given us a great gift: Because she had let go of her silence and her pride, it was at last safe for us to start becoming more open with one another in Christ Jesus.

Dear Lord, thank You for the grace that can fill Your family when someone is willing to be vulnerable and honest. Amen.

—KEITH MILLER

11 / THU   *Perfect love casteth out fear....*—I JOHN 4:18

Well, this is it—the year I turn fifty. I'm not sure I'm ready to be fifty.

I was ready to turn forty. At forty, you're just hitting your stride, poised at the demographic meridian of life and finally ready to put all your learning years to good use. At thirty, I was simply relieved to have survived my twenties. At twenty . . . well, at twenty I didn't even think about birthday milestones (except maybe turning twenty-one). Yet here I am on the precipice of fifty, and for the first time in my life I find myself troubled by a birthday. Am I one of those foolish middle-aged men trying to hang on to youth?

Here are three things I'm trying to keep in mind as I approach fifty: First, we don't live forever. Second, life is a gift, and it should only grow more valuable as we grow older. And third, the only truly important thing in life is love.

Without love we die, at least on the inside. Nothing makes us feel better than love. When love is called for, nothing will substitute, and when we try to substitute something for love it always ends badly. Without love, we cannot know each other and we cannot know God.

In fifty years, I've received an incredible amount of love, a staggering half century of it, and I've tried to give love as best I can, often clumsily and fitfully, even foolishly, to other humans, to animals, to ideas and beliefs, to my work, my country and to God. Love moves like the speed of light; it never ages, even when we do. So, I tell myself, *If you want to hold on to your youth, hold on to love.* Even as I near fifty, my learning years are not entirely over.

Let me be thankful, Lord, for every year You give me, and the love that grows with it.

—EDWARD GRINNAN

12/FRI **Give unto them beauty for ashes . . . the garment of praise for the spirit of heaviness. . . .** —ISAIAH 61:3

"Can we put up a tree?" Cindy, our assistant clinic director, asked at our Friday morning staff meeting in mid-December.

Our social service agency often receives Christmas trees and decorations for clients who wouldn't otherwise have them. I hoped we'd given them all away the previous year, for even a small tree would make the congestion worse in the crowded waiting room.

But I didn't say no, and I returned from a late afternoon meeting to find Cindy and Helen, the office manager, placing delicate silver ornaments on a flocked white tree. "Looks fine," I said.

Cindy shook her head. "It needs lights."

I fished a string out of the decoration box. "Tiny and twinkling," I told her.

She eyed me sternly. "They're on a green cord," she said. "This tree needs silver lights on a white cord." The next morning she brought the right lights plus a delicate tree skirt for the gifts of mittens, caps and candy we give neighborhood children.

It was beautiful. Still, I felt a twinge of irritation over the waste of time and space . . . until I walked out to see a small boy staring at it, transfixed. *"Es muy bonito,"* he said softly to his mother. *"Sí,"* she responded. *"Hermoso."* Throughout the days that followed that scene was repeated over and over, in English and Spanish and German: "Beautiful." "Lovely." "Perfect."

This year I won't argue over the tree. Instead, I'll encourage those who lovingly bring beauty into others' lives. Thank you, Cindy and Helen, for honoring the newborn King with a Christmas gift of beauty!

Beautiful Savior, thank You for the loveliness of this holy season.
—PENNEY SCHWAB

*13/*SAT   *Listen! The Lord is calling to the city. . . .*
                                        —MICAH 6:9 (NIV)

I've never considered the incessant ringing of bells throughout my day a blessing, but I've recently learned otherwise. Not long ago I was having lunch with friends at a family-style restaurant when the phone—mounted on a post right behind my head—rang. It rang again. And again. Then, across the room, a cell phone rang. Then a beeper sounded at the next table.

"Would you ever have thought we'd have to live with so much ringing?" my friend Kathy asked.

"And that bells ringing could be so annoying?" I said. Just then Kathy's watch alarm began beeping. We all burst out laughing.

The next day, when our bell choir played in church, the bulletin carried a brief history of church bells. Centuries ago, monks attracted a gathering by ringing bells, calling the people to worship. By the eighteenth century, some clergy referred to bells as "messengers of God," and inscribed on them *Vox Domini*, Voice of the Lord, as though their glorious sound were God's own voice calling the people to Him.

Though I wouldn't go so far as to call the ringing of a cell phone glorious (although I do like the ones that play Mozart), all that ringing carries a different message for me now. When I hear it, I pause for a moment and think of *Vox Domini*, the Voice of the Lord, calling me to remember Him throughout the day.

While it's good to silence the phone when I need to be alone with God, much of the day I can't escape the ringing. So now I've made it a reminder that no day is so busy that I can't stop to praise God and thank Him for His daily blessings upon me.

Dear God, fill my day with small reminders that You are the Lord of all things.
                                        —GINA BRIDGEMAN

A LIGHT FROM THE MANGER

14/SUN   THE THIRD SUNDAY IN ADVENT
When Joseph woke up, he did what the angel of the Lord had commanded him and took Mary home as his wife.

—MATTHEW 1:24 (NIV)

Christmas was coming. I knew it from the calendar and the decorations outside my window. But except for the Advent wreath, my apartment was bare of the season. What was there to celebrate? A month earlier, after thirty-one years of marriage, Whitney and I had separated. I was in a painful, fearful, waiting mode. I lit three candles on the wreath and reached for my Bible, sinking into the familiar story as if it were a comfortable chair. Between the lines I found something new.

The angel came to Mary with overwhelming news. Then he left her. She had to go to Joseph all by herself, with no proof except her word. Next, the story shows us a tormented Joseph tossing in his sleep, planning to divorce Mary quietly. Where and how Mary waited through this is one of the empty spaces in the story.

I, too, was living in an empty space of sorts, silent as the clouds floating by my window. I didn't know what was going to happen; the waiting was hard. But I found a thread of comfort in Mary's wait, however long, for Joseph.

Mary had the angel's message: "Do not be afraid, Mary, you have found favor with God" (Luke 1:30, NIV). In my plight, God seemed far away. *If only I could have an angel bring me a message from God,* I thought. Then from long ago I heard the voice of a favorite Sunday school teacher: "The Bible, Shari, is a love letter from God to you. All His promises in there are yours."

I began turning the pages of my Bible, aware now of God's presence beside me, waiting with me. Then a verse lit up the page—Jesus' words in Matthew 19:26 (NIV): "With God all things are possible."

Lord, thank You for Your Word, a light to comfort me.

—SHARI SMYTH

FOLLOWING JESUS

15/MON GO AND DO LIKEWISE

Then said Jesus unto him, Go, and do thou likewise.

—LUKE 10:37

I placed an order for a small Coke at the fast-food drive-through. "No ice," I emphasized. I had a terrible toothache and was afraid that ice would really set it off. But at the window, the cashier shoved a Coke overflowing with ice at me. "I need this without ice," I repeated, fixing my eyes on the plastic holiday wreath to avoid her glare.

The cashier twisted her face into a scowl, and to the astonishment of the customers lined up at the counter inside, threw the Coke toward the coffeemaker, screaming a string of expletives. "I wish you'd take your hateful self and go home!" another cashier snapped at her as she dodged the sticky puddle on the floor.

I'll take this up with the manager, I decided, silently preparing my speech. But something stopped me. That something was a sea of faces, those who have lived out the attributes of Jesus before me.

These folks have been like Jesus to me when I needed it most and deserved it least. *Help me, Lord, to see this cashier through Your eyes*, I prayed. *Who is she? A single mother up all night with a croupy baby? Worried about a car that doesn't run half the time and no extra money for Christmas? The target of endless impatient customers? Could I have been the last straw?*

Oddly, when she returned with my replacement drink, I found I wasn't irritated at all. "I'm sorry I made things harder for you," I said. "You don't know how much I appreciate this drink with no ice." I pointed to my mouth. "It's this awful toothache."

Bless her, Lord. Really touch her life, I silently prayed, smiling up at her from my car window.

"Let me get you a napkin," she said, a smile tugging at the thin line that had been a scowl. "I hope that toothache gets better."

Thank You, Lord, for those who tirelessly teach me to follow in Your steps. —ROBERTA MESSNER

READER'S ROOM

In late 2000, when I received the notice to reserve my copy of *Daily Guideposts, 2001*, I decided to order copies for my daughter and granddaughter for Christmas gifts. Here are the words I wrote under the title page in each of their books:

"Since 1977, when Fred Bauer assembled the first *Daily Guideposts*, the thoughts and prayers of the writers have been a part of my daily life.

"My fervent hope is that you, too, will take time each day to open this book and read the brief devotional and the prayer. Many days through the year, I've felt the words were written just for me.

"May this gift encourage you each day. Remember you are never alone. God is in control. He will guide and give strength for whatever the day may bring. Allow Him to help you reach out to others with a smile, a touch, a word, a prayer. As you give joy, you will receive joy."

—MARILYN WAGNON, TAMPA, FLORIDA

16/*TUE*

". . . So that a blessing may rest on your household." household.

—EZEKIEL 44:30 (NIV)

Our two oldest sons graduated from college two years ago, Jason a little late and Nathan a little early. Both finished in December, and their colleges, which did not schedule any midyear graduation ceremonies, invited them to return for the festivities in June. This seemed anticlimactic to us, but it was just fine with the boys. Joy and I wanted to do something to mark the occasion, however, so we worked together on a blessing to give them. Knowing they may return home from time to time, but are now truly out on their own, we wrote this:

Dear Sons,

Today we mark your graduation from college, an achievement of which we are extremely proud. We are proud of your effort and your success, which is the beginning of the dreams we have for you. Your mom and I want you to know that, even though we no longer have the primary responsibility for your life and well-being, we will always be there for you, always believe in you and always hope the best for you. This is because we do, and always will, love you with all our hearts.

Our love is not always perfect, but is far deeper and greater than you will ever know, because it springs from Jesus' love for us. Carry it with you as a source of strength, an anchor in the storms and warm sunshine for the journey.

Love,
Dad and Mom

I'm not positive, but I think the tears that gathered in the corners of their eyes meant this blessing was more precious to them than any of their other graduation gifts.

Why not think of someone in your life you can bless in a similar way? You don't have to wait for a big event like a graduation.

Father, may I tell, show and give my love in ways that are *unmistakable.*

—ERIC FELLMAN

17/WED   *Ask, and it shall be given you; seek, and ye shall find; knock, and it shall be opened unto you.*

—MATTHEW 7:7

Shymeka's address was simply a room number. She lived in a homeless shelter with, as her painstakingly penciled letter said, "my mom, my stepdad, big brother and baby sister." I've never met her and probably never will, but I found her letter among those received by a "Christmas Miracles" program at my church. Some writers want trips to Disneyland, but most of the requests are disarmingly modest: a coat or even a blanket. Shymeka asked for a portable cassette player, but carefully specified an inexpensive one sold in a chain drugstore.

The cassette player wasn't hard to find, and I bought it, feeling happy to have gotten precisely what she wanted. But as I walked out through the automatic sliding doors, I suddenly stopped. In a situation where there was most likely no money for food or clothes, how would a seven-year-old be able to buy batteries?

My self-satisfaction took a sharp fall and I walked back into the store to purchase a substantial package of the right batteries. Putting oneself in the shoes—or sometimes the bare feet—of others isn't just a question of giving money or things. True help requires empathy, imagination and, most of all, the involvement of prayer.

I walked home, swinging my bag of purchases. *Prayers,* I thought, *are like batteries. It's hard to make life work without them.*

Dear God, as I do my best to help others, help me to understand their needs and remember them in my prayers.

—BRIGITTE WEEKS

18/THU   *And the Lord direct your hearts into the love of God, and into the patient waiting for Christ.*

—II THESSALONIANS 3:5

Every year I've promised myself that I'd go back to my boarding school Hoosac and see the Boar's Head and Yule Log, the venerable Christmas celebration that has been held there for 108 years. This year, I kept my promise.

I went dreading the changes I'd find. The campus had been moved to a nearby hill, presided over by the baronial Tebutt mansion. I was accustomed to the school anthem, which began *Oculos meos levavi* ("I will lift up mine eyes unto the hills," Psalm 121:1), and it was to that hill we had lifted them up.

"You're here at last," said headmaster Richard Lomuscio warmly when I arrived, and after meeting with other alumni, we walked to the dining hall for the ceremony. I knew from the sight of two Beefeaters standing rigidly at the entrance that all would be well. It was.

First came the boar's head, borne on a trencher, followed by Christmas delicacies, and then the deeply reverent homage to the Christ Child. After dinner, we were ready for Elizabethan merriment. The Yule log was rolled in, and every one in the hall enjoyed the stately sword dance, the troubadours, the mummers' play—everything that I remembered. Tradition held.

The next morning I went below to find the old campus. All the buildings, save one, were gone. A thick tangle of trees and brush had taken over. I turned to the surviving structure, the old stone chapel. I felt a pang of memory and then a presentiment, something good. Here was where I had gained my first appreciation of God. Here was where the students who sang last night worshiped. What could be better than that?

And so you see, tradition held.

There's an inscription on the mantel of the fireplace where the Yule log blazed, the mantel brought up from the old campus. The words are about You, Father: **Deus Regit** *("God Reigns").*

—VAN VARNER

19/FRI   *In all things willing to live honestly.*

—HEBREWS 13:18

Last night my husband and I attended a glorious Christmas concert presented by Northwestern College in St. Paul, Minnesota. We listened enthralled, as chorale and chorus, chamber orchestra and handbell choir rang out the message of the good news of Jesus Christ.

Three quarters of the way through the concert, an interesting thing happened. On the third audience-participation carol, "Lo,

How a Rose E'er Blooming," we were to remain seated, whereas we had stood for the previous selections. But not everyone paid attention to the program note, and one after another, men and women began popping up around the auditorium. Soon islands of people, particularly those near the front, were standing and caroling in full voice.

Then an observant few began to notice that not all of us were on our feet. They quickly folded into their seats with embarrassed glances at each other. Still others realized their mistake, but were not about to acknowledge it. They stiffened their shoulders and resolutely carried on.

And then there were the clueless front-row people, oblivious to the hundreds of seated folks behind them, who remained standing and sang on. Meanwhile, the conductor valiantly waved her baton for all of us—even as amusement spread through the crowd and "Lo, How a Rose E'er Blooming" began to wilt a little.

While I smiled at the scene, it also made me take inventory. How do I react when I make a mistake? Can I—will I—admit it? And then what? Do I sink into my seat or stay on my feet pretending that I'm right and everyone else is wrong? Or am I able to accept my fallibility, sit down graciously and continue to sing on with aplomb?

Lord, my capacity for making mistakes undoubtedly comes as a bigger surprise to me than to You. But I know it's never a mistake to seek Your help in recovering from them.—CAROL KNAPP

20/SAT   Martha was distracted by all the preparations that had to be made. She ... asked, "Lord, don't you care that my sister has left me to do the work by myself? Tell her to help me!" "Martha, Martha," the Lord answered, "you are worried and upset about many things, but only one thing is needed. ..."

—LUKE 10:40–41 (NIV)

A few years ago, my mother was living with us in our house in Poughquag, New York. She had been homebound for some time with a lung ailment, and that Christmas, our church was sending some carolers by to cheer her up. I knew Mom would enjoy the visit, but the news put me in a mini-panic. I had to clean up the house!

Now, we were good housekeepers and things were quite tidy. But for some reason I felt I had to get everything superclean before the carolers arrived. I swept upstairs and down, straightening here and there, scurrying from one spot to another.

I was busy in the basement when the carolers finally rang the bell. "Ted, the carolers are here!" my wife Kathy called down to me. Over the roar of the vacuum cleaner's three-horsepower engine, I thought she was telling me they were on their way, so I kept on vacuuming. I finished the basement carpet, walked back to the furnace room and began to clean there.

When I was done, I heard, faintly but distinctly, the sounds of carols. I went upstairs and stood in the basement doorway in time to hear farewells being exchanged. When I saw my mother's face lit full of life and the faces of Kathy and the children, I knew that I'd missed an opportunity to be spiritually nourished. I could almost hear Jesus saying, "Ted, Ted, you are worried and upset about many things, but only one thing is needed."

Lord, this Christmas, help me to be less like Martha and more like Mary, "who sat at the Lord's feet listening to what he said" (Luke 10:39, NIV).　　　　　　　　　—TED NACE

A LIGHT FROM THE MANGER

$21/_{SUN}$　THE FOURTH SUNDAY IN ADVENT
And the glory of the Lord shone around them. . . .
　　　　　　　　　　　　　　　　　　—LUKE 2:9 (NIV)

Out on the cold, rocky hillside, the shepherds hadn't a clue. Same old, same old for them—tending somebody else's sheep. They were hirelings, just above the bottom rung of society's ladder. So their wildest dreams couldn't have prepared them for the one-of-a-kind gift about to be hand-delivered to them. Imagine the fearful, wonderful shock of it: the blaze of angelic glory and the news that they were important to God.

It was Christmas Eve. I was ten years old and in my customary place in the front pew. The church was packed and beautiful with draped greenery, poinsettias and a lighted tree. The program pictured shepherds on the hillside, their faces lifted radiantly to a lighted, angelic sky.

Franklin Groff was first. He was going to sing "O Little Town of Bethlehem." His mother shuffled him to the front. Franklin was about forty years old. His big head towered over a small body. His short legs ended in little feet that seemed to go every which way in their specially made shoes. In addition to his other disabilities, Franklin was blind.

Mrs. Groff sat down, beaming with pride. I wondered why she wasn't ashamed of him. Franklin, his face filled with a happiness I couldn't grasp, said, "Before I sing, I'd like to say that I'm crippled and blind. But I can see the glory of God. It fills me with love."

My literal child's mind spun. To me, the glory of God was the picture of the lighted, angelic sky on my program. Franklin said it was love. Then I looked at Mrs. Groff looking at Franklin and saw the light in her eyes.

Lord, help me to see with Your eyes, the eyes of love.

—SHARI SMYTH

22/MON *Remember the days of old, consider the years of many generations. . . .* —DEUTERONOMY 32:7

The Great Depression had taken a terrible toll on Carberry, Manitoba, a farming community in central Canada. Lost jobs meant a bleak Christmas for many families. But not for the local barber: He had just barely enough to meet the needs of his family.

As he closed up shop for Christmas, his children asked if they could take the small tabletop tree, covered with homemade cardboard ornaments, to a needy family down the block. "They've got three kids, just like us," his seven-year-old son said.

"Sure," said the barber. "Be off with you, and don't be long."

"How about tangerines?" asked the boy. Tangerines were their once-a-year-treat, bought only at Christmastime.

"I'll give one of mine," said the second child.

"Me, too," replied the third one.

It was decided. Five tangerines, with the tabletop tree.

My husband was the barber's seven-year-old son. "I'll never forget the glow of the faces," he says, "the squeals of laughter, the hands of each child as they cradled their tangerine."

The Japanese guard on duty at the POW camp was peeling a tangerine. As he put a section of fruit into his mouth, he tossed down the peel. "Eat," he muttered. The man picked up the peel and ate it slowly. That man was my father, a lieutenant with the Royal Navy. The tangerine peel was his Christmas dinner.

We have a tangerine tree in our backyard. Sweetened by the California sun, a bowl of the juicy fruit becomes a special Christmas memory. Once again my husband is seven years old, trudging through the Canadian snow . . . and with my orange, I make sure to eat a small piece of peel.

Thank You, Lord, for the traditions that help me celebrate and keep alive the blessings of the past. —FAY ANGUS

23 / TUE *"Make ready quickly three measures of fine meal, knead it, and make cakes."* —GENESIS 18:6 (RSV)

We moved into our new home on December 23. On the twenty-fourth, an unfamiliar sound woke us from our exhausted sleep. *Clickety-clack.* I looked out the window and saw ice—everywhere, ice.

"Oh, my gosh, David," I said to my husband, "it's Christmas Eve and I've got shopping left to do." In spite of the unpacked boxes, we would be hosting our annual Christmas breakfast the next morning and then dinner for our family. I hadn't even bought food!

Within the hour, we were headed for the mall, with David at the wheel. "Sorry, the weather's closed us down," a man called from inside the entrance door.

"Oh, I'm ruined," I gasped.

"Quick," David said, "Sam's will surely be open."

Slipping and sliding, we arrived in Sam's parking lot a few minutes later. In the background, the loudspeaker bellowed, "Due to inclement weather, Sam's will close in thirty minutes."

"Let's split the list," David said. "I can help."

Now David has many wonderful talents, but shopping is not one of them. And besides, I wanted Christmas my way! But I had no choice. I tore the list in half, gave him the part with the names of the people for whom I needed presents and headed for the grocery department.

I couldn't find what I'd need to prepare a homemade holiday feast, so I dashed to the frozen food section and started tossing things in the cart: quiche for breakfast, individually wrapped packets of chicken cordon bleu for dinner. I was running out of time.

"Please bring your purchases to the checkout stand," the loudspeaker urged. David was already there, his cart loaded.

In the end, Christmas came right on schedule. Our guests raved about the food; John loved his train video and Herb was delighted with his set of ten flashlights, gifts I would never have thought of buying. And for me, there was plenty of time to sit back and visit with people I love. From start to finish, it was a very good day.

Father, You turn my panic into peace. Thank You. —PAM KIDD

A LIGHT FROM THE MANGER

24/WED CHRISTMAS EVE
In him was life, and that life was the light of men.
—JOHN 1:4 (NIV)

In 1978, we lived on eighteen rolling acres in Pennsylvania. We'd acquired a cow, a few sheep, a horse and Susie, our wooly, nine-hands-high Shetland pony. Susie was past due to give birth. In her stall, her fetlocks deep in fresh straw, she waddled to me, round as a ripe pear. Her big, soft eyes were trusting. It was her first foal. Mine, too.

That night I slept in our barn. It was cold and dark and smelled of fresh hay and stale dirt and dusty cobwebs. The cow mooed. The sheep stamped and stirred. I got up and shined a light in Susie's stall, careful not to hit her eyes. She was lying down, looking miserable. She nickered softly. I shuffled back to my pallet and lay down. A growing anxiety gripped me. *What will I do if something goes wrong with the birth?* I tried to pray, but the words wouldn't come.

The next day went by. Nothing. That night I was back in the barn. The cow and sheep were strangely quiet. Moonlight flooded through the open doors. I tiptoed to Susie's stall, and there it was: just born, lying on wet straw, tiny, dark hooves flailing out of its birth sack. The new mother gently cleaned her baby with her rough tongue. It was a filly, a girl.

Like a pro, Susie nudged and nickered her filly to its thin, gangly legs. A fuzzy tuft of mane waved over a downy, cinnamon coat. Gumming her way across her mother with squeals and sucking noises, the filly latched on to a nipple.

Leaning on a rough post, I breathed the tart stable air in deep, relieved gulps. I bowed my head and, with sudden clarity, the light of Christmas shone like the stars. It really happened; the majestic, holy Creator was born a baby on a night like this, in a place like this, among His lowly animals, amid straw and dirt and the darkness of our sin.

Thank You, Jesus. —SHARI SMYTH

A LIGHT FROM THE MANGER

25/*THU* CHRISTMAS DAY

The light shines in the darkness. . . . —JOHN 1:5 (RSV)

It was Christmas morning. The dining room table was set with antique lace and hand-me-down china. The living room was arranged to suit the tall tree hung with years of treasured ornaments. Our children, home from far away, gladdened my already glad heart. I was fussing with the napkins when my husband Whitney strolled into the kitchen and hung an arm around my shoulder. I rested against him, savoring our gift of each other. It came wrapped in trust, as does the Christmas story.

"Don't be afraid," the angel said, first to Mary, then to Joseph. Joseph wanted to believe his betrothed, but he was afraid. Then the angel spoke, and in the morning he got up from his fear and took Mary as his wife.

A year earlier I had been in my apartment, waiting for God and reading the Bible. "With God all things are possible" (Matthew 19:26, NIV), I'd read. *Do You mean even my troubled marriage, Lord?* The thought of giving it another try flooded me with fear: fear of rejection, fear of change, fear of dealing with problems, fear of my fear.

Then a dear friend who'd been divorced for years gave me a nudge. "The thing to do is to get up out of your fear and take a step in the direction you think God is leading you. If you're wrong, He'll still be there. Trust me, I know."

Now my mending marriage had brought us together as a family around the Christmas table. Our plates piled high, we held hands while Whitney asked the blessing. "Thank You most of all," he

said, "for new beginnings and the courage to start in on them."
Laura and Sanna squeezed my hands. I squeezed back and looked
at Whitney across the table.

*Jesus, thank You for the light of Christmas that banishes fear
and brings me the hope of new beginnings.* —SHARI SMYTH

26 / FRI *We are bound to thank God always for you . . . and the charity of every one of you. . . .*

—II THESSALONIANS 1:3

Aunt Minnie, my mother's sister, had been divorced for many
years. She earned her living as a sales clerk in a ladies' clothing
store. Sometimes sales would be very slow, and the store would
have to temporarily lay off some of its employees. When Aunt
Minnie was among them, she often lived with us because she had
no income. She was a jolly person who loved my two sisters and
me, and we were devoted to her, too.

At Christmas, Aunt Minnie always had a gift under the tree for
each of us. When she was working, it would be a nice scarf or
blouse. In her lean times, the gift was much less expensive, but
something would be there.

Today, I have among my table silver six little fruit spoons, which
I cherish. A set of these was Aunt Minnie's gift to each of us on the
last Christmas of her life. I know how she must have saved carefully
for a long time to pay for them. Now each time my family uses
them, I wash, dry and put them away carefully to make certain I
never lose one of them—but, more importantly, so I'll always
remember the love that made them mine.

*Dear God, how thankful I am for the many ways in which love
can be expressed. Amen.* —DRUE DUKE

27 / SAT *Pray one for another, that ye may be healed. . . .*

—JAMES 5:16

I've been practicing something new that I've just got to share with
you! In January, as I was sorting through the Christmas cards I'd

received, I found myself with a dilemma I have each year: what to do with the snapshots of families, friends' children and grandchildren, and other loved ones tucked inside the cards. I delight in receiving the photos, but after the holidays I don't know what to do with them.

This year, I had an inspiration for keeping the gift alive. I decided to use them as bookmarks. In addition to marking my stopping place, I also use the pictures to mark special pages I want to come back to later. Each evening before I start to read, I look at the picture that is marking my place and pray special blessings upon that person. After finishing the book, I go back and pray again for all those people whose photos are marking special passages. Then I leave them in the book, to be found sometime later.

During the past week I've been rereading a book I first read in February, so I've prayed another time for my nephew David and his family, for the cute little granddaughters of my high school friend Jeri, for a *Daily Guideposts* reader named Laurie, even for "Poor George," the fluffy white dog of Janelle in California. I feel a special bonding now with friends' children I've never met, a renewed closeness to old friends I haven't seen in years, a personal relationship with readers I may never meet. It has enriched my prayer life in a deep way, and it's going to become a tradition with me!

Thank You, God, for new ways to pray for lives that touch mine.
—MARILYN MORGAN KING

28/ SUN There failed not aught of any good thing which the Lord had spoken unto the house of Israel; all came to pass. —JOSHUA 21:45

Prayer sometimes worries me. Don't get me wrong; I do it every day. It's just that sometimes I wonder about whether I'm doing it right. For example, people tell me all the time that "God told me" to do something. This information is usually communicated with a great deal of delight and confidence. For years, I'd be happy for them, but I couldn't help but wonder how they *knew* God was talking to them. I wanted to believe God actually talked to me, giving me clear-cut direction in my life. But all God's answers to me sounded suspiciously like my own words. Then a Christmas sermon for children gave me a new perspective on the problem.

There was once a farmyard full of geese. The geese constantly fought with each other about one thing or another, and the farmyard was in chaos. God decided to do something about it: He sent a goose from heaven to the farmyard. The goose from heaven explained that the geese must stop fighting and learn to live in peace. They listened and changed, because the goose from heaven spoke in goose words, so they could understand. So when God wanted to teach us, He sent His Son, a little baby who grew up to speak in people-language so we could all understand.

The children were delighted, but they weren't the only ones who learned an important lesson. Why was I so suspicious when God answered me in words I could understand? How else would I get the message?

Lord, thank You for speaking to me in a language simple enough for me to comprehend. —MARCI ALBORGHETTI

29 / MON

"Out of the overflow of the heart the mouth speaks." —MATTHEW 12:34 (NIV)

"The Indian lady was kind of boring."

"That woman with the dark hair was sad, but she talked too long."

"I felt sorry for the mother who kept saying the same story over and over."

At the close of our monthly Mothers Against Drunk Driving Victims' Impact Panel, I ask our listeners to be honest when they fill out their comment sheets. They're first-time offenders who have been sentenced to attend the panel to learn that being arrested is the least tragic result of drinking and driving.

One of our speakers is a grandmother whose halting voice brings her granddaughter to life for several short minutes. The audience learns, in a small but significant way, the depth of a grandmother's grief. They blink back tears while a daughter tells them how lost she has been since her mother's death. And each month, a new group of forty to sixty listeners struggles with Sanjean as she tries to make sense of her son's death.

Sanjean repeats her story from four different viewpoints. She briefly recounts her life with her son and tells what it was like for her to arrive at the hospital too late to say good-bye. Like many Native Americans, she believes that an animal's viewpoint is just as valid as a human's, so she intersperses the dog's grief with the grief of her other son. She finally reads a long letter her daughter wrote the week after her son's funeral. By then, the audience is wondering if Sanjean will ever finish talking.

After reading some of the comments about Sanjean's speech, the other speakers have gently suggested that I help Sanjean shorten her story. I gently tell them no. What should she omit? The parable of the dog? The details surrounding her son's death? The shades of light and darkness in her daughter's letter?

As all of Sanjean's stories unfold, neither the audience nor the other speakers can hear me murmur, "Matthew, Mark, Luke, John. . . ."

Dear God, help me to value all the voices that lead me to light and truth.
—TIM WILLIAMS

30/TUE *"Then will I purify the lips of the peoples, that all of them may call on the name of the Lord and serve him shoulder to shoulder."* —ZEPHANIAH 3:9 (NIV)

I had just finished speaking to a Christian Women's Club in William's Lake, Canada, and was saying good-bye to the women at the door, when my host came into the room clearly agitated.

"Your son was on the phone. He and his wife are passing through town, and he wants to know if you'll meet them for lunch at the White Spot."

I was stunned. My son, who hadn't wanted to talk to me in three years, who would visit in our hometown and not let me know that he was there, now wanted to see me. "Where did he call from?" I asked. "When am I to meet them?"

"I don't know." I left the meeting room in a hurry and waited by the telephone hoping my son would call again to give me the particulars. He did, and we had a wonderful reunion. Not much was said, but both of us sensed that we had begun the healing of a strained relationship.

In my talks with women, I find that many a mother's heart has been broken because a son or a daughter is avoiding her. "My daughter's phone calls are brief and businesslike," says one. "My daughter has time for everyone else but me," says another.

I pass on to them what has helped me during this difficult time. Often an estrangement develops during a traumatic time such as a death or a divorce. Raw emotions take time to process. We need to give our children time and space to sort them out. No amount of talking will help the situation. In fact, too much talking makes it worse. It's like egg whites: The more you beat them, the bigger they get. We can't hurry up the healing process in ourselves or in others.

In the meantime, though, we can be grace-givers. Grace lets another person be, gives him or her the freedom to grow, to make decisions, to fail and to mature at his or her own rate. We can pray for our children and wait expectantly for Jesus, the great Reconciler, to bring us together again. And when He does, we can be there with a warm embrace.

Jesus, my children and I are Your people, the sheep of Your pasture. Help me to trust You with them.

—HELEN GRACE LESCHEID

31 / WED   *He maketh me to lie down in green pastures: he leadeth me beside the still waters. He restoreth my soul. . . .*

—PSALM 23:2–3

When I was a boy growing up in the Philippine Islands, New Year's Eve was always a time of intense celebration. Filipinos and Chinese love fireworks, so my friends and I would buy bags full of firecrackers and skyrockets and spend the night in deafening explosive delight. My mother always worried that I would blow my fingers off; my dad just sat back and chuckled, wishing he were a boy again.

Now my New Year's Eves are a quiet time for meditation and contemplation. I love to build a big fire in the fireplace, feel its warmth, and stare into the flames and embers. With a cup of coffee in hand, I reflect on the events of the past year in the world, in our country and in my own life. Slowly, a sense of gratitude wells up within me as I realize that God has guided me through another year. And as I face the future, I'm reminded that whatever happens, God, my Good Shepherd, will be walking with me.

As I watch the fire, I become aware that I've begun to softly hum a hymn, "He Leadeth Me":

> *He leadeth me! O blessed thought!*
> *O words with heav'nly comfort fraught!*
> *Whate'er I do, where'er I be,*
> *Still 'tis God's hand that leadeth me!*

As we celebrate New Year's Eve together, Joseph Gilmore's words, written more than a century ago, are words of faith and hope for all of us: "Whate'er I do, where'er I be, still 'tis God's hand that leadeth me!"

Happy New Year!

Father, I trust You to be with me in all events of life. May I follow You and never fear, for You are my Shepherd and I shall not want. Amen.   —SCOTT WALKER

My Daily Blessings

1 _____

2 _____

3 _____

4 _____

5 _____

6 _____

7 _____

8 _____

9 _____

10 _____

11 _____

12 _____

13 _____

14 _____

15 _____

16 _____

17 _____

18 _____

19 _____

20 _____

21 _____

22 _____

23 _____

24 _____

25 _____

26 _____

27 _____

28 _____

29 _____

30 _____

31 _____

FELLOWSHIP CORNER

For our fifty-four Daily Guideposts *contributors, as for all of us, it's been an eventful year, but through it all, God's blessings shine all the more brightly. They're waiting for you in the "Fellowship Corner," ready to tell some of the ways that they've been blessed. Cut yourself a piece of pie, pour yourself a cup of tea, and settle in for a good visit!*

LIBBIE ADAMS of Richlands, North Carolina, writes, "One of our greatest blessings this past year was the marriage of our younger son Jeff, whose union with Jordona gave us three new granddaughters: Kara, Erica and Cassidy. They have brought so much love and laughter into our home and our hearts, and add joy to our days in more ways than we can count. Our older son Greg and wife Kim live nearby with Lindsay, who is growing quickly from the baby that she was into a little girl full of character and charisma. Sharing her world has been fascinating. I find I'm now on a first-name basis with the entire cast of *Sesame Street* and catch myself humming Elmo's theme song at the oddest moments. But my most special everyday blessing of all is my husband Larry, who has faithfully supported me in every endeavor for thirty-one years and loves me still. Thanks to him—and to all my family—finding my place in the scheme of things has been much easier, and I love and thank them all."

This has been a year of everyday blessings too numerous to count for MARCI ALBORGHETTI. She married Charlie Duffy in July 2001, in a small church overlooking Bodega Bay in northern California, and they live in a wonderful condominium in Stonington Harbor, Connecticut. In May 2001, she received a contract from ACTA Publications in Chicago to write a book on fear and faith. The book, called *Freedom from Fear—Overcoming Anxiety through Faith*, came out early last year, forcing Marci to leave her computer for a series of discussion and book-signing events. Marci admits, "I've had to face my own fear of speaking when I go out to various groups and talk about the book! But it is always rewarding. I've met some wonderful people, and I've come to realize how the written word can really reach out and touch hearts." Long walks along the harbor help her to pray and cherish God's presence.

FAY ANGUS of Sierra Madre, California, writes, "Having just celebrated our forty-fifth wedding anniversary, John and I are a tribute to the theory that opposites attract. As one friend likes to tell us, 'You're Hercules married to Tinkerbell.' *Ha!* Whatever we are, this is the year that we are flexing our love, swinging it backward and forward in a perpetual motion to enlarge its dimensions. Looking backward, we draw strength from all our fondest memories. Looking forward to whatever the future may hold, we pledge a devotion that renews the commitment engraved in our wedding rings: 'One for the other, and both for God.' We've had the heights of happiness mingled with the depths of despair, and through it all we've learned that some of the most passionate words of love are 'I'm sorry!' and that forgiveness is an ultimate act of loving. Respect for the individuality of who we are has put space in our love that keeps us reaching for each other. John's greatest gift to me is letting me be me. When I recently asked what my greatest gift to him has been, he simply smiled, took me in his arms and said, 'You!' "

"Sometimes the days just seem too short to contain all the blessings packed into them," says *Daily Guideposts* editor ANDREW ATTAWAY of New York City. "Margaret Therese was born July 19, 2001, and she's made all our lives richer, if more complicated!" The Attaways' eldest, Elizabeth, who'll be 9 this year, is still hooked on math and has started learning to play the violin; John, who turns 7, is the family's history buff; Mary, who'll be 5 in November, is slated to add ballet to gymnastics. "Being a father is a greater blessing—and a greater challenge—than I could ever have imagined before I became one. And so is working on *Daily Guideposts*. Not a day goes by without God using a reader, a writer or a colleague to surprise me with His grace." The Attaways are particularly thankful for the messages of concern and the prayers they received after 9/11. "Readers from as far away as California called to make sure we were all right. "What a blessing to belong to the *Daily Guideposts* family!"

In New York City, where having one child is considered brave, two daring and three heroic, a family with four young children borders on epic. Thus it is that since the birth of Margaret Therese, JULIA ATTAWAY frequently notices people counting up her progeny as she gets on the subway. "Invariably they goggle and ask, 'Are they all yours?'" she writes. "To which I reply with a big grin, 'Sure are!' Sometimes I add with a wink, 'I count them all the time, too!'" Counting her blessings in this way is a daily event that Julia treasures. "As a mom, I know there will always be days when the thing I am most thankful for is bedtime. But each and every day with my family is a blessing, no matter how hard that day may be."

KAREN BARBER and her husband Gordon have enjoyed the everyday blessings of seeing their three sons grow and mature. Jeff and his wife Leah celebrated their first wedding anniversary in a new home in Colorado Springs. Chris, who is on an ROTC scholarship at the University of Southern California, met the challenges of Army summer camp basic training. Their youngest, John, learned how to find his way from classroom to classroom and to keep his studies organized in middle school. Karen says, "My latest project is experimenting with new prayer times that will work in our busy lives. One of my favorites is my Sunday afternoon walk here in Alpharetta, Georgia, where I only allow myself to thank God for things. The first time I tried it, after about five minutes I ran out of ideas, so I began to thank God for the things I saw and heard. A car drove by, and I thanked God for paved roads. I heard piano music from a neighbor's window, and I thanked God for music. I heard dogs and children and saw trees and anthills, and thanked God for each one. I returned from my walk refreshed, much more aware of the everyday wonders in our world that I often take for granted."

ALMA BARKMAN of Winnipeg, Canada, writes, "Our whole year was one of everyday blessings. We had health enough to tend our large garden and even sufficient determination to outwit a 'wascally wabbit!' My hubby Leo continued to make weekly visits to veterans at a local hospital. I led an adult Sunday school class studying the book of Ephesians. In the evenings, I managed to piece together three quilts for family members. Switching from darkroom to digital photography has been an enjoyable challenge. I share my photos on the editorial pages of the Steinbach *Carillon* newspaper. I also found out that two of my devotional books, *Rise and Shine* and *Light Reflections*, were going to be reprinted. The highlight of the year occurred in late fall, when a fine young man phoned to ask for our only daughter's hand in marriage. We rejoice with them as we make plans for a May wedding in Toronto."

When FRED BAUER of Englewood Beach, Florida, and State College, Pennsylvania, found out the theme for *Daily Guideposts, 2003* was "Everyday Blessings," he says, "My first thought was of that old hymn 'Showers of Blessings.' I've always been particularly fond of the last verse: 'There shall be showers of blessing, If we but trust and obey. There shall be seasons refreshing, If we let God have His way.' I confess that I have not always trusted and obeyed God, nor have I always let Him have His way, but when I have, manifold blessings in the form of peace and happiness have surely followed. As I've gotten older, I've come to appreciate God's little gifts, those daily strokings that warm my heart and tickle my soul: a mid-morning cup of Constant Comment, a whiff of newly blossomed jasmine just out the front door, a sunset walk on the beach with my E.L. (Ever Lovin' Shirley), an advice-seeking phone call (disguised as something else) from one of the kids or grandkids. And life's greatest blessing, knowing Who to thank for my daily treasures, the One Who holds me securely and lovingly in the very palm of His hand."

EVELYN BENCE of Arlington, Virginia, is a newcomer to *Daily Guideposts*, though not to the larger Guideposts family. She remembers, "In 1980, as a young and restless book editor in New York City, I interviewed at Guideposts for a job I didn't get. Instead, I accepted one in northern Virginia, where I've settled in. But I stayed in contact with Guideposts, writing for the *Home Bible Study Program* and editing several collections of angel stories. This year, to help commemorate my fiftieth birthday, I went on a two-day silent retreat. Then, to debrief, I found my journal from ten years ago and compared notes. What a difference. At forty, I was fighting fear. At fifty, I am grasping faith. The difference doesn't reflect major changes in my life: I was self-employed then and now. I live in the same apartment a few miles from the Pentagon. Actually, in some ways life feels more unsettled now after my parents' recent deaths. No, the big difference is in my spirit. I now am more consciously grateful for the little blessings God sends every day."

In so many ways, RHODA BLECKER and her husband Keith have had a wonderful year. "The big news is that we made the final mortgage payment on our home in Los Angeles, and now own it outright. Yea!" Rhoda said. "My third published novel, *The Soldier's Daughter*, was well-received by the people who managed to get hold of it. Keith and I took our first real vacation in two years and met our one-year-old granddaughter Emily, who is a little angel." The rest of the family— Perky, Hobo, Jessif, Tau and Chi—are all thriving, despite trips to the animal dentist for teeth cleanings. And Rhoda has been honored and challenged by requests from two friends to provide them with spiritual guidance. She is trying to rise to the occasion so that she will be worthy of their trust.

It has been an extraordinary year of change for MELODY BONNETTE of Mandeville, Louisiana. "Roy and I are first-time grandparents to Indy Schoen Nebeker, our beautiful grandson. Our daughter Misty is fortunate enough to be a stay-at-home mom and has shared with us all of the milestones in his first months of life. Just tonight she called from New York City to say he laughed out loud for the first time! Kristen, our daughter who lives in New Orleans, is expecting a baby this year. We won't have to be long-distance grandparents to this one, which is very exciting. Our son Christopher is now a firefighter and engaged to be married to a beautiful girl, also named Kristin. Kevin graduates from high school in May, after a great senior year where he lettered in football. There have been changes in jobs, too. Roy is now the director of a new master's degree program at Southern Louisiana University, and I've left the classroom to produce and anchor our district's educational access TV channel. Through it all, one thing is certain: Faith is what allows us to embrace the challenges and changes in our lives as simply opportunities to walk closer to the Lord."

"When I think about the past year," says GINA BRIDGEMAN of Scottsdale, Arizona, "it's not so much the big events that stand out but the small blessings I'm thankful for every day." Maybe it's a Friday movie night, when Gina and her husband Paul bring out one of their old favorites like *The Sound of Music*. "Or shuttling from school to piano lessons or gymnastics when I hear all about what's going on in my kids' lives." The year did bring some highlights: Ross, 13 and in the eighth grade, trekked to the Grand Canyon on a school field trip, while Paul went along as one of the cooks. Later in the summer, while the guys were at Boy Scouts camp, Gina and Maria, an 8-year-old second-grader, traveled to Lakeside, Ohio, where Gina taught an inspirational writing seminar. Then the whole family took a vacation together to Coronado, California, where Gina and Paul celebrated their 17th wedding anniversary. "We never could have imagined the adventure our life together would bring, and I'm thankful for every day as the adventure continues!"

Last year brought MARY BROWN of East Lansing, Michigan, new adventures, including a summer job teaching English to adult students from ten countries. An everyday blessing is the beautiful campus of Michigan State University where husband Alex teaches physics and often invites Mary to "meet him in the gardens" for a picnic lunch. Mary says, "I'm trying to savor the special moments of motherhood that come unexpectedly. Yesterday I took Mark, nine, and his buddies bowling, and enjoyed watching them cheer for one another. One of them urged me, 'C'mon, Mrs. Brown, we need a strike!' When I finally got one, the boys erupted with loud hoorays and high fives." Mary also eats lots of pizza and popcorn with teenagers as she chaperones daughter Elizabeth, 14, and friends at church lock-ins, choir trips and basketball tournaments. Another delight is daily walks around neighborhood trails with her neighbor Lisa. "We bought pedometers and set goals of 10K (10,000 steps) a day. As I reflect on all these joys in daily life with family and friends, I realize my blessings exceed 10K a day!"

 "When I was a child," remembers MARY LOU CARNEY of Chesterton, Indiana, "one of my favorite hymns was 'Showers of Blessings.' But this year has been an absolute *deluge* of blessings!" Daughter Amy Jo completed law school and spent the summer studying for her bar exam. She and husband Kirk are making plans to move into a new condo in Chicago. "Now I can sleep over when I want to go shopping or to the theater," laughs Mary Lou. Son Brett continues to build and remodel houses. This year he bought a snug cabin at the edge of the woods where he and his dog Arkus now live. He also bought a new Harley Davidson motorcycle. "He considers the bike more of a blessing than I do," Mary Lou admits. Husband Gary's health and business are both doing well. He and Mary Lou spent several days vacationing in California this year, where they rented a convertible and drove down the Pacific Coast Highway, stopping along the way to admire the view and eat lots of ice cream. Mary Lou continues to edit *Guideposts for Teens* magazine, as well as two Web sites for youth: www.gp4k.com for children and www.gp4t.com for teens. "God has especially blessed us this year. More than a million young people have been reached through these products."

 In a season of conflict (worse, a season where three of the world's great religions find themselves in tragic discord), MARK COLLINS is anxious to find the peaceful blessings of this life. Mark and his wife Sandee have already been roundly blessed with Faith, 11, Hope, 10, and Grace, 6. And if that weren't enough—and don't you think it should be?—he's also blessed with wonderful siblings: brother Kevin and sister Cindy. "Sister Cindy" has a double meaning this year, since she officially became a tertiary member of the Carmelite religious order in the Catholic Church—an extraordinary achievement under any cir-

cumstances, but even more notable for a quadriplegic. "Whatever gifts I use in this world are a direct result of my wife and my family, especially my sister," Mark says. "Cindy is one of the main metrics I use to measure what's important and what's possible. I now know what can be accomplished—with God's help and a family's help— through iron will and iron faith."

BRIAN DOYLE is the editor of *Portland Magazine* at the University of Portland in Oregon. He is the author of three collections of essays, *Credo, Saints Passionate & Peculiar*, and *Two Voices*, written with his father Jim. Brian's essays have also been reprinted in the anthology *Resurrecting Grace*. He and his wife, a painter, are the herders of three small electric children. Regarding everyday blessings, he says, "Most of the people I love aren't dead, my work matters, and I see miracles all the time— miracles so consistent and mundane that we aren't stunned by them, except when they are endangered. Miracles like clean air and teachers and food, and nurses and laughter and light, and my wife, and a government still run mostly by its citizens, and the extraordinary grace with which most people carry their burdens. But the most miraculous of all our gifts as a species are children. Without them we would laugh less, we would be bereft of innocence, we would lose hope, we would shrivel and vanish, with no one to remember what we so wished to be."

DRUE DUKE of Sheffield, Alabama, writes, "This year has brought everyday blessings to me. The previous two years tried to get me down. But, thankfully, I knew to Whom I could turn for comfort and strength. The loss of my beloved husband Bob called for lots of prayer and earnest talking with God. Then the unexpected cancer surgery that claimed my left breast only served to emphasize the continued need of that precious association with Him. He has enriched my life with dear old friends, sent me new ones to love and opened doors of physical healing far beyond my expectations. And more recently, He has afforded me the golden opportunity of editing the manuscript of a book, which a close friend is writing."

"Our family found its way to a new closeness this year as it was the first year in nearly five that we have all lived in the same city," says ERIC FELLMAN of Falls Church, Virginia. "Jason and Nathan, the older two, took full-time jobs in the Washington, D.C., area, and Jonathan returned to George Mason University, just a few miles from our home. My wife Joy also returned to George Mason for her master's degree as a nurse practitioner. Jonathan had a bit of an adjustment seeing Mom on campus with book bag and lunch box in tow. I kept up my work consulting and traveling to wonderful parts of the world, including East Africa, Europe and Peru. Finding ourselves in close proximity, but not under the same roof, has been a pleasant experience. The boys drop by to borrow Dad's SUV or to coax Mom into laundry duty or just for a family dinner together. These everyday elements make the flow of life richer and deeper as our sons grow past being our responsibility and into being our friends. Our cat Merlin is not quite sure how to respond to the empty bedrooms, but has found a couple of new favorite spots to nap or sit in the sun. In all, it has added up to a simpler, quieter life for a time, with the promise of girlfriends, weddings and, maybe, grandchildren in the years to come."

SHARON FOSTER of Glen Burnie, Maryland, writes, "The best and most enduring blessings in my life are everyday blessings. They are the blessings that come through family, friends and new situations that I face. Old relationships and memories strengthen me today. My son Chase is a high school senior now but is completing his final course work at a local community college. He is blossoming and has developed some aptitude for operatic singing. My daughter Lanea is completing graduate studies, has begun a new job and is applying for law school. It touches me to see them maturing, developing their own relationships with God, encouraging me about His faithfulness. I continue writing full-time and thus far I have completed three novels— *Passing by Samaria, Ain't No River* and *Riding through Shadows*. I am at work on the fourth book, *Passing Into Light,* busy with speaking engagements, and learning more about the Lord. Thanks for your prayers."

JULIE GARMON of Snowville, Georgia, writes, "Rick and I have been married twenty-three years in December 2002. I've been quite surprised to find out that marriage isn't at all what I expected. Marriage is much harder, deeper, fuller and more serious than I understood at eighteen years old. We have three children. Jamie is twenty-one and will soon be a senior in college. She wants to become a paralegal. Katie is eighteen and a freshman in college. She hopes to become an elementary P.E. teacher. Our son Thomas is eleven and loves to play with GI Joe's. I have discovered that one of the greatest things we can do for people we love is to let them go—release them." Julie, the daughter of *Daily Guideposts* contributor Marion Bond West, is working on a fiction piece called *The Remnant.*

OSCAR GREENE of West Medford, Massachusetts, completed his 28th year of keeping a daily writer's log. The year was one of continued service and reaching out, and one that brought an inward change in attitude. He was asked to speak at the University of Life Lenten service, and he continues to contribute to the Grace Episcopal Church newsletter. He still coconvenes the Monday evening Bible study, and he presented a Bible at the institution of his new rector in May. Oscar remains as one of the three men on his church altar guild where his wife Ruby is the directress. Several parishioners requested he serve as usher-in-charge and deliver the eulogies at the services for their departed loved ones. Initially, Oscar was reluctant to accept this responsibility, but gradually he accepted the privilege with gratitude and understanding after noting how deeply each family was comforted.

"I have an embarrassing confession to make," says EDWARD GRINNAN of New York City sheepishly. "Last year in *Daily Guideposts* I wrote a devotional for March 18, my wedding anniversary, celebrating fifteen years with Julee. That morning, I left it next to her coffee as an anniversary gift. It brought tears to her eyes. Trouble is, we'd only been married for fourteen years." Edward made it up to Julee. "Actually," he hastens to explain, "Julee is as bad as I am about keeping track of stuff like that. We just take it a day at a time." Some of Edward's nicest days last summer were spent in Barcelona, Spain, where Julee was performing. "I picked the Barcelona dates on Julee's tour schedule to join her because I had to see something there Van Varner wrote a devotional about several years ago—Antoni Gaudi's Temple de la Sagrada Familia, a truly incredible church. Climbing up inside one of its still unfinished spires was like climbing up inside a melted candle. Those who've been there know what I'm talking about." Edward is editor-in-chief and vice president of Guideposts Publications.

RICK HAMLIN of New York City writes, "My son Timothy, twelve, broke a window at church playing catch before choir rehearsal. *Why was he playing catch indoors?* 'I stayed up until 4:30 in the morning finishing my biology lab,' my older son William, fifteen, told us ruefully in a phone call from boarding school. *Couldn't he budget his time better?* My wife Carol described her frustrations at the library tracking down material for the book she's working on. 'I wish they'd store the magazines in a more convenient place,' she said, sighing. I gaze at a long to-do list and wonder how I'll get it done. Then I realize they're all blessings: the rambunctious choirboy, the perfectionist student, the hard-working researcher and all the work that piles up on my desk. Husband, father, laborer—I consider myself the most fortunate of men."

"During the four years my stepfather was in a nursing home," says PHYLLIS HOBE of East Greenville, Pennsylvania, "I used to bring my dogs Suzy and Tara to visit him. They looked forward to those meetings and so did my dad. So did some of the other residents of the nursing home. Many who didn't ordinarily talk to anyone would talk to my dogs as they ran their hands through their fur. Some who never seemed to smile would smile broadly as we came up to them and said hello. Now that Dad is gone, my dogs and I have joined a group of therapy dogs and their owners who visit people in hospitals and nursing homes. It makes us feel good just to see patients lift their heads, reach out their hands and begin to talk—not always to us, but always to our dogs. We can't make people get better, but with God's help we can bring them some of life's simple joys."

"When I retired as managing editor of *Guideposts* magazine in 1998," says HAROLD HOSTETLER of Vista, California, "my wife Carol and I had the opportunity to move back West and be with our older daughter Laurel and granddaughter Kaila. But it was hard to leave our younger daughter Kristal. Fortunately, Kristal's work with IBM has allowed her to see us on several business trips, and we flew back East for her wedding to Derrick Johnson and for Thanksgiving in their new home in Massachusetts. These days we are blessed with frequent telephone get-togethers. But in 2001, Kristal and Derrick came here for Christmas. And two days before Christmas our whole family was together for our fortieth wedding anniversary, including a sunset dinner at a restaurant overlooking the Pacific Ocean. Now we are planning to fly East for the birth of their first child in August. It's been an adjustment, but phone calls and cross-country treks are keeping our family close."

PAM KIDD says, "Thanks to my husband David's expertise with self-timers, there's always the smell of fresh coffee wafting in the air when we wake up in the early morning. A mile down our hill in Nashville, one of the most glorious parks in Tennessee waits. We walk there often. Our daughter and son-in-law Keri and Ben Cannon are settled into their new home just two miles away, and Ben's dental practice is thriving. After extended counseling, our son Brock's marriage ended civilly and little Harrison, his son, is not only doing wonderfully well, he's our entire family's favorite entertainment venue. With the help of my stepfather Herb Hester, whom my mother married nine years ago, I'm working toward becoming a decent photographer. Holding my pictures in hand, I rest awhile in daybreak, hot coffee, a happy marriage, good health, satisfying work, and the closeness of family and friends. Such everyday blessings become a launchpad propelling me out into a new day where I am bound to use the blessings God so freely gives to me to bless others."

"My husband Robert and I spent a truly delightful week in Kyoto, Japan, in April," says MARILYN MORGAN KING, "at the height of the cherry blossom season. We visited ancient buildings, ambled through varied and exquisite gardens, and walked along the 'philosopher's path,' a three-kilometer stroll under a glorious archway of cherry blossoms. On the last day, we watched the petals fall gently to the ground like pink snow, reminding us of the shortness of life and the blessedness of every moment. There were many marker moments for us during the past year. We had the very great joy of being present at the baptism of my granddaughter Saralisa and at the graduation of my son John, who received his master's degree from the University of Illinois. Robert's book was published, and we enjoyed jointly presenting a workshop on contemplative practices at St. Andrew's Episcopal Cathedral in Jackson, Mississippi. But just as precious to us were those quiet moments at home in Green Mountain Falls, Colorado, which we spent reading to each other in front of the fire, listening to music in the dark, and breathing in the changing play of light and shadow on the pine-dressed slopes of our beloved mountains."

CAROL KNAPP of Lakeville, Minnesota, says, "Memory is God's invitation to partner with Him in turning today's possibilities into tomorrow's crop of 'good remembers,' as my whimsical seven-year-old friend Cynthia calls them. Most recently my 'crop of good remembers' includes daughter Tamara's third child Caleb's newborn puffs of breath against my cheek, cooking camaraderie in my friend Kim's kitchen in Alaska, preparing for my daughter Brenda's nursing graduation party, tramping through autumn woods on a grouse hunt with husband Terry, daughter Kelly and son-in-law Brett, excited three-year-old grandson Zak reporting a caribou sighting in his new town of Barrow, Alaska, on the Arctic Ocean, an exhilarating, summer-afternoon, back-roads cruise clinging to my husband on his new motorcycle, and a day of sorrow, soothing tears and God's comfort when our son Phil returned to Alaska, having lived with us for a year. Oh, and there was two-year-old granddaughter Hannah falling asleep upright in the little red wagon that I was pulling, and rare, luxurious hours spent alongside my brother, wandering in an art museum, and. . . . Ah, yes, memories. Everyday blessings. Keep them coming!"

CAROL KUYKENDALL of Boulder, Colorado, says, "Writing devotionals for *Daily Guideposts* is a privilege that keeps my eyes wide open to God's everyday blessings, like His perfect provisions in the midst of health problems or sudden blizzards or overcrowded airports, to name just a few of the everyday challenges I experienced last year. Then there were the abundant blessings tucked into the dream-come-true, two-week vacation that my husband Lynn and I took to Italy last fall. I've always said that we enjoy such a trip in three tenses: looking forward to it, living it and savoring the memory of it. We are currently savoring the memories of the Tuscan hillsides and the family-oriented lifestyles. We are looking forward to a year of major changes in our lives. Our son Derek and his wife Alexandra are expecting our first grandchild, our daughter Lindsay who lives in San Diego, California, is getting married in July in Yosemite, and our youngest daughter Kendall and her husband David will be moving to start graduate school somewhere in the fall. I can't wait to see what potential blessings God has within each of those changes."

HELEN GRACE LESCHEID of Abbotsford, British Columbia, writes, "Last year, when I visited my five grown children living in other parts of Canada and Africa, I told them, 'Don't worry about entertaining me. Just let me traipse along on a normal day. I want to see where you live, where you shop, who your friends are, what your activities are.' Esther, my oldest daughter, maneuvered a Subaru across the dry countryside of Senegal to attend to her nursing duties in a medical clinic. We passed through villages of mud-baked huts where children waved at us, past herds of scrawny cows and sheep. One and a half hours later, at the clinic, women in colorful dresses and head scarves held children with fevers, and old men with numerous complaints waited for her. While she attended to important things like diagnosing and treating, she let me do the eyedrops and blood pressures. In Canada, I visited with my other four children. I shopped at a colorful Chinese market in North York, thrilled to the exploding sunrise behind Toronto's CN tower, and wandered in and out of antique shops in Calgary's Heritage Park. As I witnessed a slice of their lives, I remembered God's fulfilled promise to me: All your children will be taught of the Lord and great will be your children's peace."

PATRICIA LORENZ of Oak Creek, Wisconsin, says, "In 1992, when I had more guts and gusto than common sense, I quit my real job to stay home to carve out a career as a writer and speaker. Considering the fact that I've had one or more of my four children in college every single year since 1988 (and my youngest child Andrew still has a year or more to go), and my income has never surpassed the 1992 amount, I've had more blessings and joy than I ever imagined. As I free-lance my way through life, doing what, when and where I please, I count the fact that my house is paid for and that my little red 1987 car keeps on chugging (more than 175,000 miles!) among my best everyday blessings. Whether I'm speaking in Kentucky, working on a new book while house-sitting for friends in Florida, whooping it up with relatives in Kansas City or giving a women's retreat here in Wisconsin, every single day is a new adventure in freedom. Talk about everyday blessings!"

"Everyday blessings are all around us," says ROBERTA MESSNER of Huntington, West Virginia. "But you do have to keep an eye out for them." For years Roberta had heard people make the comment, "I'll *believe* it when I *see* it." Recently a turn of that phrase really got her thinking. "A friend had gone through some problems with her teenage daughter," recalls Roberta. "Yet even more troubling than the trying times was the decrease in life's little serendipities, those moments when God's fingerprints seemed to be all over her life. My friend asked the Lord to help her to be more aware of all the good things, and to her great surprise, her blessings suddenly multiplied. Now her philosophy is 'I'll *see* it when I *believe* it.' And it's become mine, too." Some of Roberta's greatest everyday blessings? *Daily Guideposts* readers. "I feel their encouragement every day of the year."

KEITH MILLER and his wife Andrea, both writers, speakers and consultants, live in Austin, Texas. Two of their three grown daughters each have two children, and one daughter has three, and these daughters and their husbands and children have a large space in Keith and Andrea's hearts. Andrea is doing some research and writing about women and spirituality, and Keith is finishing a book about the New Testament message of Jesus. Keith says, "Andrea and I have been coleading an adult spiritual adventure class at St. Matthew's Episcopal Church. God, and the members of the class, have in some way jump-started our writing careers. We both feel that we have shifted into a new gear. And we are very grateful to be on the adventure with such a wonderful bunch of loving pilgrims."

Since coming to Guideposts in 1988, TED NACE has found every day filled with blessings. His fourteen years as pastor in the culturally rich area of Berks County, Pennsylvania, granted him a wealth of sermon illustrations and life lessons that have equipped him for his work as Director of Ministries. Ted, his wife Kathy and their sons Ryan, Joel and Kyle were blessed with times with both Dr. Norman Vincent Peale and Mrs. Ruth Stafford Peale, who were role models of devotion and dedication in their personal as well as pastoral lives. This year finds Ted and Kathy, who live in Poughquag, New York, visiting Ryan, also a pastor, and Joel and his new bride near Philadelphia. Kyle, their youngest son, has begun college, another reminder of the miracle and blessings of family.

LINDA NEUKRUG still enjoys her job at the bookstore and substitute teaching in the Walnut Creek, California, area. Due to the generosity of a fabulous family with whom she celebrates the holidays every year (they surprised her with an airline ticket as a gift!), she was able to go home to New York for a week and see her own fabulous family—her parents, sister and brother-in-law, and two young nephews Adam and Glenn. Linda has begun to give blood every eight weeks (as often as it's allowed), and is always surprised to discover how completely painless the process is and how good it makes her feel afterward.

(Plus, you get all those free cookies and juice!) Spiritually, Linda is learning that it is a lot easier to trust God when things seem to be going well, but the challenge is to keep trusting God during the rough spots. "I guess you could call it spiritual exercising," she says. "I hope those rough spots are few and far between for everyone during the coming year." A Bible quote she is keeping close to her heart this year is "Fear thou not . . . and know that I am God" (Isaiah 41:10).

BILLY NEWMAN says, "For years, my wife Nan and I talked of moving out of Atlanta, Georgia's sprawling metropolis to a smaller town. This fall we finally did it. We packed up and moved fifty miles south to my wife's hometown, Newnan. None of us quite knew what to expect. Our daughter Rebecca, living in Connecticut, was relieved to know that the airport was no farther away. Porter, our oldest daughter, switched schools in midsemester, and our son William simply adjusted to a new car pool. Nan, a practicing lawyer, began mediating disputes as a way to help mend our conflicting world, and I steered my photography work closer to home. As we settled in, we soon noticed the differences of life in a smaller town. Driving through our new neighborhood, we wave a lot more. On Saturdays, we get up and dress quicker because we never know who might knock on our door unexpectedly. Porter walks to her friend's houses, and it only takes us five minutes to drive to William's baseball practice. In a small town, God's gifts seem to arrive in smaller packages."

RUTH STAFFORD PEALE of Pawling, New York, writes, "There is nothing more exciting than the unexpected things that happen in your daily life. Let me share one such event. In the mail one day, I came across a carefully wrapped package. I opened it and, behold, what I found! It was a picture of me taken at the White House in Washington, D.C., when President George W. Bush spoke to a group celebrating a Horatio Alger Award ceremony. At the end of that meeting, the President left the podium and headed for the door. I was in the front row, seated on the aisle. He stopped and motioned for me to walk with him. The photographer caught a picture of him holding my hand as we walked out. Not your average everyday blessing!"

ROBERTA ROGERS of New Market, Virginia, says, "We have had many everyday blessings this past year and at least one that was *not* everyday. Matti Prouty will marry our youngest son David and become our dear, first, long-prayed-for daughter-in-law! What fun to host a big shower here and a rehearsal dinner in Colorado! David will be stationed at Fort Carson. Our son John continues to teach golf nearby and is house-hunting. In Atlanta, our son Tom's company was bought out by his sweetheart's, creating interesting challenges. Our son Peter, called to active duty after September 11, 2001, has been to Afghanistan and may be sent to other places 'for the duration.' I keep a candle in the kitchen window for him. Among other activities, I am praying up another book, and my husband Bill has joined the Rescue Squad. His mother Marian, ninety-five, still lives nearby, but my mother Kathryn, ninety-two, has been moved up to Chambersburg, Pennsylvania. She and I had eight months to find a new relationship, and having found it, we miss each other. You, dear friend, are among my best everyday blessings! Bless you."

This year DANIEL and Sharon SCHANTZ have been married forty years. Their fathers performed the ceremony on May 10, 1963, Dan's junior year at Great Lakes Christian College in Lansing, Michigan. They spent a budget weekend honeymoon in Holland, Michigan, a small town of tulips and a wooden-shoe factory. Thirty of their forty years were spent in their current West Logan Street home in Moberly, Missouri: a big, denim-blue house with white shutters, more than one hundred years old. Former residents claim that four-star Gen. Omar Bradley used to visit his girlfriend at this house. Everyday blessings in Dan's marriage include Sharon's incredible cooking, an early-to-bed-early-to-rise lifestyle, long walks, long talks on the screened-in porch and summer vacations when they visit homes of famous writers. This year they went to Oxford, Mississippi, home of William Faulkner and John Grisham. Dan gives credit to the Lord and Sharon for their long bond. Their reception napkins read, "Let only Him who rules the thunder put this man and woman asunder." Joking, Dan says, "Here's to my wife, for putting up with me through all the trials I would never have had if I had not married her."

That old maxim "If you want to hear God laugh, just tell Him your plans" took on new significance for GAIL THORELL SCHILLING of New Durham, New Hampshire, who had *planned* to return to her beloved Wyoming after a year in New Hampshire. "Actually, I did return to Lander for five months. Then both of my parents landed in the hospital. So my daughter Trina and I packed up to cross the country again to be near enough to help. During my brief stay in Lander, I substitute taught fifth grade for nine weeks, which included fateful September 11. Mercifully, an early morning field trip high in the mountains overlooking the Red Desert gave my colleagues and me time to process the horrific news before the children found out. Reflecting on the panoramic views at 7,500 feet, glimpsing an osprey dive into a glittering pond, marveling at the intricacies of a beaver dam and watching the wide-eyed innocence of my new student from California touch his first snow—all reassured me that God is still in charge. Thus strengthened, I could offer comfort to my confused and frightened students in the following weeks. I still want to go home to Wyoming, but I haven't made any plans. God will lead me there when it's time."

PENNEY SCHWAB of Copeland, Kansas, writes, "I've always taken good health for granted, so it was a shock when my husband Don was diagnosed with cancer and then also found to have a heart irregularity. During his surgery, tests and recovery, we were upheld and strengthened by kindness and prayer. We learned firsthand the blessings found in simple things: a card, a phone call, a visit and those oh-so-important words 'I'm praying for both of you.' I'm in my seventeenth year as executive director of United Methodist Mexican-American Ministries. During my daily drive to and from work (one hundred miles round-trip), I am thankful for a reliable car and paved roads. I'm even trying to look on roadwork as a blessing, but so far I haven't succeeded. We continue to be blessed through friends and family, especially our wonderful, talented, much-more-fun-than-their-parents grandchildren Ryan, David, Mark, Caleb and Olivia."

Since the publication of her book *All the Way to Heaven*, ELIZABETH SHERRILL of Chappaqua, New York, has enjoyed an unexpected blessing. "It's so much the most personal thing I've ever written that I thought only women—and specifically wives and mothers—would relate to it." To her surprise, wives are passing it to their husbands and teenage kids, a readership she never anticipated. One thirty-year-old man wrote, "I saw myself all the way through it." "It's shown me," Elizabeth says, "that though our life experiences are different, the Father we meet in our inmost souls is the same."

"I don't mind turning eighty years old on August 2 this year," says JOHN SHERRILL of Chappaqua, New York. "But it's a shock to realize that, the previous day, our younger son Donn will be *fifty*." Since John and Donn's birthdays are thirty years and one day apart, they often share celebrations. This year a grand family reunion will mark the occasion. Some forty relatives will gather, taking up most of a rustic lodge and campground in the Adirondack Mountains. There's no electricity, but great fishing in the lake, and in the evening "instead of reading or watching TV," John says, "we'll do what families have done since there *were* families—talk, make music, get reacquainted." John has only one request for the birthday itself: no cake. His choice each year? A whole watermelon . . . with candles of course.

SHARI SMYTH writes, "This year my everyday blessings begin in outer space. I've become fascinated with what's out there. So I'm grateful for the Hubble telescope and those who gave it to us. For one, it's thrilling to see blue-green gaseous clouds spewing newborn stars and to know we, too, were formed of the same stuff. Dust. We are kin to the universe. Yet it is so vast we can never comprehend it all. But our minds are equipped to probe it. And our imaginations to travel it. Both are everyday blessings. Down here in Kingston Springs, Tennessee, my husband Whitney and I are pushing (gulp) into old age. But we don't feel it yet—another blessing. Our children thrive—blessings times four. In Hawaii, Wendy, our oldest, and her boyfriend have realized a dream with a car repair business. He's the repair. She's the business. Jon is a chef in Maine. Sanna is a hostess in Tennessee. Laura is an art student in Washington. I close with the everyday, eternal blessing that nothing can take away: the Lord Jesus, Who loves us and give us life eternal. Which makes the vastness of the universe, and all our troubles, a mere sneeze."

JOSHUA SUNDQUIST lost his left leg to cancer at age 9. After twelve months of chemotherapy, during which he spent almost one hundred days in the hospital, he was declared in remission and has since been cured. While in high school, Josh became interested in the life-changing power of motivational speaking. He teamed up with several of his peers and secured a corporate sponsor in order to create Real Life, a motivational assembly created by teens, for teens. At the age of 17, Josh finished high school early and moved to Colorado to begin training to get on the U.S. Disabled Ski Team. In the winter months, he continues to train for the 2006 Paralympics, and in the summer he competes in triathlons and bike races. He wrote *Maximum Expectations*, which he describes as a motivational book about "tapping into your storehouse of unused potential by raising your standards and changing your perspectives." Josh gives God the credit for his opportunities and successes. "I'm not really an extraordinary person," he says. "I'm just an ordinary person with extraordinary circumstances."

"I wouldn't describe myself as coming from a typical Guideposts background," says PTOLEMY TOMPKINS of New York City, who has been at *Guideposts* magazine for three years. "Not that there is such a thing." As staff editor, Ptolemy works closely with authors. Having written several books of his own, including a book of nature trivia and a history of the monkey in art, it's perhaps not surprising that he likes stories featuring animals best. "In three years I've already worked with a Florida vet who rescues manatees, an Alabama couple who befriended a group of north woods black bears and an African missionary whose assistant was almost killed by a black mamba. When I came for my initial interview, the managing editor finished things up with a simple, straightforward statement: 'It's never boring at Guideposts.' He was telling the truth." Ptolemy has written for *Angels on Earth,* another Guideposts publication, on topics ranging from Ireland's spiritual heritage to the history of Easter eggs. He's also been featured three times in the yearly anthology *The Best Spiritual Writing.*

"When I discovered that this book was about everyday blessings," says VAN VARNER of New York City, "it caught me up short. At my age, especially, the blessings in my life seem to be more in the past than the present. On those occasions when I do feel blessed, however, the event doesn't feel ordinary. Rather, I feel that my blessings today are more precious than ever. Despite having experienced a stroke a few years ago, I have my health. The fact that I have difficulty talking means that I listen more—and am listened to less. There's certainly more food for thought and more time to think. Meanwhile, I have a place to live in my favorite city, though there are those who say, 'No wonder it's your favorite, you're always leaving it.' I have my friends, who are more special to me than ever (more blessings!), and I have a dog—you know him as Shep—and so far so good. Whatever God wants me to do, I'm ready to do it, and the readiness, I find, is a kind of blessing in itself."

"The last twelve months have been good ones for the Walker family," says SCOTT WALKER of Waco, Texas. "My wife Beth continues to work with international students at Baylor University who remind us that God is the Father of us all. Drew is a sophomore at Furman University and has decided to be a history major. Luke has had an eventful year playing linebacker on the high school football team, getting his driver's license and growing four inches. Jodi is in the eighth grade, plays basketball and has decided that being a redhead is not so bad after all. I completed a ten-year writing project on the American Civil War. It is the story of my great-great-grandfather and some of his friends enduring four years of intense combat together. Using their journals, letters and diaries, I wove their stories together and in the process learned much about life and my family. One of the joys of this year has been meeting *Daily Guideposts* readers. Recently, a family from Pittsburgh moved into our neighborhood. They had been reading *Daily Guideposts* for years. When we met, we felt that we already knew each other. What a privilege it is for all of us to be a part of the *Daily Guideposts* family."

DOLPHUS WEARY believes that God has given him two passions: one, to reach out to the poor in America, especially in rural Mississippi. God allowed him and his wife Rosie to live this out through Mendenhall Ministries for twenty-seven years. Today, they are living this out through REAL Christian Foundation, which the proceeds from his book *I Ain't Comin' Back* help to build. He sees his second passion as that of reconciliation and unity within the Body of Christ, especially across racial lines. God is allowing him to live this passion out through Mission Mississippi, a statewide movement. Dolphus lives in Richland with Rosie and their son Ryan, a tenth-grader at Richland High School. Their son Reggie lives in Jackson, Mississippi, and works with Mass Mutual Insurance and Investments. Danita, their daughter, is in her last year of residency in pediatrics at the University of South Alabama in Mobile. "We now have to work harder at getting together as a family. On December 23, we drove to Mobile and prepared dinner and had an early Christmas with Danita, then drove home the evening of Christmas Eve because she had to work Christmas Day. We all praised God for that small opportunity."

BRIGITTE WEEKS of New York City has had a wonderful time this year, working with her staff to create original books for Guideposts readers. "You are an extremely demanding audience and always let us know how we are doing," she says. " 'Church Choir Mysteries' and 'The Hidden Hand of God' both had a good reception and that is every editor's dream." She has had a peaceful few months on the home front following her daughter Charlotte's wedding. But then her son Hilary got engaged and is also planning a wedding with his brother Daniel as best man. This time Brigitte has only a rehearsal dinner to host. Much improved health has enabled her to travel again: to cross Nova

Scotia on a bicycle with her husband Edward and visit London with her daughter. The whole family—by then it will number seven—has ambitious plans for a Christmas trip to Costa Rica.

MARION BOND WEST of Watkinsville, Georgia, says, "My mother died in July. Nevertheless, God blessed us greatly. At ninety-two, she left this life having beat cancer three times! One of the sweetest blessings was the peach-colored roses we selected that perfectly matched the roses in her going-home outfit. My dear husband Gene Acuff conducted Mother's service with the help of our good friends Dr. Ira Slade and Susan and Jimmy Bamberg. A couple of months before Mother's death, my son Jon made the courageous decision to ask God and others for help with longtime chemical addictions. He was accepted into Dunklin Memorial Camp in Okeechobee, Florida, a tough, eight-month, Christ-centered rehabilitation program. The honesty and humility at this nearly forty-year-old city of refuge for about seventy-five men is so startling that both my daughters wept through their first meal, which was grown, prepared and graciously served by 'the brothers.' Every man we met, we grew to love, and our lives were blessed beyond anything we'd experienced or expected."

BRENDA WILBEE says, "I still live in the Pacific Northwest in Bellingham, Washington, where I continue to teach composition at the community college and am finishing the last of my graphic design courses. I was an artist before I could read or write, but while my children Heather, Phillip and Blake were growing up, I focused on my writing. So it's been rewarding the last couple of years to return to design and integrate my two passions. What's so delightfully wonderful about computer art is I don't rub a hole in my paper erasing—I just hit delete! For the first time ever I'm able to produce exactly what I see in my head. It's like a miracle to me."

TIM WILLIAMS of Durango, Colorado, says, "This has been a strange year to try and count everyday blessings. A more apt description of the year, at least for me, would be 'Everyday Hardships.' My church and my fire department were both places of peace and refuge for me during the past seven years. This year, both are filled with the dissension that always accompanies change. The promises of an easy yoke, a light burden and a level path seem so distant at times. I am thankful for the everyday blessing of my wife's love. Dianne's own path has not been smooth, but she always finds a way to cushion my yoke, lighten my burden and remove rocks from my path. On the days I can't see Christ clearly, I can see Christ in her. She has been my everyday blessing this year."

ISABEL WOLSELEY of Syracuse, New York, says, "I realize more and more how much I have to be grateful for. I particularly thank God for my family. When my older son John Champ married, I felt deeply sorry for my younger son Kelly, as I was sure he could never find a wife as choice as Marie. But then came Christine! Like Naomi in the Book of Ruth, I am blessed with two beloved daughters-in-law, plus six grandchildren and a great-grandson. My husband died in 1998, but the Lord brought Lawrence Torrey into my heart and we married in February 2000. A year later we spent two months with Wycliffe Bible Translators in the remote, rain forest highlands of Papua New Guinea, where Lawrence, a pharmacist, dispensed medications to staff personnel and people at the missionary compound there in Ukarumpa. I taught high school students and adults how to write the incredible stories they have to tell. I have a home, food and clothes. And as someone once said, 'Everyone needs a work to do that we consider important and someone to assure us that our efforts are indeed worthwhile. Plus someone to love who loves us in return.' God has graciously given me all of these. I am content."

SCRIPTURE REFERENCE INDEX

AUTHORS, TITLES AND SUBJECTS INDEX